OXFORD STUDIES IN ANCIENT PHILOSOPHY

OXFORD STUDIES IN ANCIENT PHILOSOPHY

EDITOR: RACHANA KAMTEKAR

ASSOCIATE EDITOR: FRANCESCO ADEMOLLO

VOLUME LXIV

SUMMER 2023

OXFORD
UNIVERSITY PRESS

Great Clarendon Street, Oxford, OX2 6DP,
United Kingdom

Oxford University Press is a department of the University of Oxford.
It furthers the University's objective of excellence in research, scholarship,
and education by publishing worldwide. Oxford is a registered trade mark of
Oxford University Press in the UK and in certain other countries

© the several contributors 2025

The moral rights of the authors have been asserted

All rights reserved. No part of this publication may be reproduced, stored in a retrieval system, transmitted, used for text and data mining, or used for training artificial intelligence, in any form or by any means, without the prior permission in writing of Oxford University Press, or as expressly permitted by law, by licence or under terms agreed with the appropriate reprographics rights organization. Enquiries concerning reproduction outside the scope of the above should be sent to the Rights Department, Oxford University Press, at the address above.

You must not circulate this work in any other form
and you must impose this same condition on any acquirer

Published in the United States of America by Oxford University Press
198 Madison Avenue, New York, NY 10016, United States of America

British Library Cataloguing in Publication Data

Data available

Library of Congress Control Number: 2024946919

ISBN 978–0–19–893454–7 (hbk.)
ISBN 978–0–19–893455–4 (pbk.)

DOI: 10.1093/oso/9780198934547.001.0001

Printed and bound by
CPI Group (UK) Ltd, Croydon, CR0 4YY

Links to third party websites are provided by Oxford in good faith and
for information only. Oxford disclaims any responsibility for the materials
contained in any third party website referenced in this work.

The manufacturer's authorised representative in the EU for product safety is
Oxford University Press España S.A. of El Parque Empresarial San Fernando de Henares,
Avenida de Castilla, 2 – 28830 Madrid (www.oup.es/en or product.safety@oup.com).
OUP España S.A. also acts as importer into Spain of products made by the manufacturer.

ADVISORY BOARD

Professor Rachel Barney, *University of Toronto*

Professor Gábor Betegh, *University of Cambridge*

Professor Susanne Bobzien, *All Souls College, Oxford*

Professor Victor Caston, *University of Michigan*

Professor Riccardo Chiaradonna, *Università degli Studi Roma Tre*

Professor Alan Code, *Stanford University*

Professor Brad Inwood, *Yale University*

Professor Gabriel Lear, *University of Chicago*

Professor A. A. Long, *University of California, Berkeley*

Professor Stephen Menn, McGill *University and Humboldt-Universität zu Berlin*

Professor Susan Sauvé Meyer, *University of Pennsylvania*

Professor Jessica Moss, *New York University*

Professor Martha Nussbaum, *University of Chicago*

Professor Marwan Rashed, *Université Paris-Sorbonne*

Professor David Sedley, *University of Cambridge*

Professor Richard Sorabji, *King's College, University of London, and Wolfson College, Oxford*

Professor Raphael Woolf, *King's College, University of London*

Contributions and books for review should be sent to the Editor, Professor Rachana Kamtekar, Sage School of Philosophy, Cornell University, 218 Goldwin Smith Hall, Ithaca, New York, USA (email rk579@cornell.edu).

Contributors are asked to observe the 'Notes for Contributors to *Oxford Studies in Ancient Philosophy*', printed at the end of this volume.

Up-to-date contact details, the latest version of Notes for Contributors, and publication schedules can be checked on the *Oxford Studies in Ancient Philosophy* website:

www.oup.com/academic/content/series/o/oxford-studies-in-ancient-philosophy-osap

CONTENTS

Plato's Isolation of a Kind Being or Why in the *Sophist* to Be Is Not to Be Something   1
ROBERTO GRANIERI

Negative Forms in Plato's *Sophist*: A Re-Examination   53
SAMUEL MEISTER

Virtue and Contemplation in *Eudemian Ethics* 8. 3   95
ROY C. LEE

How Virtuous Actions Are a Means to Contemplation   139
SUKAINA HIRJI

Thought 'From Without': The Role of the Agent Intellect in Alexander's *De intellectu*   177
ROBERT ROREITNER

Index Locorum   267

PLATO'S ISOLATION OF A KIND BEING OR WHY IN THE *SOPHIST* TO BE IS NOT TO BE SOMETHING

ROBERTO GRANIERI

1. Introduction

In the *Sophist*, Plato singles out being (ὄν, οὐσία) as just one among the Kinds or Forms.[1] In doing so, he departs from another familiar use of the terms ὄν and οὐσία whereby they signify the whole intelligible realm, typically contrasted with the domain of perceptible entities, collectively often named 'becoming' (γένεσις).[2]

The ancient Platonists often proved sensitive to this distinction. In *De principiis* 2, for example, Damascius remarks:

This paper owes much to the feedback and support of Lesley Brown, to whom I am most grateful. I also benefited considerably from the written comments of Pauline Sabrier, an anonymous referee for *OSAP*, and especially Rachana Kamtekar, whose constructive criticisms and assistance were very helpful. Thanks also to Lloyd Gerson, Rachel Barney, George Boys-Stones, James Allen, and Christian Pfeiffer for advice at an earlier stage; and to audiences at the University of Toronto, the Pontificia Universidad Católica del Perú, and the LMU Munich. Research for this paper has received funding from the European Research Council (ERC) under the European Union's Horizon 2020 research and innovation programme (grant agreement No. (885273))/Advanced Grant, acronym: PlatoViaAristotle.

[1] Cf. *Soph.* 250 C 2, 256 A 1: ὄν; 250 B 10, 251 E 10, 252 A 2: οὐσία. For 'Kinds or Forms' (I capitalize these terms throughout for the proprietary Platonic concepts), cf. e.g. *Soph.* 254 C 3–4 ('of the forms...some of those called the greatest'. τῶν εἰδῶν...τῶν μεγίστων λεγομένων ἄττα) and 254 D 4 ('greatest among the kinds', μέγιστα μὴν τῶν γενῶν); cf. *Parm.* 135 A 8 ('kind', γένος) and 135 B 7 'form', εἶδος). Unless otherwise noted, Greek texts are cited after the most recent OCT editions (including E. A. Duke et al. (eds.), *Platonis opera* (Oxford, 1995), i for the first two Platonic tetralogies; S. R. Slings (ed.), *Platonis* Rempublicam (Oxford, 2003) for the *Republic*; and J. Burnet (ed.), *Platonis opera*, 2nd edn (Oxford, 1905–13), ii–v for all other Platonic dialogues), and translations are my own.

[2] Cf. e.g. *Phaedo* 66 A 8; *Rep.* 486 A 9, 508 D 4, 521 D 5, 523 A 3, 525 B 3, 525 C 6, 526 E 5, 534 A 3; *Phileb.* 58 A 2; *Tim.* 52 D 3. Arguably foundational for this second meaning is Plato's use of οὐσία for the what-it-is sought out in definitional inquiries; cf. e.g. *Euthph.* 11 A 7–8; *Meno* 72 B 1–2; *Phaedo* 65 D 13, 76 A 8–9. Thus, *Republic* 7 calls dialectic both the inquiry that attempts in each and all cases to grasp what each thing is (cf. 533 B 1–2: αὐτοῦ γε ἑκάστου πέρι ὃ ἔστιν ἕκαστον...περὶ παντός;), *viz.* its essence (cf. 534 B 3–4: ἑκάστου...τῆς οὐσίας), and the supreme science concerned with the realm of οὐσία (cf. 534 A 3).

Πρὸ δὴ πάντων τὰ σημαινόμενα διαιρετέον τῶν ὀνομάτων. Λέγεται γὰρ ὂν καὶ ἕν τι τῶν γενῶν τοῦ ὄντος, ἀντικείμενον τῷ μὴ ὄντι, καὶ ἀντιδιῃρημένον τοῖς ἄλλοις γένεσιν· εἰδητικόν γε ὂν τοῦτο ὄν, ἀλλ' εἰδῶν τῶν ἁπλῶν μετὰ τῶν ἄλλων τεσσάρων γενῶν. Καὶ ἐν <Παρμενίδῃ> πρὸ τῶν ὑποθέσεων συγκατείληχε καὶ τοῦτο τοῖς γενικοῖς εἴδεσιν. Ἕτερον δὲ λέγεται ὂν τὸ ὁλοφυὲς πλήρωμα τῶν γενῶν, ὅπερ οὐσίαν ἰδίως καλοῦμεν, ὡς ὁ Πλωτῖνος.

(Damasc., *Princ.* 2. 56. 9–16 Westerink, my emphasis).

Before all, one must distinguish the meanings of the names. For being is called <u>one of the genera of being</u>, which is opposed to not-being, and is contradistinguished from the other genera. This being is <u>form-like</u>; but it is among the simple forms, together with the other four kinds. And in the *Parmenides*, before the hypotheses, [Plato] assigned this form to the generic forms. In another sense, being is also said to be <u>the entire plenitude of kinds</u>, since we properly call it substance, as Plotinus does.[3]

Damascius speaks for himself but traces his view back to Plato (and Plotinus). His pupil Simplicius sets out a similar point, in response to a criticism by Alexander of Aphrodisias (cf. Simpl. *in Phys.* 136. 10–11 Diels) against Plato's alleged posit of absolute not-being as a Kind:

Ἐννοῆσαι δὲ χρὴ ὅτι τὸ ὑπὸ τοῦ Πλάτωνος εἰλημμένον ὄν ἐστι <u>τὸ κατ' αὐτὴν τοῦ εἶναι τὴν ἰδιότητα ψιλὴν</u> θεωρούμενον, ὃ καὶ ἀντιδιῄρηται πρός τε τὰ ἄλλα γένη καὶ πρὸς τὸ μὴ ὄν· καὶ γὰρ <u>τοῦτο γένος</u> εἶναί φησιν, ἀλλ' οὐχὶ <u>τὸ παντελῶς ὂν τὸ καὶ τὰ γένη πάντα ἐν ἑαυτῷ συνῃρηκός</u>· ᾧ τὸ παντελῶς μὴ ὂν ἀντικέοιτο, εἰ καὶ τὸ ἀντικεῖσθαι δυνατὸν ἐπ' αὐτοῦ λέγειν. τὸ δὲ τοιοῦτον ὂν οὐκ ἂν εἴη γένος, εἴπερ τὰ γένη ἐναντία διαιρέσει ἐστὶ τῇ πρὸς ἄλληλα.

(Simpl. *in Phys.* 136. 21–27 Diels, my emphasis)

It is necessary to understand that the being assumed by Plato [*sc.* in the *Sophist*] is what is studied <u>in accordance with the bare property of being</u>

---

[3] Damascius goes on to make further distinctions not directly relevant for present purposes. The distinction between being *qua* single Kind and being *qua* eidetic realm is key throughout *Princ.* 2. 56–99, see R. Granieri, 'That in Virtue of Which Something Is a Being: Note on Damascius, *De principiis* II, p. 75.10–11 Westerink' ['Damascius'], *Studia graeco-arabica* 13 (2023), 49–55. It seems instead to have eluded Seneca('s source) in *Ep.* 58 (on which, see n. 83 below). On 'plenitude' (πλήρωμα) in this context, cf. also Damasc., *Princ.* 1. 81. 17–19; 2. 62. 11, 174. 3 Westerink; Proclus, *In Parm.* 628. 24–5, 763. 18, 800. 12–13 Luna-Segonds = 628. 18–19, 763. 13, 800. 10 Steel; *in Tim.* 3. 8. 18–19 Diehl = 4. 10. 17–19 van Riel; and C. Luna and A. Segonds (ed. and trans.), *Proclus: Commentaire sur le* Parménide *de Platon* (Paris, 2010), ii. ii. 240–1. For the Plotinian reference, cf. *Enn.* 2. 6. 1.1–5. But Plotinus too refers elsewhere both to the realm of Forms (Intellect) and to the Kind Being by using ὄν and οὐσία indifferently; cf. e.g. 6. 2. 1.6, 10, 13, 18 with 6. 2. 2. 28; and 6. 2. 7. 17, 41, 43, 8. 25 with 6. 2. 7. 6 or 3. 7. 3. 9.

itself, which is contradistinguished with respect to both the other genera and not-being. For he says that this too is a genus, but not perfect being which also contains all the genera in itself. To that, complete not-being would be opposed, if it is possible to speak of opposing with regard to it. Such a being would not be a genus, if genera are opposed to one another in a division.

(P. Huby and C. C. W. Taylor (trans.), *Simplicius: On Aristotle Physics 1.3–4* (London, 2011), slightly modified; my emphasis)[4]

By contrast, modern commentators, whilst obviously alive to Plato's recognition of a Kind or Form of Being in the *Sophist*, have not shown a comparable interest in the distinction between Being *qua* single Kind and Being *qua* intelligible realm.[5] Such distinction has, of course, not escaped notice completely,[6] but neither has it been dwelt upon in detail,[7] especially as regards the motivations and implications of the *Sophist*'s isolation of a Kind Being.[8] One

---

[4] On this passage, and its background in Damasc., *Princ.* 2. 56. 9–16 Westerink, see R. Granieri, 'Not-Being, Contradiction and Difference: Simplicius *vs.* Alexander of Aphrodisias on Plato's Conception of Not-Being', *Méthexis*, 35 (2023), 185–200.

[5] Not even D. Peipers, *Ontologia platonica* [*Ontologia*] (Leipzig, 1883), still the only, if variously limited, comprehensive treatment of Plato's views on being.

[6] For cursory remarks see H. Bonitz, *Platonische Studien* [*Studien*], 3rd edn (Berlin, 1886), 201–2; S. Rosen, *Plato's Sophist* [*Sophist*] (New Haven, 1983), 230–1, 243; M. Frede, 'Sein; Seiendes. I. *Antike*. 1. *Vorsokratiker; Platon; Aristoteles*; 2. *Hellenismus*', in J. Ritter and K. Gründer (eds.), *Historisches Wörterbuch der Philosophie* (Basel, 1995), ix. 170–80 at 172–3; B. Centrone (trans.), *Platone: Sofista* (Turin, 2008), lvii; B. Hestir, *Plato on the Metaphysical Foundation of Meaning and Truth* [*Foundation*] (Cambridge, 2016), 135–6. Aspects of this issue have also been touched upon by e.g. L. Campbell (ed.), *The Sophistes and the Politicus of Plato* [*Sophist*] (Oxford, 1867), lxxviii; F. M. Cornford (trans.), *Plato's Theory of Knowledge* [*Theory*] (London, 1935), 292–3; M. Dixsaut, *Le naturel philosophe* [*Naturel*], 3rd edn (Paris, 2001), 328; M. Burnyeat, '*Apology* 30 B 2–4: Socrates, Money, and the Grammar of ΓΙΓΝΕΣΘΑΙ ['*Apology*'], *Journal of Hellenic Studies*, 123 (2003), 1–25 at 12. M.-L. Gill, *Philosophos* [*Philosophos*] (Oxford, 2012) gives an extensive and valuable account of Plato's notion of a Form of Being (more below), but does not problematize the distinction between being *qua* eidetic domain and being *qua* individual Form or Kind.

[7] Interestingly, this issue has more clearly surfaced in Plotinian studies, see e.g. L. P. Gerson, *Plotinus* [*Plotinus*] (London, 1994), 84; and L. Lavaud, 'The Primary Substance in Plotinus' Metaphysics: A Little-Known Concept', *Phronesis*, 59 (2014), 369–84.

[8] A Form of Being might be mentioned also at *Parm.* 136 B 6 (cf. Damasc., *Princ.* 2. 56. 13–14 Westerink). But even if τὸ εἶναι ('being') there should be identified with the *Sophist*'s Kind Being, the *Parmenides* offers limited insights on it, let alone a treatment comparable in scope and depth to that of the *Sophist*. Also, at *Theaet.* 185 C 9–10, οὐσία is listed among the 'common things' (κοινά) deployed by the soul, independently of its use of sense-organs. But the ontological status of the κοινά is

among various possible reasons for this is perhaps the predominantly language-focused approach characterizing most studies on Plato's conception of being (and not-being) in the *Sophist*, with their consequent concentration on the question of the distinction of the senses or uses of εἶναι ('being') in this dialogue.[9] As a result, the very fact that the *Sophist* singles out a Kind Being—which is first and foremost a metaphysical fact, not a linguistic one—has remained without a proper explanation and generally been taken for granted as an unproblematic datum. The consequences for the setting and development of the debate on Plato's views on being

notoriously controversial and it is far from clear whether they are just Forms. It is thus safe to focus on the *Sophist*.

[9] Prominent examples include J. Ackrill, 'Plato and the Copula' ['Copula'], *Journal of Hellenic Studies*, 77 (1957), 1–16 (reprinted in id., *Essays on Plato and Aristotle* (Oxford, 1997), 72–9), esp. at 2: 'Plato, no less clearly than Frege, is engaged in distinguishing and elucidating senses of "is"'; J. Moravcsik, 'Being and Meaning in the *Sophist*' ['Meaning'], *Acta Philosophica Fennica*, 14 (1962), 23–78; M. Frede, *Prädikation und Existenzaussage* [*Prädikation*] (Göttingen, 1967); J. Malcolm, 'Plato's Analysis of τὸ ὄν τὸ μὴ ὄν in the *Sophist*' ['Analysis'], *Phronesis*, 12 (1967), 130–46; G. E. L. Owen, 'Plato on Not-Being' ['Not-Being'], in G. Vlastos (ed.), *Plato: 1. Metaphysics and Epistemology: A Collection of Critical Essays* (Garden City, NY, 1971), 223–67 (reprinted in G. E. L. Owen, *Logic, Science and Dialectic* [*LSD*] (Ithaca, NY, 1986), 104–37), esp. at 223: 'Platonists who doubt that they are Spectators of being must settle for the knowledge that they are investigators of the verb "to be"'; D. Bostock, 'Plato on "Is Not"' ['Is Not'], *Oxford Studies in Ancient Philosophy*, 2 (1984), 89–119; L. Brown, 'Being in the *Sophist*: A Syntactical Enquiry' ['Being'], in G. Fine (ed.), *Plato 1: Metaphysics and Epistemology* (Oxford, 1999), 455–78 (reprinted with revisions from *Oxford Studies in Ancient Philosophy*, 4 (1986), 49–70); M. Frede, 'Plato's *Sophist* on False Statements' ['False Statements'], in R. Kraut (ed.), *The Cambridge Companion to Plato* (Cambridge, 1992), 397–424 (reprinted in D. Ebrey and R. Kraut (eds.), *The Cambridge Companion to Plato*, 2nd edn (Cambridge, 2022), 433–63); L. Brown, 'The Verb "To Be" in Greek Philosophy: Some Remarks' ['Verb'], in S. Everson (ed.), *Companions to Ancient Thought*, iii: *Language* (Cambridge, 1994), 212–36; Burnyeat, 'Apology'; J. Malcolm, 'Some Cautionary Remarks on the "is"/"teaches" Analogy' ['Remarks'], *Oxford Studies in Ancient Philosophy*, 31 (2006), 281–96; F. Leigh, 'The Copula and Semantic Continuity in Plato's *Sophist*' ['Semantic Continuity'], *Oxford Studies in Ancient Philosophy*, 34 (2008), 105–21. Kahn's large-scale work on εἶναι has surely incentivized this interpretative trend: see C. Kahn, *The Verb 'Be' in Ancient Greek* [*'Verb Be'*] (Indianapolis, 2003 [1973]); and id., *Essays on Being* [*Essays*] (Oxford, 2009). On this approach to the *Sophist*, see Neal's remarks in R. Bluck, *Plato's Sophist* [*Sophist*] (Manchester, 1975), 9–12. For more general observations on the interest of analytic philosophers in the *Sophist*, see N. White (trans.), *Plato: Sophist* [*Sophist*] (Indianapolis, 1993), vii–ix, xix–xxi. A recent attempt to illuminate the Platonic conception of being by sidestepping the controversy on the senses of εἶναι and stressing instead the notion of ontological superiority is J. Moss, *Plato's Epistemology* (New York, 2021), ch. 3, which, however, does not focus on the *Sophist*.

have been considerable. For example, discussions of Plato's uses of the verb εἶναι have not to my knowledge paused to ask whether there is a difference between situations in which 'X is' is meant to capture X's participation in the intelligible domain in general (i.e. in any given member of such domain), such as at *Rep.* 478 E 1–2 ('what participates in both, being and not-being', τὸ ἀμφοτέρων μετέχον, τοῦ εἶναί τε καὶ μὴ εἶναι),[10] and situations in which 'X is' is meant to capture X's participation in just *one* specific member of that domain, i.e. the Kind Being, which we will see regularly happens in the *Sophist*.

My aim here is to make progress in our understanding of Plato's views on being by exploring one main implication of Plato's isolation of a Kind Being. More particularly, I want to show that this exploration enables us to question aspects of an entrenched scholarly consensus about Plato's conception of being. This consensus is aptly summarized by the famous slogan, introduced by G. E. L. Owen and echoed by many, that for Plato 'to be is to be something'.[11] This slogan may allow for different readings. A widespread and plausible one is that Plato does not conceive of existence as an independent notion, but thinks that to exist always consists in exemplifying or instantiating a determinate property (different from bare being). Thus, to say that 'X is' is not to ascribe a property of existence to X, but is a way of saying that X has (or even *is*) a

[10] Cf. also *Crat.* 401 C 7–8: 'we say that what partakes in being "is"', ἡμεῖς τὸ τῆς οὐσίας μετέχον "ἔστιν" φαμέν (with F. Ademollo, *The Cratylus of Plato* [*Cratylus*] (Cambridge, 2011), 167, 276–7); *Rep.* 585 D 3: partakes in being', οὐσίας μετέχει (cf. 585 B 11: 'partake in pure being', καθαρᾶς οὐσίας μετέχειν). See Section 3 below.

[11] The slogan was first stated in G. E. L. Owen, 'Aristotle and the Snares of Ontology' ['Snares'], in R. Bambrough (ed.), *New Essays on Plato and Aristotle* (London, 1965), 69–96 (reprinted in id., *LSD*, 259–78) at 71, 76, as 'to be is to be something or other'. Then in 'Not-Being', 265 n. 78, Owen expressly shortened it as 'to be is to be something', which he presumed more perspicuous. Both sound like companions of the Quinean adages 'to be is to be the value of a bound variable' (see e.g. R. Adams, *What Is & What Is In Itself* (New York, 2021), 23–6) and 'no entity without identity', as well as of (a certain reading of) the Kantian maxim 'existence is not a real predicate', in turn already foreshadowed in P. Gassendi, *Disquisitio metaphysica*, in id., *Opera omnia* (Lyons, 1658; reprinted Stuttgart, 1964), iii. 380b–381b; and D. Hume, *A Treatise on Human Nature*, ed. by D. F. Norton and M. J. Norton (Oxford, 2007 [1739–40]), 1. 2. 6. Unlike Owen's equally famous attempt to backdate the *Timaeus*, promptly refuted by H. F. Cherniss, 'The Relation of the *Timaeus* to Plato's Later Dialogues' ['Relation'], *American Journal of Philology*, 78 (1957), 225–66, and on which Schofield declared in 1990 'a consensus that the proposal doesn't work' (M. Schofield, 'Editor's Notes', *Phronesis*, 35 (1990), 327–34 at 327–8), Owen's 'to be is to be something' slogan managed to take root as orthodoxy.

certain nature or is variously characterized.[12] For example, when Plato says 'Motion is'—regardless of whether this sentence should be construed as an elliptical statement of predication—he does not mean that Motion just has existence as an independent property, but that Motion is *as moving*, or is *in motion*, or is *in motion by its own nature*, i.e. it is *motion itself*, the *essence* or *nature* of motion.[13]

It should be emphasized that the overall understanding of the Platonic conception of being expressed by Owen's slogan acts as a common denominator to a cluster of interpretations that differ from each other in sometimes significant ways. Thus, it has predictably been championed by those who, like Owen, have contended that in Plato's dialogues, particularly the *Sophist*, occurrences of one-place εἶναι ('*X* is') must be construed, not as existence claims, but as elliptical for two-place εἶναι ('*X* is...'), i.e. as predicative claims with elided complements.[14] But it has also been subscribed to by those who, with Lesley Brown, have argued that, in both Plato and ancient Greek more generally, the verb εἶναι, unlike its modern counterparts in English or other languages, is not ambiguous between existential and predicative sense when it is used respectively as a one-place and a two-place predicate; instead, it exhibits a semantic continuity across these syntactically different uses, analogous to

---

[12] See e.g. the helpful summary by G. Galluzzo, *Breve storia dell'ontologia* (Rome, 2011), 37–8; and E. N. Lee, 'Plato on Negation and Not-Being in the *Sophist*' ['Negation'], *Philosophical Review*, 81 (1972), 267–304 at 276, 277 n. 14.

[13] See n. 38 below. Some context on the origins of this view: Owen, along with Frede (*Prädikation*) and Malcolm ('Analysis'), was reacting against such readings as those of P. Shorey, *The Unity of Plato's Thought* [*Unity*] (Chicago, 1903), 53–4 (see also id., *What Plato Said* [*WPS*] (Chicago, 1933), 298); Cornford, *Theory*, 263–6, 278–9, 282–5, 296; Ackrill, 'Copula'; Moravcsik, 'Meaning'; and I. M. Crombie, *An Examination of Plato's Doctrines*, 2 vols. (London, 1963), ii. 498–50. Whilst defending considerably different interpretations, these commentators converged in acknowledging Plato's full awareness of existential εἶναι. Their concern with the problem of the senses of εἶναι was in turn most likely prompted by Mill's famous stigmatization of the Greeks' purported neglect of the logical distinction between copulative and existential 'is'; see J. S. Mill, *A System of Logic* (Toronto, 1974 [1843]), i. 79; with Shorey, *Unity*, 54 n. 391 and *WPS*, 298.

[14] Cf. e.g. Frede, 'False Statements', 409: 'being for Plato always is a matter of being something or other'; Malcolm, 'Remarks', 286: 'to exist is to be something' (Malcolm voices this claim in a discussion of Parmenides, but cf. p. 289: 'that which exists must be something'). While Owen, Frede, and Malcolm agreed that in the *Sophist* Plato solved the paradox of falsehood by singling out two incomplete senses or uses of 'εἶναι', their readings differ as regards what those senses or uses are: identifying and predicative senses for Owen and Malcolm, definitional and predicative uses for Frede.

the one involved in the transitive and intransitive uses of such verbs as 'to teach', so that complete uses of εἶναι do not need to be supplied with an elided complement and do express existence, but are not thereby regarded as sharply distinct *semantically* from incomplete uses.[15] Thus, granted that this reading must be kept distinct from those of e.g. Owen, John Malcolm and Michael Frede,[16] Brown too does not refrain from approvingly voicing (a version of) the Owenian slogan (as she puts it: 'the core of being is being something'),[17] and neither do her followers.[18]

Further, it is also worth noting that this opinion is not unique to (though perhaps more fashionable among) scholars broadly working in Owen's footsteps, or to analytically trained historians more generally. In fact, Étienne Gilson had already independently come,

---

[15] Cf. Brown, 'Being' and 'Verb'; followed by, among others, White, *Sophist*, xxiii–xxviii (but cf. Brown, 'Being', 461, n. 9*); J. van Eck, 'Not-Being and Difference: On Plato's *Sophist*, 256 D 5–258 E 3' ['Not-Being and Difference'], *Oxford Studies in Ancient Philosophy*, 23 (2002), 63–84, esp. 70–2; Kahn, '*Verb Be*', ix–xii; Burnyeat, 'Apology', 10–13; J. Szaif, *Der Sinn von 'sein'* (Freiburg, 2003), 19 n. 13; Ademollo, *Cratylus*, 278; N. Zaks, *Apparences et dialectique: Un commentaire du* Sophiste *de Platon* [*Apparences*] (Leiden, 2023), 2 n. 5, 108–9, 229–34.

[16] It is not quite correct to saddle Brown with the view that complete uses of εἶναι are elliptical forms of incomplete uses (see e.g. M. M. McCabe, *Plato's Individuals* [*Individuals*] (Princeton, 1994), 206, n. 37, and N. Notomi, 'Plato on *What Is Not*', in D. Scott (ed.), *Maieusis* (Cambridge, 2007), 254–75 at 259), or with the view that 'in ontologically charged contexts, existential expressions, strictly speaking, must be taken predicatively' (Hestir, *Foundation*, 138; something similar may also be suggested by Kahn, '*Verb Be*', xi: 'existential uses of *einai* are potentially predicative'), or to associate Brown with a '"non-existential" interpretation of *einai*' (C. Smith, 'Against the Existential Reading of *Euthydemus* 283 E–284 C, with Help from the *Sophist*', *Ancient Philosophy*, 42 [2022], 67–81). Brown explicitly distances herself from what she calls 'the ellipse interpretation' ('Verb', 224–8; cf. 'Being', §§II and III), and, by the same token, argues neither that for Plato existence claims should be reduced to predicative claims nor that complete uses of εἶναι fail to express existence (cf. e.g. 'Being', 469–74). But see also nn. 18 and 39 below.

[17] L. Brown, 'Negation and Not-Being: Dark Matter in the *Sophist*' ['Dark Matter'], in R. Patterson et al. (eds.), *Presocratics and Plato* (Las Vegas, 2012), 233–54 at 288. But see ead., 'Verb', 228: 'complete being is *intimately related* to, and *derived from*, incomplete being – being such and such – without merely reducing to it' (italics mine).

[18] See e.g. van Eck, 'Not-Being and Difference', 71, 82; Kahn, '*Verb Be*', ix–x; id., *Essays*, 4; Ademollo, *Cratylus*, 278; Zaks, *Apparences*, 111, 229–34; also D. N. Sedley, 'Presocratic Themes: Being, Not-Being and Mind', in R. Le Poidevin et al. (eds.), *The Routledge Companion to Metaphysics* (London, 2009), 8–17 at 11. In this respect, there are some grounds to place 'Brown's view...in the same family as Owen's' (S. Menn, 'Aristotle on the Many Senses of Being' ['Many Senses'], *Oxford Studies in Ancient Philosophy*, 59 (2021), 187–263 at 203 n. 18). See also n. 39 below.

for different reasons, to a broadly similar conclusion, contending that:

> to the question: in what sense can it be said that a Platonic Idea is, there is but one answer: it *is* in the sense that it is wholly and exclusively that which it is... the Platonic notion of being is not only entirely foreign to existence, but inconsistent with it.
>
> (É. Gilson, *Being and Some Philosophers* [*Being*] (Toronto, 1952), 15, 33)

This interpretation of Plato's conception of being is, therefore, orthogonal to the analytic-continental divide, and defences of it have come from various quarters.[19]

It seems to me that a full exploration of Plato's notion of a Kind Being enables us to realize that there is at least one important context in which this received view does not capture what Plato is doing. Here I aim to take a first step in this direction and argue that when '*X* is' is metaphysically analysed by Plato in terms of *X*'s participation in or combination with the Kind or Form of Being, it does not mean for *X* to be something, or to be itself, or to be variously characterized (or similar), but to exist.[20] And since scholars endorsing Owen's slogan typically go so far as to say, with Kahn, that 'existence does not emerge as a distinct concept in Greek philosophy',[21] then one of the ambitions of this study is to contribute

---

[19] See e.g. also E. Berti, 'Che cos'è l'essere?' ['L'essere'], in id., *In principio era la meraviglia* (Rome, 2007), 41–73 (originally published in M. Barbanti et al. (eds.), *Unione e amicizia* (Catania, 2002), 25–42) at 49; B. Collette-Dučić, '*Sophiste*' ['*Sophiste*'], in A. Motte and P. Somville (eds.), *Ousia dans la philosophie grecque des origines à Aristote* (Louvain-la-Neuve, 2008), 143–58 at 144–8.

[20] I have no intention of making a case about translation. My point is not that (uncomplemented) εἶναι should be translated with the English 'to exist' (or corresponding verbs in other modern languages), as e.g. Cornford, *Theory* or N.L. Cordero (trans.), *Platon: Sophiste* (Paris, 1993) often do. This would, in fact, probably spoil Plato's argument, as O'Brien, 'To Be' argues. Instead, my point concerns our philosophical understanding of Plato's conception of participation in the Kind Being.

[21] See C. Kahn, 'Why Existence Does Not Emerge as a Distinct Concept in Greek Philosophy' ['Existence'], *Archiv für Geschichte der Philosophie*, 58 (1976), 323–34 (reprinted in id., *Essays*, 62–74). But note that Owen claimed that 'for Plato, *to be* is *to be something*, and surely this is an account of existence' ('Not-Being', 265; my emphasis). Kahn did not, of course, merely insist that ancient Greek did not possess separate words for the English 'to exist' and 'to be' (or corresponding verbs in other modern languages). The problem is not even that *existentia* (or *exsistentia*) is a word of late appearance, which is in any case true; see V. Carraud, 'L'invention de l'existence: Note sur la christologie de Marius Victorinus', *Quaestio*, 3 (2003), 3–25, esp. 7–8 and n. 19. Kahn's point is rather the more ambitious one that 'the topic of existence is not thematized in Greek discussions of Being' (Kahn, *Essays*,

Plato's Isolation of a Kind Being 9

to revising aspects of the mainstream narrative about the history of ancient metaphysics.

My plan is as follows: I begin, in Section 2, by providing a selective analysis of *Soph.* 250 A 8–D 3, the chief passage of my discussion, and argue that it speaks against the orthodoxy. I then turn to show, in Section 3, that this passage also broaches a conception of being whereby something *is*, due to its combination (κοινωνία, ἐπικοινωνία) or mixing (σύμμειξις) with or participation (μέθεξις) in[22] the Kind Being. This conception will turn out to implement a familiar explanatory strategy whereby something's possession of a given property is metaphysically explained through its combination with or participation in a Form or Kind which is that property by its own nature and whose name names that property. Thus, just as something's beauty is explained in the *Phaedo*, the *Hippias Major*, and the *Symposium* through its participation in the Form of Beauty, so too something's being is explained in the *Sophist* through its participation in the Kind Being. This property of being (*simpliciter*, not being *something*), I contend, is best understood as existence. Section 4 shows that the explanatory pattern broached at *Soph.* 250 A 11–B 11 is consistently deployed throughout the *Sophist*. Section 5 criticizes a rival construal of the notion of a Kind Being, whereby the Kind Being is a most comprehensive genus of all genera, and which may be taken to underpin the consensus's slogan.

4; this remark seems to dispose of the caveat enunciated in 'Existence', which restricted the thesis to the classical age, up to Aristotle)—a point that could be disputed, it seems to me, also by considering the Stoic theory of the supreme genus, on which, see the classic J. Brunschwig, 'The Stoic Theory of the Supreme Genus and Platonic Ontology' ['Theory'], in id., *Papers in Hellenistic Philosophy* (Cambridge, 1994), 92–157 (originally in French in J. Barnes and M. Mignucci (eds.), *Matter and Metaphysics* (Naples, 1988), 19–127). A view consonant with Kahn's has recently been upheld in what promises to be the most extensive reconstruction of the history of the concept of existence (only the first volume has so far appeared), namely J.-C. Bardout, *Penser l'existence* (Paris, 2013), i, esp. 19–84. Bardout argues that reflection on being prior to the age of Victorinus constitutes 'an ontological landscape deprived of existence' (p. 50), though he also lets slip that 'if the word [*sc.* 'existentia'] was long in coming, the need to exhibit a non-essential sense of being (*on*) or essence had already manifested itself' (p. 64; translations mine).

[22] For the indifferent use of these terms (and their cognates), cf. e.g. 251 E 9 and 252 D 2–3 with 252 B 2; 254 E 4 with 255 B 3; 256 A 1, 256 A 7 with 256 B 10; 256 B 1 with 256 B 2. *Phaedo* 100 D 5–6 stresses the marginal importance of a rigid technical vocabulary to express the notion of a participatory relation. It is hardly the only occasion on which Plato warns against quibbling over names: see e.g. *Rep.* 533 D 6–9; *Theaet.* 184 C 1–3; *Polit.* 261 E 1–7.

Section 6 appends a brief contrast between Plato's and Aristotle's conceptions of being, and some closing remarks.

2. To be is not to be something

2.1. Context: The Sophist's inquiry into being and the 'children's prayer'

The *Sophist*'s avowed purpose to provide an account of what a sophist is (218 B 7–C 1) soon turns out to involve a series of progressively more fundamental problems whose treatment gives the dialogue a Chinese-box structure. It emerges that defining the sophist requires the preliminary disarming of the paradox of falsehood. This demands in turn a prior assessment of Parmenides' ban of not-being. But since not-being proves intractable, because unthinkable and inexpressible, the Eleatic Stranger (hereafter ES) proposes to start off by focusing on being, 'the most important and chief thing' (243 D 1: τοῦ μεγίστου τε καὶ ἀρχηγοῦ).

There begins an inquiry into *what being is*,[23] governed by a typical definitional question reminiscent of those habitually raised in Plato's earlier dialogues, but also partly unprecedented, insofar as the definiendum is for the first time, not *a* being, but being itself (τὸ ὄν, τὸ εἶναι). This inquiry starts off by sifting through the views of other thinkers who made pronouncements about being: the dualists (243 D 8–244 A 2), the monists (244 B 6–245 D 11), and the two opposing parties of the Gigantomachy (245 E 6–249 D 4). All succumb to the ES's critical scrutiny.

A last attempt to provide an account of being is made by the ES himself, through what he calls 'the children's prayer': 'being and the all are as many things as are both immovable and in motion' (249 D 3–4: ὅσα ἀκίνητα καὶ κεκινημένα, τὸ ὄν τε καὶ τὸ πᾶν συναμφότερα). The thrust of this notoriously controversial conclusion seems to me not, as often claimed, that the totality of being should include

---

[23] See e.g. *Soph.* 243 D 9–E 2, 244 A 5–6, 246 A 1–2, with M. Frede, 'Die Frage nach dem Seienden: Sophistes' ['Frage'], in T. Kobusch and B. Mojsisch (eds.), *Platon* (Darmstadt, 1996), 181–99; and P. Sabrier, 'Plato's Method of Enquiry in the *Sophist*', in J. K. Larsen et al. (eds.), *New Perspectives on Platonic Dialectic* (New York, 2022), 233–48. Thus, unlike other readers (e.g. McCabe, *Individuals*, 199–200), I doubt the agenda is set at 242 C 4–6 through the 'how many and of what sort'(πόσα τε καὶ ποιά) questions.

Plato's Isolation of a Kind Being 11

two different classes of things, those in motion and those immovable, or that (all or some) things in motion should be raised from the status of mere becoming to which the Friends of the Forms had relegated them (246 B 9–C 2; 248 A 7–8) to the status of being.[24] Instead, I believe the ES means to stress that the inhabitants of the realm of being (τὸ ὄν) and the all (τὸ πᾶν)[25] are both in motion and at rest.[26] A proper defence of this interpretation would require a global examination of the Gigantomachy, with a consequent distraction from my current argument.[27] The foregoing remarks are mostly meant to provide a minimal explanatory framework for the proposed translation,[28] and I will not rest anything heavy on them.

---

[24] See e.g. A. Diès (ed. and trans.), *Platon: Le sophiste* [*Sophiste*] (Paris, 1925), 275–6, 358; Cornford, *Theory*, 241–2; W. D. Ross, *Plato's Theory of Ideas* (Oxford, 1951), 110; D. Keyt, 'Plato's Paradox That the Immutable Is Unknowable' ['Paradox'], *Philosophical Quarterly*, 74 (1969), 1–14 at 6; V. Politis, 'The Argument for the Reality of Change and Changelessness in Plato's *Sophist* (248 E 7–249 D 5)', in F.-G. Herrmann (ed.), *New Essays on Plato* (Swansea, 2006), 149–75 at 169–71; P. Crivelli, *Plato's Account of Falsehood* [*Account*] (Cambridge, 2012), 92–5.

[25] I leave it open whether τε καί at 249 D 4 is epexegetical, and therefore τὸ ὄν and τὸ πᾶν have one and the same reference, as various scholars mentioned in both n. 24 and n. 26 have claimed. See also n. 27 below.

[26] See e.g. Bonitz, *Studien*, 168; the references in Gill, *Philosophos*, 98 n. 46; and, more recently, E. Perl, 'The Motion of Intellect on the Neoplatonic Reading of *Sophist* 248 E –249 D', *International Journal of the Platonic Tradition*, 8 (2014), 135–60 at 152–3; Hestir, *Foundation*, 121–6; and T. Irani, 'Perfect Change in Plato's *Sophist*', *Oxford Studies in Ancient Philosophy*, 60 (2022), 45–93.

[27] The issue cannot in any case be adjudicated on reasons of textual criticism or grammar. The text of the MSS is not to be altered. Schleiermacher's proposed emendation of ὅσα into ὡς (F. Schleiermacher (trans.), *Platons Werke* (Berlin, 1807), ii. ii. 493), even when judged favorably (see L. F. Heindorf (ed.), *Platonis dialogi selecti* (Berlin, 1810), iv. 392, repeated by I. Bekker (ed.), *Platonis scripta graece omnia* (London, 1826), iv. 429), has never actually been followed by any of the editors, unanimous in printing ὅσα; and even if it were followed, it would be interpretatively inconclusive. The more invasive attempt by Badham and Schanz (see the apparatus ad loc. of Diès, *Sophiste*, and O. Apelt (ed.), *Platonis Sophista* [*Sophista*] (Leipzig, 1879)) to excise the entire phrase ὅσα ἀκίνητα καὶ κεκινημένα, just like Steinhart's variation of the word order (ξυναμφότερα λέγειν τὸ ὄν τε καὶ τὸ πᾶν, καὶ ὅσα ἀκίνητα καὶ κεκινημένα), has also been rejected, and would in any case be equally inconclusive. As regards the grammar, it may be contended that if ἀκίνητα and κεκινημένα had different references, we should expect ὅσα to be repeated before κεκινημένα (cf. e.g. Perl, 'Motion', 153), as in Euseb. *PE* 14. 8. 1. 1 Mras = Numen. fr. 27 Des Places: Καρνεάδης δὲ ἐκδεξάμενος παρ' Ἡγησίνου, χρεὼν φυλάξαι ὅσα ἀκίνητα καὶ ὅσα κεκινημένα ἦν (cf. Apelt, *Sophista*, 155). But this alone is uncompelling; cf. e.g. *Polit.* 288 B 3–4; *Laws.* 823 A 4–5; *Epin.* 981 D 2–3. Similarly, τε καί may (cf. e.g. *Soph.* 256 E 3) or may not (cf. e.g. *Soph.* 242 C 6) be epexegetical.

[28] Keyt, 'Paradox', 6 (approved by Crivelli, *Account*, 92, n. 64) judges a translation like mine grammatically legitimate, but unnecessary and unfeasible. But all the motivations he sets out are specifically directed against the interpretation of

I do think, however, that this reading fits better with the ES's indirect reformulation of the 'prayer' in the subsequent lines.[29] It is this reformulation that matters for my present purposes, and I shall now turn to it.

2.2. The argument against the 'children's prayer' and its implications

Theaetetus deludes himself that with the *logos* ('account') of the 'children's prayer' a satisfactory conclusion to the definitional inquiry about being has finally been achieved (249 D 6–8). But the ES immediately disenchants him by raising a further difficulty. That *logos*, he rejoins, is open to the same objection raised earlier against the dualists (243 D 6–244 B 5). Just as being could not be the hot and the cold, so too it cannot be motion (κίνησις) and rest (στάσις).[30] The ES's argument can be schematized as follows:

1. [250 A 8–9] Motion and Rest are most contrary to each other (ἐναντιώτατα... ἀλλήλοις);
2. [250 A 11–12] and yet 'to be' (εἶναι) is said *in the same way* (ὁμοίως) of *both and each* (ἀμφότερα αὐτὰ καὶ ἑκάτερον) of them;
3. [250 B 2–7] for *both and each* of them 'to be' does not mean either 'to be in motion' (κινεῖσθαι) or 'to be at rest' (ἑστάναι);
4. [250 B 8–C 8] instead, Motion and Rest are said 'to be', due to their combination with Being (πρὸς τὴν τῆς οὐσίας κοινωνίαν),

---

G. E. L. Owen, 'Plato and Parmenides on the Timeless Present', *Monist*, 50 (1966), 317–40 (reprinted in id., *LSD*, 27–44), which is not the only one that can be underpinned by that translation.

[29] See n. 30 below and also Bonitz, *Studien*, 168–9 n. 2 and Gill, *Philosophos*, 98–9.

[30] The 'children's prayer', however, stated that being (and the all) is ὅσα ἀκίνητα καὶ κεκινημένα, not that being is στάσις and κίνησις. Now, suppose that in the 'prayer' ἀκίνητα and κεκινημένα had different references. If so, the ES would fallaciously infer from the claim that the totality of being includes both things in motion and things unmoved that being itself is both motion and rest. By contrast, if the 'prayer' states that the inhabitants of the realm of being (and the all) are both in motion and at rest, no such fallacy is committed. The ES would legitimately infer from the extensional claim that being (and the all) include things that are both in motion and at rest the intensional claim that being itself should therefore be identified with motion and rest. See Bluck, *Sophist*, 104. I hereafter capitalize 'Motion', 'Rest', and 'Being' because I take Plato to start singling out here the first three *megista genē* ('greatest Kinds'), as shown by the back-reference at 254 D 4–5: 'Greatest of the kinds we have just been talking about are being itself, rest and motion', μέγιστα μὴν τῶν γενῶν ἃ νυνδὴ διῇμεν τό τε ὂν αὐτὸ καὶ στάσις καὶ κίνησις.

which is a third thing alongside motion and rest (τρίτον ἄρα τι παρὰ ταῦτα) and encompassing them (περιεχομένην);
5. [250 C 3–4] Therefore (ἄρα), Being is not Motion and Rest together (συναμφότερον) but something other than these (ἕτερον τούτων).

Thus, not even the account of being delivered by the 'children's prayer' withstands scrutiny. But this time the refutation leads the two interlocutors to a dead end, an *aporia* about being bigger than any of those faced so far in the dialogue (250 E 1–4). For the ES draws two implications from statement (5):[31]

6. [250 C 6–7] by its own nature (κατὰ τὴν αὑτοῦ φύσιν), Being is neither in motion nor at rest (τὸ ὂν οὔτε ἕστηκεν οὔτε κινεῖται);
7. [250 C 12–D 3] so Being falls outside both Motion and Rest (ἐκτὸς τούτων ἀμφοτέρων), which means that it does not instantiate either motion or rest, i.e. it neither moves (μὴ κινεῖται) nor rests (οὐχ ἕστηκεν).

The problem is that statement (1) established that Motion and Rest are 'most contrary' to each other. This is apparently taken to entail that the attributes of being in motion and being at rest are not only mutually exclusive, but also jointly exhaustive. It seems, therefore, inconceivable that something neither moves nor rests. Thus, prompted by a rhetorical question of the ES (D 3: ἦ δυνατὸν οὖν τοῦτο; 'Is that possible, then?'), Theaetetus immediately judges statement (7) 'absolutely impossible' (250 D 4: πάντων μὲν οὖν ἀδυνατώτατον). The dead end, the greatest *aporia* about being, is, therefore, triggered by the *impossible* consequence (Being neither rests nor moves) derived, seemingly validly, from the *sound* conclusion of the argument against the account of being delivered by the 'prayer' (Being is not Motion and Rest together, but something other than these, a third thing).

---

[31] Unlike other commentators (e.g. Crivelli, *Account*, 95–7), I take the refutation of the account of being delivered by the 'children's prayer' to be completed at 250 C 5. Statements (1)–(5) give a self-contained argument, and the conclusion that Being 'is not motion and rest together' (οὐκ ἄρα κίνησις καὶ στάσις ἐστὶ συναμφότερον) is naturally interpreted as contradicting the 'prayer' (ὅσα ἀκίνητα καὶ κεκινημένα... συναμφότερα). The subsequent lines (250 C 6–D 4), as I understand them, do not, therefore, contain further steps in the argument against the 'prayer', but implications drawn from the argument's conclusion.

The literature abounds with examinations of this stretch of text.[32] The debate has largely been dominated by the attempt to unravel some surreptitious misstep in the chain of inferences leading to statement (7) and to explore its consequences in the subsequent developments of the dialogue's argument. The wrong step is usually detected in the later moves (statements (6) and (7)). Thus, scholars have variously suggested, for example, that two types of statements (e.g. of identity and predication) or predication (e.g. ordinary and definitional) are conflated; or that the adverbial phrase 'by its own nature' (250 C 6) is misunderstood; or that placing Being 'outside' (250 D 2) Motion and Rest is erroneous. The problem is surely genuine. But it has eclipsed, I submit, a key point in the argument against the 'prayer', namely its rejection of analyses of to be as to be *something*.

2.3. *Being vs. being something*

Look again at statements (2) and (3). In the former, the ES avers that εἶναι is said *in the same way* (ὁμοίως)[33] of Motion, Rest, and both Motion and Rest together. That is, when we say 'Motion is', 'Rest is', and 'both Motion and Rest are', 'to be' is predicated *in the same way* respectively of Motion, Rest, and both Motion and Rest taken together.

In what way exactly? Plato first proceeds *via negativa*, by immediately clearing the field, through statement (3), of a possible misconceived answer: *for both and each* of Motion and Rest, 'to be' means neither 'to be in motion' nor 'to be at rest'. The emphasis on the ἀμφότερα καὶ ἑκάτερον ('both and each') pair[34] (250 A 11–12, 250 B 2) calls for special attention. It suggests that neither for Motion and Rest *taken together* nor for each of them *taken individually* does εἶναι mean either 'to be in motion' or 'to be at rest'. Contrast, for example, the predicate 'two', which is (truly) attributed to Motion

---

[32] Critical surveys in Crivelli, *Account*, 95–101 and Gill, *Philosophos*, 16–17, 206–11, 227–9.

[33] Cf. 243 E 4–6, 256 A 12, and 258 A 1–3. I return to the meaning of this adverb shortly.

[34] Not a pleonasm: see Crivelli, *Account*, 140 and nn.108–110. Bostock, 'Is Not', 101 protests that the inference from the (disjunctive) claim at 250 C 1–2 'that being is not to be identified with change or rest' to the (collective) claim at 250 C 3–4 'that being is not to be identified with change and rest together...already seems to be a fallacy'. But 250 C 3–4 capitalizes on the whole argument starting from 250 A 8–9, which lays emphasis on both ἀμφότερα and ἑκάτερον.

Plato's Isolation of a Kind Being

and Rest together (they are *two* Kinds), but not to each of them individually (each of them is *one* single Kind).[35] Accordingly, the recurrence of the ἀμφότερα καὶ ἑκάτερον pair invites us to reformulate statement (3) in a slightly different but perfectly equivalent phraseology, by breaking it down into the following three distinct claims:

3a. for Motion, 'to be' means neither '*to be in motion*' nor 'to be at rest';
3b. for Rest, 'to be' means neither 'to be in motion' *nor* '*to be at rest*';
3c. for both Motion and Rest, 'to be' means neither 'to be in motion' nor 'to be at rest'.

What reasons does Plato have to hold these three claims? He does not say, but the following seems a safe guess.[36] Suppose 'to be' meant 'to be in motion'. Since 'to be in motion' expresses the nature of Motion, and since 'to be' is *ex hypothesi* said *in the same way* of both and each of Motion and Rest, it would follow that 'to move' would express the nature of Rest too, i.e. that Rest is by its own nature in motion. But this seems impossible, especially since Motion and Rest are, also *ex hypothesi*, 'most contraries'. An analogous case could obviously be made if 'to be' were taken to mean 'to be at rest'. Thus, for both and each of Motion and Rest, 'to be' means neither 'to be in motion' nor 'to be at rest'.

Now, (3a)–(3c) are phrased as statements about the semantics of the verb 'to be': they concern what this verb does not *mean*, when predicated of both and each of Motion and Rest. This manner of phrasing such statements is intended to reflect the frequent use throughout 250 A 8–D 3 of *verba dicendi* or comparable verbs related to signification.[37] But surely Plato's point here does not just concern what we mean by certain linguistic expressions. It pertains also to how things *are*. In the *Sophist*, both in the stretch of text under discussion (250 A 8–D 3) and throughout the subsequent section on the 'communion' of Kinds (but arguably elsewhere as well in both this and other dialogues), language analysis, conceptual

---

[35] Cf. *Rep.* 476 A 1–3, 524 B 7–C 1; *Theaet.* 185 B 2; *Parm.* 143 D 1–5.
[36] Following Crivelli, *Account*, 139–40.
[37] Cf. e.g. 250 A 9: λέγεις; 250 A 11: φής; 250 B 1: φημί; 250 B 2: λέγων; 250 B 5: σημαίνεις; 250 B 11: προσεῖπας.

analysis, and metaphysical analysis are tightly intertwined, and Plato freely transitions from one into another—often he starts from the analysis of what we say or think about X and continues to the analysis of how or what X is, a procedure which seems to me dictated by primarily illustrative needs and which does not imply, of course, that for Plato things are a certain way *because* we speak or think about them in a certain way. Here are a few examples:

 i. At 250 B 8, as a result (cf. 250 B 7: ἄρα) of statements (2) and (3), *viz.* the semantic claims that 'to be' is *said* in the same way of both and each of Motion and Rest, and that for both and each of them 'to be' does not *mean* either 'to be in motion' or 'to be at rest', the ES suggests that Being (τὸ ὄν) is to be singled out 'in the soul' (ἐν τῇ ψυχῇ) as a third thing (τρίτον τι), apart from Motion and Rest. But just a few lines later (250 C 3–4) he infers (cf. 250 C 3: ἄρα) that Being (τὸ ὄν) simply *is not* both Motion and Rest, but something different from them (οὐκ ἄρα κίνησις καὶ στάσις ἐστὶ συναμφότερον τὸ ὂν ἀλλ' ἕτερον δή τι τούτων). And statement (6), at 250 C 6–7, capitalizes (cf. 250 C 6: ἄρα) on this conclusion by making a point about Being's own *nature* (κατὰ τὴν αὐτοῦ φύσιν).

 ii. At 250 B 10–11, the ES suggests that one *says* (προσεῖπας) that Motion and Rest *are*, by considering (ἀπιδών) that they both combine with Being. But later, as we shall see in Section 4, virtually the same point is rephrased without any *verbum dicendi* or comparable verbs related to signification (cf. e.g. 254 D 10, 256 A 1, 256 D 9): Motion and Rest *are* (not merely: are *said* to be), because of their combination or participation in the Kind Being.

 iii. Similarly, at 255 A 7–B 1, the ES freely transitions from a claim about what we can *say* (προσείπωμεν) in common about both Motion and Rest, to a claim about their own *nature* (τῆς αὐτοῦ φύσεως).

 iv. Yet again, at 255 B 8–C 4, the ES asks whether one should *think* (διανοητέον) of Being and Identity as one single thing, then argues that they cannot *mean* (σημαίνετον) the same, and concludes that they cannot *be* (εἶναι) one thing.

Sundry further examples could be mentioned. But the foregoing suffices to show that Plato's point at 250 A 8–D 3 should not be interpreted as concerning just the semantics of the verb 'to be'

Plato's Isolation of a Kind Being

when it is predicated of Motion and Rest, but also what it is for Motion and Rest to be. After all, were 250 A 11–B 7 intended to make only a point of semantics and not also of ontology, one would hardly see how Plato could infer from statements about the meaning of 'to be' that Being should be singled out as a third thing (τρίτον τι) endowed with its own nature. I therefore conclude that statements (3a)–(3c) license the following reformulation:

3a.i. for Motion, to be is *neither to be in motion* nor to be at rest;
3b.i. for Rest, to be is neither to be in motion *nor to be at rest*;
3c.i. for both Motion and Rest, to be is neither to be in motion nor to be at rest.

Now, suppose the consensus view on Plato's conception of being were true. To take Motion as a specimen, 'Motion is' would have to be understood as meaning that Motion is *something* (cf. e.g. Owen, 'Snares', 76–7). This is, in turn, most plausibly to be unpacked as Motion is *in motion*, or is *as moving*, or is *in motion by its own nature*, i.e. it is *motion itself*, or the *essence* or *nature* of motion. Such is exactly the move that various champions of the consensus view explicitly make.[38]

I submit that statement (3a.i) speaks against readings of this type; and to the extent that (3a.i) can be generalized, it provides us with evidence that the consensus view does not reliably represent Plato's conception of being in the *Sophist*. Statement (3a.i) *denies*

---

[38] See e.g. Frede, *Prädikation*, 49: '"Motion is" should not be completed as "Motion is motion", but rather as "Motion is in motion."' (my translation). The point is preserved even when talk of completion is dropped or overshadowed; see e.g. P. Seligman, *Being and Not-Being* (The Hague, 1974), 69: 'when [Plato] says "motion is" or "motion and rest are", he does not use the verb "to be" in our "existential" sense. Motion *is* as moving, and only as moving, it *is* as a "what", a "nature"'; A. Silverman, *The Dialectic of Essence* [*Essence*] (Princeton, 2002), 157: 'Being is predicated of [Motion and Rest]. While this can be read as an existence claim, it is best understood to signify that each of them has its own distinctive nature'; Gill, *Philosophos*, 165:

> the statement, 'Change is, because it partakes of Being' (256 A 1), states of Change something quite definite...: Change is *itself* (changing) *by itself* (in virtue of Change). That is...what it means to say 'Change is' (full stop) or 'Change partakes of being'. The 'is' is complete, since we need not look outside the subject to determine what Change is; instead we analyze the subject—look inside it—to uncover its nature.

Zaks, *Apparences*, 234: 'there is nothing to prevent...saying that "change is" implies, presupposes that it exists in such and such a way, that is to say, in the present case, that it exists as change' (my translation).

that for Motion to be is to be in motion (κινεῖσθαι)—or, for that matter, to be at rest (ἑστάναι). As to-be-in-motion captures the nature of the Kind Motion, statement (3a.i) refuses metaphysical analyses of 'Motion is' whereby it signifies that Motion has (or even is) its own distinctive nature, *viz.* the nature of being-in-motion, or is motion itself, or is in motion.

Note that this is not a point about whether, and if so how, the verb εἶναι must be complemented to constitute a meaningful grammatical unit when predicated of a given subject—an issue that has been a major concern of a large number of interpreters. Instead, it is a point about the metaphysical state of affairs underlying 'Motion is'.[39] On the consensus view, this is not simply that Motion exists, but that Motion exemplifies or is itself the nature or essence of a determinate property, *viz.* Motion itself. My claim is that (3a.i) contradicts this construal.

[39] Accordingly, my argument is also not meant to counter directly the 'semantic-continuity thesis', authoritatively defended by Brown (see 'Being' and 'Verb'; the label is not Brown's own, but freely inspired by the title of Leigh, 'Semantic Continuity'). It nonetheless questions certain aspects of it. Brown formalizes her thesis as follows (numbering is mine for ease of reference): '[1] X *is* (complete use) entails X *is something* and [2] X *is* F entails X *is*. X *is not* (complete use) is equivalent to X *is not anything at all*' ('Being', 477). One plausible way of understanding entailment in [2] is that statements of predication have an existential component (cf. e.g. Crivelli, *Account*, 7–8, 202). The inference from 'X is F' to 'X is' is licensed because part of the claim made by 'X is F' is that 'X is', namely an existential claim (cf. G. E. Moore, 'Is Existence a Predicate?' [Symposium with W. Kneale], *Proceedings of the Aristotelian Society*, suppl. vol. 15 (1936), 175–88 at 187: 'It seems to me that "This exists" (in this usage) always forms part of what is asserted by "This is a book", "This is red", etc.'). We may ask, however, whether the same notion of entailment is operative in [1], that is, whether statements of existence have a copulative component, such that the inference from 'X is' to 'X is *something*' is licensed because part of the claim made by 'X is' is that 'X is *something*', i.e. '$\exists F\ (X$ is $F)$'. If this is the correct way of understanding this aspect of the 'semantic-continuity thesis', then the distance Brown claims for herself from Owen's view, as summarized by the slogan 'to be is to be something', seems to shrink. Relatedly, remember that Brown overtly agrees that 'the core of being is being something' ('Dark Matter', 288; but see 'Verb', 228) and that a number of scholars (even some sympathetic to Brown's reading) have read the 'semantic-continuity thesis' as a variation on, or an advancement of, or in the same family as, Owen's; see n. 18 above. This and other objections notwithstanding, it remains possible that the 'semantic-continuity thesis' correctly captures a phenomenon of the Greek language, namely that an existential use of εἶναι can easily lead to use of the same verb as a copula (see also O'Brien, 'Form', 225), and, conversely, that the copula has existential import. But neither insight, in my opinion, need be tied to either the idea that 'to be is to be something' or that 'X is' *entails* 'X is something' (construed as a claim that statements of existence have a copulative component).

In addition, note that nowhere does the argument against the 'prayer' say or even suggest that according to one sense or use of εἶναι but not another, or according to one reading of the sentence 'Motion is in motion' but not another, one can say that for Motion to be is to be in motion. It is, instead, agreed that in no case (250 B 3: οὐδαμῶς; cf. 250 B 7) can it be conceded that for both and each of Motion and Rest to be is to be in motion—and an analogous case holds for Rest or any other Form. Thus, the claim that for both and each of Motion and Rest 'to be' means neither 'to be in motion' nor 'to be at rest' is never called into question in the rest of the dialogue. Nor is any new doctrinal element introduced at later stages that implicitly demands its recantation.[40] Cases of self-predication

[40] According to Gill, *Philosophos*, esp. chs. 5 and 7, the development of the dialogue's argument should prompt the reader to realize that the Kind Being is a structural, internal factor co-responsible for making each being *what* it is. Thus, for Motion *to be*, by participation in Being, would mean that Motion is *itself* (moving) *by itself* (in virtue of Motion itself) (165). For Gill this conception of the Kind Being is part of the solution to the greatest *aporia* about Being (250 E 1–2), a solution which Plato leaves to the reader to work out. To resolve this *aporia*, Gill believes, one must realize: (a) against statement (1) (echoed at 254 D 7–8; possibly also at 256 B 6–c3, though see Crivelli, *Account*, 161–6), that Motion and Rest are not most contrary to each other (ἐναντιώτατα ἀλλήλοις), but, being structural Kinds, must mutually participate (227–9); and (b) against 250 C 12–D 3, that Being is not *outside* Motion and Rest, 'as a necessary external attribute they share' (229), but 'a form that structures all beings and together with some other content *makes them what they are*...Being is *inside* the nature of every being as its structural core enabling it to fit together with other things outside its specific nature' (240, italics and emphasis mine). The recognition of (a) and (b) would make it possible, so the argument goes, to remove every obstacle to the acceptance of the account of being stated by the 'children's prayer'. This interpretation is open to various objections. I focus on the two more directly relevant to the present account. (1) Gill assumes that when at 250 C 12–D 3 the ES states that Being is 'outside' (ἐκτός) both Motion and Rest, he means that Motion and Rest participate in Being 'as a necessary external attribute they share' (229). But what he actually means is that Being is neither in motion nor at rest. For he first states that if something is not in motion, then it must be at rest, and that if something is not at rest, then it must be in motion (250 C 12– D 2: εἰ γάρ τι μὴ κινεῖται, πῶς οὐχ ἕστηκεν; ἢ τὸ μηδαμῶς ἑστὸς πῶς οὐκ αὖ κινεῖται); then he concludes that Being has now appeared *outside* both Motion and Rest (250 D 2–3: τὸ δὲ ὂν ἡμῖν νῦν ἐκτὸς τούτων ἀμφοτέρων ἀναπέφανται), which should mean that it instantiates neither, i.e. it neither moves nor rests. As a matter of fact, Gill herself at one point paraphrases 250 C 12–D 3 by saying that 'rest and change are not accidents or necessary external attributes *of it*' (though earlier in the same page she asserts, rather differently, that the *aporia* about being maintains that 'change and rest partake of being as a necessary external attribute *of them*'; my italics in both cases). The problem is, therefore, not whether Being is or is not an internal constitutive part of the nature of Motion and Rest, but whether Being can legitimately be said neither to move nor to rest (and note that the νῦν ('now') at 250 D 2 suggests a

of the type '*X* is *X*' are, of course, countenanced (e.g. 258 B 11–C 3), but never regarded as analyses of '*X* is', or metaphysically explained through *X*'s participation in the Kind Being, as instead the ES systematically does—we will see that in a moment—to account for the fact that *X is*. After all, statement (3) contributes decisively to concluding that being is a 'third thing', i.e., as will be clarified shortly thereafter in the dialogue, an independent Kind or Form, a conclusion never dismissed in the *Sophist* and playing a key role in its argument.

Further, it would also be rather puzzling if for Motion to be were to be in motion. For in statement (4), as we shall see better in Section 3, Plato states that Motion and Rest *are*, due to their combination with a 'third thing' (τρίτον τι), namely (what will soon thereafter be identified as) the Kind or Form of Being. But Motion is in motion by its own nature, being itself the essence of Motion (see n. 44 below), and not due to its participation in or combination with some other thing.[41] One may perhaps say that *ousia*, like knowability, comes to Motion (and all other Forms) from the Good, as per

back-reference to 250 C 6–7, which does not deny *tout court* that Being moves or rests, but that it does so *by its own nature*). (2) Even granted that Motion and Rest should mutually participate (*contra*, see e.g. D. O'Brien, *Le non-être* [*Non-Être*] (Sankt Augustin, 1995), 103–10), the point of statement (3) in the argument above against the 'prayer' would remain untouched. For even if Motion and Rest shared in each other, 'to be' would still mean, for both and each of them, neither to-be-in-motion nor to-be-at-rest. For even if Motion were predicated of Rest, and Rest of Motion, the fact remains that to-be-in-motion expresses the nature of Motion, but not of Rest, and cannot therefore be predicated *in the same way* of both and each of Motion and Rest; by the same token, to-be-at-rest expresses the nature of Rest, but not of Motion, and cannot therefore be predicated *in the same way* of both and each of Motion and Rest.

[41] *Pace* Bonitz, *Studien*, 201–2. Whilst commendably being among the few to address the problem, Bonitz resolves it by dubiously suggesting that the isolation of a Kind Being causes:

a modification for the theory of ideas…While, on the one hand, the content of every concept is in itself because it is the object of knowledge, on the other hand, its being comes from its communion with the idea of being, and the reality attributed to it in itself thereby becomes *a conditioned reality, borrowed from the relationship to another idea*' (translation and italics mine).

Similarly, Silverman, *Essence*, 146 (but without any developmentalist claim): 'what follows from the fact that a Form partakes of Being, i.e., possesses its *ousia*'. If a Form is in itself (*viz.* not due to its participation in something else) no longer even the essence of which it is the Form, which it would purportedly borrow from the Kind Being, that Form is in itself no longer anything. The doctrine of Forms would not simply be modified, but deprived of its distinctive philosophical meaning.

Rep. 509 B 5–9 (cf. e.g. Dixsaut, *Naturel*, 328; see also n. 89 below). Yet Plato never describes this as an instance of participation or combination,[42] and at any rate the Good never makes an appearance in the *Sophist*.

Furthermore, statement (2) established that 'to be' is said *in the same way* (ὁμοίως) of *both and each* (ἀμφότερα καὶ ἑκάτερον) of Motion and Rest. So in both 'Motion is' and 'both Motion and Rest are' the verb 'to be' should carry the same meaning (cf. Arist., *Metaph*. Z. 4, 1030ª21–ᵇ3, esp. 1030ª21: 'being belongs to everything, but not in the same way', τὸ ἔστιν ὑπάρχει πᾶσιν, ἀλλ' οὐχ ὁμοίως; *EE* 7. 2, 1236ª28–9: but the others are [*sc*. friendships], though they are *not similarly* [*sc*. so]', αἱ δ' εἰσὶ [*sc*. φιλίαι] μέν, ἀλλ' οὐχ ὁμοίως εἰσίν). But if 'Motion is' should be understood as indicating, not that Motion simply *is*, i.e. exists, but that it has (or even is) its own nature, or even just *a* nature, then it is difficult to see how 'to be' could mean *the same* in 'Motion is' and 'both Motion and Rest are'. No single nature or essence could be shared by both Motion and Rest. The possible rejoinder that the latter phrase means simply that Motion and Rest have each their own nature brushes away the semantic difference between ἀμφότερα and ἑκάτερον. We have seen, however, that Plato's emphasis on both is scarcely redundant.[43]

---

[42] Aristotle does say that Forms 'come from (ἐξ) the Great and the Small by participation in the One (κατὰ μέθεξιν τοῦ ἑνός)' (*Metaph*. A. 6, 987ᵇ21–2), and other remarks of his may suggest a similar point (cf. e.g. *Metaph*. A. 9, 987ᵇ29–33, B. 3, 998ᵇ9–11). But the reconciliation of this claim with the *littera* of the dialogues encounters notorious difficulties (including that of the relation between the One and the Good), such that its use here would mean trying to explain *obscurum per obscurius*.

[43] One may legitimately protest that ὁμοίως need not mean 'in the same way', but can be understood in the weaker sense of 'equally'. Now, in the *Sophist* there are six further occurrences of the adverb 'ὁμοίως': 243 C 5, 243 E 5, 252 B 4, 252 B 5, 256 A 12, and 258 A 1. Those at 252 B 4–5 are philosophically irrelevant. Of the remaining four: (i) 243 C 5 allows both readings: it can indicate both that, with respect to being and not-being, the two interlocutors are in a condition of equal *aporia*, or that they are in *aporia* in the same way, i.e. by failing to understand the meaning of both the terms 'being' and 'not-being'. (ii) Regarding 243 E 5 (which 249 E 6–250 A 2 explicitly refers back to), Crivelli, *Account*, 74–5 gives compelling reasons for preferring a robust reading, and I refer to his discussion for further details. (iii) 256 A 12 clearly supports a robust reading of ὁμοίως: the ES asserts that when we assert that Motion is identical and not identical, we do not say so ὁμοίως; surely he does not mean that we do not affirm it to an equal degree, but that we do not do so in the same sense. The different senses involved reflect two different metaphysical states of affairs: Motion's partaking in Identity with respect to itself and its partaking in Difference with respect to Identity. (iv) 258 A 1 seems to support a weaker reading, because

Further objections may arise about the unpacking of the notion that Motion is *something* as Motion is *as moving*, or is *in motion*, or is *in motion by its own nature*. Thus, some critics may protest that the claim that Motion is *something* should be understood in terms of self-identity, as indicating that Motion is Motion, or that Motion is itself, or that Motion is the same as itself. Other critics might insist that since Plato, both in the *Sophist* and elsewhere, avers that every 'something' (τι) is also a 'being' (ὄν), he should also be taken to commit to the 'to be is to be something' slogan. I shall consider each of these objections in Sections 3.1 and 3.2.

3. To be is to combine with the Kind Being

Statement (2) established that εἶναι is said in the same way of Motion, Rest, and both Motion and Rest taken together. Statement (3) denies that for both and each of Motion and Rest to be is either to be in motion or to be at rest. So what is it for both and each of Motion and Rest—or, for that matter, anything else—to be?

3.1. *The property of being and the Kind Being*

Look back at statement (4). It posits that Motion and Rest *are* because of their combination with Being (πρὸς τὴν τῆς οὐσίας κοινωνίαν), which is a third thing along Motion and Rest (τρίτον ἄρα τι παρὰ ταῦτα) and encompassing them (περιεχομένην). The intentionally underdetermined phrase 'third thing' prefigures the claim explicitly made a few Stephanus pages later that Being is an independent Kind or Form (254 E 3; 255 E 1; 257 A 4–9; 259 A 4–5, 259 B 1–2). So statement (4) broaches a conception of what it is for something to be, whereby X *is* in virtue of its combination with the Kind or

---

there ὁμοίως is contrasted with 'more' (μᾶλλον) and 'less' (ἧττον)—the not-big, the not-beautiful, etc. are, no less and no more, but ὁμοίως with respect to Big and Beautiful. But this need not be so. The point here is not about alleged degrees of being, but that each part of Difference *is* in the same way as the Kind to which it is opposed, i.e. by partaking in Being. Of course, a difficulty arises about the part of Difference opposed to the Kind Being. For the former is not in the same way as the latter—the latter does not participate in, but just *is*, Being. But this issue, which would require a separate treatment, also arises for the rival interpretation. I therefore conclude that, on balance, a robust reading of 'ὁμοίως' is preferable.

Form of Being, i.e. one of the *megista genē*. This is a key move and calls for attention.

I submit that Plato is here implementing two familiar explanatory strategies. First is the one whereby something's possession of a given property is metaphysically accounted for by appealing to its combination with or participation in a Form or Kind which is that property by its own nature and whose name names that property.[44] Plato does not say that Motion is, by being part of the domain of essences, a member the realm of true being contrasted with that of the transient objects of perception (γένεσις, 'becoming'). If he did say so, we could perhaps have interpreted him as saying that Motion *is*, in that it is itself an essence, a nature, a member of 'the domain of definable entities' (Code, 'Essence', 426). Instead, he asserts that Motion *is*, due to its combination with a single, independent Kind, i.e. the Kind Being, which will explicitly be called different from *each* and *all* other kinds ('Being, for its part, by sharing in difference, will be different from the other kinds, and in being different from all of them it is not each of them or all the rest together', τὸ δὲ ὂν αὖ θατέρου μετειληφὸς ἕτερον τῶν ἄλλων ἂν εἴη γενῶν, ἕτερον δ' ἐκείνων ἁπάντων ὂν οὐκ ἔστιν ἕκαστον αὐτῶν οὐδὲ σύμπαντα τὰ ἄλλα), 259 B 2–4). Thus, just as, for example, the beauty of a plurality of objects was explained in the *Phaedo* (100 B 3–D 7), the *Hippias Major* (300 A 9–B 2), and the *Symposium* (210 B 1–211 B 3) through

---

[44] On participation, see F. Fronterotta, *METHEXIS [METHEXIS]* (Pisa, 2001), esp. 42–4, 148–51, 195–8. On the Forms' *being* by their own nature the property their name names and their participants *have*, see esp. Cherniss, 'Relation', 258–62; and A. Code, 'Aristotle: Essence and Accident' ['Essence'], in R. Grandym and R. Warner (eds.), *Philosophical Grounds of Rationality* (Oxford, 1986), 411–39, esp. 425–9. This seems the gist of formulae such as τὸ ὅ ἐστι ("what is"'), e.g. *Phaedo* 75 D 1) or τὸ ὅ ἐστι ὂν ὄντως ('what really is what it is', e.g. *Phdr.* 247 E 2), often deployed by Plato to refer to Forms; see F. Ademollo, 'Plato's Conception of the Forms: Some Remarks', in R. Chiaradonna and G. Galluzzo (eds.), *Universals in Ancient Philosophy* (Pisa, 2013), 41–85 at 56–65. It also provides for the appropriate conceptual framework to understand uses of the term φύσις with the genitive singular referring to a Form ('the nature of *F*'); cf. e.g. e.g., in the *Sophist*, 255 D 9, 255 E 5, 256 C 2–3, 256 E 1, 257 A 9, 257 C 7, 257 D 4, 257 D 31, 258 A 8, 258 A 11. On this meaning of φύσις, see D. Mannsperger, *Physis bei Plato* (Berlin, 1969), 175–91; and Ademollo, *Cratylus*, 129 on *Crat.* 389 B 8–11. My reading commits Plato to the view that the Kind Being is *being* by its own nature (cf. *Soph.* 250 C 6), i.e. the essence of being. I take it that a view along these lines is targeted by Aristotle's criticism of Plato in the eleventh aporia of *Metaph.* B. 4, 1001ᵃ4–ᵇ1; cf. E. Berti, 'Le problème de la substantialité de l'être et de l'un dans la *Métaphysique* d'Aristote', in P. Aubenque (ed.), *Études sur la 'Métaphysique' d'Aristote* (Paris, 1993), 89–129 (Ital. trans. in E. Berti, *Studi aristotelici* (Brescia, 2012), 221–52).

their participation in the Form of Beauty, so too in our *Sophist* passage the being of Motion and Rest is explained through their combination with the Kind or Form of Being.

Note that, although the cross-examination of rival views on being (starting from 242 C 4) arguably paved the way for the isolation of a Kind Being, it is only with the assessment of the 'children's prayer' that this Kind, though still generically referred to just as a 'third thing', is singled out as an entity in its own right.[45] To be sure, the hypothesis that being is a 'third thing' was envisaged already at 243 E 3–4, in the refutation of the dualists—alluded to by the ES at 249 E 6–250 A 2. But in that context it had a merely refutatory role and was quickly set aside. Instead, in the assessment of the 'children's prayer', while also being involved in a refutation, that hypothesis is entertained and indeed formally established, *for the first time* in the dialogue, as a positive conclusion, following what I have interpreted as a disproof of the slogan (statement (3)). This is also worth emphasizing, because, to deny that participation in (or combination with) Being should be interpreted in purely existential terms, proponents of the 'to be is to be something' slogan have often neglected or underestimated this passage and focused on others (e.g. 256 A 1 and 259 A 6–8; see Section 4).[46] It is interesting, on this note, that Runciman, who believed that the thesis 'that Plato marks off the existential sense of εἶναι from at least one other sense... requires at least a degree of modification', could not help but recognize that at 250 A 11 (and 254 D 10) 'the purely existential sense does appear to be what is meant' (W. G. Runciman, *Plato's Later Epistemology* (Cambridge, 1971), 84, 86).

The second familiar explanatory strategy implemented in our passage is that of (a version of) the 'One-Over-Many' argument.[47] The ES postulates the existence of a Kind or Form of Being as the adequate metaphysical principle responsible for the possession by

---

[45] *Pace* Bostock, 'Is Not', 101: ' "τὸ ὄν" is consistently treated as a phrase used to *generalize* over *whatever is*; it is not used to *name* an abstract entity called "being".' In my view, exactly the opposite is true. Here τὸ ὄν is an independent τι ('something'), shortly after termed γένος and εἶδος, involved in participatory relations, just like any familiar Form in other dialogues which is obviously an abstract entity (i.e. immaterial and outside space and time, cf. *Sym.* 211 A 7–8; *Phdr.* 247 C 2; *Tim.* 52 B 3–5).

[46] Perhaps this may at least partly be due to Ackrill ('Copula'), who defended his 'existential' reading by giving special emphasis to those passages.

[47] On this argument, cf. Alex. Aphr. *In Metaph.* 80. 8–81. 22 Hayduck, with G. Fine, *On Ideas* (Oxford, 1993), 103–19.

a plurality of objects other than that Form, and partaking in that Form, of the property that Form's name names. The interconnection of the two strategies I evoked is clear: precisely when the ES first proposes to account for the being of Motion and Rest by appealing to their combination with the Kind Being, he is also *isolating* that very Kind as the appropriate metaphysical principle responsible for the possession of the property of being by Motion and Rest.

Two further remarks on this. First, both strategies are silently based on the additional (and admittedly unargued) two-pronged premiss that the property of being is a *natural* one and that the predicate signifying it is univocal. For one thing, Plato simply assumes that the (uncomplemented) verb εἶναι refers to a joint-carving property and is not merely a common attribute such as the one signified by 'barbarian', from which he withholds a corresponding Form (*Polit*. 263 A 2–B 11). For another, the adverb ὁμοίως at 250 A 11 shows that Plato takes the verb εἶναι to be predicated in one and the same sense of the various subjects it holds true of—unsurprisingly, given that the property it signifies is obtained through participation in a single Form.

Second, we are now also in a position to resist interpretations of Plato's notion of being in the *Sophist* in terms of self-identity, whereby 'Motion is' signifies that Motion is identical to itself.[48] Such exegeses sit uneasily with Plato's argument for the non-identity of the Kind Identity and the Kind Being (255 B 8–C 8).[49] The property of being the same as itself is due to sharing in the former, not in the latter (256 B 1–2). The truthmakers of 'X is' and 'X is identical to itself' are two distinct states of affairs: the former is X's participation in the Kind Being, the latter X's participation in the Kind Identity. The property obtained by combination with the Kind Being is just being (*simpliciter*) and not being itself or the same as itself.

---

[48] See e.g. Malcolm, 'Analysis'; and Owen, 'Not-Being' (echoed by many, e.g. G. Fine, 'Immanence', in ead., *Plato on Knowledge and Forms* (Oxford, 2003), 301–25 (reprinted from *Oxford Studies in Ancient Philosophy*, 4 (1986), 71–97) at 313: 'Each [*sc*. Form] is (insofar as each is *the same as itself* and has many predicates true of it)' (italics mine); V. Harte, *Plato on Parts and Wholes* (Oxford, 2002), 154: 'if the kind Change is to combine with other kinds, it must both *be* and be distinct; *that is*, it must be the same as itself and different from the rest' (italics original; emphasis mine)).

[49] Analysis of the argument in Crivelli, *Account*, 136–40.

The following interim conclusion results: the argument against the 'children's prayer' suggests that to be is, not to be something, as the consensus view would have it, but to enjoy a distinctive property, *viz.* being, obtained through the combination with a distinctive Kind, i.e. the Kind Being.

Before we move on to explore this property in more detail, a further point needs to be stressed. When in statement (4) Plato asserts that Motion and Rest are, due to their combination with Being, the notion of combination with Being at issue must be distinguished from the one at issue in such passages as *Rep.* 478 E 1–2 (see n. 10 above). Here, speaking of the intermediate ontological status of objects of opinion, earlier said both to be and not to be (e.g. 477 A 6; 478 D 5–7), Plato says that they participate in being and not-being (τὸ ἀμφοτέρων μετέχον, τοῦ εἶναί τε καὶ μὴ εἶναι). In this case, by participation in being, he should be meaning participation in intelligible Being in general (τοῦ εἶναι at 478 E 2 picks up τοῦ εἰλικρινῶς ὄντος ('what purely is') at 478 D 6; cf. 477 A 6–9), i.e. in any given member of the eidetic domain. This is, of course, the Being which, together with the sensible realm, forms the being/becoming dichotomy, key to the argument at the end of *Republic* 5. In such a context, the claim that one of the many beautiful things *is*, by participation in being, may be interpreted as establishing that that thing is beautiful in virtue of it partaking in Beauty itself, or the Form of Beauty (combine e.g. *Rep.* 476 C 7–D 3, 477 A 6–9, 478 D 5–7, and 478 E 7–479 D 5). By contrast, in statement (4), just as in sundry other passages we will examine below in Section 4, the metaphysical scenario is very different: by combination with (or participation in) Being, Plato means combination with Being *qua* single, independent Kind or Form. In such a context, I submit, to say that Motion *is* no longer allows for an interpretation like the one mentioned earlier regarding *Republic* 5. By combining with (or partaking in) Being, Motion just *is* (*simpliciter*), not is something.

As I anticipated in Section 1, it seems to me that the difference between these two contexts—participation in Being *qua* intelligible realm in general and participation in Being *qua* single Kind—has not been sufficiently appreciated in Platonic scholarship. For example, when Kahn states in his monumental study on εἶναι that 'both in the *Sophist* and in the *Republic*...we can say that Plato has only one concept of Being, expressed by *einai*, *ousia*, and *on*, a concept that will cover the notions of existence, predication, identity, truth, and perhaps more' ('*Be*', xii), it seems to me that he is overlooking that difference.[50] Of course, this is neither to say that the being/becoming dichotomy, which also famously comes up in the *Gigantomachia* passage (cf. esp. 246 B 6–C 4; 248 A 7–13), has escaped any commentator on the *Sophist*, nor that scholars have denied or failed to recognize that Plato introduces a Kind Being in the *Sophist*. Instead, what I want to stress is that most modern commentators, unlike ancient ones, have paid insufficient attention to the different metaphysical contexts in which Plato talks about being and that this has not come without consequences for the interpretation of his conception of being and uses of εἶναι.

3.2. *The property of being and existence*

I see no impediment to an understanding of the property of being obtained through the combination the Kind Being as existence. This is, in my view, the most natural way of interpreting the notion of a property of being (*simpliciter*), once the contention that for Plato to be always means to be something, including when it is metaphysically analysed in terms of participation in or combination with the Kind Being, has been proved unpersuasive.[51]

I take the property of being so conceived to be what Simplicius calls 'the bare property of being itself' (*in Phys.* 136. 22 Diels: αὐτὴν τοῦ εἶναι τὴν ἰδιότητα ψιλήν; cf. text to n. 4 above), thereby unmistakably echoing his master Damascius (*Princ.* 2. 62. 12 Westerink: τὰς ἰδιότητας ψιλάς).[52] The latter also calls it 'being alone in itself', which

---

[50] Similarly Burnyeat, 'Apology', 12; and also Brown, 'Verb', 228–33, who detects between the *Republic* and the *Sophist* a modification in the Platonic conception of non-being, but not of being.

[51] For perceptive (if rather brief) remarks in this direction, see M. Mignucci, 'In margine al concetto aristotelico di esistenza' ['Esistenza'], in G. Bernardi Pierini et al., *Scritti in onore di † Carlo Diano* (Bologna, 1975), 227–61 at 257–61; and G. Matthews, 'Aristotle on Existence' ['Aristotle on Existence'], *Bulletin of the Institute of Classical Studies*, 40 (1995), 233–8 at 236.

[52] Note that, apart from the less specific occurrences at Simpl. *in Phys.* 18. 6 and 19. 16 Diels, these are the only occurrences of the phrase ἰδιότης ψιλή in all ancient Greek literature. 'Bare properties' are also termed by Damascius 'simple properties' (cf. *Princ.* 2, esp. 62.24; 62.27–63.1 Westerink: αἱ ἁπλαῖ ἰδιότητης; cf. also 75.7: 'Some properties are simpler', διότητές εἰσιν αἱ μὲν ἁπλούστεραι), i.e. those bestowed by the simple or first Kinds or Forms (75.5–6: τῶν ἁπλῶν γενῶν; 75.7–8: τῶν πρώτων εἰδῶν), including, of course, the Kind Being, which comes first among them (cf. Damasc., *Princ.* 3. 150.2–3 Westerink: ἐν τοῖς γένεσι τοῦ ὄντος τὸ ὂν προηγεῖται τῶν ἄλλων). See

he claims to differ from being considered conjointly with other things, just as ὕπαρξις ('subsistence') differs from οὐσία (cf. *Princ.* 3. 152.13–15 Westerink: 'Subsistence will differ from substance in the same way that *being alone in itself* differs from being considered jointly with the other properties', ἄρα διοίσει τῆς οὐσίας ἡ ὕπαρξις, ᾗ τὸ εἶναι μόνον καθ' αὑτὸ τοῦ ἅμα τοῖς ἄλλοις ὁρωμένου). And both Damascius and Simplicius aptly contrast this notion of being with the one related to being as the full domain of Forms.

My construal is also in harmony with the ES's repeated emphasis on the Kind Being's all-pervasiveness (256 D 12–E 3, 259 A 5–6), which suggests that the property of being cannot fail to obtain (at least for real unities which are not a matter of mental fabrication).[53]

Note that in both passages the ES speaks about Kinds. But the point can arguably be extended to sensible particulars, thereby providing a fresh explanatory framework to a point at least as old as *Phaedo* 79 A 6 ('two sorts of *beings*', δύο εἴδη τῶν ὄντων).[54] Consider

also Damascius' discussion at *Princ.* 2. 74. 23–79, 6 Westerink, with Granieri, 'Damascius'.

[53] See H. F. Cherniss, *Aristotle's Criticism of Plato and the Academy* (Baltimore, 1944), 254; D. O'Brien, *Non-Être*, 76–7; id., 'La forma del non essere nel *Sofista* di Platone' ['Forma del non essere'], in F. Fronterotta and W. Leszl (eds.), *Eidos-Idea* (Sankt Augustin, 2005), 115–60 at 144; C. Thomas, 'Speaking of Something: Plato's *Sophist* and Plato's Beard' ['Beard'], *Canadian Journal of Philosophy*, 38 (2008), 631–68 at 659–66; Crivelli, *Account*, 8. According to S. Kripke, *Reference and Existence* (Oxford, 2013), 4, 'no problem has seemed to represent a more perplexing philosophical conundrum than that of the use of names which have no reference', like 'imaginary entities'. I doubt that this is also true of Plato, who seems to me much less concerned with the problem of fictional entities than contemporary analytic philosophers. Nor do I believe that the riddle of not-being in the *Sophist* concerns centaurs and chimaeras, as e.g. Owen, 'Not-Being', 244, 246, 265 seems to suggest, but Philop., *in GC* 44. 12–18 Vitelli aptly denied. More generally, I doubt that the so-called 'Plato's beard', at least as habitually presented, was actually ever Plato's own. For Plato's attitude towards other types of non-existent objects, cf. R. Heinaman, 'Being in the *Sophist*' ['Being'], *Archiv für Geschichte der Philosophie*, 65 (1983), 1–17 at 12–13.

[54] Cf. *Tim.* 48 E 3–4 ('we distinguished two sorts', δύο εἴδη διειλόμεθα (cf. 27 D 5–28 A 4)), and *Rep.* 509 D 1–4 ('there are these two things, one reigning over the intelligible kind and place, the other over the visible.... In any case, you have two sorts of thing, visible and intelligible', δύο αὐτὼ εἶναι, καὶ βασιλεύειν τὸ μὲν νοητοῦ γένους τε καὶ τόπου, τὸ δ' αὖ ΟΡΑΤΟ ... διττὰ εἴδη, ὁρατόν, νοητόν); also Arist. *Metaph.* A. 8, 989^{b}24–6: 'those who study all beings, and of beings posit some to be perceptible and others not perceptible, evidently investigate both kinds (ὅσοι δὲ περὶ μὲν ἁπάντων τῶν ὄντων ποιοῦνται τὴν θεωρίαν, τῶν δ' ὄντων τὰ μὲν αἰσθητὰ τὰ δ' οὐκ αἰσθητὰ τιθέασι, δῆλον ὡς περὶ ἀμφοτέρων τῶν γενῶν ποιοῦνται τὴν ἐπίσκεψιν. According to Frede, *Prädikation*, 49, in the *Sophist* 'Being is *no longer* limited to forms alone, but applies to everything' (translation and italics mine). It never was. What was and

Plato's Isolation of a Kind Being

the two examples of true and false statements at 263 A 2–D 5: 'Theaetetus sits' and 'Theaetetus flies'. Both statements are *about* (περί) Theaetetus (263 A 5, 11, 263 B 4–5, 263 C 1, 263 D 1). At 262 E 6–7 the ES had claimed that every *logos* must be 'of something' (τινος). The same point is reasserted, with unimportant variations, at 263 C 9–11. Theaetetus is, therefore, a *something* (τι). But Plato, unlike the Stoics or Meinong, is also committed to the view that every *something* (τι) is also a *being* (ὄν).[55] This further aspect of Plato's account, famously judged by Aubenque 'une occasion manquée' ('a missed opportunity'; cf. n. 55), is proved by passages both within and outside the *Sophist*. Thus, one of the governing premisses (left unquestioned by Plato) of the paradox of falsehood is that to say *something* is to say something that *is* (237 D 1–4), a point repeated at 246 E 5–9 in the refutation of the materialists, where the legitimacy of the transition from τι ('a mortal creature is *a something*') to τι τῶν ὄντων ('they therefore posit soul as *one of the beings*') is simply assumed. But see also *Theaet.* 189 A 6–8, where it is agreed that one who opines *something* opines something that *is* ('Isn't the one who opines some one thing opining something that is?' — 'Necessarily', ὁ δ' ἕν τι δοξάζων οὐκ <u>ὄν</u> τι; — ἀνάγκη.). This suggests the (perhaps obvious) conclusion that Theaetetus is not only a *something* (τι), but also a *being* (ὄν). But we have seen the ES explaining something's being a being by evoking its participation in the Kind Being; and Section 4 will show that he does so systematically in the dialogue. We are, therefore, invited to surmise that Theaetetus, a perceptible particular, partakes in Being too, and accordingly,

---

remains limited to Forms alone is the perfect, true, unchanging, and uncontaminated being. Sensible particulars were never considered by Plato complete not-beings. By the same token, I find it doubtful that 'for Plato... forms alone possess being [and] in the Stranger's doctrine, they do so by combination with the form *being*' (Rosen, *Sophist*, 233). It is also a legitimate question whether my account implies Plato's commitment to a distinction between essence and existence. To the extent that this is interpreted modally, as implying a distinction between *possibilia* and *actualia*, the answer is no (see also n. 63 below). But if it is understood as pointing to a distinction between what a Form is in and by itself, that is the *essence* of which it is the Form, and the property (of *existence*) obtained through participation in the Kind Being, the answer is yes. Motion is itself, i.e. the essence of Motion, by its own nature; it *is*, i.e. exists, by partaking in something else, namely the Kind Being.

[55] Cf. Brunschwig, 'Theory'; P. Aubenque, 'Une occasion manquée: La genèse avortée de la distinction entre l'"étant" et le "quelque chose"', in id. (ed.), *Études sur le Sophiste de Platon* (Paris, 1991), 365–85; and Thomas, 'Beard'.

that Being's all-pervasiveness is not confined to Kinds, but extends to sensible particulars.[56]

Three clarifications of this account of the property of being in terms of existence. First, it does not entail that we should end up interpreting Plato's calling X a *not*-being (οὐκ ὄν, μὴ ὄν) as indicating that X does not exist, thereby reintroducing the impossible absolute not-being (τὸ μηδαμῶς ὄν) long ruled out by the ES, and still declared off limits at 258 A 6–259 A 1. This implication would follow if calling X a *not*-being indicated that X does not partake in Being. But Plato makes it clear that by calling something a not-being he only means that it is *different* from the Kind Being, not that it does not partake in it. Thus, 'Motion really is a not-being' (256 D 8: ἡ κίνησις ὄντως οὐκ ὄν ἐστι) in that it 'is different from Being' (256 D 5: τὴν κίνησιν ἕτερον εἶναι τοῦ ὄντος), but also 'is a being, because it partakes in Being' (256 D 8–9: ἔστι καὶ ὄν, ἐπείπερ τοῦ ὄντος μετέχει—see Section 4 below for more details on this passage). This is possible, Plato explains, because when a negative particle is prefixed to a term, it can simply indicate *difference* from and not necessarily *contrariety* to what that term designates (257 B 9–C 3); and it is contrariety, not mere difference, that excludes participation.[57]

Second, the above claim that Plato, both in the *Sophist* and elsewhere, is committed to the idea that every 'something' (τι) is also a 'being' (ὄν) is not, contrary to appearances, liable to bolster the 'to be is to be something' slogan. It is one thing to make the claim (of coextensivity) that [a] for every X, if X is something, then X is also a being (which is all Plato needs to be meaning; he may be also committed to the view that if X is a being, then X is also something, but cf. n. 91); it is quite another thing to make the claim (of intension) that [b] for every X, to be is to be something. For [a], unlike [b], does not entail that X's being resolves into its being

---

[56] I therefore do not commit Plato to the claim that there are things that do not exist (see n. 53 above). Note also that I have argued that the all-pervasiveness of Kind Being is not a *proof* of my interpretation, but *in harmony* with it. For one could in principle maintain that being-something is as pervasive as being. That said, O'Brien, 'Form', 231 has also rejoined that the Kind Difference's participation in Being and constitutive fragmented structure (257 C 7–E 5, 258 D 7–E 2) prevent it from being *something*. And while one could reply that the Kind Difference is, nevertheless, said to have a φύσις (256 D 11–E 1, 257 C 7, 257 D 4, 258 D 7), it is admittedly quite difficult to account for *what* Difference is, if (each part of) it is constitutively parasitic on what it is opposed to.

[57] Cf. *Phaedo* 102 D 6–7 (also 104 B 6–C 1); *Soph.* 252 D 2–10; with O'Brien, 'Forma del non essere', 129–33; 'To Be', esp. 94–103.

something and therefore that X's being something is explanatory of X's being a being.[58] Participation in the Kind Being explains *that* something is, not *what* it is.[59]

More generally, it should be noted, I by no means deny that Kind Being can *also* be involved in the combination between other Kinds (expressed by predicative judgements), as suggested by the so-called 'vowel analogy', whatever interpretation one may give of it.[60] Nor do I deny that Being can *also* be predicated 'relatively to other' (πρὸς ἄλλο)—that is, according to what we may identify as a possible conception of the copula—as suggested by *Soph.* 255 C 13–D 5.[61] What I do deny is that when Being is predicated *simpliciter* or, according to the terminology of 255 C 13–14, 'in and by itself' (αὐτὸ καθ' αὑτό), and this is explained just in terms of combination or participation in the Kind Being alone, this is to be understood as indicating being *something*, rather than existing.[62]

Third, my present account does not commit Plato to any specific conception of what it is for something to exist, apart from its enjoying a distinctive property obtained in virtue of its participation in the Kind Being. Notably, it does not entail that Plato subscribed to either a *quantified* or a *modal* conception of existence—this seems

---

[58] This distinction may have eluded some readers, e.g. Collette-Dučić, '*Sophiste*', 144–8; and Zaks, *Apparences*, 229–34. I have encountered the objection that at *Soph.* 247 A 5–B 4 the general principle is worded in terms of εἶναί τι (247 A 9–10) and the conclusion drawn from it is worded in terms of plain εἶναι (247 B 1–4: οὔσης). And this seems to point to the thesis that for Plato 'to be is to be something'. But all this passage shows is that Plato is comfortable inferring 'is' from 'is something', which I take to be an application of the principle that for every X, if X is a something, then X is also a being.

[59] Dixsaut, *Naturel*, 326–35 rightly stresses that something's participation in the Form of Being does not suffice to determine *what* something is (327), and that for something *to be*, i.e. to exist, is a condition for (and not identical to) its being the determinate thing it is (332). She also adds, however, that an uncomplemented occurrence of εἶναι 'calls for determination' and 'has to be determined' (326–7; translation mine). This claim, paired with the remark that Being, as much as Difference, is fragmented into parts (which Plato never says; see Lee, 'Negation', 283–4; and esp. O'Brien, *Non-Être*, 113–14) and has a relative character (332), suggests an interpretation ultimately in line with the Owenian slogan.

[60] Cf. e.g. 252 A 5–10. For a valuable and updated critical overview of the debate, see Zaks, *Apparences*, 188–204.

[61] Overviews of the main readings of this controversial passage are to be found in Crivelli, *Account*, 140–9; Gill, *Philosophos*, 173–6; and Zaks, *Apparences*, 213–24.

[62] The attribution of this dual role to the Kind Being could fit well with the so-called 'semantic-continuity thesis' advocated by Brown. But see n. 39 above for reservations on the way Brown formalizes her reading, which involves, among other things, an endorsement of the Owenian slogan.

to have been a major reason for denying to Plato *any* notion of existential being (independent of being *something*).[63] Nor do I think it would be suitable to saddle Plato with either, although I cannot pause here to defend this position. More generally, I believe no straightforward solution to this issue is to be found in the *Sophist* (or, for that matter, in any other dialogue).[64]

Some might complain that an account of existence as a property of everything that exists seems unilluminating unless more can be said about that property.[65] This objection can be answered by distinguishing three types of questions about existence:[66] (1) What does exist? (2) What is it for something to exist? (3) What is the general *status* of existence?, i.e. What sort of situation, or fact, or state of affairs, is the existence of something—Is existence a property? Question (3) can be regarded as more fundamental than (2), and prior in the order of inquiry. The claim that being or existence is a property obtained by participation in the relevant Platonic Kind provides an answer to (3). To this end, it is a sufficiently informative claim, contrary to how it may first appear. This is not intended to suggest that Plato was not committed to any specific conception of what it is for something to exist. Instead, it means that the claim that being or existence is a property obtained by participation in the Kind Being stands on its own legs and is independent of possible further analyses of the Platonic concept of existence. Analogously, the claim in the *Phaedo* or the *Hippias Major* that something is beautiful due to participation in the Form of Beauty

---

[63] For example, when Gilson and Kahn denied to Plato (as well as to ancient Greek thought in general) any concept of existence, they most likely had in mind the modal one that came to prominence with monotheistic religions and was dominant in the Middle Ages and the Early Modern Age; see Gilson, *Being*, 33; Kahn, 'Existence'. 323–4 (see n. 54 above). And when Thomas asked whether Plato anticipated 'the concept of existence we post-Fregeans, post-Russellians possess' (cf., on this, Mignucci, 'Esistenza', 259 n. 149), she voiced a widespread preoccupation in analytic Platonic scholarship; see Thomas, 'Beard', 658 (see n. 9 above). See also Zaks, *Apparences*, 230–1.

[64] One promising candidate answer is the so-called '*dunamis* proposal', namely the ὅρος of being put forward at 247 d 8–E 4, whereby to be is to have 'the power to act or to be acted upon'. See, for discussion, Fronterotta, *METHEXIS*, 333–79 and F. Leigh, 'Being and Power in Plato's *Sophist*', *Apeiron*, 43 (2010), 1–23. But this too is an issue I must leave for another occasion.

[65] Cf. e.g. C. Dale, 'To Be', in R. Le Poidevin et al. (eds.), *The Routledge Companion to Metaphysics* (London, 2009), 225–33 at 231.

[66] For the following threefold distinction (and the priority of question (3)), see P. Butchvarov, *Being Qua Being* (Bloomington, 1979), 82–3.

stands on its own legs and is independent of possible further analyses of the Platonic concept of beauty.

4. A recurrent pattern

Statement (4) of the argument against the 'prayer' is not an isolated case. The explanatory pattern it inaugurates is consistently deployed by Plato throughout the *Sophist*. I shall now discuss the passages where it reappears. None of them supplies *direct* evidence for denying that for Plato to be is to be something, but only for corroborating that Plato sticks to the conception of being put forward in statement (4). For none of these passages echoes the point of statement (3). But should we expect anything different? We have seen that statement (3) sets out what it does *not* mean, for both and each of Motion and Rest, to be. Statement (4) builds on that *negative* result and broaches a *positive* conception of what it is for something to be. Once this conception has been introduced and the Kind Being isolated, Plato no longer has any need to repeat the negative point. Instead, he can take it for granted and limit himself to restating, where the argument requires it, the positive conception introduced by statement (4). Nevertheless, since statement (4) builds on statement (3), Plato's repeated emphasis on the explanatory pattern broached in the former can also be interpreted, I submit, as *indirectly* confirming the point taken home in the latter, and therefore as underpinning the contention that for Plato to be is not to be something. Here are the passages where that pattern reappears:

(1) 254 D 10: *'Being is mixed with both [Motion and Rest]; for both presumably are'* (τὸ δέ γε ὂν μεικτὸν ἀμφοῖν· ἐστὸν γὰρ ἄμφω που). The verb μιγνύναι (whence comes μεικτόν) is used in the dialogue, especially in the compound form συμμιγνύναι, interchangeably with other verbs or locutions indicating participation, such as μετέχειν, μεταλαμβάνειν, κοινωνεῖν, ἐπικοινωνεῖν, or ἔχειν κοινωνίας (see n. 22 above). Accordingly, 254 D 10 points out, consistently with statement (4), that Motion and Rest are, i.e., as I argued, enjoy the property of being (*simpliciter*, not being *something*) in virtue of[67] their sharing in the Kind Being.

---

[67] The γάρ has an elucidatory and confirmatory function, not causal; see R. Kühner and B. Gerth, *Ausführliche Grammatik der Griechischen Sprache* (Hanover, 1904),

(2) 256 A 1: '*And yet [Motion] is, because of its partaking in being*' (ἔστι δέ γε διὰ τὸ μετέχειν τοῦ ὄντος). The genitive τοῦ ὄντος refers to the Kind Being. The line is naturally read as pointing in the same direction as 250 A 11–B 11 and 254 D 10: Motion is, i.e. possesses the property of being, in virtue of its participation in the Kind Being.

This passage, however, has proved more controversial and requires us to pause. In fact, some proponents of the 'to be is to be something' slogan have contended that it may even bolster their case.[68] They have observed that 256 A 1 is embedded in a stretch of reasoning that has an interim conclusion at 256 E 3–4, with a remark that generalizes to all Kinds the same point 256 A 1 makes about Motion: 'since [all Kinds, cf. 256 D 12–E 2: πάντα τὰ γένη... σύμπαντα] participate in being, we will say that they are and call them beings' (trans. Crivelli). But then at 256 E 6–7—so the argument goes—the ES seems also to infer *uniquely* from that remark that in relation to each of the Forms being is *manifold* (256 E 6: περὶ ἕκαστον ἄρα τῶν εἰδῶν πολὺ μέν ἐστι τὸ ὄν). Now, assuming that the latter claim must mean that 'there are many predicates which may be truly affirmed [of a Form]' (Malcolm, 'Analysis', 130), it follows that 256 E 3–4 cannot be taken to make an existential claim ('all Forms exist, because they partake in Being'), or else we would saddle Plato with a fallacious inference from an existential to a predicative claim. Accordingly, the same should apply to 256 A 1.

The governing premiss of this argument is that the conclusion at 256 E 6 is inferred *uniquely* from the claim that all Kinds partake in Being, and that the latter claim explains the former.[69] So it is precisely because each Kind partakes in Being that there are many predicates truly affirmed of a Kind, i.e. that each Kind has many attributes.

However, there are reasons to be doubtful about this premiss. Consider the context of the ES's remark. Starting from 255 E 8, he gives a sample of how Kinds combine with each other—the second

ii.ii. 331–2. It is the former sentence that explains the latter, not the other way round (compare: 'the sun has risen; for there is light').

[68] See e.g. Malcolm, 'Analysis', 130, and Owen, 'Not-Being', 253–5.

[69] This is a charitable reading of the rival interpretation. For suppose the contention were that '*if* [not *since*] a Form exists, then there are many attributes that belong to it' is fallacious. This could be proved wrong on purely logical grounds, because the inference is, in fact, valid, as Heinaman, 'Being', 8 already observed.

project of the twofold agenda set at 254 C 4–6. He singles out Motion as a specimen and explores its combinatory relations with the other four of the selected greatest Kinds:

(a) [255 E 11–15] Motion is not Rest, because it is entirely different from Rest;
(b) [256 A 1–2] but Motion is (*simpliciter*), because it partakes in Being;
(c) [256 A 3–6] yet again, Motion is not Identity, because it is different from Identity;
(d) [256 A 7–8] but Motion is identical, because it partakes in Identity;
(e) [256 C 4–5] yet again, Motion is not Difference, because it is different from Difference;
(f) [256 C 7–11] but Motion is different, namely from Identity, Difference, and Rest;
(g) [256 C 11–D 8] yet again, just as Motion is different from three of the five selected Kinds, so too it is different from Being, and is, therefore, a not-being;
(h) [256 D 8–9] but remember, Motion *is* (as per (b)), because it partakes in Being.

The crucial steps for the dialogue's overall aim are (g) and (h). Thus, the ES naturally goes on at 256 D 11–E 4 to stress the conclusion reached through (g) and (h) and to generalize it to all Kinds:

Ἔστιν ἄρα ἐξ ἀνάγκης τὸ μὴ ὂν ἐπί τε κινήσεως εἶναι καὶ κατὰ πάντα τὰ γένη· κατὰ πάντα γὰρ ἡ θατέρου φύσις ἕτερον ἀπεργαζομένη τοῦ ὄντος ἕκαστον οὐκ ὂν ποιεῖ, καὶ σύμπαντα δὴ κατὰ ταὐτὰ οὕτως οὐκ ὄντα ὀρθῶς ἐροῦμεν, καὶ πάλιν, ὅτι μετέχει τοῦ ὄντος, εἶναί τε καὶ ὄντα.

It is therefore necessarily the case that not-being be about motion and with respect to all kinds: for, with respect to all of them, the nature of the different, by rendering each one different from being, makes it a not-being, and thus we will correctly call them all together in the same way not-beings, and again, since they participate in being, we will say that they are and call them beings.

(trans. Crivelli, minimally modified)[70]

But when at 256 E 6–7 the ES infers further (ἄρα) that in relation to each of the Forms 'being is manifold' and 'not-being is unlimited

---

[70] For the so-called 'converse use of "to be"' at work in this and other passages of the *Sophist*, see Crivelli, *Account*, 167–8.

in multiplicity', we are under no obligation to think that this conclusion is drawn *uniquely* from (g) and (h). It is surely possible, and indeed probable, that it is meant to follow from the whole chain of inferences initiated at 255 E 8, i.e. (a)–(h). Thus, the 'manifold being' does not, and surely need not, indicate the property obtained by participation in the Kind Being alone. Instead, it should be interpreted as collectively indicating the set of properties a Kind possesses (including, but not restricted to, the property of being) in virtue of its participation in several other Kinds (including, but not restricted to, the Kind Being)—take, for example, Motion: since it partakes in Being (254 D 10, 256 A 1, 256 D 8–9), Identity (256 A 7–8, 256 B 1), and Difference (256 B 2–3), then it is many things, i.e. it is a being (256 D 8–9), identical (256 A 7, 256 B 1–2), and different (256 B 3–4) (see e.g. Crivelli, *Account*, 168–9). Two further textual signposts corroborate this reading. I will bring them out inspecting the next passage.

(3) 256 D 8–9: *'Clearly then Motion really is a not-being—and a being, since it partakes in Being'* (ἡ κίνησις ὄντως οὐκ ὄν ἐστι καὶ ὄν, ἐπείπερ τοῦ ὄντος μετέχει). The ES has just pointed out that Motion shares in Difference in relation to Being (256 D 5–6). By foreshadowing the forthcoming semantic analysis of negation as expressing not necessarily contrariety but also just difference (257 B 3–C 3), he infers that Motion 'really is a not-being' (ὄντως οὐκ ὄν ἐστι). On top of this, he adds that, despite its being a not-being, Motion is still also a being (ἐστι καὶ ὄν), because it partakes in Being (ἐπείπερ τοῦ ὄντος μετέχει). Both οὐκ ὄν and ὄν are governed by one and the same copula (ἐστι).

The first textual signpost supporting my reading of 256 A 1 lies in the grammar of the phrase 'Motion *is a being*' (256 D 8: κίνησις ἐστι ὄν). Notice the repetition of the verb εἶναι in the participial form complementing the copula (ἐστι ὄν). This redundant formula gives a sense equivalent to the uncomplemented ἔστι (cf. in a different context Alex. Aphr., *In An. Pr.* 15. 15–22 Wallies and Ammon., *In Int.* 57. 29–32 Busse). For both ἔστι at 256 A 1 and ἐστι ὄν at 256 E 7 are equally explained in terms of participation in Being (cf. 256 A 1: 'due to partaking in being', διὰ τὸ μετέχειν τοῦ ὄντος; 256 D 9: 'because it partakes in being', ἐπείπερ τοῦ ὄντος μετέχει). The question, therefore, arises why Plato does not just say ἔστι at 256 D 8 too, instead of ἐστι ὄν. In my view, he intends to stress that being is a property on a par with others, obtained by participation in a

Kind.[71] Just as Motion's possession of the properties of identity (with respect to itself) and difference (with respect to something else) was expressed by the locution copula + participle (256 A 7: 'it was identical', ἦν ταὐτόν; 256 A 10: 'it is identical', ταὐτόν τ' εἶναι; 256 C 4: 'it is different', ἐστιν ἕτερον), so too is Motion's possession of the property of being (256 D 8: ἐστι ὄν). Thus, since the phrasing suggests that the property obtained by participation in the Kind Being is a property on a par with others, it seems unnatural to regard the conclusion at 256 E 5–6 as suggesting that being is instead some sort of supererogatory property that comprises all the properties signified by predicates that hold true of a Kind.

It might be objected that my interpretation of the 'manifold being' (πολὺ τὸ ὄν) at 256 E 6 entails a cumbersome ambiguity in the meaning of ὄν: on the one hand, ὄν refers to the property obtained by partaking in the Kind Being, and on the other hand, (πολὺ τὸ) ὄν stands for the *ensemble* of properties signified by the predicates that hold true of a given Form. I bite the bullet: there is indeed an ambiguity, but one that is clearly intended and flagged by Plato and, far from being cumbersome, is instead pivotal—together, of course, with the aforementioned analysis of negation (257 B 3–C 3)— for the accomplishment of the dialogue's overall project.[72]

This becomes clear if we turn to 263 B 4–12, the second textual signpost supporting my reading of 256 A 1. The ES has just mentioned the two famous examples of true and false statement: 'Theaetetus sits' and 'Theaetetus flies' (263 A 2–9). The latter statement, he says, is false because it 'says things that are different from those that are... in which case it says the things that are not as if they are' (263 B 7–9: ὁ δὲ δὴ ψευδὴς ἕτερα τῶν ὄντων.... τὰ μὴ ὄντ' ἄρα ὡς ὄντα λέγει). The things said by this false statement, thus, are not an impossible blank nothing, as the sophist would tendentiously baulk. They are not, in other words, the 'absolute not-being' (μηδαμῶς ὄν, 237 B 7–8), involved in the Parmenidean dictum, the thought and utterance of which was said to entail a 'contradiction' (ἐναντιολογία, 236 E 5),[73] thereby triggering the paradox of falsehood. At 258 E

[71] Similarly Heinaman, 'Being', 9; Leigh 'Semantic Continuity', 117–19; and O'Brien, 'To Be', 98–9.

[72] What follows is based on R. Granieri, 'The Referents of "Being" in Plato's *Sophist*', in L. Brisson et al. (eds.), *Plato's Sophist* (Baden-Baden, forthcoming).

[73] A Platonic hapax (cf. 268 B 4: ἐναντιολογεῖν, itself a Platonic hapax; cf. Arist. *GC* 1. 7, 323^{b}17 Rashed), just like ὀρθολογία at 239 B 4, attested again only half a millennium later; cf. Herodian. Gr. 3. 2, 513.6 Lentz.

6–259 A 1 the ES declared that *that* non-being, now crucially reconceived of as *the contrary of the Kind Being* (258 E 6: τοὐναντίον τοῦ ὄντος),[74] had long since been abandoned.[75] Instead, as 263 B 7–9 expounds, the things said by this false statement are still [i] 'things that are' (263 B 11: ὄντων), but just [ii] different from those that are *about Theaetetus* (263 B 11: ὄντα ἕτερα περὶ σοῦ). That is to say: [i] flying is an existing attribute, in that it partakes, like everything else, in the Kind Being; but [ii] it is also different from all the attributes signified by predicates that hold true of Theaetetus. It is at this stage that the ES makes an explicit back-reference to the point made at 256 E 6–7, which is now restated in a slightly, if meaningfully, different phraseology: 'for we said, I think, that there are many things that are about each and every thing, and many that are not' (263 B 11–12: πολλὰ μὲν γὰρ ἔφαμεν ὄντα περὶ ἕκαστον εἶναί που, πολλὰ δὲ οὐκ ὄντα). I cannot dwell here on the substitution of 'unlimited in multiplicity' (256 E 7: ἄπειρον πλήθει) for 'many' (263 B 12: πολλά) (see O'Brien, '*Non-Être*', 79–81 for discussion). What matters for present purposes is that the πολὺ τὸ ὄν of 256 E 6 is rephrased as πολλὰ ὄντα ('many beings'). This confirms that the 'manifold being' referred to in the earlier passage was not meant to indicate *only* the property obtained by participation in the Kind Being, but all the positive properties a Kind possesses (including, but not restricted to, the property of being) in virtue of its participation in several other Kinds.

Thus, the fact that τὸ ὄν can have different referents contributes saliently (without being the only key) to the disentanglement of the paradox of falsehood. For it enables Plato, among other things, to display and dispel a sophistical confusion between, on the one hand,

---

[74] That τοῦ ὄντος refers here to the Kind Being can be proved as follows. First, when a few lines above, at 257 B 3–4, the ES concludes in the same vein that τὸ μὴ ὄν ('not-being') is not something contrary, but only different from ὄν (οὐκ ἐναντίον τι λέγομεν τοῦ ὄντος ἀλλ' ἕτερον μόνον), he should have in mind what was said about Motion at 256 D 5–9, that since it is different from ὄν, it is an οὐκ ὄν ('a not-being'), and about Difference at 256 D 12–E 4, that by rendering each a different thing from being (ἕτερον ἀπεργαζομένη τοῦ ὄντος ἕκαστον), it makes it a not-being (οὐκ ὄν ποιεῖ). In both cases ὄν stands for the Kind Being. Second, this Kind is universally participated in; but since contrariety implies absence of participation (cf. *Phaedo* 102 D 6–7, 104 B 6–C1; *Soph.* 252 D 2–10; with O'Brien, 'Forma del non essere', 129–33), there can be no contrary of Being. Hence the μὴ ὄν involved in the Parmenidean ban, as reformulated in the *Sophist*'s analysis, is the (impossible) contrary of the Kind Being.

[75] See on this D. O'Brien, 'The Stranger's Farewell (258 E 6–259 A 1)', in A. Havlíček and F. Karfík (eds.), *Plato's* Sophist (Prague, 2011), 199–220.

Plato's Isolation of a Kind Being

'being' as the *ensemble* of properties something possesses and, on the other hand, 'being' as existence—and therefore between, on the one hand, 'not-being' as the *ensemble* of properties that are *different from* (and therefore *are not*) all those signified by the predicates that hold true of something and, on the other hand, 'not-being' as non-existence. By showing that these two meanings of τὸ ὄν are grounded in two distinct metaphysical states of affairs, Plato is able to distinguish what the sophist had muddled up.

(4) 256 E 3–4: *all Kinds are not-beings—and then again, since they partake in Being, are and are beings* (σύμπαντα...οὐκ ὄντα...καὶ πάλιν, ὅτι μετέχει τοῦ ὄντος, εἶναί τε καὶ ὄντα). This passage generalizes the point made at 256 D 9 and, for present purposes, the foregoing remarks suffice as an interpretation of it.

(5) 259 A 6–7: *'Difference, participating in Being, is, because of that participation, but not what it partakes in, but something different'* (259 A 6–7: τὸ μὲν ἕτερον μετασχὸν τοῦ ὄντος ἔστι μὲν διὰ ταύτην τὴν μέθεξιν, οὐ μὴν ἐκεῖνό γε οὗ μετέσχεν ἀλλ' ἕτερον). The point generalized at 256 E 3–4 is now applied to the Kind Difference. The scenario is by and large comparable to that of the previous passages. Yet although the first ἔστι ('is') is emphatically twice explained in terms of participation in Being, scholars have expressed doubts on the existential interpretation of this verb, mostly due to the second clause of the passage ('but not what it partakes in, but something different', οὐ μὴν ἐκεῖνό γε οὗ μετέσχεν ἀλλ' ἕτερον), which complicates the picture. For since in that clause the verb is missing, it must be supplied from the first (ἔστι); but in the second clause the implicit 'is' should be copulative; thus, it appears that the same should hold for the 'is' in the first clause too.

However, it has been observed that the ἐστί[76] in the second clause might have been simply elided, rather than supplied from the first clause,[77] or that even if it is supplied from the first clause, nothing compels us to take it univocally, for it might be used existentially in the former clause, copulatively in the latter.[78] Nor is this shift logically fallacious or grammatically anomalous.

---

[76] In writing ἐστί, I follow the modern standard convention known as 'Hermann's rule', for which ἔστι (orthotone accent) expresses the existential sense but ἐστί (enclitic accent) the copulative sense. But see Kahn, '*Verb Be*', 420–34 for critical remarks on this convention (p. 420 n.1 references the relevant work of Hermann).

[77] See Heinaman, 'Being', 10; Leigh, 'Semantic Continuity', 115.

[78] See again Heinaman, 'Being', 10.

I take it, therefore, as proved that the explanatory pattern introduced in statement (4) is not an isolated case. The *Sophist* consistently appeals to combination or mixing with or participation in the Kind or Form of Being to account for the fact that something *is*, i.e., as I argued, possesses the property of being (*simpliciter*, not being *something*).[79]

5. The Kind Being is not a genus of all genera

One might raise an objection based on the perhaps intuitive view that the Platonic Kind Being is best interpreted not as a metaphysical principle bestowing being upon what partakes in it, but as a most generic genus of all genera. The germ of this reading can arguably be traced back to Aristotle.[80] It has in any case expressly been supported by various modern commentators.[81] On this interpretation,

---

[79] An analysis of the second deduction of the second part of the *Parmenides* would further strengthen this reading. Here I can only sketch the essentials of it. Starting from *Parm.* 142 B 1, it is argued that 'one is one' (ἓν ἕν) and 'one is' (ἓν ἔστιν) cannot mean the same, because the being of the one is not the same as the one (ἡ οὐσία τοῦ ἑνὸς εἴη ἂν οὐ ταὐτὸν οὖσα τῷ ἑνί) and 'is' and 'one' signify different things (ἄλλο τι σημαῖνον τὸ ἔστι τοῦ ἕν). Twice in this passage (142 B 6, 142 C 5–6) is the attribute signified by the predicate 'is' (ἔστιν)—the one's being—analysed in participatory terms that should by now be familiar to us, i.e. as *participation in being* (οὐσίας μετέχειν). So, on the one hand, the second deduction prefigures the conception of being whereby something *is* in virtue of participation in Being; on the other hand, it confirms that when the being of something is thus explained, 'to be is not to be something' (the being of the one is not the same as the one; 'the one is' and 'the one is one' mean different things). Admittedly, being is here not overtly described as a γένος or εἶδος. Still, the vocabulary of participation does point in the direction of the *Sophist*'s sustained account of being.

[80] It is implicit in the (anti-Platonic) argument that being is not a *genos* at *Metaph.* B. 3, 998ᵇ22–7.

[81] Cf. e.g. R. Bury (ed.), *The Philebus of Plato* (Cambridge, 1897), lxxi, 210–11; J. Stenzel, *Studien zur Entwicklung der platonischen Dialektik von Sokrates zu Aristoteles*, 2nd edn (Leipzig, 1931), 94–7; Diès, *Sophiste*, 286; Seligman, *Being*, 43; Frede, 'Frage', 197–8 (but see *Prädikation*, 92); Berti, 'L'essere', 54–5; F. Lewis, 'Aristotle on the Homonymy of Being', *Philosophy and Phenomenological Research*, 68 (2004), 1–36 at 12–13, 27 n. 64; M. Loux, 'Being, Categories, and Universal Reference in Aristotle', in L. Haaparanta and H. J. Koskinen (eds.), *Categories of Being* (Oxford, 2012), 17–35 at 18–20, 31–3; and Peipers, *Ontologia*, 34, 332–3. We have the same idea in M. Heidegger, *Gesamtausgabe* vi.1–2: *Nietzsche II* (Frankfurt, 1996–7 [1936–46]), 211. Heidegger corresponded with Stenzel and was acquainted with (both editions of) his *Studien*: see H.-C. Günther, 'Briefe Martin Heideggers an Julius Stenzel (1928–1932)', *Heidegger Studies*, 16 (2000), 11–33, esp. 25, 30). So he probably borrowed this idea from him.

purportedly underpinned by the ES's stress on the Kind Being's all-pervasiveness (256 D 12–E 3, 259 A 5–6), this Kind is located atop a sort of universal Porphyrian tree, which branches out into all the various species and subspecies of reality.[82] The Kind Being is thus regarded as an overarching highest genus of 'whatness', which we encounter when we get to the summit of a hierarchical classificatory account of Kinds, based on the extensional criterion of the generality of their intelligible content. As we work upwards from the various lowest species (or even from individuals) by asking '*What* is it?' at each step, the Kind Being will be the point of arrival of our ascent. It will thus be, to use later terminology, a genus of maximal extension and minimal intension. So, on the one hand, the range of objects falling under this genus, and therefore the range of applicability of the term that designates it, will be universal—all beings, including those Aristotle would have placed in different categories (e.g. Socrates and his complexion), will fall under this genus and will thereby equally be called 'beings'. On the other hand, the set of features that constitute the intelligible nature of this genus and therefore determine the applicability of the term that designates it will be minimal, and for this reason able to contain within itself all the various natures of the objects it subsumes.[83]

---

[82] For the sake of precision, Porphyry himself in fact denies that there is a highest genus of being encompassing all the categories and equally predicated in quid of them all; cf. Porph., *Isag*. 6. 5–11 Busse; *in Cat*. 86. 7–13 Busse; *in Phys*. 129. 61–72 F Smith = Simpl. *in Phys*. 94. 5–13 Diels. Interestingly, various commentators on the *Isagoge* took Porphyry to side with Aristotle *against* Plato, thereby ascribing to the latter the idea of a highest genus of being; cf. Elias, *in Isag*. 70. 15–17 Busse; David, *in Isag*. 158. 2–9 Busse; Arethas, *in Isag*. 49. 14 Share.

[83] Gerson, *Plotinus*, 84–5 ascribes a reading along these lines to Plotinus and takes it to be a fair reading of Plato. I leave it open whether this is an accurate representation of Plotinus' own view or his reading of Plato. It does seem, at any rate, to capture the essentials of Seneca's doctrine of the supreme genus at *Ep*. 58. 8–14, on which, see Brunschwig, 'Theory', 110–11 and J. Mansfeld, *Heresiography in Context* (Leiden, 1992), 84–107. (M. Rashed, 'Posidonius et le traité d'Albinus *Sur les incorporels*', *Elenchos*, 42 (2021), 165–98 at 177–82 has recently argued that Seneca's reform of the Stoic theory of the supreme genus is already Posidonian. He has also explored aspects of the Islamic reception of Posidonius' version of that theory, transmitted through the Syriac tradition; cf. his 'Hišām ibn al-Ḥakam et Sulaymān ibn Ǧarīr entre stoïcisme et kalām: De la négation du tiers-exclu à la distinction entre "chose" et "existant"', *Discipline filosofiche*, 31 (2021), 9–26.) Note, however, that while this doctrine of Seneca is embedded in a discussion of the (six) meanings that, according to Seneca's anonymous Platonist friend, Plato assigned to τὸ ὄν (hesitantly rendered by Seneca as *quod est*), Seneca 'does not present [the classification of species and genera in ascending order of magnitude, ending with *quod*

This understanding of the notion of a *genos* of Being—which, for the sake of clarity, should not be conflated with the πολὺ τὸ ὄν of 256 E 6, the latter being the determinate set of properties signified by predicates that hold true of a given subject—may appear to chime with the slogan 'to be is to be something'. For if the Kind Being is a most generic genus of 'whatness', one may perhaps surmise that, by partaking in Being, something gets its own determinate nature, its *what*-it-is.

However, this interpretation faces a difficulty. It accounts for the relation between the Kind Being (which, remember, is explicitly said at 259 B 2–4 not to be the sum of the other Kinds) and its participants as a genus–species relation. This relation, at least on Aristotle's description of it in the *Organon* (cf. e.g. Arist. *Cat.* $2^b 20$–1 and *Top.* 4. 1, $121^a 10$–14) that is implicit in the above account, can never be symmetrical. A genus is predicated of its species; a species is never predicated of its genus. Consider, by contrast, the relationship between Being and Difference: each is predicated of the other. For Being partakes in Difference; but Difference also partakes in Being (259 A 4–B 7). Their relationship is, therefore, symmetrical. Hence, they do not stand to each other as genera stand to their species (in the Aristotelian sense).[84] One could make an analogous case about Being and Identity, which are both all-pervasive (256 A 7–8; 256 D 12–E 3; 259 A 5–6) and must consequently be taken to partake in each other. The possible rejoinder that my counterexample applies only to all-pervasive Kinds leaves untouched the points that, first, the participated–participant relation, in which all-pervasive Kinds are as much involved as non-all-pervasive ones, is not correctly understood in terms of the genus–species relation; second, that the *Sophist*'s intelligible domain is not adequately represented as a pyramid-shaped ontological hierarchy.[85]

---

est as the first and supreme genus] as a Platonic classification' (Brunschwig, 'Theory', 111). Rather, it is Aristotle's name that appears at the beginning of Seneca's account; cf. *Ep.* 58. 9. 13–14: *homo species est, ut Aristoteles ait*. See Mansfeld, *Heresiography*, 85–90 for discussion.

[84] This argument is also effective as a reply to Aristotle's criticism at *Top.* 4. 1, $121^a 14$–17. Crivelli, *Account*, 16 aptly observes that the central concept of Plato's method of division is that of 'subordination', which is irreducible to extensional inclusion. See Cornford, *Theory*, 268–9.

[85] Gill agrees that the Kind Being should not be conceived of 'as a highest genus of which all the Aristotelian categories are species—an indefinite indeterminable

The objection that the Kind Being is not a principle metaphysically responsible for the property its name names, i.e. the property of being, but *a genus of all genera*, is accordingly uncompelling.

6. Conclusion: Plato and Aristotle

I have argued that in the *Sophist* Plato is committed to a conception of being whereby something *is*, i.e. exists, due to its participation in the Kind Being. To appreciate the significance of this position fully, a comparison with Aristotle proves instructive.

Menn has recently argued that according to Aristotle the correct method to make existential sentences involving one-place being ('F is') amenable to causal analysis is to rewrite them by [i] turning them into sentences involving two-place being, [ii] moving the subject term ('F') to predicate position, and [iii] introducing a subject (primarily the per se subject of F) of which the new predicate holds ('S is F').[86] Thus, to explain the fact that F exists we need not look for a cause that supplies existence to F, but for something that supplies F-ness to some subject S (primarily the per se subject of F). The 'cause of the being' (αἴτιον τοῦ εἶναι) of F is, for Aristotle, the οὐσία of F. Thus, the second meaning of οὐσία listed at *Metaph. Δ.* 8, 1017^{b}14–16 is 'that which, being present in such things as are not predicated of a subject, is the cause of being (αἴτιον τοῦ εἶναι), as the soul is of the being of animals'. The example of the soul makes it

---

from which all categorial content has been stripped away' (*Philosophos* 229). It is not obvious, however, that this can be reconciled with her view that the Kind Being is a Form that 'dictates a focus on the nature of things and gives the philosopher a distinctive perspective on any topic he studies', 'a form that structures all beings and together with some other content makes them what they are', so that it enables the philosopher to fulfil her interest 'in *all beings*' and her desire 'to understand the *nature* of things' (241–2; my emphasis, Gill's italics). For if the study of the Kind Being gives a focus on the *nature* of all beings, on *what* each being is, then either the notion of the Kind Being intensionally contains that of all beings or it does not. If it does, then it is unclear in what sense it is not a genus of all genera or a most indeterminate determinable of all determinates. If it does not, then it is unclear how by studying the Kind Being the philosopher can fulfil her desire to know *what* each being is.

[86] Cf. Menn, 'Many Senses', esp. 212–13. For comparable remarks, see Matthews, 'Aristotle on Existence', and D. Charles, 'Some Comments on Prof. Enrico Berti's "Being and Essence in Contemporary Interpretations of Aristotle"', in A. Bottani et al. (eds.), *Individuals, Essence and Identity* (Dordrecht, 2002), 109–26. A shared target of these three works is Owen, 'Snares'.

clear that Aristotle is thinking of the formal cause as something's internal cause of being (cf. e.g. *Metaph.* B. 2, 996^{b}13–14 and *DA* 2. 4, 415^{b}10–14).[87]

The *Sophist*, I submit, is committed to precisely the alternative view.[88] As I have argued throughout this paper, Plato avers that to explain the fact that F *is* (i.e. exists) we need to look for an entity that supplies being to F. This entity is not the οὐσία of F, as Aristotle would have it, but a metaphysical principle which, by its own nature, provides being to all the objects bearing the appropriate relation (i.e. participation) with it. This entity is the Kind Being.[89] And if Aristotle, as some have argued, judged that at least part of the ground for the doctrine of the multivocity of being lies in the thesis that being is not a genus, which is in turn supported by an argument in *Metaph.* B 3 probably directed against Plato (see nn. 80 and 82 above), then we can suppose that Aristotle himself judged his doctrine of the many senses of being at odds with Platonic ontology.

Such a hiatus between Plato's and Aristotle's conceptions of beings is worth special notice because the supporters of the view that for Plato to be is to be something have also claimed this to be common ground between Plato and Aristotle. Thus, when Owen introduced his slogan, he added that if it is true that for Plato to be is always to be something, then '[Plato's] analysis becomes the direct parent of Aristotle's' ('Snares', 71).[90] If the interpretation

---

[87] Cf. Boeth., *De Trin.* 2. 83, p. 169 Moreschini: *omne namque esse ex forma est* ('For every being is from the form').

[88] See Matthews, 'Aristotle on Existence', 236; and also Menn, 'Many Senses', esp. 204, 242.

[89] At *Rep.* 509 B 7–8 Plato says that the being and essence (τὸ εἶναι τε καὶ τὴν οὐσίαν) of the Forms is bestowed upon them by the Idea of the Good (ὑπὸ τοῦ ἀγαθοῦ παρεῖναι), which is itself beyond essence in rank and power (ἐπέκεινα τῆς οὐσίας πρεσβείᾳ καὶ δυνάμει). One way of construing this famous claim is that the Idea of the Good is the cause of the being of the other Forms (at 516 C 2 the Sun, which is the sensible analogue of the Good, is said to be 'in a certain sense cause of all things (τρόπον τινὰ πάντων αἴτιος)'). A thorny problem, though one that is rarely tackled in the scholarship, is how this squares with the *Sophist*'s claim that something *is* because it combines with or partakes in the Kind Being. See for a first discussion Dixsaut, *Naturel*, 328 and N.-L. Cordero, 'La participation comme être de la forme dans le *Sophiste* de Platon', in id. (ed.), *Ontologie et dialogue* (Paris, 2000), 33–46 (the latter attempting a developmental solution). I cannot discuss this issue here.

[90] See also Brown, 'Being', 478; 'Verb', 233–6; Ademollo, *Cratylus*, 278; but see Gilson, *Being*, 49.

defended in this paper is sound, we are in a position to resist both the slogan and the juxtaposition with Aristotle.

Working through the *Sophist*'s concept of a Kind Being enables us to see that there is at least an important context in which the consensus view on Plato's conception of being does not accurately represent Plato's view. I have argued that when being is metaphysically analysed by Plato in terms of participation in the Kind Being (*X is*, because it partakes in or combines with the Kind Being), as is so often the case in the *Sophist*, 'to be' does not stand for 'to be something', or 'to be itself', or 'to be variously characterized' (or similar), but should be understood in terms of existence. And while I think the consensus view is open to further objections and does not easily account, for example, for the ontological status of the *Timaeus*' receptacle or the *Republic*'s Idea of the Good,[91] I have not intended to show that for Plato to be is *never* to be something. My argument does not in itself rule out the possibility, which goes well beyond the scope of this paper to ascertain, that the slogan may help us to make sense of other Platonic texts, such as the so-called sight-lovers argument at *Republic* 5. But even so, that dialogue, like virtually all others except the *Sophist*, does not isolate a Kind Being. Instead, it treats being (τὸ ὄν, οὐσία) as indicating the intelligible domain *in general*, typically contrasted with that of perceptible entities, the realm of becoming (γένεσις). And this alone makes all the difference.

Università Roma Tre

BIBLIOGRAPHY

Ackrill, J., 'Plato and the Copula' ['Copula'], *Journal of Hellenic Studies*, 77 (1957), 1–16 (reprinted in id., *Essays on Plato and Aristotle* (Oxford, 1997), 72–9).
Adams, R., *What Is & What Is In Itself* (New York, 2021).
Ademollo, F., *The Cratylus of Plato* [*Cratylus*] (Cambridge, 2011).

---

[91] It is far from clear, for example, in what sense the receptacle could be 'something', while being deprived of every attribute (cf. *Tim.* 50 D 7, 51 A 3, 51 A 7), or in what sense the Idea of the Good evoked at *Republic* 509 B 9–10 could be 'something', being 'beyond essence in rank and power' (ἐπέκεινα τῆς οὐσίας πρεσβείᾳ καὶ δυνάμει). Both, however, certainly exist: cf. *Tim.* 52 A 8; *Rep.* 518 C 9, 526 E 3–4, 532 C 6.

Ademollo, F., 'Plato's Conception of the Forms: Some Remarks', in R. Chiaradonna and G. Galluzzo (eds.), *Universals in Ancient Philosophy* (Pisa, 2013), 41–85.

Apelt, O. (ed.), *Platonis Sophista [Sophista]* (Leipzig, 1879).

Aubenque, P., 'Une occasion manquée: La genèse avortée de la distinction entre l'"étant" et le "quelque chose"', in id. (ed.), *Études sur le Sophiste de Platon* (Paris, 1991), 365–85.

Bardout, J.-C., *Penser l'existence* (Paris, 2013), i.

Bekker, I. (ed.), *Platonis scripta graece omnia* (London, 1826), iv.

Berti, E., 'Che cos'è l'essere?' ['L'essere'], in id., *In principio era la meraviglia* (Rome, 2007), 41–73 (originally published in M. Barbanti et al. (eds.), *Unione e amicizia* (Catania, 2002), 25–42).

Berti, E., 'Le problème de la substantialité de l'être et de l'un dans la *Métaphysique* d'Aristote', in P. Aubenque (ed.), *Études sur la 'Métaphysique' d'Aristote* (Paris, 1993), 89–129 (Ital. trans. in E. Berti., *Studi aristotelici* (Brescia, 2012), 221–52).

Bluck, R., *Plato's Sophist [Sophist]* (Manchester, 1975).

Bonitz, H., *Platonische Studien [Studien]*, 3rd edn (Berlin, 1886).

Bostock, D., 'Plato on 'Is Not'' ['Is Not'], *Oxford Studies in Ancient Philosophy*, 2 (1984), 89–119.

Brown, L., 'Being in the *Sophist*: A Syntactical Enquiry' ['Being'], in G. Fine (ed.), *Plato 1: Metaphysics and Epistemology* (Oxford, 1999), 455–78 (reprinted with revisions from *Oxford Studies in Ancient Philosophy*, 4 (1986), 49–70).

Brown, L., 'Negation and Not-Being: Dark Matter in the *Sophist*' ['Dark Matter'], in R. Patterson et al. (eds.), *Presocratics and Plato* (Las Vegas, 2012), 233–54.

Brown, L., 'The Verb "To Be" in Greek Philosophy: Some Remarks' ['Verb'], in S. Everson (ed.), *Companions to Ancient Thought*, iii: *Language* (Cambridge, 1994), 212–36.

Brunschwig, J., 'The Stoic Theory of the Supreme Genus and Platonic Ontology' ['Theory'], in id., *Papers in Hellenistic Philosophy* (Cambridge, 1994), 92–157 (originally in French in J. Barnes and M. Mignucci (eds.), *Matter and Metaphysics* (Naples, 1988), 19–127).

Burnet, J. (ed.), *Platonis opera*, 2nd edn (Oxford, 1905–13), ii–v.

Burnyeat, M., '*Apology* 30 B 2–4: Socrates, Money, and the Grammar of ΓΙΓΝΕΣΘΑΙ' ['Apology'], *Journal of Hellenic Studies*, 123 (2003), 1–25.

Bury, R. (ed.), *The Philebus of Plato* (Cambridge, 1897).

Butchvarov, P., *Being Qua Being* (Bloomington, 1979).

Campbell, L. (ed.), *The Sophistes and the Politicus of Plato* (Oxford, 1867).

Carraud, V., 'L'invention de l'existence: Note sur la christologie de Marius Victorinus', *Quaestio*, 3 (2003), 3–25.

Centrone, B. (trans.), *Platone: Sofista* (Turin, 2008).

Charles, D., 'Some Comments on Prof. Enrico Berti's "Being and Essence in Contemporary Interpretations of Aristotle"', in A. Bottani et al. (eds.), *Individuals, Essence and Identity* (Dordrecht, 2002), 109–26.
Cherniss, H. F., *Aristotle's Criticism of Plato and the Academy* (Baltimore, 1944).
Cherniss, H. F., 'The Relation of the *Timaeus* to Plato's Later Dialogues' ['Relation'], *American Journal of Philology*, 78 (1957), 225–66 (reprinted in id., *Selected Papers* (Leiden, 1977), 298–339).
Code, A., 'Aristotle: Essence and Accident' ['Essence'], in R. Grandym and R. Warner (eds.), *Philosophical Grounds of Rationality* (Oxford, 1986), 411–39.
Collette-Dučić, B., '*Sophiste*' ['*Sophiste*'], in A. Motte and P. Somville (eds.), *Ousia dans la philosophie grecque des origines à Aristote* (Louvain-la-Neuve, 2008), 143–58.
Cordero, N.-L., 'La participation comme être de la forme dans le *Sophiste* de Platon', in id. (ed.), *Ontologie et dialogue* (Paris, 2000), 33–46.
Cordero, N.-L. (trans.), *Platon: Sophiste* (Paris, 1993).
Cornford, F. M. (trans.), *Plato's Theory of Knowledge* [*Theory*] (London, 1935).
Crivelli, P., *Plato's Account of Falsehood* [*Account*] (Cambridge, 2012).
Crombie, I. M., *An Examination of Plato's Doctrines*, 2 vols. (London, 1963).
Dale, C., 'To Be', in R. Le Poidevin et al. (eds.), *The Routledge Companion to Metaphysics* (London, 2009), 225–33.
Diès, A. (ed. and trans.), *Platon: Le Sophiste* [*Sophiste*] (Paris, 1925).
Dixsaut, M., *Le naturel philosophe* [*Naturel*], 3rd edn (Paris, 2001).
Duke, E. A. et al. (eds.), *Platonis opera* (Oxford, 1995), i.
Fine, G., 'Immanence', in ead., *Plato on Knowledge and Forms* (Oxford, 2003), 301–25 (reprinted from *Oxford Studies in Ancient Philosophy*, 4 (1986), 71–97).
Fine, G., *On Ideas* (Oxford, 1993).
Frede, M., 'Die Frage nach dem Seienden: Sophistes' ['Frage'], in T. Kobusch and B. Mojsisch (eds.), *Platon* (Darmstadt, 1996), 181–99.
Frede, M., 'Plato's *Sophist* on False Statements' ['False Statements'], in R. Kraut (ed.), *The Cambridge Companion to Plato* (Cambridge, 1992), 397–424 (reprinted in D. Ebrey and R. Kraut (eds.), *The Cambridge Companion to Plato*, 2nd edn (Cambridge, 2022), 433–63).
Frede, M., *Prädikation und Existenzaussage* [*Prädikation*] (Göttingen, 1967).
Frede, M., 'Sein; Seiendes. I. Antike. 1. Vorsokratiker; Platon; Aristoteles; 2. Hellenismus', in J. Ritter and K. Gründer (eds.), *Historisches Wörterbuch der Philosophie* (Basel, 1995), ix. 170–80.
Fronterotta, F., *METHEXIS* (Pisa, 2001).
Galluzzo, G., *Breve storia dell'ontologia* (Rome, 2011).

Gassendi, P., *Disquisitio metaphysica*, in id., *Opera omnia* (Lyons, 1658; reprinted Stuttgart, 1964) iii.

Gerson, L. P., *Plotinus [Plotinus]* (London, 1994).

Gill, M.-L., *Philosophos [Philosophos]* (Oxford, 2012).

Gilson, E., *Being and Some Philosophers [Being]* (Toronto, 1952).

Granieri, R., 'Not-Being, Contradiction and Difference. Simplicius *vs*, Alexander of Aphrodisias on Plato's Conception of Not-Being', *Méthexis*, 35 (2023), 185–200.

Granieri, R., 'The Referents of 'Being' in Plato's *Sophist*', in L. Brisson et al. (eds.), *Plato's Sophist* (Baden-Baden, forthcoming).

Granieri, R., 'That in Virtue of Which Something Is a Being: Note on Damascius, *De principiis* II, p. 75.10–11 Westerink' ['Damascius'], *Studia graeco-arabica*, 13 (2023), 49–55.

Günther, H.-C., 'Briefe Martin Heideggers an Julius Stenzel (1928–1932)', *Heidegger Studies*, 16 (2000), 11–33.

Harte, V., *Plato on Parts and Wholes* (Oxford, 2002).

Heidegger, M., *Gesamtausgabe* vi.1–2: *Nietzsche II* (Frankfurt, 1996–7 [1936–46]).

Heinaman, R., 'Being in the *Sophist*' ['Being'], *Archiv für Geschichte der Philosophie*, 65 (1983), 1–17.

Heindorf, L. F. (ed.), *Platonis dialogi selecti* (Berlin, 1810), iv.

Hestir, B., *Plato on the Metaphysical Foundation of Meaning and Truth [Foundation]* (Cambridge, 2016).

Huby, F., and Taylor, C. C. W. (trans.), *Simplicius: On Aristotle Physics 1.3–4* (London, 2011).

Hume, D., *A Treatise on Human Nature*, ed. by D. F. Norton and M. J. Norton (Oxford, 2007 [1739–40]).

Irani, T., 'Perfect Change in Plato's *Sophist*', *Oxford Studies in Ancient Philosophy*, 60 (2022), 45–93.

Kahn, C., *Essays on Being [Essays]* (Oxford, 2009).

Kahn, C., *The Verb 'Be' in Ancient Greek ['Be']* (Indianapolis, 2003 [1973]).

Kahn, C., 'Why Existence Does Not Emerge as a Distinct Concept in Greek Philosophy', *Archiv für Geschichte der Philosophie*, 58 (1976), 323–34 (reprinted in id., *Essays*, 62–74).

Keyt, D., 'Plato's Paradox That the Immutable Is Unknowable' ['Paradox'], *Philosophical Quarterly*, 74 (1969), 1–14.

Kripke, S., *Reference and Existence* (Oxford, 2013).

Kühner R., and Gerth, B., *Ausführliche Grammatik der Griechischen Sprache* (Hanover, 1904), ii. ii.

Lavaud, L., 'The Primary Substance in Plotinus' Metaphysics: A Little-Known Concept', *Phronesis*, 59 (2014), 369–84.

Lee, E. N., 'Plato on Negation and Not-Being in the *Sophist*' ['Negation'], *Philosophical Review*, 81 (1972), 267–304.

Leigh, F., 'Being and Power in Plato's *Sophist*', *Apeiron*, 43 (2010), 1–23.
Leigh, F., 'The Copula and Semantic Continuity in Plato's *Sophist*' ['Semantic Continuity'], *Oxford Studies in Ancient Philosophy*, 34 (2008), 105–21.
Lewis, F., 'Aristotle on the Homonymy of Being', *Philosophy and Phenomenological Research*, 68 (2004), 1–36.
Loux, M., 'Being, Categories, and Universal Reference in Aristotle', in L. Haaparanta and H. J. Koskinen (eds.), *Categories of Being* (Oxford, 2012), 17–35.
Luna, C., and Segonds, A. (ed. and trans.), *Proclus: Commentaire sur le Parménide de Platon* (Paris, 2010), ii. ii.
Malcolm, J., 'Plato's Analysis of τὸ ὄν τὸ μὴ ὄν in the *Sophist*' ['Analysis'] *Phronesis*, 12 (1967), 130–46.
Malcolm, J., 'Some Cautionary Remarks on the "is"/"teaches" Analogy' ['Remarks'], *Oxford Studies in Ancient Philosophy*, 31 (2006), 281–96.
Mannsperger, D., *Physis bei Plato* (Berlin, 1969).
Mansfeld, J., *Heresiography in Context* (Leiden, 1992).
Matthews, G., 'Aristotle on Existence' ['Aristotle on Existence'], *Bulletin of the Institute of Classical Studies*, 40 (1995), 233–8.
McCabe, M. M., *Plato's Individuals* [*Individuals*] (Princeton, 1994).
Menn, S., 'Aristotle on the Many Senses of Being' ['Many Senses'], *Oxford Studies in Ancient Philosophy*, 59 (2021), 187–263.
Mignucci, M., 'In margine al concetto aristotelico di esistenza' ['Esistenza'], in G. Bernardi Pierini et al., *Scritti in onore di † Carlo Diano* (Bologna, 1975), 227–61.
Mill, J. S., *A System of Logic* (Toronto, 1974 [1843]), i.
Moore, G. E., 'Is Existence a Predicate?' [Symposium with W. Kneale], *Proceedings of the Aristotelian Society*, suppl. vol. 15 (1936), 175–88 (reprinted in id., *Philosophical Papers* (London, 1959), 115–26).
Moravcsik, J., 'Being and Meaning in the *Sophist*' ['Meaning'], *Acta Philosophica Fennica*, 14 (1962), 23–78.
Moss, J., *Plato's Epistemology* (New York, 2021).
Notomi, N., 'Plato on *What Is Not*', in D. Scott (ed.), *Maieusis* (Cambridge, 2007), 254–75.
O'Brien, D., 'La forma del non essere nel *Sofista* di Platone' ['Forma del non essere'], in F. Fronterotta and W. Leszl (eds.), *Eidos-Idea* (Sankt Augustin, 2005), 115–60.
O'Brien, D., 'A Form That "Is" of What "Is Not": Existential *einai* in Plato's *Sophist*' ['Form'], in G. Boys-Stones et al. (eds.), *The Platonic Art of Philosophy* (Cambridge, 2013), 221–48.
O'Brien, D., *Le non-être* [*Non-Être*] (Sankt Augustin, 1995).
O'Brien, D., 'The Stranger's Farewell (258 E 6–259 A 1)', in A. Havlíček and F. Karfík (eds.), *Plato's* Sophist (Prague, 2011), 199–220.

O'Brien, D., 'To Be and Not To Be in Plato's *Sophist*' ['To Be'], in D. Barry (ed.), *Passionate Mind* (Sankt Augustin, 2020), 17–36.
Owen, G. E. L., 'Aristotle and the Snares of Ontology' ['Snares'], in R. Bambrough (ed.), *New Essays on Plato and Aristotle* (London, 1965), 69–96 (reprinted in id., *LSD*, 259–78).
Owen, G. E. L., *Logic, Science and Dialectic* [*LSD*] (Ithaca, NY, 1986).
Owen, G. E. L., 'Plato and Parmenides on the Timeless Present', *Monist* 50 (1966), 317–40 (reprinted in id., *LSD*, 27–44).
Owen, G. E. L., 'Plato on Not-Being' ['Not-Being'], in G. Vlastos (ed.), *Plato: 1. Metaphysics and Epistemology: A Collection of Critical Essays* (Garden City, NY, 1971), 223–67 (reprinted in id., *LSD*, 104–37).
Peipers, D., *Ontologia platonica* [*Ontologia*] (Leipzig, 1883).
Perl, E., 'The Motion of Intellect on the Neoplatonic Reading of *Sophist* 248 E–249 D', *International Journal of the Platonic Tradition*, 8 (2014), 135–60.
Politis, V., 'The Argument for the Reality of Change and Changelessness in Plato's *Sophist* (248 E 7–249 D 5)', in F.-G. Herrmann (ed.), *New Essays on Plato* (Swansea, 2006), 149–75.
Rashed, M., 'Hišām ibn al-Ḥakam et Sulaymān ibn Ǧarīr entre stoïcisme et kalām: De la négation du tiers-exclu à la distinction entre "chose" et "existant"', *Discipline filosofiche*, 31 (2021), 9–26.
Rashed, M., 'Posidonius et le traité d'Albinus *Sur les incorporels*', *Elenchos*, 42 (2021), 165–98.
Rosen, S., *Plato's Sophist* [*Sophist*] (New Haven, 1983).
Ross, W. D., *Plato's Theory of Ideas* (Oxford, 1951).
Runciman, W. G., *Plato's Later Epistemology* (Cambridge, 1971).
Sabrier, P., 'Plato's Method of Enquiry in the *Sophist*', in J. K. Larsen et al. (eds.), *New Perspectives on Platonic Dialectic* (New York, 2022), 233–48.
Schleiermacher, F. (trans.), *Platons Werke*, 2.2 (Berlin, 1807).
Schofield, M., 'Editor's Notes', *Phronesis*, 35 (1990), 327–34.
Sedley, D. N., 'Presocratic Themes: Being, Not-Being and Mind', in R. Le Poidevin et al. (eds.), *The Routledge Companion to Metaphysics* (London, 2009), 8–17.
Seligman, P., *Being and Not-Being* (The Hague, 1974).
Shorey, P., *The Unity of Plato's Thought* [*Unity*] (Chicago, 1903).
Shorey, P., *What Plato Said* [*WPS*] (Chicago, 1933).
Silverman, A., *The Dialectic of Essence* [*Essence*] (Princeton, 2002).
Slings, S. R. (ed.), *Platonis* Rempublicam (Oxford, 2003).
Smith, C., 'Against the Existential Reading of *Euthydemus* 283 E–284 C, with Help from the *Sophist*', *Ancient Philosophy*, 42 (2022), 67–81.
Stenzel, J., *Studien zur Entwicklung der platonischen Dialektik von Sokrates zu Aristoteles*, 2nd edn (Leipzig, 1931).

Szaif, J., *Der Sinn von 'sein'* (Freiburg, 2003).
Thomas, C., 'Speaking of Something: Plato's *Sophist* and Plato's Beard' ['Beard'], *Canadian Journal of Philosophy*, 38 (2008), 631–68.
van Eck, J., 'Not-Being and Difference: On Plato's *Sophist*, 256 D 5–258 E 3', *Oxford Studies in Ancient Philosophy*, 23 (2002), 63–84.
White, N. (trans.), *Plato: Sophist* [*Sophist*] (Indianapolis, 1993).
Zaks, N., *Apparences et dialectique: Un commentaire du* Sophiste *de Platon* [*Apparences*] (Leiden, 2023).

NEGATIVE FORMS IN PLATO'S *SOPHIST*

A Re-Examination

SAMUEL MEISTER

In Plato's *Sophist*, a visitor from Elea (henceforth, 'the Visitor') and his interlocutor Theaetetus set out to answer Socrates' question what the sophist is (218 C 5–7). Because the Visitor casts the sophist as one who thrives on what appears to be but is not, and who says things that are not true (236 E 1–2), the Visitor must vindicate 'is not' claims and the possibility of false speech. This, in turn, requires him to argue against Parmenides that being and not-being mix: being is not, and not-being is. On an increasingly popular view, in arguing that not-being is, the Visitor posits negative kinds or forms, such as the not-beautiful.[1] In this paper, I will oppose this trend to argue that, in the *Sophist*, the Visitor relies

An earlier version of this paper has been presented at the *Symposium Platonicum* 2022 in Athens, GA, and I would like to thank the audience for their valuable feedback. I developed my first thoughts on the topic in commenting on a paper by Jan Szaif (in which he defended the opposite view) at a workshop at Brown University in 2019 organized by Mary Louise Gill and Anna Pavani, and I am very grateful to him not only for making me think about the topic but also for his comments on a draft of the present paper. I also owe a great debt to Mary Louise Gill for discussing these issues with me over many years and for prompting me to continue working on them. Finally, I want to thank Rachana Kamtekar and two anonymous referees for their extremely helpful comments that have allowed me to improve the paper greatly.

[1] See e.g. J. M. E. Moravcsik, 'Being and Meaning in the *Sophist*' ['Being'], *Acta Philosophica Fennica*, 14 (1962), 23–78 at 68–9; M. Frede, *Prädikation und Existenzaussage* [*Prädikation*] (Göttingen, 1967), 92–4; E. N. Lee, 'Plato on Negation and Not-Being in the *Sophist*' ['Negation'], *Philosophical Review*, 81 (1972), 267–304; J. Szaif, *Platons Begriff der Wahrheit* [*Wahrheit*] (Freiburg, 1996), 434–45; L. Brown, 'Negation and Not-Being: Dark Matter in the *Sophist*' ['Dark Matter'], in R. Patterson, V. Karasmanis, and A. Hermann (eds.), *Presocratics and Plato: Festschrift in Honor of Charles Kahn* (Las Vegas, 2012), 233–54; P. Crivelli, *Plato's Account of Falsehood: A Study of the* Sophist [*Falsehood*] (Cambridge, 2012), 204–14; P. Crivelli, 'Negative Kinds in Plato's *Statesman*' ['Negative Kinds'], in S. Delcomminette, van Daele (eds.), *La méthode de division de Platon à Érigène* (Paris, 2020), 19–40. It used to be common to dismiss the attribution of negative forms to the Visitor out of hand (see e.g. F. M. Cornford, *Plato's Theory of Knowledge* [*Knowledge*] (London,

only on positive kinds or forms, especially the kind or form difference, to confront Parmenides.

It is worth reconsidering the issue of negative forms in the *Sophist* for at least two reasons. The first touches on Platonic metaphysics at large. Already Aristotle objected to the Platonists on the grounds that they are committed to negative forms (*Metaph.* A. 9, 990^{b}13–14=M. 4, 1079^{a}9–10; *De ideis* 80. 16–81. 8), and regardless of whether his objection is a good one, it shows that the stakes are high: it is important for our understanding of Plato whether he countenances negative forms. The second reason concerns the *Sophist* itself. Since the Visitor engages with Parmenides to vindicate 'is not' claims and false speech, it would be a weakness of his account if he made gratuitous appeal to entities that are not needed for this vindication. A proper appreciation of the Visitor's account, then, calls for a careful examination of whether he is committed to negative kinds or forms.

My argument against the attribution of negative kinds or forms to the Visitor in the *Sophist* has a textual and a philosophical side. On the textual side, I will argue that the Visitor does not posit negative kinds or forms. On the philosophical side, I will argue that the Visitor does not *need* to posit any such entities because he can reach his goals by appeal to difference. The latter conclusion suggests that an appeal to negative kinds or forms would be gratuitous and hence weaken the Visitor's account. The textual result implies that we need not saddle him with this unsatisfactory view. Rather,

---

1935), 292–4; H. Cherniss, *Aristotle's Criticisms of Plato and the Academy* [*Criticisms*] (Baltimore, 1944), 262–8; W. D. Ross, *Plato's Theory of Ideas* [*Ideas*] (Oxford, 1951), 167–9), but resistance to negative forms has waned more recently, with a few exceptions (M. Dixsaut, 'La négation, le non-être et l'autre dans le *Sophiste*' ['Négation'], in P. Aubenque and M. Narcy (eds.), *Études sur le Sophiste de Platon* (Naples, 1991), 165–213; G. Fine, On Ideas: *Aristotle's Criticism of Plato's Theory of Forms* [*Forms*] (Oxford, 1993), 113–16; S. Berman, 'Plato's Explanation of False Belief in the Sophist' ['False Belief'], *Apeiron*, 29 (1996), 19–46; M. L. Gill, *Philosophos: Plato's Missing Dialogue* [*Philosophos*] (Oxford, 2012),162). The two main objections to attributing negative forms to the Visitor in the *Sophist* have been that, in principle, negative forms are unpalatable and should not be ascribed to Plato (T. Penner *The Ascent from Nominalism: Some Existence Arguments in Plato's Middle Dialogues* [*Ascent*] (Dordrecht, 1987), 369, n. 53; Berman, 'False Belief', 35–7), and that the Visitor supposedly rejects negative forms in the *Politicus* (Cornford, *Knowledge*, 293; Ross, *Ideas*, 168; Dixsaut, 'Négation', 195–7; Fine, *Forms*, 113–16; Gill, *Philosophos*, 162). As they stand, these objections are not persuasive (see Section 1), which has surely contributed to the renaissance of the attribution of negative forms to the Visitor.

Negative Forms in Plato's Sophist

by appeal to difference, the Visitor offers a unified account of 'is not' claims and false speech that relies on remarkably economical ontological resources.

Notably, the issue of negative forms intersects with another problem, namely whether in the *Sophist* we get an account of Platonic forms at all. The Visitor uses the words *genos* and *eidos* (and occasionally, *idea*) to refer to the entities under discussion, such as the 'greatest of the *genē*' (μέγιστα τῶν γενῶν) (254 D 4): being, rest, change, sameness, and difference. But *genē* or *eidē* could be either Platonic forms or simply kinds. My opponents disagree on this issue. For instance, Frede (*Existenz*) claims that the Visitor posits negative forms, whereas Crivelli (*Falsehood*; 'Negative Kinds') argues merely that he posits negative kinds and Szaif (*Wahrheit*) speaks neutrally of negative *eidē*. I will translate *genos*, *eidos*, and *idea* as 'kind' but without taking a stand on whether, ultimately, this talk of 'kinds' should be understood in terms of forms. I assume only that *if* there are forms in the *Sophist*, they are referred to as *genē* or *eidē*, or in my translation, 'kinds'. Thus, I will argue that the Visitor does not posit negative kinds, which implies also that he does not posit negative forms, regardless of whether *genē* or *eidē* are forms.

In the following, I begin by introducing the issue of negative kinds in the *Sophist* (Section 1), before working my way through the Visitor's argument against Parmenides. First, I address his discussion of the communion of kinds and the argument that being is not (255 E 8–257 A 12). These passages matter because, as I argue, they introduce the resources on which the Visitor relies later in his argument that not-being is and his vindication of 'is not' claims and false speech. These resources include the kind difference as well as a triadic participation relation by which one entity partakes of difference with regard to another entity, but not negative kinds (Section 2).

Against this backdrop, I turn to the Visitor's argument that not-being is (257 B 1–258 E 5), which contains the main evidence for negative kinds in the *Sophist*. First, I discuss the *introductory exchange* (257 B 1–C 4), where, in my view, the Visitor begins to vindicate negative predication without negative kinds (Section 3). Second, I argue that the account of entities such as the not-beautiful in the *passage on the parts of difference* (257 C 5–258 A 10) does not introduce negative kinds (Section 4). Third, I extend my argument to show that the kind not-being in the *passage on not-being* (258 A 11–E 5) is not a negative kind either but rather identical with the positive kind difference (Section 5). Finally, I sketch how the Visitor can vindicate negative predication and false speech with recourse to difference and without appeal to negative kinds (Section 6).

1. The *Sophist* and negative forms

According to the Visitor, the claim that the sophist 'says things but not true things' (τὸ λέγειν μὲν ἄττα, ἀληθῆ δὲ μή, 236 E 2) relies on the assumption that not-being is (237 A 3–4).[2] Hence, the project of the dialogue, namely to say what the sophist is (218 C 5–7), requires a refutation of Parmenides, who argued that only being is, and not-being is not (237 A 4–B 3). Against Parmenides, then, the Visitor concludes both that being is not (257 A 1–7) and that not-being is (257 A 11–258 E 8). The goal of his arguments for these conclusions is to vindicate 'is not' claims and false speech, and thus to allow the Visitor to complete the definition of the sophist.[3]

Prominent scholars have claimed that, in arguing that not-being is, the Visitor posits negative kinds or forms.[4] Since most recent interpreters who consider the issue of negative kinds or forms in detail hold this view, I will call it the *standard interpretation*. There are textual and philosophical grounds for adopting the standard interpretation. The chief textual evidence is contained in two contiguous passages where the Visitor introduces parts of difference (257 C 5–258 A 10) and a kind not-being (258 A 11–E 5). The philosophical motivation is harder to gauge because the advocates of negative kinds disagree on their import. A motivation implicit in most discussions is that negative kinds are needed to vindicate

---

[2] All translations are mine, but I have greatly profited from other translations, especially C. Rowe, *Plato:* Theaetetus *and* Sophist [Theaetetus *and* Sophist] (Cambridge, 2015). For the Greek text of the *Sophist* (and the *Politicus*), unless noted otherwise, I rely on E. A. Duke et al., *Platonis Opera* [*Opera*] (Oxford, 1995), i.

[3] For the question whether there can be a genuine definition of sophistry and the sophist, see J. Beere, 'Faking Wisdom: The Expertise of Sophistic in Plato's *Sophist*', *Oxford Studies in Ancient Philosophy*, 57 (2019), 153–89.

[4] See Moravcsik, 'Being', 68–9; Frede, *Prädikation*, 92–4; Lee, 'Negation'; Szaif, *Wahrheit*, 434–45; Brown, 'Dark Matter'; Crivelli, *Falsehood*, 204–14; 'Negative Kinds'.

negative predication.[5] For instance, one may argue that it is permissible to say that Socrates is not beautiful because this claim can be spelled out in terms of Socrates' partaking of the negative kind of the not-beautiful.

A second philosophical motivation for the standard interpretation is more controversial among its proponents. It would be natural to use negative kinds to give an account of false speech. For instance, one could argue that the claim that Helen is guilty is false just in case Helen partakes of the negative kind of the not-guilty. But although Crivelli (*Falsehood*, 5–7, 256–7) proposes such an application, other advocates of the standard interpretation do not bring in negative kinds to explain the account of false speech (Frede, *Prädikation*, 94–5), or even argue against the application (Szaif, *Wahrheit*, 486, 500). Still, I will assume that there are, in principle, two ways of motivating the standard interpretation philosophically: first, the Visitor needs negative kinds to vindicate negative predication, and second, he needs them to vindicate false speech.

All that said, what are negative kinds? Since, in my view, the *Sophist* does not give an account of negative kinds, this question is not easy to answer. But we can get a sense of these entities if we consider how they might be introduced (or discovered). One option is to assume a stock of positive kinds, such as the human kind, and posit negative kinds that include all the entities that are not members of the relevant positive kind. For instance, one can posit a non-human kind which includes all entities that are not human.[6] Another option is to generate negative kinds (or forms) by means of the One-Over-Many argument: just as there must be a human kind for all things that are human, there must be a kind non-human for all things that are not human (Aristotle, *Metaph*. A. 9, 990^{b}13–14=M. 4, 1079^{a}9–10; *De ideis* 80. 16–81. 8).

There are two classic objections to the standard interpretation. The first rests on Plato's own remarks elsewhere. In the *Politicus*, the Visitor argues against dividing the human kind into Greek and barbarian kinds (262 C 8–D 6). This may be read as an objection to negative kinds, such as the barbarian or non-Greek. Hence, one

---

[5] See Frede, *Prädikation*, 94; Lee, 'Negation', 288–98; Szaif, *Wahrheit*, 243–5; Crivelli, *Falsehood*, 5–6, 220.

[6] See e.g. Crivelli (*Falsehood*, 205): 'for every kind there is another kind that is its complement, namely a kind that holds of all and only the things of which the given kind does not hold'.

might infer that he cannot posit negative kinds in the *Sophist* either.[7] I am not persuaded by this objection. For in the *Politicus*, the Visitor rejects primarily the claim that every part of something is a kind (263 B 7–10). The rejection of this claim may rule out a negative kind of the non-Greek, but it need not prohibit negative kinds in general. After all, it is hardly obvious that if only some parts of a kind are themselves kinds, there are no legitimate divisions that lead to negative kinds. Generally, in the *Politicus*, the Visitor seems to object to a misapplication of the method of division, not to negative kinds as such.[8]

The second objection is a philosophical one that targets the profligacy of an ontology that includes negative kinds. Aristotle is a famous representative of this objection.[9] Indeed, in the passages cited above, he considers it a strike against the Platonists that they are committed to kinds (or forms) of negations (*Metaph.* A. 9, 990^{b}13–14=M. 4, 1079^{a}9–10; *De ideis* 80. 16–81. 8). As it stands, this objection is not effective either. For if the standard interpretation is true, negative kinds are needed to vindicate negative predication and perhaps also the possibility of false speech. In that case, the introduction of negative kinds is not profligate but well motivated.

However, as I hope to show, there is a more powerful version of the profligacy objection. This version does not assume that it is in principle ontologically profligate to posit negative kinds but rather shows that, by the Visitor's own lights in the *Sophist*, it would be profligate to do so. For, in fact, he does not need negative kinds to reach his argumentative goals. The kind difference is sufficient not only to show that not-being is but also to vindicate negative predication and the possibility of false speech, and thus to lay the foundations for defining the sophist.

---

[7] See Cornford, *Knowledge*, 293; Ross, *Ideas*, 168; Dixsaut, 'Négation', 197; Fine, *Forms*, 113–16; Berman, 'False Belief', 36, n. 39; Gill, *Philosophos*, 162.

[8] Cf. Crivelli, *Falsehood*, 212–13; 'Negative Kinds'. At 'Negative Kinds', 31–6, Crivelli argues that the *Politicus* rules out that certain parts of a kind are species *of* that kind, but *not* that they are kinds. Thus, the not-beautiful is a part of difference, but not a species of difference, and yet the not-beautiful is, on Crivelli's view, a kind. This reading requires a distinction between a kind and a species or kind *of* a larger kind (Crivelli, 'Negative Kinds', 30). But even without this distinction, it remains far from clear that rejecting the view that every part of a kind is a kind implies that there cannot be any negative kinds.

[9] See also Penner, *Ascent*, 290–1; Berman, 'False Belief'.

Of course, these considerations alone do not rule out that the Visitor posits negative kinds. For he might well be a profligate philosopher. Hence, the profligacy objection has to be paired with a detailed analysis of the text. Our focus will be on the argument that not-being is (257 B 1–258 E 5), which contains the main evidence for negative kinds. But first we should consider the context from which this argument arises, namely the Visitor's discussion of the communion of kinds and the claim that being is not (254 D 4–257 A 12). For I will argue that, in this stretch of text, the Visitor introduces the ontological resources on which he will later rely in his argument that not-being is, prominently including the kind difference but excluding any negative kinds.

2. The communion of kinds (254 D 4–257 A 12)

At 254 B 8–D 2, the Visitor singles out some kinds that are considered the greatest to ask 'of what sort' (ποῖα) they are, and 'how they are capable of being in communion with each other' (κοινωνίας ἀλλήλων πῶς ἔχει δυνάμεως) (254 C 4–6). An answer will allow us to get clearer on being and not-being (254 C 5–8), and to show that we can say that not-being (τὸ μὴ ὄν) *is*, as when we say that it *is* (ἔστιν) something that is not (μὴ ὄν) (254 D 1–2).[10] Hence, before arguing that not-being is (257 B 1–258 E 5), the Visitor embarks on a long discussion of the communion of kinds (254 D 4–257 A 12), which includes arguments for distinguishing the five greatest kinds (being, rest, change, sameness, and difference) (254 D 4–255 E 7), an explanation of how they are related (255 E 8–256 E 8), and the conclusion that being is not (257 A 1–12).

Almost every turn in this discussion of the communion of kinds is controversial, and I cannot address all these debates in detail. My goal is rather to defend two general claims. First, the Visitor analyses what I call 'difference claims' in terms of a triadic participation relation: for any *x* and *y*, for *x* to be different from *y* is for *x* to partake of difference *with regard to y*. Second, he vindicates non-identity claims by appeal to difference, and thus begins his broader vindication of 'is not' claims. Both results will be crucial for understanding the later argument that not-being is.

[10] Cf. Cornford, *Knowledge*, 273; Szaif, *Wahrheit*, 443.

The Visitor begins the discussion of the communion of kinds by recalling the three kinds to which he has appealed so far: being, rest, and change (254 D 4–5). He concludes that 'each of them is *different* from the other two, and *the same* as itself' (αὐτῶν ἕκαστον τοῖν μὲν δυοῖν ἕτερόν ἐστιν, αὐτὸ δ' ἑαυτῷ ταὐτόν) (254 D 14–15). This prompts him to launch a series of arguments that distinguish sameness and difference from being, rest, and change as two further kinds (254 E 17–255 E 7). For us, the most interesting argument is the final one that distinguishes difference from being (255 C 8–E 2) and thereby elucidates the character of the kind difference.

The argument rests on a distinction between entities that are said 'themselves by themselves' (*auta kath' hauta*) and entities that are always said 'towards others' (*pros alla*) (255 C 12–13). The Visitor claims that being can be said either itself by itself or towards another, whereas difference is always said towards another (255 D 4–6)—and hence the two kinds must be distinct (255 D 6–7). The *auta kath' hauta/pros alla* distinction, especially as applied to being, has proven extremely controversial.[11] But we do not need to enter this debate to learn something from the Visitor's argument about his construal of difference claims.

According to the Visitor, 'what is different is always said towards something different' (τὸ δέ γ' ἕτερον ἀεὶ πρὸς ἕτερον) (255 D 1). Moreover,

[11] On a classic view, the *auta kath' hauta/pros alla* distinction is between absolute and relative predicates (Cornford, *Knowledge*, 282; Szaif, *Wahrheit*, 353–4, n. 31; R. M. Dancy, 'The Categories of Being in Plato's *Sophist* 255 C–E', *Ancient Philosophy*, 19 (1999), 45–72; J. Malcolm, 'A Way Back for *Sophist* 255 C 12–13', *Ancient Philosophy*, 26 (2006), 275–89). Both M. Frede (*Prädikation*; 'The *Sophist* on False Statements' ['False Statements'], in R. Kraut (ed.), *The Cambridge Companion to Plato* (Cambridge, 1992), 397–424) and G. E. L. Owen ('Plato on Not-Being' ['Not-Being'], in G. Vlastos (ed.), *Plato I: Metaphysics and Epistemology: A Collection of Critical Essays* (Garden City, NY, 1971), 223–67 at 252–8) opposed this view. In application to being, Frede took the *auta kath' hauta/pros alla* distinction to amount to a distinction between essential and non-essential predication, whereas Owen understood it in terms of the distinction between the 'is' of identity and the 'is' of predication. See L. Brown, 'Being in the *Sophist*: A Syntactical Enquiry', *Oxford Studies in Ancient Philosophy*, 4 (1986), 49–70, for influential criticisms of Owen, and Gill, *Philosophos*, 173–6 for a survey. Recent readings include F. Leigh's ('Modes of Being at *Sophist* 255 C–E' ['Modes of Being'], *Phronesis*, 57 (2012), 1–28 at 11–17), which takes the *auta kath' hauta/pros alla* distinction to be between absolute and relative properties, and Crivelli's (*Falsehood*, 144–5), which argues that the Visitor distinguishes things that are beings only relative to something else (namely perceptible particulars) from things that are beings also by being identical with kinds (namely kinds). See also M. Wiitala, 'That Difference is Different from Being: *Sophist* 255 C 9–E 2', *Oxford Studies in Ancient Philosophy*, 62 (2022), 85–103.

'whatever is different, it simply turns out from necessity to be this very thing it is relative to another' (νῦν δὲ ἀτεχνῶς ἡμῖν ὅτιπερ ἂν ἕτερον ᾖ, συμβέβηκεν ἐξ ἀνάγκης ἑτέρου τοῦτο ὅπερ ἐστὶν εἶναι) (255 D 6–7). In the first of these claims, *to heteron* seems to refer to an entity that is different from another, not difference itself, which in this passage is marked as *to thateron* (255 D 3).[12] Something that is different is different relative to, or from, another. The Visitor spells this out further: '[we will say that] each one thing is different from the others not because of its own nature but because it partakes of the idea of difference' (ἓν ἕκαστον γὰρ ἕτερον εἶναι τῶν ἄλλων οὐ διὰ τὴν αὑτοῦ φύσιν, ἀλλὰ διὰ τὸ μετέχειν τῆς ἰδέας τῆς θατέρου) (255 E 4–6). Thus, difference claims involve three relata: a first entity is different from a second entity, and third, there is the 'kind' (ἰδέα) difference of which the first entity partakes. But this picture raises the further question whether these relata are all related by a single triadic relation or by two distinct dyadic relations.

There are good reasons to think that it is a single triadic relation. Suppose we want to analyse the claim that apples are different from oranges. In the Visitor's terms, the kind apple partakes of difference. Moreover, the difference in question is difference from the kind orange. But there are not two facts: the fact that the kind apple partakes of difference and the fact that the difference in question is difference from the kind orange. Rather, there is a single fact, namely that the kind apple partakes of difference from the kind orange. Hence, the three relata are related by a single triadic participation relation, where the first entity partakes of difference from

---

[12] At 255 C 9, the Visitor said that *to thateron* is 'the fifth' (sc. kind). Hence, it is quite clear that *to thateron* in our passage refers to the kind difference. As for *to heteron* at 255 D 1, I partially agree with Leigh ('Modes of Being', 18) who says that it does not refer to the kind (or form) of difference. However, on her view, *to heteron* refers not to an entity that is different but to the *property* difference. Thus, the Visitor says that the property difference is always said towards something different: difference is always difference from something different. The resulting reading of 255 D 1 is difficult. Although it is plausible that difference is difference from *something*, it is hard to make sense of the claim that difference is difference from something different. For what is the latter entity different from? If it is difference, the Visitor says that difference is difference from something different *from difference*, which seems beside the point. If it is an entity that is different, he says that difference is difference from something that is different, and we will keep asking what the latter entity is different from. It is more natural, then, to take *to heteron* to refer to an entity that is different which is always said towards something that is different from it, e.g. Socrates is different from Kallias, who is different from Socrates.

the second entity. Triadic participation can be expressed as follows (where e_1, e_2, and e_3 are any entities):

> Triadic participation: e_1 partakes of e_3 with regard to e_2.

In the case that interests us, we can substitute 'difference' for e_3 and thus get differential triadic participation:

> Differential triadic participation: e_1 partakes of difference with regard to e_2.

The ensuing 'change passage' (255 E 8–256 D 10), as I will call it, supports this reading. There, the Visitor uses change to illustrate the communion of kinds. Change is different from rest, and hence *is not* rest (255 B 11–15). But change *is* because it partakes of being (256 A 1–2). Further, change is different from sameness, and hence *is not* sameness, but it also partakes of sameness because it is the same as itself, and thus, change *is* the same (256 A 3–B 5). Indeed, if change partook of rest, it would not be surprising to say that change *is* at rest, although it *is not* rest (256 B 6–7).[13] Also, change is different from difference, and hence *is not* difference, although change is different insofar as it partakes of difference (256 C 6–10). Finally, although change partakes of being, it is different from being, and hence *is not* being (256 C 11–D 9).

According to the Visitor, then, seemingly inconsistent claims (e.g. that change is the same and that change is not the same) turn out to be consistent. Scholars disagree on his explanation.[14] But

---

[13] At 252 D 2–11 and 255 A 7, the Visitor denied that change and rest partake of each other. Since G. Vlastos ('An Ambiguity in the *Sophist*' ['Ambiguity'], in G. Vlastos, *Platonic Studies*, 2nd edn (Princeton, 1973), 270–322), there has been a debate on how to reconcile these remarks with the claim that every object of knowledge is at rest (249 B 12) and whether this claim is consistent with the view that an entity is affected and changed when it is known (248 D 4–E 4). See C. D. C. Reeve ('Motion, Rest, and Dialectic in the *Sophist*', *Archiv für Geschichte der Philosophie*, 67 (1985), 47–64 at 47–9) for a statement of these issues and T. Irani ('Perfect Change in Plato's *Sophist*', *Oxford Studies in Ancient Philosophy*, 60 (2022), 45–93) for a recent discussion.

[14] On one reading, he distinguishes the predicative 'is' from the 'is' of identity. For instance, change is the same (as itself) in the predicative sense of 'is', but change is not identical with the same (J. L. Ackrill, 'Plato and the Copula: *Sophist* 251–9' ['Copula'], *Journal of Hellenic Studies*, 77 (1957), 1–6; Owen, 'Not-Being'; Vlastos, 'Ambiguity'; J. van Eck, 'Plato's Logical Insights: On *Sophist* 54 D–57 A', *Ancient Philosophy*, 20 (2000), 53–79). A related view locates the ambiguity not in the copula but the predicate, for instance, 'the same': change is the same (as itself), but it is not sameness (L. Brown, 'The *Sophist* on Statements, Predication, and Falsehood'

what concerns us is again the role of difference, especially in the following segment:

ΞΕ. Τὴν κίνησιν δὴ ταὐτόν τ' εἶναι καὶ μὴ ταὐτὸν ὁμολογητέον καὶ οὐ δυσχεραντέον. οὐ γὰρ ὅταν εἴπωμεν αὐτὴν ταὐτὸν καὶ μὴ ταὐτόν, ὁμοίως εἰρήκαμεν, ἀλλ' ὁπόταν μὲν ταὐτόν, διὰ τὴν μέθεξιν ταὐτοῦ πρὸς ἑαυτὴν οὕτω λέγομεν, ὅταν δὲ μὴ ταὐτόν, διὰ τὴν κοινωνίαν αὖ θατέρου, δι' ἣν ἀποχωριζομένη ταὐτοῦ γέγονεν οὐκ ἐκεῖνο ἀλλ' ἕτερον, ὥστε ὀρθῶς αὖ λέγεται πάλιν οὐ ταὐτόν.

(256 A 10–B 4)

V: It should be agreed, then, without chagrin that change is the same and not the same. For when we say that it is the same and not the same, we do not speak in the same way, but when [we say that] it is the same, we speak in this way because of its participation of the same towards itself, and when [we say that] it is not the same, [we speak in this way] because of the communion in turn with difference because of which it is separated from the same and turns out to be not that but something different so that it is in turn again correctly said to be not the same.

Change is the same, namely the same as itself, because it partakes of sameness 'towards itself'. Change is not the same because it 'communes' with difference by which it is 'separated from' sameness. In the terminology from above, change partakes of difference 'towards' something else, namely sameness.[15] Thus, change, difference, and sameness are related by a triadic participation relation: change partakes of difference with regard to sameness.[16]

['Statements'], in G. Fine (ed.), *The Oxford Handbook of Plato* (Oxford, 2008), 437–62; cf. D. Bostock, 'Plato on "Is Not"' ['Is Not'], *Oxford Studies in Ancient Philosophy*, 2 (1984), 89–119 at 97–8). Frede's (*Prädikation*; 'False Statements') alternative reading utilizes the distinction between essential and non-essential predications mentioned above. For instance, change is non-essentially the same because it partakes of sameness, but change is not essentially the same because sameness is not part of the essence of change (cf. Crivelli, *Falsehood*, 149–66; Leigh, 'Modes of Being'). I will shortly return to one aspect of this debate, namely whether 'is not' claims are non-identity claims here.

[15] I assume that *methexis* (256 B 1) and *koinōnia* (256 B 2) have the same meaning, since *koinōnia* is construed with the genitive (see Ackrill, 'Copula', 5–6; Szaif, *Wahrheit*, 414, n. 92). For an overview of participation language in this part of the *Sophist* (249 D 9–264 B 8), see F. J. Pelletier, *Parmenides, Plato, and the Semantics of Not-Being* [*Not-Being*] (Chicago, 1990), 106–13.

[16] One might wonder whether sameness claims are also analysed in terms of a triadic participation relation, as is suggested by the expression 'participation of the

The passage also sheds light on the Visitor's treatment of 'is not' claims. After all, in arguing that change 'is the same and not the same' (ταὐτόν τ' εἶναι καὶ μὴ ταὐτὸν) (256 A 10), he seems to vindicate the claim that change is not the same: we can correctly say that change is not the same, since this is just to say that change partakes of difference with regard to sameness. One might object to this reading because the Visitor attaches negations not to 'is' but to kind terms.[17] For instance, he does not say that change is-not the same, but that it is not-the-same. Hence, it may seem misleading to say that the Visitor is concerned with the vindication of 'is not' claims in the change passage.

However, as we will see in Section 3, it is a feature of the Visitor's account of 'is not' claims that negations (μή and οὐ) are 'put before the subsequent expressions' (προτιθέμενα τῶν ἐπιόντων ὀνομάτων), or the entities to which those expressions refer (257 C 1–2). For instance, 'not' (μή) is attached to 'large' or the large (256 B 6). Hence, in the change passage, 'is not' claims are construed in just the way we should expect. This holds even though later the Visitor twice attaches a negation to 'is' rather than a kind term when he says that 'however many the others are, as many times [being] is not' (ὅσαπέρ ἐστι τὰ ἄλλα, κατὰ τοσαῦτα οὐκ ἔστιν) (257 A 4–5) and that being 'is not the others' (τἆλλα οὐκ ἔστιν) (257 A 6). These sentences do not contain a kind term to which the negation can be attached, since the Visitor says generically that being is not the other kinds. Hence, he attaches the negation to 'is'. But this does not undermine the point that, *typically*, negations are attached to the kind term. Overall, then, there is little reason to doubt that the Visitor begins to vindicate 'is not' claims in the change passage, and that he does so by appeal to difference.

same towards itself' (256 B 1): change is the same (as itself) because it partakes of sameness towards itself. This account of sameness claims implies that every kind or form is related to itself (assuming that every kind or form is the same as itself) but not that it partakes of itself in the dyadic sense of 'participation' required for self-participation. For example, change partakes not of itself but *of sameness with regard to itself*. Notably, as tempting as it may be to extend my account of difference claims to sameness claims, this is not required for the purposes of this paper. Many thanks to an anonymous referee for bringing the issue to my attention.

[17] See J. McDowell, 'Falsehood and Not-Being in Plato's *Sophist*' ['Not-Being'], in M. Schofield and M. Nussbaum (eds.), *Language and Logos* (Cambridge, 1982), 115–34 at 117–18; J. van Eck, 'Not-Being and Difference: On Plato's *Sophist* 256 D 5–58 E 3' ['Difference'], *Oxford Studies in Ancient Philosophy*, 23 (2002), 63–84 at 69; Crivelli, *Falsehood*, 170–1.

Negative Forms in Plato's Sophist

This reading of the change passage also helps us understand the transition to the next passage where 'not-being' (τὸ μὴ ὄν) is explicitly mentioned and the Visitor concludes that being is not:

ΞΕ. Ἔστιν ἄρα ἐξ ἀνάγκης τὸ μὴ ὂν ἐπί τε κινήσεως εἶναι καὶ κατὰ πάντα τὰ γένη· κατὰ πάντα γὰρ ἡ θατέρου φύσις ἕτερον ἀπεργαζομένη τοῦ ὄντος ἕκαστον οὐκ ὂν ποιεῖ, καὶ σύμπαντα δὴ κατὰ ταὐτὰ οὕτως οὐκ ὄντα ὀρθῶς ἐροῦμεν, καὶ πάλιν, ὅτι μετέχει τοῦ ὄντος, εἶναί τε καὶ ὄντα.
ΘΕΑΙ. Κινδυνεύει.
ΞΕ. Περὶ ἕκαστον ἄρα τῶν εἰδῶν πολὺ μέν ἐστι τὸ ὄν, ἄπειρον δὲ πλήθει τὸ μὴ ὄν.
ΘΕΑΙ. Ἔοικεν.
ΞΕ. Οὐκοῦν καὶ τὸ ὂν αὐτὸ τῶν ἄλλων ἕτερον εἶναι λεκτέον.
ΘΕΑΙ. Ἀνάγκη.
ΞΕ. Καὶ τὸ ὂν ἄρ' ἡμῖν, ὅσαπέρ ἐστι τὰ ἄλλα, κατὰ τοσαῦτα οὐκ ἔστιν· ἐκεῖνα γὰρ οὐκ ὂν ἓν μὲν αὐτό ἐστιν, ἀπέραντα δὲ τὸν ἀριθμὸν τἆλλα οὐκ ἔστιν αὖ.
ΘΕΑΙ. Σχεδὸν οὕτως.

(256 D 7–257 A 5)

V: From necessity, then, it is possible that not-being is both in the case of change and for all kinds. For, for all things, the nature of difference makes each thing something that is not by fashioning it different from being, and along the same lines in this way, we will correctly speak of all things as things that are not, and again, because they partake of being, [we will correctly say that] they are and [speak of them] as things that are.
T: Probably.
V: Concerning each of the kinds, therefore, there is a lot of being, and an unlimited amount of not-being.
T: So it seems.
V: So, it has to be said that being itself too is different from the others.
T: Necessarily.
V: And therefore we [have to say that], however many the others are, as many times being is not. For not being those, it is itself one, and again it is not the others that are unlimited in number.
T: Presumably.

Commentators have been puzzled by the Visitor's reasoning in this passage.[18] Initially, he appears to say that, just like change, any kind is not because it is different from *being* (256 D 11–E 3). But the claim that there is an unlimited amount of not-being concerning each kind (256 E 6–7), including being (257 A 4–6), seems to presuppose that a kind is not because it is different from *all* other kinds—not specifically from being. What, then, underwrites 'is not' claims here? Difference from being or difference from *any* other kind?

Van Eck ('Difference', 64–72) responds that, even in 256 D 11–E 3, what is at stake is difference from *any* kind. His reading rests on translating κατὰ πάντα τὰ γένη at 256 D 12 as 'in respect of all the kinds': change is not 'in respect of all the kinds', and hence is not because it is different from all kinds. But as others have noted, *pace* van Eck ('Difference', 69–71), since ἐπί τε κινήσεως ('in the case of change') and κατὰ πάντα τὰ γένη are linked by τε...καί ('both...and'), these two expressions here seem to play parallel syntactic roles: not-being is both in the case of change and 'for' or 'in the case of' (κατά) all other kinds.[19] In turn, Crivelli (*Falsehood*, 171) suggests that once a negation has been attached to being, one can infer that each kind is not *any* other kind. But it remains hard to see how the claim that each kind is different from being is supposed to *imply* that it is different from all kinds, and thus that there is an unlimited amount of not-being concerning it, as the 'therefore' (ἄρα) at 256 E 5 requires.

Instead, we can draw on my interpretation of the change passage. At 256 D 8–9, the Visitor concludes that change is not because it is different from being, and this result is generalized at 256 D 11–E 3: each kind is not because it is different from being. But the claim that change is not because it is different from being was only one of the 'is not' claims defended in the change passage. The Visitor also argued that change is not the same because it is different from the same (256 A 10–B 4), and so forth for each of the greatest kinds. My suggestion, then, is that the explicit generalization of one 'is not' claim concerning change (namely that change is not because it is different from being) implicitly serves as a generalization of all the 'is not' claims established in the change passage. Just as change is different from all other kinds, each kind is different from all other kinds, and thus, just as change is not any of the other

---

[18] See van Eck, 'Difference'; Crivelli, *Falsehood*, 168–75.
[19] D. O'Brien, *Deux études sur le* Sophiste *de Platon* [*Études*] (Sankt Augustin, 1995) at 52, n. 1; Crivelli, *Falsehood*, 173–4.

kinds, each kind is not any of the other kinds. Hence, at 256 E 5, the Visitor can conclude that there is an unlimited amount of not-being concerning each kind, even concerning being.

On the proposed reading, then, the Visitor offers a vindication of 'is not' claims that begins in the change passage and continues through the argument that being is not. But what sort of 'is not' claims are we dealing with here? On the majority view, in the passages surveyed so far, 'is not' claims are non-identity claims, and it is only from 257 B 1 that the Visitor begins to tackle negative *predicative* claims.[20] But Frede (*Prädikation*; 'False Statements') has argued that, already in the argument that being is not, 'is not' claims are negative predicative claims. One of his main arguments is that we cannot explain how not-being has a single nature (258 A 11; 258 B 10) if, at 257b, the Visitor moves from non-identity claims to negative predicative claims ('False Statements', 407–8).

However, when 'is not' claims come to the fore in the change passage, the Visitor recapitulates his arguments for distinguishing the five kinds (255 E 11–12). In these arguments, he concluded that each kind is *distinct* from, or not identical with, the other kinds. Hence, the 'is not' claims in the change passage should also be non-identity claims, as should the conclusions drawn from the change passage, including the claim that being is not the other kinds. Moreover, it is not difficult to see why, although he moves from non-identity claims to negative predicative claims at 257 B, the Visitor thinks that not-being has a single nature. For one kind, namely difference, is enough to vindicate both sorts of 'is not' claims.[21]

Overall, then, we can draw two conclusions from the Visitor's discussion of the communion of kinds: first, he construes difference claims in terms of a differential triadic participation relation, and second, he vindicates non-identity claims by appeal to difference. Negative kinds have not played any role so far. Next, I want to show that, in arguing that not-being is, the Visitor extends his account to negative predicative claims with the same resources, including the kind difference and the differential triadic participation relation but *not* negative kinds.

---

[20] Owen, 'Not-Being'; McDowell, 'Not-Being'; Szaif, *Wahrheit*, 428–33; Gill, *Philosophos*, 157.
[21] See Section 6 below; cf. J. van Eck, 'Falsity without Negative Predication: On *Sophistes* 255 E–63 D' ['Falsity'], *Phronesis*, 40 (1995), 20–47.

3. Not-Being is: First steps (257 B 1–C 4)

After he has concluded that being is not, the Visitor argues that not-being is (257 B 1–258 E 5). It is on the basis of this argument that scholars have attributed negative kinds to the Visitor in the *Sophist*. In Sections 3–5, I will revisit the argument and oppose the attribution of negative kinds to the Visitor. Instead, I will argue that he continues to operate with the kind difference alongside the differential triadic participation relation.

I divide the argument that not-being is into three sections. In an introductory exchange (Section 3), the Visitor argues that when we speak of not-being or the not-large, we refer not to their opposite but to something different from them (257 B 1–C 4). Next (Section 4), he analyses entities such as the not-large as parts of difference (257 C 5–258 A 10). Finally (Section 5), he concludes that not-being is and that there is a kind not-being (258 A 11–E 5). The last two passages are the main evidence for negative kinds. But first let us look at the introductory exchange which sets the tone for the entire argument. I want to show that the Visitor extends his vindication of 'is not' claims to negative predicative claims by appeal to difference, not negative kinds. Hence, the set-up of the argument that not-being is should not make us expect the imminent introduction of negative kinds.

The introductory exchange reads as follows:

ΞΕ. Ἴδωμεν δὴ καὶ τόδε.
ΘΕΑΙ. Τὸ ποῖον;
ΞΕ. Ὁπόταν τὸ "μὴ ὄν" λέγωμεν, ὡς ἔοικεν, οὐκ ἐναντίον τι λέγομεν τοῦ ὄντος ἀλλ' ἕτερον μόνον.
ΘΕΑΙ. Πῶς;
ΞΕ. Οἷον ὅταν εἴπωμέν τι "μὴ μέγα", τότε μᾶλλόν τί σοι φαινόμεθα τὸ σμικρὸν ἢ τὸ ἴσον δηλοῦν τῷ ῥήματι;
ΘΕΑΙ. Καὶ πῶς;
ΞΕ. Οὐκ ἄρ', ἐναντίον ὅταν ἀπόφασις λέγηται σημαίνειν, συγχωρησόμεθα, τοσοῦτον δὲ μόνον, ὅτι τῶν ἄλλων τι μηνύει τὸ "μὴ" καὶ τὸ "οὒ" προτιθέμενα τῶν ἐπιόντων ὀνομάτων – μᾶλλον δὲ τῶν πραγμάτων περὶ ἅττ' ἂν κέηται τὰ ἐπιφθεγγόμενα ὕστερον τῆς ἀποφάσεως ὀνόματα.
ΘΕΑΙ. Παντάπασι μὲν οὖν.

(257 B 1–C 4)

V: So, let us look at this as well.
T: Which thing?

V: When we speak of 'not-being', it seems, we do not say something opposite to being but merely something different [from being].
T: How so?
V: For example, when we call something 'not large', then do we seem to you to refer to the small any more than the equal by that expression?
T: How could we?
V: So, we will not concede that when a negation is said, it indicates an opposite, but merely this much, that the 'non-' and 'not' put before the subsequent expressions (and more so before the things over which the expressions uttered after the negation are set) signal one of the others.
T: By all means.

According to the Visitor, in speaking of not-being, we do not speak of something 'opposite' (ἐναντίον) to being but something 'different' (ἕτερον) from it (257 B 3–4). For instance, when we say 'Socrates is not large', by 'not large' we do not (necessarily) refer to the opposite of the large, that is, the small, but might equally refer to the equal (257 B 6–8).[22] Thus, when one attaches 'non-' and 'not' (τὸ μὴ καὶ τὸ οὔ) to expressions or, better, to the entities to which those expressions refer, the resulting expressions or entities indicate not the opposite of the negated entity but 'one of the others' (τῶν ἄλλων τι), that is, an entity different from the negated entity. For instance, if one attaches 'not' to 'large' (or the large), 'not large' does not (necessarily) refer to the small but simply to something different from the large, including the small and the equal.

These lines have been hotly debated. The less controversial issue concerns the sort of 'is not' claims at stake. As I mentioned, most scholars think that the discussion from 257 B 1 onwards (if not already before) concerns negative predication.[23] But van Eck ('Falsity', 29–33) has claimed that the Visitor is not interested in negative predication here. His main argument is that, although the Visitor alludes to negative predicative claims, he does so merely to elucidate the meaning of negation ('not'), not the meaning of negative

[22] Contrast with Crivelli (*Falsehood*, 198), who argues that we refer to *neither* the small *nor* the equal. But the Visitor's question whether we refer 'any more' (μᾶλλόν τί) to the small than the equal suggests that, on his view, we might equally well refer to one or the other, not that we refer to neither.
[23] Frede, *Prädikation*; Owen, 'Not-Being'; McDowell, 'Not-Being'; Szaif, *Wahrheit*, 428–33; Gill, *Philosophos*, 157.

predicates ('is not large') (van Eck, 'Falsity', 33). However, even if the Visitor's focus is on negations rather than negative predication, it is hard to believe that the discussion of negations does not also serve the purpose of giving an account of negative predicative claims. For the Visitor begins with an example of a negative predicative claim (that something is not large), and the subsequent discussion of negations is surely motivated at least in part by the intention to vindicate claims of that sort, that is, negative predicative claims.

The much more contentious issue is the interpretation of the Visitor's construal of negative predicative claims. My preference is for the reading which Szaif (*Wahrheit*, 490–1) and Brown ('Statements', 456) call the 'incompatibility range' interpretation:[24] when we say that Socrates is not large, we ascribe to Socrates a property F different from largeness, where largeness and the property F are on a *range* of incompatible properties. For instance, we ascribe smallness or equality to Socrates, which are on the same range of incompatible size properties as largeness. But a proper defence of this reading is beyond the scope of this paper; I will assume it merely for illustrative purposes.[25] For us, what matters is a more basic point that does not depend on the incompatibility range interpretation: the

---

[24] See also M. Ferejohn, 'Plato and Aristotle on Negative Predication and Semantic Fragmentation', *Archiv für Geschichte der Philosophie*, 71 (1989), 257–82; Gill, *Philosophos*, 160–1.

[25] There are at least three alternatives. On the first, in saying 'something that is different' from being, one ascribes to Socrates a property that is incompatible with largeness (see e.g. Pelletier, *Not-Being*, 39–44). This view implies that *heteron* at 257 B 4 *means* 'incompatible', although up to this point of the dialogue it meant 'different'. The incompatibility range interpretation avoids this implication: *heteron* means 'different', but the property that is different from being is taken from a range of incompatible properties that includes the property to be negated (Szaif, *Wahrheit*, 491; Brown, 'Statements', 456). On the second alternative interpretation, in saying 'something different from' being, one ascribes to Socrates a property different from *all* of his properties (see e.g. Frede, *Prädikation*, 95; Owen, 'Not-Being'; J. van Eck, 'Plato's Theory of Negation and Falsity in *Sophist* 257 and 263: A New Defense of the Oxford Interpretation', *Ancient Philosophy*, 34 (2014), 275–88). As I see it, this reading neglects the example at 257 B 6–7: smallness and equality are drawn specifically from a range of properties that also includes largeness. Finally, Crivelli (*Falsehood*, 186) defends an extensional reading: in claiming that Socrates is not large, one says that Socrates is different from any large entity. Thus, at 257 B 9–C 3, the name following a negation refers not to a property or kind but to an entity that has a property or partakes of a kind (e.g. a large thing, not largeness) (cf. Bostock, 'Is Not', 115). But *pace* Crivelli (*Falsehood*, 193), it is not clear that the 'things' (πράγματα) 'about' (περί) which names 'are set' are objects rather than kinds. For in the ensuing sections on the parts of difference (257 C 5–258 A 10), the 'things' of interest are kinds such as the beautiful and not, say, beautiful people or objects.

Visitor vindicates not only non-identity claims but also negative predicative claims by appeal to difference.

The Visitor concedes to Parmenides that we could not speak of not-being if this implied that we are speaking of the 'opposite' (ἐναντίον) of being (cf. Szaif 1996: 446–53). But he denies this implication. For in speaking of not-being, we may speak merely of something different from being. In the case of negative predicative claims, we can say, for instance, that Socrates is not large without appeal to the opposite of the large. Our claim merely requires an appeal to some entity different from the large. More generally, in attaching a negation to an expression or, better, to the entity to which the expression refers, we are not committed to any reference to the opposite of being, but merely to 'one of the others' (τῶν ἄλλων τι), that is, an entity other than, or different from, the negated entity.[26]

None of this seems to require negative kinds. For instance, we are not told that the ascription of a property different from largeness to Socrates implies that Socrates partakes of the not-large. More plausibly, given the central role of difference, the ascription of the relevant property to Socrates requires him to partake of an entity that is different from the large, where the difference claim involved is analysed as set out above: the entity of which Socrates partakes in turn partakes of difference with regard to the large. Let us say that the entity in question is equality. Hence, Socrates partakes of equality which in turn partakes of difference with regard to the large.

This analysis of negative predicative claims is more complex than the analysis of non-identity claims. For in the case of negative predicative claims, alongside the differential triadic relation, an ordinary dyadic participation relation is needed. For instance, the claim that Socrates is not beautiful is analysed as follows: Socrates partakes of a property (for instance, the moderately good-looking), where this property in turn partakes of difference with regard to

---

[26] The truthmaker, then, of the claim that Socrates is not large is the fact that Socrates partakes of *some* property that is incompatible with, but on the same range as, largeness. What this property is may vary. At a young age, Socrates partook of a property that is further removed from largeness than the property of which he partook as an adult, and Theaetetus may partake of yet another size property. If the properties differ from largeness and are drawn from the right range, if something partakes of one of these properties, it will be true that it is not large. One might worry that, in certain cases, this implies that there are lowly kinds or forms. For instance, one might think that the truthmaker of the claim that Socrates is not beautiful may be his participation in ugliness (and thus that there is a kind or even form ugliness). But the Visitor's account does not require, for example, a kind or form ugliness. For one may partake of all sorts of properties that differ from beauty but fall short of ugliness.

beauty. By contrast, non-identity claims are spelled out simply in terms of the triadic relation. For example, the claim that Socrates is distinct from beauty is analysed as follows: Socrates partakes of difference with regard to beauty. In addition, in the case of negative predicative claims, further conditions on the differing entities hold, for instance, that they must be on the same range of incompatible properties (if one adopts the incompatibility range interpretation). For example, for Socrates to be not beautiful, it is not sufficient for him to partake of redness even though redness is distinct from beauty and hence partakes of difference with regard to beauty. By contrast, non-identity claims may involve any distinct entities, including properties from different ranges.[27]

Thus, non-identity claims and negative predicative claims are not analysed in the same way. But the basic ontological resources required for the two analyses are the same: the kind difference and participation, especially differential triadic participation. In this sense, then, the Visitor extends his earlier treatment of non-identity claims to negative predicative claims to provide a unified account of both. And just as he did not require negative kinds to vindicate non-identity claims, he does not need them to vindicate negative predicative claims.

This intermediate verdict does not defeat the standard interpretation yet. For the main evidence for negative kinds is still to come. But given the Visitor's strategy against Parmenides so far, it would be surprising if he did go on to introduce negative kinds. After all, he has been able to vindicate 'is not' claims, and thus to counter Parmenides, by appeal to difference and without recourse to negative kinds. I will now argue that as expected from the introductory exchange, the Visitor keeps operating only with positive kinds to complete the argument that not-being is.

4. Parts of difference (257 c 5–258 a 10)

In the introductory exchange, the Visitor has argued that, in making negative predicative claims, we refer to something different

---

[27] The conditions will vary with one's interpretation of the construal of negative predicative claims. In particular, if one thinks that the negated property must be different from all properties of the relevant entity (e.g. largeness is different from all of Socrates's properties), one must add a different sort of condition, namely that all entities of which Socrates partakes in turn partake of difference with regard to largeness. This condition too is absent from the analysis of non-identity claims where one is interested simply in the difference of one entity from another.

from, not the opposite of, the negated entity. But we might want to know more about the entities to which we refer when we make negative predicative claims. In the aftermath of the introductory exchange, then, the Visitor argues that the entities in question, such as the not-large or not-beautiful, are parts of difference (257 C 5–258 A 10), before proceeding to argue that not-being is (258 A 11–E 5). On the standard interpretation, the analysis of entities such as the not-large as parts of difference implies that they are kinds. But I will argue instead that the parts of difference are simply entities that partake of difference. Thus, the Visitor does not posit any 'partial' negative kinds that correspond to the parts of difference. In Section 5, I will argue that he does not posit a negative kind not-being either.[28]

The Visitor introduces the parts of difference in analogy with knowledge:

ΞΕ. Τόδε δὲ διανοηθῶμεν, εἰ καὶ σοὶ συνδοκεῖ.
ΘΕΑΙ. Τὸ ποῖον;
ΞΕ. Ἡ θατέρου μοι φύσις φαίνεται κατακεκερματίσθαι καθάπερ ἐπιστήμη.
ΘΕΑΙ. Πῶς;
ΞΕ. Μία μέν ἐστί που καὶ ἐκείνη, τὸ δ' ἐπί τῳ γιγνόμενον μέρος αὐτῆς ἕκαστον ἀφορισθὲν ἐπωνυμίαν ἴσχει τινὰ ἑαυτῆς ἰδίαν· διὸ πολλαὶ τέχναι τ' εἰσὶ λεγόμεναι καὶ ἐπιστῆμαι.
ΘΕΑΙ. Πάνυ μὲν οὖν.
ΞΕ. Οὐκοῦν καὶ τὰ τῆς θατέρου φύσεως μόρια μιᾶς οὔσης ταὐτὸν πέπονθε τοῦτο.
ΘΕΑΙ. Τάχ' ἄν· ἀλλὰ πῇ δὴ λέγωμεν;
ΞΕ. Ἔστι τῷ καλῷ τι θατέρου μόριον ἀντιτιθέμενον;
ΘΕΑΙ. Ἔστιν.
ΞΕ. Τοῦτ' οὖν ἀνώνυμον ἐροῦμεν ἤ τιν' ἔχον ἐπωνυμίαν;
ΘΕΑΙ. Ἔχον· ὃ γὰρ "μὴ καλὸν" ἑκάστοτε φθεγγόμεθα, τοῦτο οὐκ ἄλλου τινὸς ἕτερόν ἐστιν ἢ τῆς τοῦ καλοῦ φύσεως.
ΞΕ. Ἴθι νυν τόδε μοι λέγε.
ΘΕΑΙ. Τὸ ποῖον;
ΞΕ. Ἄλλο τι τῶν ὄντων τινὸς ἑνὸς γένους μέρος ἀφορισθέν, καὶ πρός τι τῶν ὄντων αὖ πάλιν ἀντιτεθέν, οὕτω συμβέβηκεν εἶναι τὸ μὴ καλόν;

---

[28] Some scholars think that not-being is itself a part of difference (see e.g. Lee, 'Negation'; O'Brien, *Études*, 44–5; Crivelli, *Falsehood*, 218), but I will argue below that not-being is identical with, not a part of, difference.

ΘΕΑΙ. Οὕτως.
ΞΕ. Ὄντος δὴ πρὸς ὂν ἀντίθεσις, ὡς ἔοικ', εἶναί τις συμβαίνει τὸ μὴ καλόν.
ΘΕΑΙ. Ὀρθότατα.
ΞΕ. Τί οὖν; κατὰ τοῦτον τὸν λόγον ἆρα μᾶλλον μὲν τὸ καλὸν ἡμῖν ἐστι τῶν ὄντων, ἧττον δὲ τὸ μὴ καλόν;
ΘΕΑΙ. Οὐδέν.
ΞΕ. Ὁμοίως ἄρα τὸ μὴ μέγα καὶ τὸ μέγα αὐτὸ εἶναι λεκτέον;
ΘΕΑΙ. Ὁμοίως.
ΞΕ. Οὐκοῦν καὶ τὸ μὴ δίκαιον τῷ δικαίῳ κατὰ ταὐτὰ θετέον πρὸς τὸ μηδέν τι μᾶλλον εἶναι θάτερον θατέρου;
ΘΕΑΙ. Τί μήν;
ΞΕ. Καὶ τἆλλα δὴ ταύτῃ λέξομεν, ἐπείπερ ἡ θατέρου φύσις ἐφάνη τῶν ὄντων οὖσα, ἐκείνης δὲ οὔσης ἀνάγκη δὴ καὶ τὰ μόρια αὐτῆς μηδενὸς ἧττον ὄντα τιθέναι.
ΘΕΑΙ. Πῶς γὰρ οὔ;

(257 C 5–258 A 10)

V: Let us think through this, if it agrees with you as well.
T: Which thing?
V: The nature of difference seems to me to be chopped up just like knowledge.
T: How so?
V: [Knowledge], too, is one, I suppose, but each part of it that is about a certain thing is separated and has some peculiar name of its own; which is why we speak of many crafts and branches of knowledge.
T: By all means.
V: The same thing, then, holds also for the parts of the nature of difference, although [the nature] is one.
T: Perhaps, but how can we spell this out?
V: Is there some part of difference set against the beautiful?
T: There is.
V: Will we speak of that as nameless or as having some name?
T: As having [some name]; for what, on each occasion, we call 'not beautiful', this is not different from anything other than the nature of the beautiful.
V: Well, then, tell me this.
T: Which thing?
V: Separated from some one kind as a part, and in turn again set against one of the things that are, in this way, the

	not-beautiful has turned out to be another one of the things that are?
T:	In this way.
V:	The not-beautiful, then, it seems, turns out to be some setting of a thing that is against a thing that is.
T:	That's right!
V:	What then? According to that reasoning, do we think of the beautiful as being more among the things that are, and the not-beautiful less?
T:	Not at all.
V:	So, we should say that the not-large and the large itself are in the same way?
T:	In the same way.
V:	Hence, the not-just too should be posited along the same lines as the just with respect to one being nothing more than the other?
T:	Sure.
V:	And about the other things we will speak in the same manner, since the nature of difference has emerged as one of the things that are, and if it is, it is necessary to posit its parts, too, as things that are, and no less so.
T:	What else?

According to the Visitor, (the nature of) difference is 'chopped up' (κατακεκερματίσθαι) just like 'knowledge' (ἐπιστήμη) (257 C 7–8):[29] just as there are parts of knowledge, individuated by their objects, which form different crafts and 'branches of knowledge' (ἐπιστῆμαι), there are parts of difference individuated by being 'in turn again set against one of the things that are' (πρός τι τῶν ὄντων αὖ πάλιν ἀντιτεθέν) (257 E 2), such as the beautiful (257 D 7; 257 E 2–4; 257 E 6–7). For instance, just as medicine is a part of knowledge, individuated by its object, namely health, the not-beautiful is a part of difference individuated by (being set against) the beautiful. It is concluded further that the parts of difference belong to the 'things that are' (ὄντα) no less than the things against which they are set (258 A 7–10).

---

[29] The Visitor repeatedly speaks of the 'nature' (φύσις) of difference (255 D 9; 256 D 12–E 1; 257 D 4; 258 A 8–9; 258 D 7). Sometimes, this is taken to emphasize that difference is a kind (Crivelli, *Falsehood*, 210). But we can also read it in a less loaded way as stressing against Parmenides that difference *is* or exists (compare my response to the objection of ontological parity below). For the mention of the nature of a *part* of difference at 258 A 11, see Section 5.

How should we understand the analogy? The standard interpretation takes it to imply that the parts of difference are kinds just as the branches of knowledge are kinds of knowledge.[30] But it is not clear that this is the salient analogical feature. For, in our passage, the Visitor does not make explicit that the branches of knowledge are kinds, nor does he explicitly treat the parts of difference that way (cf. Gill, *Philosophos*, 162). Instead, the focus seems to be on individuation: the parts of difference, like the parts of knowledge, are individuated by the objects they are set over, that is, the objects of knowledge or the things against which the parts of difference are set.

One could retort that the Visitor speaks of a 'kind' ($\gamma\acute{\epsilon}\nu o s$) at 257 E 2. He says that the not-beautiful 'has turned out to be' ($\sigma\upsilon\mu\beta\acute{\epsilon}\beta\eta\kappa\epsilon$ $\epsilon\tilde{\iota}\nu\alpha\iota$) 'another one of the things that are' ($\mathring{\alpha}\lambda\lambda o$ $\tau\iota$ $\tau\hat{\omega}\nu$ $\mathring{o}\nu\tau\omega\nu$) in two steps: first, it is 'separated off ($\mathring{\alpha}\phi o\rho\iota\sigma\theta\grave{\epsilon}\nu$) from a unified *kind*, namely difference, and second, it is set against a thing that is, namely the beautiful (257 E 2–4).[31] The claim that a part of difference is separated off from the kind difference may be taken to suggest that the part is itself a kind. But as we know from the *Politicus* (262 C 6–D 6), it does not follow from the fact that something is a part of a kind that the part is itself a kind.[32] On a less inflationary reading, then, although the parts of difference are separated off from a kind, they are not themselves kinds. Since the Visitor refrains from calling the parts of difference 'kinds' ($\gamma\acute{\epsilon}\nu\eta$ or $\epsilon\mathring{\iota}\delta\eta$), this reading seems preferable to me.

Instead, I suggest that the relation between difference and its parts is elucidated by the Visitor's claim that the nature of difference is

---

[30] See e.g. Lee, 'Negation', 267–304; R. S. Bluck, *Plato's Sophist: A Commentary* [*Commentary*] (Manchester, 1975) at 166–7; Szaif, *Wahrheit*, 437; Brown, 'Dark Matter', 246–7; Crivelli, *Falsehood*, 206; 'Negative Kinds', 24–6. According to Crivelli ('Negative Kinds', 35), the parts of difference are kinds but not species or kinds *of* difference (see n. 8 above). Bluck (*Commentary*, 168–70) wavers on whether parts of difference are negative forms.

[31] For this interpretation, see also Diès, A., *Platon: Œuvres*, viii. iii: Le Sophiste [*Œuvres*] (Paris, 1925) at 372, n. 2; Frede, *Prädikation*, 86–7; Lee, 'Negation', 279, n. 16. Cornford (*Knowledge*, 291, n. 1) claims that the not-beautiful is separated off from the beautiful, but the not-beautiful seems to be set against the beautiful, not separated off from it. Gill (*Philosophos*, 160) argues that the not-beautiful is separated off from a larger kind that characterizes the relevant incompatibility range (namely the aesthetic). However, the Visitor has not explicitly mentioned a larger kind such as the aesthetic anywhere in his account of negative predication. More plausibly, the kind in question is difference.

[32] I do not assume that, in the *Politicus*, the Visitor rules out negative kinds but merely that he rejects the claim that every part of something is a kind (see Section 1 above).

'chopped up' (κατακεκερματίσθαι) like knowledge (257 C 7–8) (cf. Dixsaut, 'Négation', 196–7). The word *katakermatizein* ('chop up') occurred earlier in the *Sophist* to describe a part of 'refutative' speech (ἀμφισβητητικόν) (225 B 1) that is 'chopped up into questions relative to answers' (κατακεκερματισμένον ἐρωτήσεσι πρὸς ἀποκρίσεις) which the Visitor calls 'controversialist' (ἀντιλογικόν) (225 B 9–11).[33] It is also used in the *Politicus* to mark the division of animal inasmuch as it is tame and gregarious (266 A 1–4).[34] But the most fruitful parallel is with a passage in the second deduction of the *Parmenides* where the expression is applied to being (144 B 4–5) and the one (144 E 4).

Plato's Parmenides says that 'being' (οὐσία) 'is chopped up into the smallest and largest possible and into any of the things which are at all, and it is the most divided thing of all, and there are unboundedly many parts of being' (144 B 4–C 1).[35] As in the *Sophist*, being chopped up is associated with parthood: being is chopped up and hence has many parts. But in the *Parmenides*, this does not imply that those parts are kinds of being but rather that they have a share in, or partake of, being.[36] I propose that we understand the relation between difference and its parts in the *Sophist* in the same way: the parts of difference are entities that partake of difference, without the implication that they are 'kinds' (εἴδη) of difference, or kinds at all.

But as I argued earlier, participation in difference should (typically) involve three relata.[37] For instance, change is different *from sameness*, and hence partakes of difference with regard to sameness. Therefore, for something to be a part of difference, it should partake of difference with regard to something else, namely the entity

[33] In this division, sophistry turns out to be, among other things, a 'controversialist' (ἀντιλογική) craft (226 A 1–4).

[34] Dixsaut ('Négation', 197) claims that the Visitor uses the word *katakermatizein* at *Polit.* 266 A 2 to insinuate that a mistake has occurred which trades on treating each part of something as a kind (that is, the assumption rejected at 263 B 7–10). But it is not clear that the Visitor intends any such criticism *at this point of the division*. He says that animal, inasmuch as it is tame and gregarious, has been divided except for two kinds (setting aside dogs), and then, apparently unperturbed, continues with the division (266 A 9–10).

[35] Κατακεκερμάτισται ἄρα ὡς οἷόν τε σμικρότατα καὶ μέγιστα καὶ πανταχῶς ὄντα, καὶ μεμέρισται πάντων μάλιστα, καὶ ἔστι μέρη ἀπέραντα τῆς οὐσίας (*Parm.* 144 B 4–C 1 Burnet).

[36] In the immediate vicinity of this passage in the *Parmenides*, there is no explicit mention of participation. But the first move in the second deduction was to say that if the one is, then it 'partakes of being' (οὐσίας μετέχει) (142 B 5–7). The later claims about the distribution of being should be read in the same vein.

[37] I put aside the self-participation of difference. See Leigh, 'Modes of Being', 22–3 for a discussion.

'against which it is set' (ἀντιτεθέν). Thus, a triadic participation relation obtains between a part of difference, difference itself, and the entity against which the part of difference is set. Moreover, the first relatum is a *part* of difference because it partakes of difference with regard to something else. For example, the not-beautiful is a part of difference because it partakes of difference with regard to the beautiful. None of this implies that the parts of difference, such as the not-beautiful, are kinds.[38]

What, then, *is* the not-beautiful? In the introductory exchange, the Visitor said that when attached to an expression or the corresponding object, 'not' refers not to the 'opposite' (ἐναντίον) of the object but to 'one of the others' (τῶν ἄλλων τι) (257 B 9–C 3), that is, something 'different' (ἕτερον) from it (257 B 4). This suggests that the not-beautiful is not a kind on par with the positive kind against which it is set. For if the not-beautiful were such a kind, surely it would be the opposite of the beautiful.[39] Instead, I suggest that 'the not-beautiful' simply refers to any entity different from the beautiful. For instance, on the incompatibility range interpretation, 'the not-beautiful' refers to any property different from the beautiful that is on the same range of incompatible properties as the beautiful.[40]

This conclusion may seem to fly in the face of what we can call the 'ontological parity' of the parts of difference and the entities against which they are set (Szaif, *Wahrheit*, 441–2). After all, the

[38] According to a friendly alternative reading, the parts of difference are constitutive of difference without being kinds of it (many thanks to an anonymous referee for this suggestion). I prefer spelling out parthood in terms of the triadic participation relation because this account allows us to tie in the Visitor's claim that the parts of difference are set against (positive) entities with the differential triadic participation relation as formulated above.

[39] One could retort that the Visitor denies only that when attached to the beautiful, 'not' refers to the opposite of *being*, but does not deny that it refers to the opposite of the beautiful (cf. Szaif, *Wahrheit*, 41). But although at 257 B 3–4 the Visitor says that, when we call something 'not large' we do not speak of the opposite of being, he goes on to claim that, in speaking of the not-large, we refer to something different from the large, not its opposite (257 B 6–C 3).

[40] Cf. Cornford, *Knowledge*, 290; Cherniss, *Criticisms*, 263–4. But unlike Cornford and Cherniss, I do not take 'the not-beautiful' to refer to *all* entities that are not the beautiful. For if we adopt the incompatibility range interpretation, 'the not-beautiful' refers only to entities that are on the same range of incompatible properties as the beautiful. Moreover, 'the not-beautiful' need not refer to all entities on this range but may refer to only one, or several, of them. For recall that, according to the Visitor, we need not refer to the small when we speak of 'the not-large' (257 B 6–7). But if 'the not-large' referred to all entities on the incompatibility range, it would *have to* refer to the small as well.

Visitor says that the not-beautiful, not-large, and not-just are among 'the things that are' (τὰ ὄντα) no 'less' (ἧττον) than and 'in the same way' (ὁμοίως) as the beautiful, the large, and the just (258 A 1–2; 258 A 7–9). For instance, he says that 'the not-just too should be posited along the same lines as the just with respect to one being nothing more than the other' (καὶ τὸ μὴ δίκαιον τῷ δικαίῳ κατὰ ταὐτὰ θετέον πρὸς τὸ μηδέν τι μᾶλλον εἶναι θάτερον θατέρου) (258 A 4–5). This seems to imply that whatever ontological status is accorded to the beautiful or the just, the not-beautiful or not-just have the same status: if the former are kinds, so are the latter. In addition, the Visitor asserts the parity of difference and its parts. For he argues that if difference is among the things that are, then 'it is necessary to posit its parts too as things that are, and no less so' (ἀνάγκη δὴ καὶ τὰ μόρια αὐτῆς μηδενὸς ἧττον ὄντα τιθέναι) (258 A 8–9). But difference is a kind, and hence its parts, such as the not-beautiful or not-just, should be kinds as well.

In response, we can give ontological parity a weaker spin. Since there is not just a kind of the beautiful, but also the kind difference, and since those kinds can mix, the not-beautiful is no less than the beautiful, even if there is no kind of the not-beautiful. This weaker version of ontological parity is sufficient for the Visitor's dialectical goals against Parmenides. The motivation for engaging with Parmenides was to show that not-being is, and this has been achieved for the parts of difference, regardless of whether they have the status of kinds. Similarly, the claim that if difference is, then its parts too must be 'things that are' (ὄντα) need imply only the result that they *are*, not that they are kinds.[41]

I have argued that the Visitor does not introduce what I called 'partial' negative kinds, such as the not-beautiful or not-just. On a positive note, I have suggested that the Visitor's argument against Parmenides requires only the kind difference and a triadic participation relation: the not-beautiful or not-just are parts of difference, and included among the things that are, because they partake of

---

[41] Moreover, on my reading, the parts of difference *are* or exist independently of us. For they are simply entities that partake of difference with reference to something else (e.g. equality in size that partakes of difference with regard to largeness). Thus, we need not embrace the more radical view defended by A. Silverman (*The Dialectic of Essence: A Study of Plato's Metaphysics* (Princeton, 2002) at 183, 200) that the parts of difference are merely 'conceptual items' produced by us as we speak and think.

difference with regard to positive kinds such as the beautiful. Next, I will argue that the Visitor does not commit himself to a negative kind not-being either.

5. Not-Being (258 A 11–E 5)

After the Visitor has concluded that the parts of difference, such as the not-beautiful and not-just, are among the things that are, he completes his argument that not-being is and concludes that there is a 'kind' or 'form' (εἶδος) of not-being:

ΞΕ. Οὐκοῦν, ὡς ἔοικεν, ἡ τῆς θατέρου μορίου φύσεως καὶ τῆς τοῦ ὄντος πρὸς ἄλληλα ἀντικειμένων ἀντίθεσις οὐδὲν ἧττον, εἰ θέμις εἰπεῖν, αὐτοῦ τοῦ ὄντος οὐσία ἐστίν, οὐκ ἐναντίον ἐκείνῳ σημαίνουσα ἀλλὰ τοσοῦτον μόνον, ἕτερον ἐκείνου.
ΘΕΑΙ. Σαφέστατά γε.
ΞΕ. Τίν' οὖν αὐτὴν προσείπωμεν;
ΘΕΑΙ. Δῆλον ὅτι τὸ μὴ ὄν, ὃ διὰ τὸν σοφιστὴν ἐζητοῦμεν, αὐτό ἐστι τοῦτο.
ΞΕ. Πότερον οὖν, ὥσπερ εἶπες, ἔστιν οὐδενὸς τῶν ἄλλων οὐσίας ἐλλειπόμενον, καὶ δεῖ θαρροῦντα ἤδη λέγειν ὅτι τὸ μὴ ὂν βεβαίως ἐστὶ τὴν αὑτοῦ φύσιν ἔχον, ὥσπερ τὸ μέγα ἦν μέγα καὶ τὸ καλὸν ἦν καλὸν καὶ τὸ μὴ μέγα <μὴ μέγα> καὶ τὸ μὴ καλὸν <μὴ καλόν>, οὕτω δὲ καὶ τὸ μὴ ὂν κατὰ ταὐτὸν ἦν τε καὶ ἔστι μὴ ὄν, ἐνάριθμον τῶν πολλῶν ὄντων εἶδος ἕν; ἤ τινα ἔτι πρὸς αὐτό, ὦ Θεαίτητε, ἀπιστίαν ἔχομεν;
ΘΕΑΙ. Οὐδεμίαν.

(258 A 11–C 5)

V: So, it seems, the setting against of the nature of a part of difference and the nature of being, which lie opposed to each other, is no less of a being, if we may say so, than being itself, not indicating an opposite of [being] but merely this much, something different from it.
T: Exactly!
V: What should we call it?
T: Clearly, not-being, which we sought on account of the sophist, is this very thing.
V: As you said, then, it does not fall short in being of the others in the least, and it is necessary to take courage and now say that not-being firmly has a nature of its own, and just as the

> large was large, the beautiful was beautiful, the not-large not large, and the not-beautiful not beautiful, in this way, along the same lines, not-being was and is something that is not, counted as one kind among the many things that are? Or do we still have any distrust regarding it, Theaetetus?
>
> T: None.

Often, the Visitor's conclusion that there is a 'kind' (εἶδος) of not-being is taken to imply that he is committed to a negative kind not-being.[42] One may infer further that he posits a negative form not-being, if kinds are forms. But there is an alternative that has fallen out of fashion, namely that the kind not-being is identical with the kind difference.[43] I hope to show that this old-fashioned view, although in need of a more detailed textual defence, is correct.[44] The Visitor does not posit a new negative kind not-being but rather argues that the positive kind difference *is* (identical with) the kind not-being.

To see this, we have to understand how the Visitor arrives at the conclusion that there is a kind not-being. In the first sentence of our passage, the Visitor says about the 'setting against', or simply *antithesis* (ἀντίθεσις),[45] between the nature of a part of difference and the nature of being that it is a 'being' (οὐσία) no less than 'being itself' (τοῦ ὄντος αὐτοῦ) (258 A 11–B 3).[46] Echoing his remarks from the introductory exchange, he stresses that the *antithesis* 'indicates'

---

[42] See e.g. Frede, *Prädikation*, 93–4; Szaif, *Wahrheit*, 442–6; Crivelli, *Falsehood*, 212.

[43] See e.g. F. Schleiermacher, *Platon: Werke*, vi: Theaitetos, Der Sophist, Der Staatsmann [*Werke*] (Darmstadt, 1970) at 369; Diès, *Œuvres*, 373, n. 1; Cornford, *Knowledge*, 292–4; Ross, *Ideas*, 168; Vlastos, 'Ambiguity', 288–9, n. 44; Bluck, *Commentary*, 170; Fine, *Forms*, 114.

[44] Berman ('False Belief', 35–7) also argues against attributing negative forms to the Visitor but takes not-being to be a relation between positive forms, including difference, and distinct from difference. By contrast, on my view, the Visitor does not need to posit a further entity (not-being) distinct from difference, regardless of whether this entity is characterized as 'positive' or 'negative'.

[45] 'ἀντίθεσις' and its cognates are difficult to translate. Perhaps the most natural translation would be 'opposition', but I already used this term to render 'ἐναντίον'. Cornford (*Knowledge*, 292) has 'contrast', but this is too weak to capture the ἀντί- ('against') in 'ἀντίθεσις'. Rowe (*Theaetetus and* Sophist, 161) translates 'ἀντίθεσις' as 'contraposition' which is stronger, but I prefer the English 'setting against' for the cognates and the transliteration for 'ἀντίθεσις' itself.

[46] As I mentioned in Section 4, the Visitor likes to speak of the 'nature' (φύσις) of difference. Here, he similarly speaks of the nature of *a part* of difference (258 A 11). One could take this to imply that the part of difference is a *kind*. But I suggested a weaker reading in Section 4, namely that the Visitor speaks of the 'nature' of something to emphasize against Parmenides that it *is*. Similarly, in this passage, he emphasizes that the part of difference *is*. At any rate, the occurrence of the word

(σημαίνουσα) not an 'opposite' (ἐναντίον) of being but 'something different' (ἕτερον) from being (258 B 3). The Visitor then calls the *antithesis* 'not-being' (τὸ μὴ ὄν) (258 B 6–7), which has a nature of its own (258 B 10) and is a kind (258 C 3).

How innovative is this passage ontologically? In my view, it is not innovative at all. Earlier, the not-beautiful was said to be 'set against' (ἀντιτιθέμενον), that is, in *antithesis* to, the beautiful (257 D 7). As I argued above, this claim is understood best in terms of difference: the not-beautiful partakes of difference with regard to the beautiful. The not-beautiful, then, is set against, or in *antithesis* to, the beautiful in the sense that it is *different from* it. Similarly, in the present passage, when the Visitor speaks of the *antithesis* of a part of difference and being, he presumably refers to the difference of a part of difference, such as the not-beautiful, from being. Thus, the *antithesis* just is difference, and to be in *antithesis* to something, or set against it, is to stand in a triadic participation relation to it, that is, to partake of difference with regard to it.[47]

The Visitor goes on to claim that the *antithesis* is a 'being' (οὐσία) (258 B 2), and then calls 'it' (αὐτήν) (258 B 5) 'not-being' (τὸ μὴ ὄν) (258 B 6–7). 'It' (αὐτήν) refers to 'ἀντίθεσις', which is the subject of the previous sentence: the *antithesis* is not-being. If the *antithesis* is difference, the Visitor here identifies the kind difference with the kind not-being (cf. Cornford, *Knowledge*, 293–4). Thus, the claim that there is a kind not-being (258 C 3) does not introduce a new entity into the ontology. For the kind not-being is the familiar kind difference. Hence, the Visitor does not introduce a novel negative kind not-being. Rather, he continues to operate only with the (positive) kind difference, just as throughout the argument against Parmenides.

One could object to my interpretation of the Visitor's talk of *antithesis*. I claimed that the *antithesis* between a part of difference and being is difference. But one might argue instead that the *antithesis* is an *entity* which is *different from* being, not difference itself. For at 257 E 6–7, the not-beautiful itself was characterized as the

'nature' cannot settle whether an entity is a kind. Its strength must be determined on the basis of an interpretation of the Visitor's overall theory.

[47] Dixsaut ('Négation', 204) claims that the antithesis is an 'operation', namely 'la mise en opposition' ('putting into opposition'). But I struggle to see what performs the operation on this view, and where in the text this operation has been introduced.

Negative Forms in Plato's Sophist 83

antithesis of a thing that is. Similarly, one could hold that, in the present passage, the *antithesis* is something different from being. On this view, the Visitor does not identify difference with not-being. Rather, he identifies *something* different from being with not-being, and this is a new kind that must be distinct from difference.

But at 258 A 11–B 3, the Visitor is quite clear that the *antithesis* is *between* a part of difference and being. But surely the *antithesis* between two entities is not itself one of these two entities. Notably, the claim that the *antithesis* 'indicates' (σημαίνουσα) 'something different' (ἕτερον) (258 B 3) is compatible with this reading. Since the antithesis is a 'being' (οὐσία), not a mere expression, 'indication' should not be taken linguistically. The Visitor's claim is not that '*antithesis*' *refers* to something different from being but rather that the *antithesis* itself *discloses* or *reveals* something different from, but not opposite to, being, namely whatever is in *antithesis* to being.[48] This is compatible with, or even requires, the view that the antithesis itself is difference. For the *antithesis* can indicate something different from being precisely because, by being in *antithesis* to being, the entity indicated is different from being.

Similarly, the earlier claim that 'the not-beautiful turns out to be, as it seems, some setting of a thing that is against a thing that is' (ὄντος δὴ πρὸς ὂν ἀντίθεσις, ὡς ἔοικ', εἶναί τις συμβαίνει τὸ μὴ καλόν) (257 E 6–7) is shorthand for the fuller statement that came before, namely that the not-beautiful is 'set against' (ἀντιτιθέν) one of the things that are (257 E 2–4) (not that it is the setting against or *antithesis* itself). In general, a part of difference is not *the antithesis* between itself and being, or a thing that is, but *in antithesis* to it because it is different from it. The *antithesis* itself is the difference of a part of difference from being or from a thing that is.

These remarks notwithstanding, the objector could continue to insist that the Visitor does not identify the kind not-being with the kind difference. For before he says that not-being is a kind (258 C 3), he claims that 'not-being' (τὸ μὴ ὄν) is 'something that is not' (μὴ ὄν) 'in this way' (οὕτω) and 'along the same lines' (κατὰ ταὐτόν), that is, in the same way in which, for instance, the not-beautiful is

---

[48] Lee ('Negation', 274–5) claims that Plato 'fails to say' that the *expression* that refers to the *antithesis*, rather than the *antithesis* itself, does the indicating here. But in my view, it is better to take the text at face value and understand the talk of 'indication' non-linguistically.

not beautiful (258 B 10–C 3). This could be taken to imply that not-being, like the not-beautiful, is itself one of the parts of difference (O'Brien, *Études*, 44–5), and hence distinct from difference itself.

But the claim that not-being is 'something that is not' in the way in which the not-beautiful is not beautiful need not imply that not-being is a part of difference. The Visitor is coming to the close of his argument against Parmenides and revisits the targeted conclusion, namely that we can correctly say that not-being is, as when we say that not-being is something that is not (254 D 1–2). He has now achieved this, just as he has shown that we can correctly say that something is not beautiful. But this extension of the conclusion does not require that not-being is a *part* of difference. There may be another reason why we can correctly say that not-being is something that is not, for instance, because the kind not-being just is the kind difference itself.

But the objection might gain new strength from a later summary passage:

ΞΕ. Ἡμεῖς δέ γε οὐ μόνον τὰ μὴ ὄντα ὡς ἔστιν ἀπεδείξαμεν, ἀλλὰ καὶ τὸ εἶδος ὃ τυγχάνει ὂν τοῦ μὴ ὄντος ἀπεφηνάμεθα· τὴν γὰρ θατέρου φύσιν ἀποδείξαντες οὖσάν τε καὶ κατακεκερματισμένην ἐπὶ πάντα τὰ ὄντα πρὸς ἄλληλα, τὸ πρὸς τὸ ὂν ἑκάστου μόριον αὐτῆς ἀντιτιθέμενον ἐτολμήσαμεν εἰπεῖν ὡς αὐτὸ τοῦτό ἐστιν ὄντως τὸ μὴ ὄν.

(258 D 4–E 3)

V: But not only have we shown that the things which are not are, but we have also exhibited just what the kind of not-being is. For having shown the nature of difference as being and as chopped up over all the things that are related to each other, we dared to say concerning the part of the nature of difference set against the being of each thing that that very thing is truly not-being.

Once again, the Visitor speaks of a 'the kind of not-being' (τὸ εἶδος τοῦ μὴ ὄντος) (258 D 5). As we saw, this does not by itself imply that he posits a negative kind not-being *in addition to* difference. Still, the end of the passage may suggest this conclusion. For the Visitor says about a *part* of difference that it is 'not-being' (τὸ μὴ ὄν) (258 E 2–3). Once again, it seems that the kind of not-being is a part of difference and distinct from difference itself.

But this reading neglects the ἑκάστου ('of each thing') at 258 E 2.[49] The Visitor says that the part of difference is set against 'the being of each thing' (τὸ ὂν ἑκάστου), not being *tout court*. Presumably, 'the being of each thing' refers to each of the entities against which the parts of difference are set, for instance, the beautiful and the large. If this is right, the Visitor relies on the earlier claim that each part of difference is set against some entity (e.g. the not-large is set against the large). He does not, then, introduce a part of difference set against being *tout court*, namely not-being. Nor is he committed to a kind not-being distinct from difference.

Still, the Visitor says that a *part* of difference, rather than difference, is not-being. This seems hard to square with my interpretation. Surely, he does not think that, say, the not-large just is not-being. In response, we can deny that the Visitor's claim concerns a particular part of difference. He first makes a general claim that holds for *any* part of difference: that it is set against 'the being of each thing' (258 E 2). His further claim that 'that very thing is truly not-being' (258 E 3) should be equally general: *any* part of difference is not-being. One might thus think that not-being is identical with any part of difference but still distinct from difference itself.[50] But another reading is possible: on the basis of an observation about any *part* of difference, namely that it is set against 'the being of each thing', the Visitor concludes that difference itself is not-being.

This interpretation is supported by the summary of the Visitor's argument against Parmenides (258 E 6–259 D 8). The Visitor first reiterates that his claim is not that there is an opposite of being (258 E 6–7) and then restates how and why it is legitimate to speak of not-being. He does so by formulating two 'oppositions' (ἐναντιώσεις) (259 C 8), that is, two pairs of seemingly inconsistent claims, as we encountered them, for instance, in the change passage (255 E 8–256 D 10). One pair of claims concerns difference; the other pair concerns being. As for being, he reminds us that being is in many ways and is not in many ways (259 B 1–6). Being is not the other kinds because 'partaking of difference, it would be different from the other

---

[49] Following Rowe (Theaetetus *and* Sophist, 182), I adopt 'ἑκάστου' not 'ἕκαστον' (as in Duke et al., *Opera*) because it has better manuscript support (cf. Owen, 'Not-Being', 239–40, n. 33).
[50] See e.g. van Eck, 'Difference', 73–83; Brown, 'Dark Matter', 248–52.

kinds' (ὁ δὲ ὂν αὖ θατέρου μετειληφὸς ἕτερον τῶν ἄλλων ἂν εἴη γενῶν) (259 B 1–2).

Similarly, difference both is and is not (the Visitor is speaking):

ὃ δὲ νῦν εἰρήκαμεν εἶναι τὸ μὴ ὄν, ἢ πεισάτω τις ὡς οὐ καλῶς λέγομεν ἐλέγξας, ἢ μέχριπερ ἂν ἀδυνατῇ, λεκτέον καὶ ἐκείνῳ καθάπερ ἡμεῖς λέγομεν, ὅτι συμμείγνυταί τε ἀλλήλοις τὰ γένη καὶ τό τε ὂν καὶ θάτερον διὰ πάντων καὶ δι' ἀλλήλων διεληλυθότε τὸ μὲν ἕτερον μετασχὸν τοῦ ὄντος ἔστι μὲν διὰ ταύτην τὴν μέθεξιν, οὐ μὴν ἐκεῖνό γε οὗ μετέσχεν ἀλλ' ἕτερον, ἕτερον δὲ τοῦ ὄντος ὂν ἔστι σαφέστατα ἐξ ἀνάγκης εἶναι μὴ ὄν·

(259 A 1–B 1)

As for what we have said now, namely that not-being is, either someone should question and persuade us that we do not speak well or, as long as he cannot do that, he too must say as we say that the kinds are mixed together with each other, and that since being and difference pervade all things and each other, difference which partakes of being *is* because of that partaking, not that of which it partakes but something different, and because it is different from being, it is very clearly and from necessity possible that it is something that is not.

Being and difference pervade all things, including each other. Thus, difference too partakes of being, and hence *is*. But difference is not thereby being. Rather, difference itself is different from being, and in this sense, it is, or at least it is possible that it is, 'something that is not' (μὴ ὄν).

Prima facie, this passage is puzzling. Although the Visitor begins the summary with the claim that not-being is (259 A 2), he does not mention 'not-being' (τὸ μὴ ὄν) in what follows. In particular, we might have expected him to restate that 'not-being' (τὸ μὴ ὄν) is 'something that is not' (μὴ ὄν), since this claim was stated at crucial junctures of the argument against Parmenides, namely at its outset (254 D 1–2) and at the end of the argument that not-being is (258 B 10–C 3). Instead, all we get is the claim that *difference* is 'something that is not' (μὴ ὄν) because it is different from being (259 A 8–B 1). This looks like a disappointing denouement. For one might think that the same claim could have been made about any kind other than being. Why could the Visitor not also have said that change is something that is not because it is different from being?

The answer is that difference is special. The passages cited above (254 D 1–2; 258 B 10–C 3) were the only places in the Visitor's argument against Parmenides where he said that something is 'something that is not' (μὴ ὄν, without the definite article), and in both cases, he said this about 'not-being' (τὸ μὴ ὄν, with the definite article). Of course, he is happy to say about each kind that it 'is not' (οὐ ἔστιν), as he does about being in the summary (259 B 4–6). He also said that 'not-being' (τὸ μὴ ὄν) is concerning each kind, as discussed in Section 2 (256 E 5–6). But the only entity about which he has claimed that it is 'something that is not' (μὴ ὄν) is 'not-being' (τὸ μὴ ὄν). The most straightforward explanation, then, why the Visitor says about *difference* that it is something that is not, and not about any other kind, is that he takes the kind difference to be (identical with) the kind not-being. Thus, in claiming that difference is something that is not, he restates the central claim that not-being is something that is not, as we should have expected.[51]

Indeed, if the Visitor did not assume that difference just is not-being, it is hard to see how the summary would be pertinent to the conclusion that not-being is. The two pairs of oppositions in the summary concern being and difference. Hence, no claim to the effect that not-being is could be made here unless difference just is not-being. Again, if the standard interpretation were true and the Visitor had established a negative kind not-being distinct from difference, why does he not frame the summary in terms of being and *not-being* rather than difference? He could easily have formulated a pair of oppositions about this alleged kind not-being, including a claim that not-being is, which would have mirrored the claim that being is not. Instead, he talks about difference. The explanation, I submit, is that the Visitor has not posited a negative kind not-being in addition to difference at all. The kind not-being just is the kind difference.

6. Negative predication and false speech: A sketch

I have argued that the text of the *Sophist* does not support the ascription of negative kinds to the Visitor. He is committed neither to partial negative kinds, such as the not-beautiful, nor to a kind not-being. We can infer further that the Visitor is not committed to negative *forms* either. For if there are forms in the *Sophist*, they are

---

[51] My interpretation should be distinguished from Schleiermacher's (*Werke*, 369) who translates 'μὴ ὄν' at 259 B 1 as 'das Nichtseiende', that is, 'not-being', as if Plato had written 'τὸ μὴ ὄν' (with the definite article). This reading would directly imply that difference is not-being but is based on a mistranslation, corrected in Staudacher's revision of Schleiermacher (*Werke*, 369, first note): the Visitor says only that difference is 'μὴ ὄν' ('nichtseiend'; 'something that is not').

presumably called 'kinds' (γένη or εἴδη), just like the 'greatest kinds' (μέγιστα τῶν γενῶν 254 D 4). Hence, the conclusion that the Visitor does not introduce negative kinds also undermines the evidence for negative forms in the *Sophist*. But besides the textual motivation for the standard interpretation, there is a philosophical one: that negative kinds or forms are needed to vindicate negative predication and, according to some scholars, the possibility of false speech.[52] What alternative can my interpretation provide, if any?

Regarding negative predication, I have already suggested that the Visitor does not need negative kinds or forms: negative predicative claims can be vindicated solely by appeal to difference and two participation relations (an ordinary dyadic one and a differential triadic one). For example, the claim that Socrates is not large can be spelled out as the claim that Socrates partakes of a property that in turn partakes of difference with regard to the large. This suffices to show against Parmenides that we can make negative predicative claims without commitment to an 'opposite' (ἐναντίον) of being. But I have not yet said anything about the possibility of false speech which, as I mentioned at the beginning, is of particular importance for defining the sophist. The topic is too large to be addressed in detail here.[53] Still, I want at least to sketch how the Visitor can vindicate the possibility of false speech without negative kinds or forms.

After the Visitor has concluded that being and not-being mix, one further step is needed before he can return to the definition of the sophist: to show that 'speech' (λόγος) and 'opinion' (δόξα) can partake of not-being (260 D 5–261 A 3).[54] For if speech and opinion cannot partake of not-being, there is no 'falsehood' (ψεῦδος) (260 E 2–3), and the definition of the sophist cannot be completed. The Visitor begins with false speech and extends the account to 'thinking' (διάνοια), 'opinion' (δόξα), and 'imagination' (φαντασία) (263 D 6–264 B 8). I restrict my attention to false speech.

---

[52] See especially Crivelli, *Falsehood*, 256–7. As mentioned in Section 1, some proponents of the standard interpretation deny that negative kinds are needed to vindicate false speech (Szaif, *Wahrheit*, 486).

[53] For full treatments, see e.g. Szaif, *Wahrheit*, 454–509; Crivelli, *Falsehood*, ch. 6; B. E. Hestir, *Plato on the Metaphysical Foundation of Meaning and Truth* [*Foundation*] (Cambridge, 2016), ch. 8.

[54] I translate 'λόγος' as 'speech' rather than 'sentence' or 'statement', as is sometimes done, because the Visitor characterizes it as 'the stream going from [the soul] through the mouth with sound' (264 A 7–8) (cf. Rowe, Theaetetus *and* Sophist).

In his analysis of speech, the Visitor distinguishes 'names' (ὀνόματα) from 'verbs' (ῥήματα) (262 A 1) and also claims that 'it is necessary that a speech, whenever it is, is a speech of something, and it is impossible for it to be of nothing' (λόγον ἀναγκαῖον, ὅτανπερ ᾖ, τινὸς εἶναι λόγον, μὴ δὲ τινὸς ἀδύνατον) (262 E 5–6). For instance, the speech 'Theaetetus is sitting' consists of a name ('Theaetetus') and a verb ('sits'), and it is about Theaetetus (263 A 5).[55] Moreover, some speeches are true, others false (263 B 3). For example, 'Theaetetus, to whom I am talking now, is flying' is also about Theaetetus, but unlike 'Theaetetus is sitting', it is a false speech (263 B 3).

The distinction between true and false speeches is drawn as follows:

ΞΕ. Λέγει δὲ αὐτῶν ὁ μὲν ἀληθὴς τὰ ὄντα ὡς ἔστιν περὶ σοῦ.
ΘΕΑΙ. Τί μήν;
ΞΕ. Ὁ δὲ δὴ ψευδὴς ἕτερα τῶν ὄντων.
ΘΕΑΙ. Ναί.
ΞΕ. Τὰ μὴ ὄντ' ἄρα ὡς ὄντα λέγει.
ΘΕΑΙ. Σχεδόν.
ΞΕ. Ὄντως δέ γε ὄντα ἕτερα περὶ σοῦ. πολλὰ μὲν γὰρ ἔφαμεν ὄντα περὶ ἕκαστον εἶναί που, πολλὰ δὲ οὐκ ὄντα.[56]
ΘΕΑΙ. Κομιδῇ μὲν οὖν.

(263 B 4–13)

V: And among these, the true [speech] says the things that are as they are about you.
T: What else?
V: And the false [speech says] things different from the things that are?
T: Yes.
V: So, it says things that are not as things that are?
T: Presumably.
V: Namely, different things about you that truly are. For we said, I guess, that there are many things that are about each thing, and many that are not.
T: Quite so.

---

[55] In Greek, the predicate consists of a single verb ('κάθηται' or 'sits'), but in English, the right sense of the sentence is better captured by the present continuous, and hence the two-part predicate 'is sitting'. The same goes for 'is flying' (in Greek 'πέτεται' or 'flies').

[56] At 263 B 11, I adopt the manuscript reading 'ὄντως' rather than Cornarius' emendation 'ὄντων', as in Duke et al., Opera. For a discussion, see Frede, Prädikation, 57; Szaif, Wahrheit, 475–8.

A true speech says about some entity 'the things that are as they are' (τὰ ὄντα ὡς ἔστιν) (263 B 4). We can parse this in terms of the ascription of activities: a true speech ascribes activities (or properties) to an entity which it is in fact performing.[57] For instance, 'Theaetetus is sitting' ascribes sitting to Theaetetus 'as it is' (ὡς ἔστιν), since Theaetetus is, in fact, sitting. By contrast, a false speech says about some entity 'things different from the things that are' (ἕτερα τῶν ὄντων) (263 B 7). We might say that a false speech ascribes activities to an entity which are different from activities it is, in fact, performing. For instance, 'Theaetetus is flying' ascribes an activity (flying) to Theaetetus which is different from an activity he is performing, namely sitting.

Crucially, the Visitor offers two formulations of his account of false speech. The first formulation, which I just explicated, relies on difference. The second formulation involves not-being or, more precisely, 'things that are not' (τὰ μὴ ὄντα): a false speech treats things that are not as things that are (263 B 9). For instance, 'Theaetetus is flying' treats flying, which is something that is not (relative to Theaetetus), as if it were something that is (relative to Theaetetus).[58] The two formulations are equivalent, and the first explicates the second. For 'the things that are not' (τὰ μὴ ὄντα) are 'different things about you that truly are' (ὄντως δέ γε ὄντα ἕτερα περὶ σοῦ) (263 B 11). As in the argument against Parmenides, not-being is spelled out in terms of difference.

The exegetical options are the same as for the introductory exchange of the argument that not-being is.[59] On the incompatibility range interpretation adopted earlier, a speech is false just in case it ascribes an activity to an entity which is different from an activity which the entity is, in fact, performing, where both activities are drawn from a range of incompatible activities. For instance, 'Theaetetus is flying' is false because it ascribes flying to Theaetetus, although Theaetetus is sitting, where flying is different from sitting, and both flying and sitting are on the same range of incompatible activities. Once again, however, what matters for us is not

---

[57] In what follows, I will speak of 'activities' because the Visitor's examples involve activities (πράξεις, 262 A 3). But the account of true and false speech can easily be extended to (ordinary) property ascriptions.

[58] Cf. J. Szaif, 'Plato and Aristotle on Truth and Falsehood', in M. Glanzberg (ed.), *The Oxford Handbook of Truth* (Oxford, 2018), 9–49 at 31.

[59] See Crivelli, *Falsehood*, 238–9; Hestir, *Foundation*, 191–9.

the exact interpretation of the Visitor's claim but the basic point that not-being is spelled out in terms of difference. For this allows us to see how false speech can be vindicated without appeal to negative kinds or forms.

I suggested that negative predication can be vindicated by appeal to difference: the claim that Theaetetus is not flying is spelled out as the claim that Theaetetus partakes of an activity that in turn partakes of difference with regard to flying. This account can be extended to vindicate the possibility of false speech. Let us distinguish positive from negative speeches, where the former makes a positive predicative claim (e.g. that Theaetetus is flying), and the latter makes a negative predicative claim (e.g. that Theaetetus is not flying). A positive speech about an entity, then, is false just in case this entity partakes of an activity (or property) that in turn partakes of difference with regard to the activity (or property) ascribed to the entity by the speech. For instance, 'Theaetetus is flying' is false just in case Theaetetus partakes of an activity that in turn partakes of difference with regard to flying. Moreover, and more simply, a negative speech about an entity is false just in case this entity directly partakes of the activity (or property) which, according to the speech, it does not have. For example, 'Theaetetus is not flying' is false just in case Theaetetus partakes of flying.

Of course, I have offered only a rough sketch of the Visitor's account of false speech. But this should suffice to show that negative kinds or forms are not *required* for a vindication of the possibility of false speech. Indeed, we saw the Visitor invoke the same analysis of not-being in terms of difference as in the argument against Parmenides. If that earlier argument did not rely on negative kinds or forms precisely because of the analysis of not-being in terms of difference, as I argued, it is plausible that the later account of false speech does not rely on negative kinds or forms either. The Visitor offers a unified account of non-identity claims, negative predication, and false speech in terms of the kind difference, without appeal to negative kinds or forms.

7. Conclusion

I have argued that the Visitor vindicates negative predication and false speech by appeal to the kind difference and two participation relations (where one relation is dyadic and the other triadic, involving difference). The resulting view achieves the same goals as an account that includes negative kinds or forms but with a more economical ontology. Hence, a modified version of the profligacy objection to the standard interpretation is on target after all: it would be profligate for the Visitor to posit negative kinds or forms, not because it is *in principle* gratuitous to posit such entities but because he does not need them to confront Parmenides or, therefore, to define the sophist. Not only, then, is the textual evidence for the standard interpretation weaker than is often thought, but the philosophical motivation for it has been undercut as well.

University of Geneva

BIBLIOGRAPHY

Ackrill, J. L., 'Plato and the Copula: *Sophist* 251–9' ['Copula'], *Journal of Hellenic Studies*, 77 (1957), 1–6.

Beere, J., 'Faking Wisdom: The Expertise of Sophistic in Plato's *Sophist*', *Oxford Studies in Ancient Philosophy*, 57 (2019), 153–89.

Berman, S., 'Plato's Explanation of False Belief in the Sophist' ['False Belief'], *Apeiron*, 29 (1996), 19–46.

Bluck, R. S., *Plato's Sophist: A Commentary* [*Commentary*] (Manchester, 1975).

Bostock, D., 'Plato on "Is Not"' ['Is Not'], *Oxford Studies in Ancient Philosophy*, 2 (1984), 89–119.

Brown, L., 'Being in the *Sophist*: A Syntactical Enquiry', *Oxford Studies in Ancient Philosophy*, 4 (1986), 49–70.

Brown, L., 'Negation and Not-Being: Dark Matter in the *Sophist*' ['Dark Matter'], in R. Patterson, V. Karasmanis, and A. Hermann (eds.), *Presocratics and Plato: Festschrift in Honor of Charles Kahn* (Las Vegas, 2012), 233–54.

Brown, L., 'The *Sophist* on Statements, Predication, and Falsehood' ['Statements'], in G. Fine (ed.), *The Oxford Handbook of Plato* (Oxford, 2008), 437–62.

Cherniss, H., *Aristotle's Criticisms of Plato and the Academy* [*Criticisms*] (Baltimore, 1944).

Cornford, F. M., *Plato's Theory of Knowledge* [*Knowledge*] (London, 1935).

Crivelli, P., 'Negative Kinds in Plato's *Statesman*' ['Negative Kinds'], in S. Delcomminette and R. van Daele (eds.), *La méthode de division de Platon à Érigène* (Paris, 2020), 19–40.

Crivelli, P., *Plato's Account of Falsehood: A Study of the Sophist* [*Falsehood*] (Cambridge, 2012).
Dancy, R. M., 'The Categories of Being in Plato's *Sophist* 255 C–E', *Ancient Philosophy*, 19 (1999), 45–72.
Diès, A., *Platon: Œuvres complètes*, viii. iii: Le Sophiste [*Œuvres*] (Paris, 1925).
Dixsaut, M., 'La négation, le non-être et l'autre dans le *Sophiste*' ['Négation'], in P. Aubenque and M. Narcy (eds.), *Études sur le Sophiste de Platon* (Naples, 1991), 165–213.
Duke, E. A., Hicken, W. F., Nicoll, W. S. M., Robinson, D. B., and Strachan, J. C. G., *Platonis Opera* [*Opera*] (Oxford, 1995), i.
Ferejohn, M., 'Plato and Aristotle on Negative Predication and Semantic Fragmentation', *Archiv für Geschichte der Philosophie*, 71 (1989), 257–82.
Fine, G., On Ideas: *Aristotle's Criticism of Plato's Theory of Forms* [*Forms*] (Oxford, 1993).
Frede, M., *Prädikation und Existenzaussage* [*Prädikation*] (Göttingen, 1967).
Frede, M., 'The *Sophist* on False Statements' ['False Statements'], in R. Kraut (ed.), *The Cambridge Companion to Plato* (Cambridge, 1992), 397–424.
Gill, M. L., *Philosophos: Plato's Missing Dialogue* [*Philosophos*] (Oxford, 2012).
Hestir, B. E., *Plato on the Metaphysical Foundation of Meaning and Truth* [*Foundation*] (Cambridge, 2016).
Irani, T., 'Perfect Change in Plato's *Sophist*', *Oxford Studies in Ancient Philosophy*, 60 (2022), 45–93.
Lee, E. N., 'Plato on Negation and Not-Being in the *Sophist*' ['Negation'], *Philosophical Review*, 81 (1972), 267–304.
Leigh, F., 'Modes of Being at *Sophist* 255 C–E' ['Modes of Being'], *Phronesis*, 57 (2012), 1–28.
Malcolm, J., 'A Way Back for *Sophist* 255 C 12–13', *Ancient Philosophy*, 26 (2006), 275–89.
McDowell, J., 'Falsehood and Not-Being in Plato's *Sophist*' ['Not-Being'], in M. Schofield and M. Nussbaum (eds.), *Language and Logos* (Cambridge, 1982), 115–34.
Moravcsik, J. M. E., 'Being and Meaning in the *Sophist*' ['Being'], *Acta Philosophica Fennica*, 14 (1962), 23–78.
O'Brien, D., *Deux études sur le* Sophiste *de Platon* [*Études*] (Sankt Augustin, 1995).
Owen, G. E. L., 'Plato on Not-Being' ['Not-Being'], in G. Vlastos (ed.), *Plato I: Metaphysics and Epistemology: A Collection of Critical Essays* (Garden City, NY, 1971), 223–67.
Pelletier, F. J., *Parmenides, Plato, and the Semantics of Not-Being* [*Not-Being*] (Chicago, 1990).

Penner, T., *The Ascent from Nominalism: Some Existence Arguments in Plato's Middle Dialogues* [*Ascent*] (Dordrecht, 1987).

Reeve, C. D. C., 'Motion, Rest, and Dialectic in the *Sophist*', *Archiv für Geschichte der Philosophie*, 67 (1985), 47–64.

Ross, W. D., *Plato's Theory of Ideas* [*Ideas*] (Oxford, 1951).

Rowe, C., *Plato:* Theaetetus *and* Sophist [Theaetetus *and* Sophist] (Cambridge, 2015).

Schleiermacher, F., *Platon: Werke*, vi: Theaitetos, Der Sophist, Der Staatsmann [*Werke*] (Darmstadt, 1970).

Silverman, A., *The Dialectic of Essence: A Study of Plato's Metaphysics* (Princeton, 2002).

Szaif, J., 'Plato and Aristotle on Truth and Falsehood', in M. Glanzberg (ed.), *The Oxford Handbook of Truth* (Oxford, 2018), 9–49.

Szaif, J., *Platons Begriff der Wahrheit* [*Wahrheit*] (Freiburg, 1996).

van Eck, J., 'Falsity without Negative Predication: On *Sophistes* 255 E–63 D' ['Falsity'], *Phronesis*, 40 (1995), 20–47.

van Eck, J., 'Not-Being and Difference: On Plato's *Sophist* 256 D 5–58 E 3' ['Difference'], *Oxford Studies in Ancient Philosophy*, 23 (2002), 63–84.

van Eck, J., 'Plato's Logical Insights: On *Sophist* 54 D–57 A', *Ancient Philosophy*, 20 (2000), 53–79.

van Eck. J., 'Plato's Theory of Negation and Falsity in *Sophist* 257 and 263: A New Defense of the Oxford Interpretation', *Ancient Philosophy*, 34 (2014), 275–88.

Vlastos, G., 'An Ambiguity in the *Sophist*' ['Ambiguity'], in G. Vlastos, *Platonic Studies*, 2nd edn (Princeton, 1973), 270–322.

Wiitala, M., 'That Difference Is Different from Being: *Sophist* 255 C 9– E 2', *Oxford Studies in Ancient Philosophy*, 62 (2022), 85–103.

VIRTUE AND CONTEMPLATION IN *EUDEMIAN ETHICS* 8. 3

ROY C. LEE

1. Introduction

The end of *Eudemian Ethics* (*EE*) 8. 3 makes a notable addition to the work's overall account of virtue. Aristotle thinks that a doctor looks to some standard (ὅρος) not only to judge whether a body is healthy but also to evaluate potential medical interventions as healthy rather than excessive or deficient. In the same way, Aristotle proposes, the virtuous person should have a standard, at least for a certain sphere of action. Concluding an argument that ends the work, Aristotle identifies that standard:

Therefore, whatever choice or acquisition of natural goods will most promote the contemplation of god—whether of bodily goods, property, friends, or the other goods—this is best, and this standard is finest.

(1249^{b}18–21)[1]

This is Aristotle's clearest statement of the standard in *EE* 8. 3. The standard requires promoting the contemplation of god, and, as stated here, it applies to actions that involve the acquisition of

---

I am grateful to Christopher Bobonich, Alan Code, Willie Costello, Corinne Gartner, Terence Irwin, Rachana Kamtekar, and two anonymous referees for their generous comments on earlier versions of this paper. Additional thanks to Ashley Attwood, Grant Dowling, Daniel Ferguson, Landon Hobbs, Josh Ober, Matthew Pincus, Thomas Slabon, and Rupert Starling for their helpful suggestions and feedback. I presented parts of this paper to audiences at the APA Central Division Meeting and Stanford University and benefited from their questions and discussions. This research was completed with the financial support of the Mellon/ACLS Dissertation Completion Fellowship from the American Council for Learned Societies.

[1] Citations of the Greek text are to C. Rowe (ed.), *Aristotelis Ethica Eudemia* (Oxford, 2023), also considering C. Rowe, *Aristotelica: Studies on the Text of Aristotle's* Eudemian Ethics [*Aristotelica*] (Oxford, 2023); F. Susemihl (ed.), *Aristotelis Ethica Eudemia* (Leipzig, 1884); and R. R. Walzer and J. M. Mingay (eds.), *Aristotelis Ethica Eudemia* (Oxford, 1991). Translations are adapted from B. Inwood and R. Woolf (eds.), *Eudemian Ethics* (Cambridge, 2013).

natural goods, which are goods whose value depends on their user's character—often thought to be external goods (1248^{b}27–31).[2]

So, which actions exactly fall within the scope of the standard? Aristotle states the standard's scope twice in the chapter, using slightly different language each time; yet he does not explain why the standard should only be used in a limited domain. The interpretive options commentators have favoured fall into three groupings. Each interpretation results in a different view of contemplation's relation to ethical virtue and its place within a happy life. On the Most Restrictive Reading, the standard applies only to actions concerning natural goods specifically in excess of virtue's needs.[3] On this view, Aristotle has already completed his considered account of virtue prior to the discussion of contemplation in *EE* 8. 3, so the standard only directs the use of natural goods that are not needed for virtuous actions. A fully happy life would involve attending first to the demands of ethical virtue, acquiring whatever natural goods are needed for these virtuous actions, and then, only after meeting virtue's demands, additionally securing the quantity of natural goods needed to promote contemplation. So, the standard of promoting contemplation does not contribute in any way to Aristotle's account of ethical virtue, and contemplation should be sought only after satisfying virtue's requirements.

On the Less Restrictive Reading, the standard directs all actions concerning natural goods, not just the actions concerning natural goods that exceed virtue's needs.[4] This means that all actions

---

[2] Some, like A. Kenny, *The Aristotelian Ethics: A Study of the Relationship between the* Eudemian *and* Nicomachean Ethics *of Aristotle* [*Aristotelian Ethics*], 2nd edn (Oxford, 2016), 182–3, believe that this standard for natural goods is supplemented by another standard (1249^{b}21–5). But the chapter anticipates only the one standard for natural goods (1249^{a}23–^{b}7), and the doctor uses only one standard. I argue below that the other formulations are not substantively different.

[3] Its proponents include C. Rowe, *The* Eudemian *and* Nicomachean Ethics*: A Study in the Development of Aristotle's Thought* [*Study*] (Cambridge, 1971); J. M. Cooper, *Reason and Human Good in Aristotle* [*Reason*] (Indianapolis, 1986); S. Broadie, *Ethics with Aristotle* (Oxford, 1991); G. Bonasio, 'Natural Goods in the *Eudemian Ethics*' ['Natural Goods'], *Ancient Philosophy*, 41 (2021), 123–42; and D. Wolt, '*Phronêsis* and *Kalokagathia* in *Eudemian Ethics* VIII. 3' ['*Phronêsis*'], *Journal of the History of Philosophy*, 60 (2022), 1–23.

[4] For this view, see J. D. Monan, *Moral Knowledge and Its Methodology in Aristotle* (Oxford, 1968), 127–32; Kenny, *Aristotelian Ethics*, 181–3; J. L. Ackrill, 'Aristotle on *Eudaimonia*', in A. O. Rorty (ed.), *Essays on Aristotle's Ethics* (Berkeley, 1980), 15–33 at 30–1; F. Buddensiek, *Die Theorie des Glücks in Aristoteles'* Eudemischer

concerning natural goods, including those prescribed by virtue, must promote contemplation. The standard supplements the foregoing account of ethical virtue by specifying what virtue requires, but only for actions and choices concerning natural goods. Other virtuous actions may be determined in other ways, or perhaps relative to other standards. So, on this view, contemplation is an aim that some, but only some, virtuous actions must promote and is not a defining aim for virtue as such.

On the Unrestricted Reading, the standard applies to all virtuous actions.[5] Since the standard is not restricted to any domain of action related to natural goods, all virtuous actions, in order to count as virtuous, must reflect directly or indirectly the aim of promoting the most contemplation. This represents a substantive, informative addition to Aristotle's account of virtue as a mean: the standard helps to determine where exactly the virtuous mean between excess and deficiency lies. The aim of promoting contemplation is an essential element of Aristotle's considered account of ethical virtue that he has alluded to but not made explicit until the very end.

This paper argues against the two Restrictive Readings of the standard and in favour of the Unrestricted Reading. The Most Restrictive Reading tacitly relies on an important assumption that an earlier Eudemian passage contradicts. On the Less Restrictive Reading, following the standard seems sometimes to lead to instrumental irrationality. However, defenders of the Unrestricted Reading bear the burden of explaining why the standard's apparent restriction to natural goods is not only repeated in the passage but even illustrated with examples. The existing strategies for defending the

---

Ethik [*Theorie*] (Göttingen, 1999), 252–4; F. Buddensiek, 'Contemplation and Service of the God: The Standard for External Goods in *Eudemian Ethics* VIII 3' ['Contemplation'], *Bochumer Philosophisches Jahrbuch für Antike und Mittelalter*, 14 (2011), 103–24; P. Simpson (trans. and comm.), *The* Eudemian Ethics *of Aristotle* [*Eudemian Ethics*] (New York, 2013), 392–4; and M. D. Walker, *Aristotle on the Uses of Contemplation* [*Uses*] (Cambridge, 2018), 136–9, 162–3.

[5] Here I include T. M. Tuozzo, 'Contemplation, the Noble, and the Mean: The Standard of Moral Virtue in Aristotle's Ethics' ['Standard'], *Apeiron*, 28 (1995), 129–54; C. D. C. Reeve, *Action, Contemplation, and Happiness: An Essay on Aristotle* [*Essay*] (Cambridge, 2012), 134–40; D. Devereux, '*Theoria* and *Praxis* in Aristotle's Ethics' ['*Theoria*'], in P. Destrée and M. A. Zingano (eds.), *Theoria: Studies on the Status and Meaning of Contemplation in Aristotle's Ethics* (Louvain-la-Neuve, 2014), 178–92; and, arguably, R. Kraut, *Aristotle on the Human Good* (Princeton, 1989), 169–70.

Unrestricted Reading appeal to certain textual parallels, but they are inconclusive.

I think the challenge to the Unrestricted Reading should be met instead by considering the argumentative context of *EE* 8. 3. The references to actions concerning natural goods are not meant to restrict the scope of the standard but rather situate it as part of Aristotle's extended criticism of the Spartan disposition, which prizes actions that acquire natural goods. It is through criticizing the Spartan disposition, especially its improper relation to natural goods, that Aristotle makes his own account of virtue clear. Indeed, the chapter's focus on natural goods and the Spartan disposition, and even its framing interest in the comprehensive virtue *kalokagathia* ('fine-and-goodness')[6] all serve to foreground the protreptic consequence of this account of virtue. If comprehensive virtue requires observing the standard of promoting the most contemplation, then the happy life of complete virtue must turn towards philosophy. I confirm this reading by showing that the core inference of the argument given for the standard supports the Unrestricted Reading.

In addition to revealing a more unified structure to a chapter that has struck most commentators as disjointed, these arguments support the view that in the *Eudemian Ethics,* the mean in accordance with correct reason is not the last word on what ethical virtue is. Virtue's mean is determined by the standard of promoting contemplation. The mean, at least, is not uncodifiable. This resulting account of virtue requires explaining how an external standard promoting the most contemplation might be integrated into an account of virtue, given virtue's other requirements, especially that the agent choose virtuous action for its own sake or for the sake of the fine, rather than for the sake of contemplation. In light of the Eudemian function ($ἔργον$) argument, I argue that the standard should be understood to require the indirect promotion of contemplation. Contemplation should be promoted only through

---

[6] The term *kalokagathia* is the noun form of the adjective *kalos k'agathos*, which describes someone who is fine and good. The adjective form is composed of the word for fine (*kalos*) and the word for good (*agathos*) joined by a conjunction (*kai*, which is often elided to *k'* but in some appearances can also be written out in full or combined with the conjunction *te*). The term has a social meaning, indicating nobility or high birth, as well as a related evaluative meaning, indicating ideal excellence, discussed further below.

virtuous activity, whose own nature sets further boundaries on one's pursuit of that aim.

Though this interpretive dispute in *EE* 8. 3 is about the scope of the standard, it mirrors the interpretive controversy arising from Aristotle's elevation of the philosophical life over the political life in *Nicomachean Ethics* (*EN*) 10. 7–8. There, Aristotle thinks that the philosophical life, distinctively characterized by theoretical contemplation, is superior to the political life, distinctively characterized by its focus on the ethical virtues. Even so, interpreters of the *Nicomachean Ethics* disagree about how prominent a place theoretical contemplation should occupy within the philosophical life, whether a contemplative life is even possible for ordinary humans, and if it is, why and to what extent a contemplative life should observe the ethical virtues. I acknowledge the interest of this parallel only to set it aside for the present inquiry, which focuses only on the *Eudemian Ethics*.

2. The Most Restrictive Reading

The Most Restrictive, Less Restrictive, and Unrestricted Readings of the standard of *EE* 8. 3 disagree over what subset or sphere of actions fall under the scope of the standard given in 1249^{b}18–21, quoted above. The other passage important to this dispute introduces the context of the standard and how it should be used:

Since there is some standard also for the doctor, to which they look when they judge that the body is healthy or not, and with reference to which they judge to what extent they should produce each thing, and if it is done well, then the body is healthy, but if less or more then it would be healthy no longer—in the same way too for the virtuous person (σπουδαίῳ), concerning the actions and choices of things by nature good but not praiseworthy, there must be some standard for the possession, choice, and avoidance of how much or how little property and fruits of good fortune. It was said before about these matters to be as reason says. But this is like saying in matters of nutrition to do as medicine and its reason say. While true, this is not clear.

(1249^{a}23–^{b}7)

The doctor, *qua* doctor, aims to produce health. In doing so, they look to a standard of health to determine whether health is present and how to bring it about. Aristotle compares the doctor to the virtuous person, who also looks to a standard. But though the standard helps the doctor achieve their primary aim, for the virtuous person, the standard here is specifically said to be for actions and choices concerning natural goods that are not praiseworthy.

On the Most Restrictive Reading, the standard only applies to actions concerning natural goods in excess of what is needed for virtue. Ordinary virtuous actions will require natural goods, but the quantity and variety the virtuous person should acquire for these purposes is straightforwardly dictated by what is instrumentally necessary. Supposing that the agent already has the natural goods needed for ethically virtuous actions, the standard instructs them to pursue a further quantity of goods: whatever is needed to promote contemplation.

Defenders of the Most Restrictive Reading have offered two different textual considerations in support of the view.[7] The first, following John Cooper, is a literal reading of the phrase, 'things by nature good but not praiseworthy' ($\tau\hat{\omega}\nu$ $\phi\acute{\upsilon}\sigma\epsilon\iota$ $\mu\grave{\epsilon}\nu$ $\mathring{\alpha}\gamma\alpha\theta\hat{\omega}\nu$ $o\mathring{\upsilon}\kappa$ $\mathring{\epsilon}\pi\alpha\iota\nu\epsilon\tau\hat{\omega}\nu$ $\delta\acute{\epsilon}$). Things by nature good are natural goods, which were introduced earlier in *EE* 8. 3 as competitive goods ($\pi\epsilon\rho\iota\mu\acute{\alpha}\chi\eta\tau\alpha$), thought by some to be the greatest: honour, wealth, bodily strength, luck, and power. These goods benefit the virtuous but harm the vicious (1248^{b}27–31). Next, the description 'not praiseworthy' seems to pick out those goods that are not fine. Aristotle describes what is fine at two points in *EE* 8. 3. First, he names as fine what is praiseworthy on its own account: the virtues and virtuous actions (1248^{b}20–4). On this first telling, no natural goods are praiseworthy, because they are not virtues or virtuous actions. But later, Aristotle expands what is fine: things are fine whenever the end for which they are managed and acquired is fine (1249^{a}6–7). On the expanded account, natural goods do count as fine and so as praiseworthy when they are used for the sake of virtuous actions. So, natural goods that are *not* praiseworthy would be natural goods that are not used for the sake of virtues or virtuous actions. Only the actions concerning these goods would fall under the standard of promoting contemplation.

---

[7] Notable defences of the Most Restrictive Reading include Cooper, *Reason*, 136–43 and Broadie, *Ethics with Aristotle*, 383–8, who present the first and second points respectively. Bonasio, 'Natural Goods', 139 loosely follows Broadie, while Wolt, '*Phronêsis*', 18–19 follows Cooper. Rowe, *Studies*, 110–12 is less explicit but describes the standard as severely restricted and can reasonably be read with this group.

Perhaps virtue may require us to undertake certain actions but underdetermine what actions we must perform or how we must complete them.[8] It would be in this discretionary sphere that the standard applies.

There is a serious problem for the Most Restrictive Reading in this form.[9] This interpretation requires that there be a class of unpraiseworthy goods which do not further any fine purpose but should be acquired and used to promote contemplation. This implicitly assumes that contemplation is not itself a fine, praiseworthy purpose. However, Aristotle is explicit when he first distinguishes the ethical from the intellectual virtues in the *Eudemian Ethics* that 'we praise not only the just, but also the intelligent [συνετούς] and the wise [σοφούς]' (1220ᵃ5–7; cf. *EN* 1103ᵃ4–10).[10] If theoretical wisdom is praiseworthy in itself, then it is fine, and its corresponding activity, contemplation, would also be fine. This point destabilizes the key distinction for the Most Restrictive Reading, between praiseworthy and unpraiseworthy goods. Natural goods are fine and praiseworthy when they are managed and chosen for a fine aim. But if contemplation is fine, then unpraiseworthy natural goods acquired for the purpose of meeting the standard (i.e. promoting contemplation) themselves thereby become fine and praiseworthy. So, if the standard applies only to unpraiseworthy natural goods, then the standard does not apply to natural goods acquired for the purpose of meeting the standard.

To illustrate, the standard says to manage and acquire unpraiseworthy natural goods, like money exceeding what is needed for virtue, to promote contemplation. Before the money has been earmarked for some contemplation-promoting expense, it may well count as unpraiseworthy, because it serves no fine aim. But once the sum of

---

[8] See especially Cooper, *Reason*, 141.

[9] Buddensiek, *Theorie*, 252–4 raises other issues for the Most Restrictive Reading.

[10] Some commentators dispute that the uniquely *Eudemian* books use the words *sophia* or *sophos* to refer to theoretical wisdom in the sense developed in *EE* 5 (=*EN* 6). See D. Frede, 'On the So-Called Common Books of the *Eudemian* and the *Nicomachean Ethics*' ['Common Books'], *Phronesis*, 64 (2019), 100–5; cf. C. Rowe, '*Sophia* in the *Eudemian Ethics*' ['*Sophia*'], in G. Di Basilio (ed.), *Investigating the Relationship between Aristotle's* Eudemian *and* Nicomachean Ethics (London, 2022), 122–36. Even so, theoretical wisdom would be part of what makes a wise person (*sophos*) praiseworthy. Aristotle's aim is to vindicate as praiseworthy the class of intellectual virtues, which includes theoretical wisdom. Given that he has already described Anaxagoras as choosing to live for the sake of knowledge of the universe (1216ᵃ15), this theoretical dimension to intellectual achievement is not unexpected.

money is acquired and set aside for contemplation, it becomes fine, because it now has a fine aim, contemplation. So, having acquired the money for contemplation's sake, the agent's subsequent use of it for that intended purpose now cannot satisfy the standard, because the standard applies only to natural goods that are not fine, and the money became fine after it was acquired. In order to satisfy the standard, the agent would have to promote contemplation with money that was never acquired or earmarked for the purpose of promoting contemplation. Indeed, natural goods, when they are used to satisfy the standard, thereby become fine and praiseworthy, falling outside the standard's scope.[11] It is hard, then, to see how someone could ever acquire unpraiseworthy natural goods for the purpose of promoting contemplation and then use them while they are unpraiseworthy to satisfy the standard. If contemplation is fine, the standard becomes practically unfollowable. The designation 'not praiseworthy' is ill-suited for picking out those natural goods exceeding what is needed for virtuous actions.[12]

The order of the chapter's argumentative progression has been cited as another textual consideration in support of the Most Restrictive Reading. Sarah Broadie thinks that the first half of the chapter (1248^{b}9–1249^{a}17) presents a picture of *kalokagathia* 'as if it were *complete without reference to theôria*', while the chapter's second half (1249^{a}23–^{b}25) supplements complete virtue with the

[11] There may be another way of understanding when goods become fine. Perhaps things become fine only after they have been acquired *and* used for the fine purpose (καλὰ γάρ ἐστιν ὅταν οὗ ἕνεκα πράττουσι καὶ αἱροῦνται καλὸν ᾖ, 1249^{a}6–7). Merely acquiring goods for future contemplation does not make them praiseworthy, since they have not yet also been used for the sake of a fine end, and so my objection may be avoided. Against this suggestion, I worry that πράττουσι, in its transitive sense, cannot comfortably sustain the meaning 'use' here. The verb might more naturally mean 'achieve' or 'effect', but that would work against this suggestion. I prefer 'manage', but goods can be managed prior to use. More to the point, Aristotle explains at 1249^{a}7–10 that natural goods are fine for the *kalos k'agathos* because their possession accords with a just distribution, which is a just and so fine end. So, for the *kalos k'agathos*, merely acquiring a natural good for future contemplative use makes it fine, even before it is used for contemplation, because simply by being possessed it is for the sake of the fine (i.e. achieving a just distribution). This makes all the natural goods had by a *kalos k'agathos* fine and so ineligible for use to meet the standard. See also Section 6 below for a discussion of this argument.

[12] Could 'unpraiseworthy natural goods' refer to types of good, rather than to tokens whose status changes situationally? Aristotle lists types of goods at 1249^{b}20 (bodily goods, wealth, friends), but these types of goods do not seem, as types, to be unpraiseworthy (e.g. wealth may typically be used for generosity). Any class of goods that is typically used to promote contemplation would, for that reason, be praiseworthy as a class and so fall outside the standard's scope.

standard of promoting contemplation.[13] After all, Aristotle has already concluded that '*kalokagathia* is complete virtue' (1249^{a}16–17) prior to adding the additional requirement to promote contemplation. Assuming further that ethical virtue suffices to determine the quantity of natural goods needed for virtuous actions, someone with complete virtue needs no standard for natural goods used in virtuous actions. So, the standard of promoting contemplation can only be for the natural goods that remain unaccounted for after the preceding discussion of complete virtue.

The problem for this approach is that Aristotle never explicitly excludes contemplation from *kalokagathia* in the first half of the chapter. He says *kalokagathia* is composed of (ἐκ) the virtues discussed earlier (1248^{b}9–12). But by this point in the work, Aristotle has already discussed the intellectual virtues, including theoretical wisdom, so theoretical wisdom should be a part of *kalokagathia*. In the common books, Aristotle says that theoretical wisdom is part of the whole of virtue (1144^{a}5), and the Eudemian function argument identifies complete virtue with the whole of virtue (1219^{a}36–9). And virtue includes the intellectual virtues (1220^{a}5). So, prior to *EE* 8. 3 Aristotle has already said that complete virtue includes theoretical wisdom. Broadie assumes that Aristotle's audience would not be willing to regard contemplation as a fine activity alongside other virtuous activities. Yet Aristotle justifies considering the intellectual virtues to be virtues by appealing to the thought that the wise person is praiseworthy; this appeal would succeed only if his audience was, in fact, willing to accept that, beyond ethical excellence, intellectual excellence is also praiseworthy. So, neither the phrase 'not praiseworthy' nor the order of the chapter's exposition supports the Most Restrictive Reading's distinction between natural goods used for virtuous action and those that should be used for contemplation.

3. The Less Restrictive Reading

The Less Restrictive Reading does away with the Most Restrictive Reading's distinction between natural goods needed for virtuous actions and those in excess of virtue's needs. On this view, the

---

[13] Broadie, *Ethics with Aristotle*, 385 (emphasis original). Though Broadie's position largely aligns with Cooper's here, she does not cite in support of her view the phrase 'good but not praiseworthy', as Cooper understands it.

standard of promoting contemplation applies to actions concerning all natural goods, not only unpraiseworthy natural goods. Even though the formulation of the standard at 1249^b1 includes the qualification 'not praiseworthy', the formulation at 1249^b19 omits it. One might even read 'by nature' in the phrase 'by nature good but not praiseworthy' (1249^b1) as modifying not only 'good' but also 'not praiseworthy'.[14] Since natural goods are fine only if they are managed or acquired for a virtuous purpose, all natural goods are by nature not praiseworthy, so the standard applies to actions concerning all natural goods.

On the Less Restrictive Reading, the key distinction is between those actions that involve managing natural goods and those that do not. All actions that involve managing natural goods should aim to promote contemplation. What virtue requires for actions that do not involve natural goods is, presumably, determined in some other way. It is important for defenders of the Less Restrictive Reading to explain why a standard is needed only for virtuous actions that manage natural goods. Peter Simpson holds that practical wisdom suffices to guide most particular virtuous actions, but being focused on particulars, it lacks long-term planning capacity, which is supplemented by the standard. Practical wisdom's focus on immediate, particular actions 'does not determine how much and which of the natural goods one should have on hand, just as the doctor's perception of what medicine to give in what quantity and to which patients does not determine how much and which medicines and other instruments he should keep in store ready for use'.[15] Taking another path, Anthony Kenny takes Aristotle to divide the ethical virtues into those that concern natural goods (generosity, magnificence, magnanimity) and those concerned with passions (courage, temperance, mildness).[16] The former are guided by the standard for natural goods, while the latter are governed by another standard, 'that one be least aware of the other part of the soul as such' (1249^b24-5).

[14] For the suggestion, see Buddensiek, 'Contemplation', 116 n. 16. Less explicitly, Ackrill, 'Aristotle on *Eudaimonia*', 30–1 may be understood to take this route too.
[15] Simpson, *Eudemian Ethics*, 392.
[16] See A. Kenny, *Aristotle on the Perfect Life* [*Perfect Life*] (Oxford, 1992), 100 and Kenny, *Aristotelian Ethics*, 182–3. Similarly, Walker, *Uses*, esp. 136–9, holds that there are various standards for practical reasoning in different domains of action. Contemplation is a standard for the domain concerning natural goods, while other domains are determined by other standards.

The main difficulty with the Less Restrictive Reading, in either version, is that the standard of promoting contemplation could require agents to be instrumentally irrational. Suppose that a virtuous agent ought to undertake some actions, not having to do with natural goods, that have some aim other than contemplation. Though these actions do not directly manage or acquire a certain quantity of natural goods, they may still require certain natural goods as means. For instance, repelling invaders from one's own city or an ally's city might require weapons and ships. But actions that acquire those natural goods are required to follow the standard of promoting contemplation. Yet the quantity and kinds of weapons and ships needed to promote contemplation might not be appropriate or adequate to repel invaders. If in all actions concerning natural goods, the agent sought only the quantity appropriate for contemplation, they would not have enough to achieve some of the non-contemplative aims set by virtue. Nothing guarantees that the standard of promoting contemplation will yield the right quantity and variety of natural goods for the virtuous person's non-contemplative actions and aims.

The problem arises because the Less Restrictive Reading divides agency up into one domain having to do with natural goods, subject to the standard, and another domain not having to do with natural goods, with goals or standards of its own. But these two domains are not easily understood to be naturally autonomous from one another since agents regularly act in both domains when they pursue courses of action. So, a standard that applies only to the domain concerning natural goods could cause problems for actions involving the other domain unless the other domain is also subject to the same or at least a corresponding standard. Yet if the threat of conflict leads us to stipulate that the standard for actions concerning natural goods must also have significant, irrationality-barring implications for actions in the other domain, then the former standard is no longer restricted to natural goods.

One way of avoiding the worry about instrumental irrationality is by recasting contemplation as the sole, ultimate, organizing aim of all virtuous actions. If every ordinary virtuous action is thought of as aiming ultimately to promote contemplation, then the quantity or variety of natural goods apt for promoting contemplation will never conflict with what is needed for ordinary virtuous actions. To support this construal, one might point out that virtually all virtuous actions concern natural goods in some way, so that, by the standard, virtually all virtuous actions should promote contemplation. Even the virtues Kenny categorizes as passions-directed involve managing natural goods: courage defends them, temperance takes pleasure in them, and mildness directs anger at threats to them. This modified view combines the standard's restriction to actions concerning natural goods with the new claim that all actions concern natural goods. This renders the restriction to natural goods vacuous and ends up similar to the Unrestricted Reading, which denies that the standard is restricted to natural goods in any way. Let us call this modified view the Vacuous Restriction Reading.[17]

Still, the Vacuous Restriction Reading raises questions and, because of its similarity to the Unrestricted Reading, faces problems like those the Unrestricted Reading will face. If the restriction to natural goods ends up being vacuous, why does Aristotle include it? Though natural goods are needed in the right quantity for happiness (1153^b14–26), there is no textual indication that *all* virtuous actions are concerned with their acquisition or management. Virtue as such is a mean between excess and deficiency, but in the earlier books of the *EE*, this mean was not specific to the management of natural goods. Likewise, in the earlier passages that introduce the notion of a standard (cited below), Aristotle never indicates that the standard only applies, even vacuously, to natural goods. Why is the standard in *EE* 8. 3 qualified in this way? I argue in Section 5 below for an answer that is available to the Unqualified Reading but not to the Vacuous Restriction Reading. So, the Vacuous Restriction Reading owes an explanation for why the standard is formulated in a roundabout way in terms of natural goods when its effect is to direct all of our virtuous actions towards contemplation.

4. The Unrestricted Reading

The Unrestricted Reading takes the standard to guide all virtuous actions, not just a subset of them. If the standard is completely unrestricted in scope, then all virtuous actions, in order to count as

---

[17] Buddensiek, 'Contemplation', 117–23 may be understood as defending a version of this view. Cf. Broadie, *Ethics with Aristotle*, 385; Buddensiek, *Theorie*, 252–4.

virtuous, must, in some way, promote contemplation.[18] This introduces a new, essential feature of virtue—that the mean, as such, is determined by the standard of promoting contemplation. The Unrestricted Reading faces a serious problem: the text of *EE* 8. 3 is clear that the standard given is a standard for actions concerning natural goods. It repeats this qualification and even twice lists examples of these natural goods. How can the standard be thought to apply directly to all virtuous actions, when its presentation is repeatedly restricted to actions acquiring or managing natural goods?

Defenders of the Unrestricted Reading often position the standard in *EE* 8. 3 as fulfilling promises made earlier in the treatise to specify a standard to determine virtue's mean.[19] Two passages from earlier in the *Eudemian Ethics* anticipate the standard of *EE* 8. 3. The first forms part of a longer conditional sentence summarizing features of ethical virtue established throughout Aristotle's general discussion of virtue in *EE* 2. 1–5:

We have grasped the division of states corresponding to the various affections, both of those that are excesses and deficiencies, and of the states opposed to these by which people are in accord with the correct reason— what the correct reason is, and what standard we should look to in stating the mean, must be examined later.

(1222^b5–9)

The other begins the second common book at *EE* 5. 1, which introduces the treatment of the intellectual virtues, anticipating their role in expanding the earlier account of virtue as a mean, specifically in accordance with the correct reason and its standard:

---

[18] Though the Unrestricted Reading may also hold that all actions are concerned with natural goods, as the Vacuous Restriction Reading does, this commitment is not necessary for the Unrestricted Reading and plays no role in its defence.

[19] Tuozzo ('Standard', 143), Reeve (*Essay*, 134–40), and Devereux ('*Theoria*') all take the standard in *EE* 8. 3 not to be limited to actions concerning natural goods, and they all follow the general strategy outlined in this section. They disagree about how the standard guides actions. Tuozzo thinks that the prescription for actions concerning natural goods and the prescription to minimize perception of the non-rational part of the soul (1249^b23–5) together 'dictate, in particular cases, actions and feelings appropriate to one another.' These two formulations cover, respectively, the outward- and inward-facing aspects of moral virtue. Devereux and Reeve deny that the standard applies to particular cases, taking it to guide the choice of a career or to illustrate the structure of practical reason in general, respectively.

In all the states discussed, just as in other matters, there is some mark (σκοπός) at which the person with reason looks as he tightens and loosens, and there is some standard (ὅρος) of the mean states, which we say lie between excess and deficiency, being in accordance with the correct reason. Now this claim is true, but not at all clear. For in other concerns governed by knowledge this is true to say, that one ought to work and to ease off neither too much nor too little, but moderately and as the correct reason says. But assuming that this is all one has, one would be none the wiser, for instance, about how to treat the body if one were to say, 'what medicine and the doctor order'. That is why when it comes to the states of the soul this claim, though true, is not enough, but we must also determine what the correct reason is and what its standard is.[20]

(1138^{b}21–34)

Both passages describe states of virtue as lying in a mean between excess and deficiency, relative to correct reason and a standard that helps determine the mean. Moreover, both passages are about virtue in general; neither limits itself to acquiring natural goods.

Like these two passages, *EE* 8. 3, 1249^{a}23–^{b}7 (quoted above) describes a mean between excess and deficiency, relative to reason and a standard. Furthermore, like the *EE* 5. 1 passage, the *EE* 8. 3 passage compares the virtuous agent's reasons with the doctor's but rejects the verbal formula 'as reason says' as inadequate for determining the mean, because, while true, it is not clear.[21] Since these earlier passages anticipate a standard for virtue in general, not just for actions that concern natural goods, if the standard in *EE* 8. 3 answers the earlier passages' forward references, it would guide all virtuous actions, not just those that concern natural goods.

Yet resting the Unrestricted Reading's case on the textual parallels is tenuous because the parallels are inexact. In *EE* 8. 3 the standard is specifically for 'actions and choices of things by nature good but not praiseworthy' and 'whatever choice or acquisition of natural goods...whether of bodily goods, property, friends, or other goods'. Yet the *EE* 2. 5 and 5. 1 passages give no indication that the standard for virtue as such was one that would be limited to or articulated in terms of choices of natural goods.[22] It may be

---

[20] Text for the common books from I. Bywater (ed.), *Aristotelis Ethica Nicomachea* (Oxford, 1894). On translating ὅρος here, see Devereux, '*Theoria*', 172–8.

[21] The method of moving from what is true but unclear to what is true and clear is introduced in *EE* 1. 6 and invoked at *EE* 1. 7 and 2. 1 but is absent from the books unique to the *EN*.

[22] See e.g. Rowe, *Study*, 110 and Broadie, *Ethics with Aristotle*, 375.

Virtue and Contemplation in EE 8. 3

tempting to redescribe the specification of natural goods in *EE* 8. 3 as a matter of emphasis, not restriction.[23] But *EE* 8. 3 does not give a standard for virtue in general and then subsequently emphasize its application for natural goods; the only standard given in the chapter is repeatedly qualified as being about natural goods. What the Unrestricted Reading needs to explain is why Aristotle states the restriction only in *EE* 8. 3 twice and with examples if the standard has no restriction.

In fact, there are alternative explanations available for this discrepancy between *EE* 2. 5/5. 1 and 8. 3 that would cut against the Unrestricted Reading. Some readers think that Aristotle answers his promise for a standard from *EE* 5. 1 later in the book when he presents his account of practical wisdom.[24] If this is so, then the question of virtue's standard has been answered long before—and without the help of—*EE* 8. 3. So, whatever the scope of the standard in *EE* 8. 3, it does not answer any need to clarify the standard for virtue in general but only virtue's relation to natural goods, as the Restrictive Readings of the standard hold. Another possibility is that Aristotle countenances multiple standards, each for a different domain of virtuous actions. In *Protrepticus* 10, the politician is said to have certain standards (τινὰς ὅρους) with reference to which they judge what is just, what is fine, and what is beneficial (Iambl., *Protr.* 55. 1–3 Pistelli).[25] Reading *EE* 2. 5 and 5. 1 in light of *Protr.* 10, one might think that Aristotle implicitly countenances a number of standards of virtue, each for a different domain of action, and *EE* 8. 3 gives a standard only for the domain of action concerning natural goods. I raise these alternatives not to endorse them but to illustrate why the textual parallel from *EE* 2. 5 and 5. 1 to 8. 3 is, by itself, inconclusive if not inadequate support for the Unrestricted Reading.

---

[23] See Devereux, '*Theoria*', 187 and Reeve, *Essay*, 139.

[24] For instance, S. Peterson, '*Horos* (Limit) in Aristotle's Nicomachean Ethics' ['*Horos*'], *Phronesis*, 33 (1988), 233–50 holds that the promised standard in *EN* 6. 1 (=*EE* 5. 1) cannot be informatively described in advance of a particular situation. So, the general account of *phronēsis* in *EN* 6 is all that it is possible to say about that boundary outside a particular case. (Despite reading *EN* 6. 1 this way, Peterson favours Kenny's reading of the *EE* 8. 3 standard but sees its attempted codification as inadequate, a fault of the *EE*.)

[25] On the basis of the cited passage, Walker (*Uses*, 150) holds that practical reasoning makes use of a number of different standards, each for a different domain of action.

Defenders of the Unrestricted Reading have also sought support from subsequent formulations, which omit the restriction to natural goods:

> Therefore, whatever choice or acquisition of natural goods will most promote the contemplation of god—whether of bodily goods, property, friends, or the other goods—this is best, and this standard is finest. And whatever, through deficiency or excess, impedes serving and contemplating god is base. This holds for the soul, and this standard of the soul is best: that one be least aware of the other part of the soul as such.
>
> (1249^{b}18–25)[26]

In addition to a standard that demands the use of natural goods to promote contemplation, the passage also condemns whatever prevents the service (θεραπεύειν) and contemplation of god and includes a second standard, of the soul, to be minimally aware of the other part of the soul as such. Some commentators place weight on the formula against preventing contemplation and service to god, because serving or attending to god might require actions expressing ethical virtue, not just contemplation.[27] However, this formula only says what counts as base—it does not prescribe the pursuit of its opposite.

What about the last sentence's prescription, that one be least aware of the other (or non-rational, if one adopts Fritzsche's emendation) part of the soul as such? This is not formulated specifically in reference to natural goods. It is unclear what exactly the other (or non-rational) part of the soul refers to—whether, for instance, it refers to the vegetative part or to the part that naturally obeys reason's commands (which, for short, I call the subject part).[28] Perhaps this means that one should allow the soul's rational part to contemplate unencumbered by concern for nutrition and digestion, or perhaps it means we should avoid having the subject part act irrationally in disobeying the rational part. But neither construal would seem to offer the kind of clear practical guidance that would

---

[26] See Section 7 for notes on how I take the text here.

[27] See Kenny, *Perfect Life*, 102, who notes a parallel to Plato's *Euthyphro*.

[28] Either might be thought of as the 'other' part of the soul by taking the part that is other than to be either the commanding part or the reason-involving part that includes both the commanding and the subject parts. If one adopts Fritzsche's emendation, both the vegetative and the subject parts are described as non-rational (ἄλογον, 1219^{b}33; 1219^{b}38–9; 1221^{b}31), though the subject part has a share in reason (τὰ λόγου μετέχοντα, 1219^{b}30; cf. 1219^{b}40–1220^{a}3).

mark a distinct improvement on 'as reason says'. How much, after all, is it possible to minimize the other psychic activities? Might one, for instance, neglect one's health to do so?[29] Furthermore, minimizing obstacles to contemplation is, strictly speaking, a separate act from undertaking contemplation. Minimizing obstacles to contemplation might, after all, be followed by inactivity or dreamless sleep. And the question that troubled the Vacuous Restriction Reading remains for the Unrestricted Reading: why does Aristotle not just say in the first standard to promote contemplation in all actions, not only in those concerning natural goods? So, the alternative formulations at 1249^{b}21–5 do not seem to be meaningfully more informative than the statements at 1249^{b}4–7 or 1249^{b}18–21. And if the original standard should be understood according to the Unrestricted Reading, its apparent restriction to natural goods—a feature which sets *EE* 8. 3 apart from *EE* 2. 5 and 5. 1—must still be explained.

5. Natural goods and Spartan virtue

I propose a different kind of defence of the Unrestricted Reading. I concede that the explicit textual statements of the standard imply that Aristotle is thinking specifically about natural goods. Still, I think there are two considerations that strongly favour taking Aristotle's point to apply to virtue in general and not just to those actions concerning natural goods. I present the first consideration in Sections 5–6 and turn to the second in Section 7. The first consideration is the dialectical context of the standard, which explains why Aristotle's specific interest in natural goods is actually part of a broader account of virtue in general.[30] Commentators often treat the presentation of the standard as the beginning of a new discussion after the conclusion of Aristotle's criticism of the political disposition

---

[29] For instance, Peterson, '*Horos*', 249: 'The phrase "as little as possible" invites the question, "And exactly how little is that?" It thus seems to be no helpful advance to the question, "What is the limit?"' I take part of Peterson's point here to be that on a certain reading, this formulation of the standard could be too demanding, requiring the self-abnegation of ordinary human activities for contemplation's sake.

[30] Here I am using 'dialectical' to mean responding to an argumentative opponent—not relating to the ancient practice or philosophical method of dialectic.

attributed to the Spartans.[31] However, it is precisely because Spartan virtue wrongly aims at natural goods that the standard is presented as a corrective for actions and choices concerning natural goods. Taking the standard out of its argumentative context is what causes the interpretive difficulties discussed above. Aristotle is not just stipulating how natural goods should be used; he is showing how a mistaken account of virtue should be corrected. Aristotle's own view is the corrected account of virtue. This comports with the Unrestricted Reading.

Commentators have focused on the phrase 'things by nature good but not praiseworthy' (1249^{b}1) as a way of delimiting the standard's scope. However, Aristotle's earlier criticism of the Spartans supports an overlooked explanation for why he is interested specifically in a standard for unpraiseworthy natural goods. There is a connection between two claims: first, natural goods are fine whenever they are managed and acquired for the sake of a fine aim (1249^{a}6–7), like virtue or virtuous action; second, those with the Spartan disposition do fine things only accidentally (1249^{a}14–16).[32] Doing some action that is accidentally fine or accidentally virtuous means that the agent's aim was not a fine or virtuous thing, but the action turned out to be virtuous (or sufficiently like a virtuous action) due to coincidence. Since Spartans characteristically do fine actions for the sake of an aim that is not fine, natural goods are not fine for them. Since what is fine is explained in terms of what is praiseworthy (1248^{b}20–1), natural goods are not fine or praiseworthy for

---

[31] For short, I call this 'Spartan virtue', even though the civic disposition (ἕξις πολιτική) in question is not, in my view, genuine virtue, and the Spartans are but one group to whom Aristotle attributes this disposition.

[32] The literature disagrees about how exactly the Spartans err and whether their error makes them unhappy. See J. Whiting, 'Self-Love and Authoritative Virtue: Prolegomenon to a Kantian Reading of *Eudemian Ethics* VIII 3' ['Self-Love'], in S. Engstrom and J. Whiting (eds.), *Aristotle, Kant, and the Stoics: Rethinking Happiness and Duty* (Cambridge, 1996), 162–99; R. Barney, 'Comments on Sarah Broadie "Virtue and Beyond in Plato and Aristotle"', *Southern Journal of Philosophy*, 43 suppl. 1 (2005), 115–25; S. Broadie, 'The Good, the Noble, and the Theoretical in *Eudemian Ethics* VIII. 3' ['The Good'], in J. Cottingham and P. M. S. Hacker (eds.), *Mind, Method, and Morality: Essays in Honour of Anthony Kenny* (Oxford, 2010), 3–25; T. Irwin, 'The Wild and the Good' ['Wild'], in G. Di Basilio (ed.), *Investigating the Relationship between Aristotle's* Eudemian *and* Nicomachean Ethics (London, 2022), 188–206; and Wolt, '*Phronêsis*'. Since I think that the standard in *EE* 8. 3 is a corrective to Spartan virtue, and the standard specifically applies to 'actions and choices', my view is that the Spartans at least in some cases act and choose wrongly, as a genuinely virtuous person would not.

those with Spartan virtue. So, the phrase 'things by nature good but not praiseworthy' picks out exactly the Spartans' natural goods.

The fact that the Spartans are the ones who have unpraiseworthy natural goods is especially salient because, for those with Spartan virtue, natural goods play a specific role. Spartan virtue is introduced and described primarily by its aim. In characterizing Spartan virtue, Aristotle says, 'For though they think they should have virtue, it is for the sake of natural goods' (1248^b40–1). Since natural goods are unpraiseworthy for the Spartans, the Spartans think they should have virtue for the sake of what turns out to be 'things by nature good but not praiseworthy'. Because Spartan virtue aims at unpraiseworthy natural goods, actions and choices concerning unpraiseworthy natural goods have a kind of special, final status for someone with Spartan virtue. For such an agent, learning that natural goods should actually promote contemplation would change which actions are the best, most final actions. If the actions that pursue natural goods cannot be regarded as the most final, but are only really good for bringing about contemplation, then one should have virtue for the sake of contemplation, not natural goods.

The argumentative context of *EE* 8. 3, then, suggests a specific purpose of the standard for unpraiseworthy natural goods. The phrase 'actions and choices of things by nature good but not praiseworthy' does not function restrictively, to delimit the scope of the standard. Rather, it functions dialectically, to target and correct Spartan virtue by providing a new final aim. In Spartan virtue, actions that manage and acquire natural goods may be the most choiceworthy and final actions, but these final actions also structure and organize the less final actions that contribute to the result they aim to achieve. Many actions may not directly contribute to the acquisition of natural goods, but they may prepare the way for the other actions that acquire natural goods later on. These preparatory actions will vary in their extent, duration, and expected outcome as a function of what final aim they support. For instance, courage for the sake of natural goods might seek out confrontation to achieve honour or plunder, while courage for the sake of contemplation might be satisfied with quelling aggressive threats and then turning from war to leisure.[33] So, correcting the aim of

---

[33] See also *Pol.* 7. 14, 1333^b12–18.

Spartan virtue has downstream consequences for a fuller range of actions too.

Aristotle's point, then, is not just that Spartan virtue is defective; his criticism indicates how it can be corrected. And this correction indicates a necessary condition of virtue which is a part of Aristotle's own considered view of virtue. The Spartans think that virtue is for the sake of natural goods. But virtue should really aim at what the natural goods should be used for, contemplation. So, adopting my dialectical interpretation of the phrases concerning natural goods in the second half of *EE* 8. 3 gives the Unrestricted Reading an answer to its most pressing problem. Aristotle repeats that the standard given in *EE* 8. 3 applies to actions that acquire natural goods. But the standard is for the virtuous person's actions concerning what, *for the Spartans*, is good but not praiseworthy— the goods which Spartan virtue mistakes as being most final. Since the aim of Spartan virtue eventually affects many actions done from that disposition, by correcting its central mistake, its aim, the standard in fact guides virtuous actions in general, not only some limited sphere of actions. So, Aristotle's interest in *EE* 8. 3 is not primarily in how to use natural goods, but to show that those who value them too much neglect the proper aim of both natural goods and virtue, contemplation.

6. The argumentative arc of *Eudemian Ethics* 8. 3

After Aristotle concludes that *kalokagathia* is complete virtue (1249^a16-17), he turns to the topic of pleasure (1249^a18-22), before introducing the standard at 1249^a23. Pleasure does not seem connected either to Spartan virtue or to the standard. So, why not think that Aristotle is turning to another topic? If Aristotle turns to a different topic after his discussion of the Spartans before the standard, then perhaps the chapter is not as unified as my dialectical interpretation would suppose.[34] On the contrary, I maintain that even if Aristotle has different argumentative targets in the chapter, they are unified by his overarching interest in genuine virtue's

---

[34] Many readers (e.g. Broadie, 'The Good', 4) have seen the chapter instead as divided into two separate, only loosely related parts. I am grateful to an anonymous reviewer for pressing this point.

effects and requirements. This aim is apparent in light of two often overlooked pieces of contextual information. The first is the contested meaning of the terms *kalokagathia* and *kalos k'agathos*; the second is virtue's role in harmonizing different evaluative categories. In short, Aristotle's focus on *kalokagathia* anticipates the protreptic consequence of his account of virtue by situating his account of virtue's standard within a broader discourse about the kind of life one's education should prepare one to lead. This life of virtue he is describing really is happy because it unifies the good, the fine, and the pleasant. And the standard provides clear guidance for someone to achieve this kind of life.

By the time Aristotle is writing, the term *kalos k'agathos* had come to be a contested appellation.[35] Especially among sophists, the term is used to refer to an ideal of ethical cultivation or educational achievement, which would be the expected result of the course of study they offered. Plato attests to this usage. He makes Protagoras say, 'I consider myself to be such a person, uniquely qualified to assist others in becoming *kalon kai agathon*' (*Prot.* 328 B 1–3). Socrates, in the *Laches*, laments having no money to give to the sophists, 'who professed to be the only ones able to make me *kalon te k'agathon*' (186 C 3–4).[36] In the *Apology*, Socrates recalls asking Callias who can be 'sought and hired as a supervisor for [his] sons, who would make them *kalō te k'agathō* in respect of their proper virtue' (20 A 7–B 2). Callias answers Evenus, who, like the other sophists named—Gorgias, Prodicus, and Hippias—purports to teach this for a fee. In these passages, a *kalos k'agathos* is one who has attained an ideal of cultivation and education in virtue, which sophists especially promised to their students.

---

[35] The term has both a social sense, indicating aristocratic status, and an evaluative sense, denoting a kind of ethical ideal, someone who is well brought up or who has achieved noble feats. Though the social and evaluative meanings are related, it is the evaluative sense which is contested here. My discussion has benefited from the study of F. Bourriot, *Kalos Kagathos—Kalokagathia: D'un terme de propagande de sophistes à une notion sociale et philosophique; Étude d'histoire athénienne*, 2 vols. (Hildesheim, 1995). My argument in this section does not, however, rely on Bourriot's controversial account of the term's Spartan origin; cf. P. Davies, ' "Kalos Kagathos" and Scholarly Perceptions of Spartan Society', *Historia: Zeitschrift für alte Geschichte*, 62 (2013), 259–79.

[36] Translations modified from J. M. Cooper and D. S. Hutchinson (eds.), *Plato: Complete Works* (Indianapolis, 1997). Sometimes Plato does not use the term in reference to sophists, e.g. *Theaet.* 142 B 7; *Rep.* 405 A 7, but even in these cases, the term picks out an ethical and educational ideal that is what the sophists would promise to teach. See also Xen., *Mem.* 1. 6. 13, Ar., *Clouds* 101, and Isocr., *Antid.* 220.

The term was also used by proponents of other programmes of education to elevate competing visions of the ethical ideal. Specifically, Athenian admirers of Sparta's military success and power regarded its rigorous, state-mandated education and training programme as key to its political success, regularly transforming youths into exemplars of virtue, especially courage. The Spartans' reputation for courage on the battlefield is often thought to be a credit to the training system that produced them. According to Thucydides, after hearing of the Spartan surrender at Sphacteria, an Athenian ally taunted his Spartan captive, asking him whether the Spartans who had died in battle had been their *kaloi k'agathoi* (Thuc. 4. 40). The sneer plays on Sparta's reputation for forming courageous warriors, now embarrassed by the surrender. More explicitly, Xenophon praises Sparta for exceeding all other cities in virtue, being the only one to make the teaching and cultivation of virtue and *kalokagathia* a public responsibility (*Lac.* 10. 1–4; cf. *Mem.* 3. 5. 15). And Isocrates criticizes the Spartans for committing injustices that belie the virtue of a *kalos k'agathos* (*Panath.* 183). Thus, the question of whether the Spartans are exceptional with regard to virtue was both contested and related to the discourse about what kind of an education it would take to produce a *kalos k'agathos*. When Aristotle weighs in on *kalokagathia* in *EE* 8. 3, he invokes this usage of the term in inquiring about what the ethical ideal requires and whether the Spartans, who are sometimes praised in this discourse, really are worthy of the title.[37]

Furthermore, when Aristotle calls the standard of promoting the most contemplation the standard of *kalokagathia* (1249^b26), he is positioning his own ethical ideal within the discourse. By denying that the Spartans are *kaloi k'agathoi* (1249^a1–2), he is contrasting his own virtuous ideal with their civic disposition. He is also anticipating a contrast between his ideal and any non-contemplative ethical ideal—not only that of the Spartans but also that of sophists who promised to teach *kalokagathia*. For instance, Callicles, in the *Gorgias*, discourages excessive philosophizing: 'For even if one is naturally well favoured but engages in philosophy far beyond

---

[37] *Pol.* 7. 14 describes a group of Laconophiles with whom Aristotle disagrees: 'Thibron and all the other writers' praise the Spartan lawgiver for the training that enabled their power (1333^b18–21). Thibron's work is unknown, but Xenophon would belong here.

that appropriate time of life, he will necessarily become inexperienced in everything that someone who is to be *kalos k'agathos* and well regarded needs to be experienced in' (484 C 8–D 2). Isocrates holds that study should be limited if it is not useful (see especially *Antid.*, 261–9). By denying contemplation's value, they make the same mistake the Spartans do. Aristotle's use of the term *kalos k'agathos*, then, draws out the protreptic implication of his account of virtue's standard, specifically against Spartan virtue, but also against the wider backdrop of this discourse, which is dismissive of contemplation. Yet if virtue turns out to aim at contemplation, then someone aspiring to *kalokagathia* should indeed turn their life towards philosophy. This protreptic upshot, largely absent through the preceding Eudemian account of virtue, turns out now to be a necessary part of it.

The second contextual point to note is that the good person (ἀγαθός) described in *EE* 8. 3 is someone Aristotle has introduced before. In *EE* 8. 3, the good person is someone for whom natural goods are good (1248ᵇ27–8). But natural goods can be harmful for some people because of their dispositions, if, for instance, they are foolish or unjust, just as the diet of a healthy person would be harmful to someone who is sick (1248ᵇ32–4). In *EE* 7. 2, Aristotle distinguishes things good without qualification (ἁπλῶς) from things that are good for some particular person (τινί), given their particular circumstance or condition (1235ᵇ31–6). Though what is good without qualification is good for anyone in a standard or good condition, what is good for a particular person might differ if they are in a defective condition. *EE* 7. 2 gives an example like that of *EE* 8. 3: some medical intervention might be good for someone who is sick but not someone who is healthy.[38] Though the unqualified and the particular good can come apart, 'they should harmonize, and this is what virtue brings about' (1237ᵃ2). So, both in *EE* 7. 2 and 8. 3, the things that are good by nature or good without qualification are harmful for some but beneficial to the virtuous.[39] The Greek word for virtue, ἀρετή, has no cognate adjectival form; Aristotle often

---

[38] As the example of the body shows, good ἁπλῶς and good τινί are both relatives; they differ in being related to different objects—one to a standard, good, or healthy one, the other to a defective one. Though this example illustrates what is the good and pleasant for the body, the situation for the soul is similar (1236ᵃ1–2).

[39] At *EE* 7. 2, 1237ᵃ4–5, Aristotle identifies natural goods as goods without qualification.

uses good (ἀγαθός) and excellent (σπουδαῖος) to describe someone who is virtuous, and this is how we should take the good person in *EE* 8. 3.[40]

These two points help make sense of the argumentative arc of *EE* 8. 3. The chapter begins by recalling the preceding discussions of the particular virtues and then considering the virtue that arises from them, *kalokagathia*.[41] From even the common usage of the term, it should be clear that whoever merits this appellation must have the particular virtues. Aristotle then distinguishes things that are fine from things that are good. Fine things are goods that are, furthermore, choiceworthy for their own sake and praiseworthy in themselves (1248^{b}19–21). He uses this distinction in goods to distinguish between two ways people may be described: being good and being *kalos k'agathos*. He describes a good person in terms of benefiting from good things and a *kalos k'agathos* in terms of having fine things and doing fine actions for their own sakes. While the account of the good person is familiar from *EE* 7. 2, the account of the *kalos k'agathos* is new; yet it is formulated in such a way that should be broadly acceptable to proponents of a range of different, competing ethical ideals. A *kalos k'agathos* has and does intrinsically choiceworthy, praiseworthy, good things. There may be disagreement about what things are good, choiceworthy, and praiseworthy, but neither sophist nor Laconophile would dispute the claim that someone they call *kalos k'agathos* would have and do choiceworthy, praiseworthy, good things.

---

[40] The good person of *EE* 8. 3 is sometimes thought to fall short of genuine virtue because they are contrasted with the *kalos k'agathos* and because the Spartans are called good. I reject both these claims below for relying on unsupported emendations. Further, since *EE* 7. 2 does not indicate that it is describing someone whose goodness falls short in any way, it would be surprising if in *EE* 8. 3, someone with a matching description and who is also called ἀγαθός now turns out to be so called in only a secondary or incomplete sense.

[41] Of the virtue which arises from the particular virtues already discussed, Aristotle says, 'We already called (ἐκαλοῦμεν ἤδη) [it] *kalokagathia*' (1248^{b}11–12). Perhaps this indicates that Aristotle had already discussed *kalokagathia* in a part of the common books since revised, but the discussion may also have been oral or belonged to another work. For instance, in *Protr.* 53. 1, the term appears at the end of a discussion distinguishing necessities and joint causes (συναίτια) from goods in the proper sense (ἀγαθὰ κυρίως) but is not otherwise explicated. In any case, *EE* 8. 3 gives no reason to think that Aristotle is remembering a regimented or technical usage of the term. Sophists, Spartans, and Laconophiles too would claim that their ethical ideal embodies the whole of (what they think is) virtue.

Aristotle's aim, then, is to show that even on a neutral account of *kalokagathia*, the good, virtuous person described at length in the *Eudemian Ethics* is the one who deserves that title. This is not a trivial or question-begging conclusion, because, as Aristotle notes, the good and the *kalon k'agathon* are different properties: they differ not only in name but also in themselves (1248^b17–19). Because these characteristics are explicated in terms of relations to different types of goods, if these types of goods turn out to be sufficiently different, then it would also turn out that the good person and the *kalos k'agathos* must come apart, at least in some cases.

Addressing the Laconophiles, Aristotle considers whether the sometimes esteemed Spartans might be worthy of the title. They are not, because they mistakenly regard virtue as being for the sake of natural goods: 'For this reason, they are fierce men, for while they have natural goods, they do not have *kalokagathia*' (1249^a1–2).[42] The Spartans lack *kalokagathia* because they only do fine actions coincidentally—a result of instrumentalizing virtue for the sake of natural goods (1249^a14–16)—while the *kalos k'agathos* does fine actions for their own sake. Though natural goods are not fine for the Spartans (as argued in Section 5), they are fine for the *kalos k'agathos*, who, characteristically, does and has fine things. At 1248^b37–8, these fine things were virtuous actions and virtues, but now they include natural goods too.

---

[42] Following Irwin, 'Wild', I reject the commonly accepted emendation of ἀγαθοί at 1249^a1 for the ἄγριοι of PCBL, along with Solomon's second ἀγαθά at 1249^a2 (which Rowe rejects), and Spengel's <καλῷ κ> at 1249^a13 (which Rowe accepts); the second and especially the third emendations help make sense of the first. Such extensive emendations are acceptable only if the MSS text makes no sense without them. Yet Irwin shows that there is a coherent argument without the emendations if we understand Aristotle as identifying the *agathos* with the *kalos k'agathos* at 1249^a13–14, instead of distinguishing them all the way through, as many readers think. The great advantage of Irwin's reading is that it makes sense of the text without adopting these various unsupported, meaning-changing emendations. It also makes Aristotle's treatment of the Spartans consistent between *EE* 8. 3 and *Pol.* 2. 9 and 7. 14–15. For a challenge to Irwin's reading, see C. Bobonich, 'The Good or the Wild at Aristotle *Eudemian Ethics* 8. 3?', *Classical Philology*, 118 (2023), 172–93. My interpretation expands on Irwin's result by identifying the *agathos* from *EE* 8. 3 with the good person from *EE* 7. 2 and by drawing on historical context to explain why it fits Aristotle's dialectical aim to identify the *agathos* with the *kalos k'agathos* after initially distinguishing them. Additionally, I take the argument from justice at 1249^a7–10 as supporting indirectly the identification of the good person and the *kalos k'agathos*. I take it to be further confirmation for this reading that it can unify the first half of the chapter (1248^b9–1249^a17) with the second half (see below).

At 1249ᵃ8–11, Aristotle explains why natural goods are fine possessions for the *kalos k'agathos*. Natural goods are fine when the aim for which they are managed or acquired is fine. Being a virtue, justice is fine, and justice requires a distribution of natural goods in accordance with worth. The *kalos k'agathos* is worthy of these goods, so simply by being possessed, natural goods would serve a fine aim (i.e. a just distribution of natural goods), making these goods themselves also fine.

However, the same argument from justice also shows that natural goods are fine for the good person. The good person too does many fine actions on their own account (1249ᵃ14).[43] Because the good person is virtuous, they are also just, and since they are virtuous, they are also worthy of having goods (1131ᵃ24–9). Their possession, then, of natural goods also helps to fulfil the distribution required by justice, making natural goods fine for them as well (1249ᵃ13). So, for the good person, as for the *kalos k'agathos*, the beneficial things and the fine things are the same. The explanation for this is that the good person does many fine actions. Since the *kalos k'agathos* is first described in terms of having and doing fine things, this makes the good person the true *kalos k'agathos*. Spartans, though described by their admirers as *kaloi k'agathoi*, turn out not to be because they do fine things coincidentally—a result of the kind of virtue they are taught. When Aristotle concludes that *kalokagathia* is complete virtue, he ties *kalokagathia* to the language from the *EE* 2.1 function argument, which identified the highest good as the activity of complete virtue over a complete life (1219ᵃ39–40). Aristotle is taking the title to which Laconophiles and sophists alike lay claim and showing that it really belongs to the one who lives by the account developed in the *EE*.

Next, Aristotle pivots to consider pleasure. The short section that follows (1249ᵃ18–22) reminds the reader that what is good without qualification is also pleasant and that what is pleasant

---

[43] The sentence actually has no explicit subject: 'For he, too, characteristically performed many fine things on their own account' (1249ᵃ14). Context strongly suggests that the subject of the verb should be the good person (ἀγαθῷ) mentioned at the end of the previous line. However, translators who follow Spengel's emendation to καλῷ κἀγαθῷ at 1249ᵃ13 think the subject is the *kalos k'agathos*. Aristotle is entitled to claim that the good person does fine actions because the good person is one for whom natural goods are good (1248ᵇ27–8), and *EE* 7.2 has already established that the good person's virtue, which is fine, is what makes goods without qualification good for them (1237ᵃ2).

without qualification is also fine. In fact, it was in *EE* 7. 2 that Aristotle also argued that what is good without qualification is also pleasant without qualification (1235^{b}33), and that what is fine is pleasant (1237^{a}6–7). These claims about pleasure and the fine were a part of Aristotle's account of the agent for whom goods without qualification were also good, i.e. the good person.[44] So, after declaring the good person to be the deserving recipient of the title *kalos k'agathos*, Aristotle adds what he previously established: that what is good and fine for the good person is also pleasant.

The convergence of the good, fine, and pleasant recalls the beginning of *EE* 1. 1. Aristotle disagrees with the gateway inscription at Delos, which assigns the categories of best, finest, and most pleasant to different objects: 'For happiness, being the finest and best of all things, is the most pleasant' (1214^{a}1–7). The argument for the convergence of these three evaluative categories—good, fine, and pleasant—is one of the overarching projects of the *Eudemian Ethics*.[45] The fact that these categories converge for the good person is a further sign that the good person really is in fact happy and achieves the ethical ideal—unlike the Spartan, for whom natural goods are not fine.

The section on pleasure, then, does not turn the reader's interest away from the foregoing account of *kalokagathia* but rather unites the account of the good person, now shown also to be *kalos k'agathos*, with previously established claims about the relation between the good, the pleasant, and the fine. As previously established, the convergence of the good, fine, and pleasant depends on virtue. Virtue not only enables one to benefit from unqualified goods and enjoy fine things as such but also makes one eligible to take pleasure in

[44] The claim that pleasure arises only in action points back to the conclusion from *EE* 6. 12 that pleasure is unimpeded natural activity (1153^{a}14). Though *EE* 6. 12 supports the claim that a happy life is pleasant (1153^{b}14–15), the inference at 1249^{a}20 that happiness is most pleasant is difficult; cf. G. Bonasio, 'The Pleasure Thesis in the *Eudemian Ethics*', *Journal of the History of Philosophy*, 60 (2022), 521–36.

[45] Aristotle's opening programmatic claim is not just the positive claim that the good is also fine and pleasant, but the stronger, superlative claim that the best, finest, and most pleasant converge in happiness. Though the chapter, up to 1249^{a}20, seems to focus on the convergence of the three evaluations, there are textual clues that the chapter's next aim is to vindicate the stronger, superlative claim (e.g. the truly happy person lives most pleasantly, 1249^{a}20–1; the standard of promoting contemplation is finest, 1249^{b}21; the standard of being aware of the non-rational part least is best, 1249^{b}24). However, if Aristotle has an argument for the stronger, superlative claim, it is not straightforward.

what is pleasant without qualification. After all, the unqualified pleasures of acting virtuously are available only to someone who is virtuous (1237^{a}27–8). Virtue's role in the convergence of evaluative categories that the good person achieves makes it important to determine what virtue really is, and in particular, what genuine virtue requires that Spartan virtue lacks: the aim given by the standard. So, Aristotle presents his own account of the standard as a correction to the Spartan conception of virtue. The Spartans think that virtue is for the sake of natural goods, but the actions and choices that pursue what they think virtue's end is should really serve the aim of promoting contemplation, and what counts as virtue's mean must be readjusted accordingly.

The chapter's parts, then, are all united in their interest in the genuinely virtuous, good person. There is a consistent line of thought that moves from identifying *kalokagathia* as the complete virtue of the good person to the good person's relation to the pleasant and the fine to the standard for the virtuous, good person. Perhaps Aristotle could have started the chapter from 1249^{a}23, omitting the discussion of *kalokagathia*, the Spartans, and pleasure. But then the chapter would only be about a final necessary condition of virtue, not about the ethical ideal that someone with genuine virtue achieves, and it would not reappropriate a term often used to describe non-contemplative ethical ideals for use to elevate Aristotle's own contemplative ethical ideal. The contrast with the Spartan draws out the significance of this necessary condition of virtue: it entails an ideal that requires reorienting one's life towards philosophical contemplation.

7. The aim of practical wisdom's commands

After prospectively describing the standard for the genuinely virtuous person's dealing with the goods that the Spartans regarded as virtue's aim from 1249^{a}23–^{b}7, Aristotle then gives an argument, from 1249^{b}7–25 to identify and justify it. Some aspects of the argument's text and interpretation are contested, but the argument's core inference is fortunately clear. And this central inference is my second consideration in favour of—and the clearest statement of—the Unrestricted Reading. The argument arrives at its conclusion that the standard requires promoting contemplation from a premiss

Virtue and Contemplation in EE 8. 3

that describes the contemplation of god as the aim of practical wisdom (*phronēsis*). It is because, properly speaking, practical wisdom issues commands for the sake of god that the standard promotes the contemplation of god. Because the argument's key premisses contain no restriction to any class of goods, the conclusion that is licensed from the argument should contain no such restriction either.

Here is the argument:

[1] δεῖ δὴ ὥσπερ καὶ ἐν τοῖς ἄλλοις πρὸς τὸ ἄρχον ζῆν, καὶ πρὸς τὴν ἕξιν καὶ τὴν ἐνέργειαν τὴν τοῦ ἄρχοντος, οἷον δοῦλον πρὸς δεσπότου καὶ ἕκαστον πρὸς τὴν ἑκάστου καθήκουσαν ἀρχήν. ἐπεὶ δὲ καὶ ἄνθρωπος φύσει συνέστηκεν ἐξ ἄρχοντος καὶ ἀρχομένου, καὶ ἕκαστον ἂν δέοι πρὸς τὴν ἑαυτοῦ ἀρχὴν ζῆν [2] αὕτη δὲ διττή· ἄλλως γὰρ ἡ ἰατρικὴ ἀρχὴ καὶ ἄλλως ἡ ὑγίεια· ταύτης δὲ ἕνεκα ἐκείνη· οὕτω δ' ἔχει κατὰ τὸ θεωρητικόν. οὐ γὰρ ἐπιτακτικὸς ἄρχων ὁ θεός, ἀλλ' οὗ ἕνεκα ἡ φρόνησις ἐπιτάττει. διττὸν δὲ τὸ οὗ ἕνεκα, διώρισται δ' ἐν ἄλλοις, ἐπεὶ κεῖνός γε οὐθενὸς δεῖται. [3] ἥτις οὖν αἵρεσις καὶ κτῆσις τῶν φύσει ἀγαθῶν ποιήσει μάλιστα τὴν τοῦ θεοῦ θεωρίαν, ἢ σώματος ἢ χρημάτων ἢ φίλων ἢ τῶν ἄλλων ἀγαθῶν, αὕτη ἀρίστη, καὶ οὗτος ὁ ὅρος κάλλιστος· ἥτις δ' ἢ δι' ἔνδειαν ἢ δι' ὑπερβολὴν κωλύει τὸν θεὸν θεραπεύειν καὶ θεωρεῖν, αὕτη δὲ φαύλη. ἔχει δὲ τοῦτο τῇ ψυχῇ, καὶ οὗτος τῆς ψυχῆς ὁ ὅρος ἄριστος, ἂν ἥκιστα αἰσθάνηται τοῦ ἄλλου μέρους τῆς ψυχῆς, ᾗ τοιοῦτον.

(1249^{b}7-25)

[1] Indeed it is necessary, just as in other things too, to live by that which rules and by the state and the activity of that which rules, like a slave by that of their master, and each thing by its proper ruling principle. And again, since a human being is by nature composed of that which rules and that which is ruled, each part [or: person] would also have to live by its [their] own ruling principle. [2] There are two kinds. For medicine is a ruling principle in one way and health in another: the former is for the sake of the latter. This is true for the contemplative part. For god is not a ruler who gives commands, but that for the sake of whom practical wisdom gives commands. And 'that for the sake of which' is double (the distinction has been made elsewhere); yet god is in need of nothing. [3] Therefore, whatever choice or acquisition of natural goods will most promote the contemplation of god—whether of bodily goods, property, friends, or the other goods—this is best, and this standard is finest. And whatever, through deficiency or excess, impedes serving and contemplating god is base. This holds for the soul, and this standard of the soul is best: that one be least aware of the other part of the soul as such.[46]

---

[46] Numbering added for ease of reference. I retain the place of the sentence διττὸν δὲ τὸ οὗ ἕνεκα, διώρισται δ' ἐν ἄλλοις after φρόνησις ἐπιτάττει following the MSS, rather than after οὐθενὸς δεῖται, as Rowe proposes. At 1249^{b}19, I read μάλιστα after

Interpretations of the passage have diverged on three questions. First, is it each part of the soul or each person who must live by the ruling principle in question?[47] If each part of the soul has a ruling principle, the passage gives two ruling principles, not just one. Second, does 'the contemplative part' refer to the rational part of the soul or to the specifically scientific-rational part of the soul of *EE* 5 (ἐπιστημονικόν, 1139^{a}12)?[48] Third, when Aristotle refers to god throughout the passage, does he refer to the external god of the universe, or does he mean the god within—the soul's contemplative capacity?[49]

Here is a summary that remains neutral about these disputes:

[1] Each person/part of the soul must live by their/its ruling principle.
[2] For the relevant person/part, living by their/its ruling principle requires practical wisdom to issue commands for the sake of god.
[3] Therefore, agents should live by the standard of promoting the most contemplation (in the appropriate domain).

Each step of the argument corresponds to the section of the passage above labelled with the same number. Though [3] is presented with an inferential particle (οὖν, 1249^{b}18), it is not valid to infer from [1] and [2]. There is no reason [3], a conclusion about the standard of promoting contemplation, should follow from [2], a claim about the aim of practical wisdom's commands, unless Aristotle implicitly assumes some connection like the following:

ποιήσει, following PCB, rather than after θεοῦ, which Rowe prints, following L. At 1249^{b}23, I keep the MSS τῇ ψυχῇ, which Rowe's emends to ἡ ψυχή, and τῆς ψυχῆς at 1249^{b}24, which Rowe brackets.

[47] Broadie, 'The Good' and W. J. Verdenius, 'Human Reason and God in the *Eudemian Ethics*' ['Human Reason'], in P. Moraux and D. Harlfinger (eds.), *Untersuchungen zur Eudemischen Ethik* (Berlin, 1971), 285–97 hold that there are two ruling principles, one for each part of the soul, while Kenny, *Aristotelian Ethics*, 174–8; Rowe, *Study*, 68–9; and M. Woods, *Aristotle:* Eudemian Ethics, *Books I, II, and VIII* [*Eudemian Ethics*], 2nd edn (Oxford, 1992), 181 hold that the one ruling principle in question is for each person.

[48] Rowe, *Study*, 68–9 and Woods, *Eudemian Ethics*, 180–4 think the ruler is the rational part of the soul, subparts undistinguished. Kenny, *Aristotelian Ethics*, 174–8 and Verdenius, 'Human Reason' think the ruler is the scientific-rational part.

[49] F. Dirlmeier, *Aristoteles: Eudemische Ethik* (Berlin, 1962), ad loc. is the primary defender of internal-god reading. It has been criticized by Rowe, *Study*, 69; Woods, *Eudemian Ethics*, 183–4; Kenny, *Aristotelian Ethics*, 174–8; and Buddensiek, 'Contemplation', 114.

[C] Practical wisdom's commands are issued for the sake of god only when the agent lives by the standard of promoting the most contemplation (in the appropriate domain).

This link between promoting contemplation and issuing commands for the sake of god should be acceptable to Aristotle whether one thinks that the references to god in the passage are to the internal, divine capacity for contemplation or to the external god of the universe. If god refers to the internal capacity for divine contemplation, practical wisdom would issue commands for the sake of god by issuing actions that prepare and allow the agent to engage in divine contemplative activity. If god refers to the external god of the universe, practical wisdom's commands would be for the sake of contemplation in a different sense. Plants and animals partake in the divine through reproduction, which allows them to be like god insofar as they are able, approximating divine eternity through the immortality of their species.[50] Human beings can be like god in a further respect, through human contemplation. So, practical wisdom might issue commands for the sake of god by selecting activities that allow one to approximate god's own contemplation.

With the addition of [C], the argument is straightforward. Agents should follow the standard of promoting contemplation in the appropriate domain because this standard is a necessary condition for practical wisdom to issue commands for the sake of god, which itself is necessary for living by the ruling principle, which every kind of living thing must do. The conclusion to abide by the standard of promoting contemplation follows from the premiss that practical wisdom issues commands for the sake of god, which it does through promoting contemplation. This Aristotle calls the finest standard. Aristotle then draws a second conclusion from the same premisses: whatever through excess or deficiency prevents the contemplation and service of god is base. This conclusion is supported by the same argument. If contemplation is a worthy goal, then what impedes it is bad.[51]

---

[50] See *DA* 415^{a}26–^{b}7. This construal would probably take 'for the sake of' (ἕνεκα) as involving a sense of approximation. See e.g. G. R. Lear, *Happy Lives and the Highest Good: An Essay on Aristotle's* Nicomachean Ethics (Princeton, 2004).

[51] Rhetorically, however, by adding 'serving' (θεραπεύειν), which in Greek often has religious connotations, Aristotle is making the new point that contemplation and actions that further it should be valued as religious observances. This is part of a broader project among philosophers of reappropriating the religious connotation

A second standard, this time for the soul and not just the contemplative part, follows from applying the formula for what is base that has just been given to the soul (1249^{b}23).[52] Whatever impedes contemplation is base, and when it comes to the soul as a whole, what impedes contemplation is awareness of the other part of the soul as such, so this should be minimized.[53] What is the other part of the soul as such? Since the only part of the soul mentioned by name is the contemplative part, the 'other' part in question appears to be other-than-contemplative. Since some passions of the non-contemplative part of the soul are necessary for bringing about or realizing contemplation, the requirement cannot be to minimize all such perceptions. Rather, the minimand is awareness of the non-contemplative part, insofar as it is other-than-contemplative, that is, not supporting contemplation—say, by focusing on some distracting end or by disobeying commands that bring contemplation about. So, taken together, the various formulations of the standard at the conclusion of the argument at 1249^{b}18–25 enjoin the commanding part of the soul to issue commands that promote the contemplation of god, and the subject part to support contemplation by strictly obeying these commands and nothing else.

The core thought behind the argument as a whole is that the standard of promoting contemplation (in the appropriate domain) is underwritten by practical wisdom's aim. It is because practical wisdom orders for the sake of god that the standard requires promoting contemplation. This raises a difficulty for the Restrictive Readings. Practical wisdom is a capacity that accompanies all virtuous action as the correct reason that accompanies action (1144^{b}23–4).

---

of θεωρία ('contemplation'). See A. W. Nightingale, *Spectacles of Truth in Classical Greek Philosophy: Theoria in Its Cultural Context* (Cambridge, 2004).

[52] It seems that 'this' (τοῦτο) refers to the immediately preceding account of what is base. Aristotle is applying that account now to the soul (ἔχει...τῇ ψυχῇ) to yield a standard for the soul (τῆς ψυχῆς ὁ ὅρος). The first standard (1249^{b}19–21) applies to the contemplative part and describes the aim of practical wisdom's commands, while this standard (1249^{b}23–5) applies to the soul as such and describes the 'other' part as minimizing base obstacles to contemplation as a complement to the activity of the contemplative part. This suggestion makes sense of the sentence without Rowe's changes. Cf. Rowe, *Aristotelica*, 224–5.

[53] Aristotle describes thought and perception as competing movements such that the stronger can expel the weaker: for this reason people deep in thought (ἐννοοῦντες) sometimes do not perceive what is before their eyes (*De Sensu*, 447^{a}14–16) and thought (διανοία) helps to drive illusory images out (*De insomn.*, 461^{a}1). See E. Cagnoli Fiecconi, 'Aristotle on Attention', *Archiv für Geschichte der Philosophie*, 103 (2021), 602–33.

If practical wisdom aims to promote contemplation, why should this aim find expression only in a domain of actions concerning the acquisition or disbursement of natural goods? Practical wisdom is the virtue of the part of the rational soul concerned with things that admit of being otherwise (1139ᵃ5–10), and there is no principled restriction of this part of the soul to a domain of actions concerning natural goods. Of course, many, if not all, of the actions practical wisdom prescribes may use, involve, or presuppose natural goods. But practical wisdom guides action as such, and if contemplating god is its aim, there is no reason to restrict the fulfilment of its aim to actions having to do with natural goods. So, even though Aristotle is addressing the status of natural goods in *EE* 8. 3, the argument he provides for his conclusion is stronger than the immediate context demands. In context, Aristotle is explaining why a disposition that aims at procuring natural goods, such as the Spartans', should in fact aim at contemplation. But Aristotle secures this conclusion by arguing that the intellectual virtue that accompanies *all* actions aims at contemplation.

In the *Eudemian Ethics*, Aristotle is more permissive in using the word *phronēsis* frequently outside its technical meaning as practical wisdom.[54] However, even in the books unique to the *Eudemian Ethics*, Aristotle unambiguously uses the word *phronēsis* with the specific practical meaning my interpretation requires. In *EE* 3. 7, Aristotle distinguishes genuine virtues from the other virtues better described as merely natural virtues: 'As will be discussed in what follows, each virtue exists in a way by nature and in another way with *phronēsis*' (1234ᵃ28–31). *Phronēsis* attends each of the genuine ethical virtues, and its contribution distinguishes genuine virtue from natural virtue.[55] This role for *phronēsis* is the same as the role

---

[54] *EE* 1. 1–2. 1 uses the word *phronēsis* in ways that do not follow the technical sense introduced in the common books. In these cases, the word seems to be used more broadly to mean wisdom, which includes theoretical wisdom. However, these broad uses of the word seem to be limited to the early parts of the treatise. As H. Lorenz, 'Virtue of Character in Aristotle's *Nicomachean Ethics*', *Oxford Studies in Ancient Philosophy*, 37 (2009), 177–212 at 210 points out, later uses of *phronēsis*, especially in *EE* 3. 7 and *EE* 8, do seem to convey consistently the word's specifically practical sense. Cf. G. Pearson, '*Phronêsis* as a Mean in the *Eudemian Ethics*', *Oxford Studies in Ancient Philosophy* 32 (2007), 273–95; Frede, 'Common Books'; and Rowe, '*Sophia*'.

[55] Wolt, '*Phronêsis*', 20–1 cites two other passages (*EE* 2. 11, 1227ᵇ13–17; 8. 1, 1246ᵇ24–7) that appear to allow an enkratic agent to have *phronēsis*, which should be impossible if *phronēsis* plays the role of unifying the virtues. However, in neither passage does Aristotle speak *in propria persona*. In one parenthetical remark at *EE*

described in *EE* 5. 13. So, if *phronēsis* aims to promote contemplation and *phronēsis* accompanies each genuine virtue, then the aim of promoting contemplation should apply to all of the ethical virtues. It is hard to see how Aristotle might limit this feature of *phronēsis* to actions concerning natural goods. So, the Unrestricted Reading finds its clearest positive expression in the statement in *EE* 8. 3 that practical wisdom commands for the sake of god by promoting contemplation.

From this general statement about practical wisdom's aim, it follows that actions guided by practical wisdom within any specific domain—including, but not limited to the domain concerning natural goods—should also reflect practical wisdom's aim of promoting contemplation. By drawing the narrower conclusion about actions relevant to Spartan virtue, Aristotle does not retroactively revise the general aim of practical wisdom so that its aim guides only the narrower domain. In presenting the standard for natural goods, when Aristotle says, 'It was said before about these matters to be as reason says' (1249^b4), he need not be understood as referring to a previous, now lost discussion specifically about the mean for natural goods. Rather, he is referring to the passages at *EE* 2. 5/5. 1, where the standard of virtue in general is said to be in accordance with correct reason ($1222^a8–9$; 1138^b20). So, the standard of *EE* 8. 3 is looking back to answer the promises from *EE* 2. 5 and 5. 1. However, their continuity is not an assumption required for my reading—as it is for the defences of the Unrestricted Reading considered in Section 4—but rather a consequence of my reading, and it is supported independently by my dialectical reading of the phrase 'things by nature good but not praiseworthy' and the core inference of the argument from $1249^b7–25$.

8. How to promote contemplation

On the interpretation I have advanced, the standard of *EE* 8. 3 describes the relationship between ethical virtue and contemplation

8. 1, he seems to assimilate *phronēsis* with self-control, suggesting one can be prudent without having the ethical virtues. But this claim forms part of an argument for a conclusion later rejected as strange (1246^b28). In *EE* 2. 11, Aristotle seems to say that what makes one's reason right is self-control, rather than *phronēsis*, but immediately after saying this, he clarifies that he is attributing this view to 'those who believe that virtue provides correct reason'—a view he rejects ($1227^b17–19$, $1227^b35–1228^a1$).

as productive: ethical virtue aims to promote contemplation. The promotion of contemplation is a goal for ethical virtue in the sense that it determines the mean between excess and deficiency. But how exactly does this productive relationship inform the kind of state ethical virtue is? Is ethical virtue merely a matter of promoting contemplation? I propose that virtue's productive relationship with contemplation should be understood coordinately alongside its other features, so that acting virtuously is a matter of promoting the most contemplation while preserving virtue's other essential properties.

When Aristotle turns from the virtuous person's pleasure to the standard, he introduces it in comparison to the doctor, at 1249^{a}23–^{b}7, quoted above. The doctor's standard is used to make judgements about health, namely whether it is present and what must be done to attain it. In particular, the standard helps determine what kinds of medical interventions would be excessive, deficient, or just right, since in medicine, as in other endeavours (1220^{b}21–6), what conduces to its aim, health, is a mean between excess and deficiency. On the Unrestricted Reading, the standard for the virtuous person works similarly. The standard of promoting the most contemplation determines what counts as excessive or deficient relative to virtue's mean.

Even so, saying that ethical virtue aims essentially at promoting contemplation does not specify how much contemplation should be effected or how demanding this requirement to promote contemplation might be. The word *malista* at 1249^{b}19 suggests an answer: whatever will 'most of all' promote contemplation. But most relative to what? In formulating the standard, Aristotle identifies 'whatever choice or acquisition of natural goods will most promote the contemplation of god' (ἥτις οὖν αἵρεσις καὶ κτῆσις τῶν φύσει ἀγαθῶν ποιήσει μάλιστα τὴν τοῦ θεοῦ θεωρίαν).[56] Here, *malista*

[56] The word order here (μάλιστα after ποιήσει) is in PCB and is adopted by Susemihl and Walzer and Mingay. However, L has and a Latin fragment suggests ποιήσει τὴν τοῦ θεοῦ μάλιστα θεωρίαν, which Rowe, *Aristotelica*, 224 adopts on the grounds that it is less expected. The latter order makes it more plausible to take μάλιστα with θεοῦ rather than ποιήσει or θεωρίαν (though without requiring it). If μάλιστα is understood with θεοῦ, then the standard picks out whatever action promotes the kind of contemplation (in unspecified quantity or duration) whose object is god most of all, as opposed to some other object. Perhaps the wise person can see how much contemplation to promote but not whom to contemplate. But the Spartans need to be told that a certain quantity of natural goods is too much. If Aristotle is clarifying only whom to contemplate, not how much to contemplate, then the standard would not give a clear account of how many natural goods to

could be picking out whatever action will promote contemplation more or better than any other action available would, or it could be picking out those actions that promote contemplation more than they effect any other result. Two actions might both result in more contemplation than any other product; yet one of them might still promote more contemplation than the other. The sentence immediately following suggests that Aristotle is picking out the action that promotes more contemplation than any other action would: whatever through excess or deficiency impedes contemplation is base. It seems, then, that Aristotle's concern is with the quantity of contemplation effected, not with whether contemplation is the most prominent constituent of the action's result. For between two mutually incompatible actions that promote contemplation more than any other result, it might still be that choosing one of them would impede contemplation if doing so results in significantly less contemplation than choosing the alternative would.

Though *malista* more often has the sense of 'most importantly' than 'most in quantity', actions and choices that treat promoting contemplation as most important would understandably promote the greatest quantity or duration of contemplation, other things being equal. Admittedly, Aristotle is not explicit here about how promoting the most contemplation of god should be understood— whether, for instance, focused contemplation weighs more than scatterbrained contemplation, or even whether the contemplation of others is counted or discounted relative to one's own.[57] However this is decided, a natural way to read *malista* here would be that it picks out the choices and actions that treat contemplation as most

acquire—like saying 'as medicine and its reason say to do'. So, even if we keep μάλιστα after θεοῦ, as Rowe prefers, we should still take μάλιστα to describe a quantity of contemplation that the Spartans' natural goods should enable.

[57] On the question of whose contemplation is in question, Broadie, 'The Good', 23 allows that 'some serve [god] through practical measures for advancing the position of [theoretical] studies in the *polis*, whether by political, or financial, or even legislative support'. In the *EE*, Aristotle describes virtue as having a political dimension: it is taught by the law and has the effect of making citizens treat each other justly. Yet even if the standard can be satisfied through acts that help others contemplate, since contemplation is itself (not just its promotion) a part of complete virtue, one cannot be happy without contemplating for oneself. Still, it may be possible to combine some contemplation of one's own with actions that advance the contemplation of others. This, however, does not yet say how Aristotle weighs the contemplation of others against one's own or whether this involves aggregating contemplation across individuals.

valuable and, accordingly, promote contemplation more than other actions that accord contemplation less value would.

Still, identifying contemplation as the most valuable object of promotion need not imply that it is the *only* valuable object of promotion, subordinating every other object of promotion to its maximization. In interpreting the requirement to promote the most contemplation, we can distinguish between direct promotion and indirect promotion. If Aristotle's requirement is to promote contemplation directly, then whether agents satisfy the standard depends entirely on whether they promote the greatest quantity of contemplation. This would effectively be a requirement to maximize contemplation. A direct promotion interpretation would identify contemplation (and only contemplation) with the highest good, the primary object worthy in itself of pursuit.[58] Non-contemplative considerations like the agent's motives, feelings, or character states would then only be valuable only insofar as they are instrumental or ancillary to the aim of promoting contemplation.[59] On an indirect promotion interpretation, the agent's promotion of contemplation would necessarily be mediated by rules, policies, or, in Aristotle's case, virtuous character states. When an agent acts, they should act as virtue requires, but what virtue is is determined separately in terms of what promotes the most contemplation. So, on the indirect promotion view, the requirement to promote contemplation does not apply directly to the agent but is a defining aim specifically for the agent's character states.

The case for taking Aristotle's view of contemplation to be one of indirect promotion follows from the function argument of *EE* 2. 1, whose conclusion is an account of the highest good, happiness, as 'the activity of complete virtue over a complete life' (1219^{a}39–40). 'Complete' is glossed explicitly as the whole of virtue rather than a part. So, happiness, the best thing human beings can achieve in action, is the activity of complete virtue, a whole which includes all

---

[58] This view would cohere best with strict intellectualist readings of the *EE* (though some such readers, like Kraut, *Aristotle on the Human Good*, 11–12, would resist the term 'maximize'). For instance, citing 1249^{a}23–^{b}27, D. Ferguson, 'The "Belonging to a Kind" Reading of the Eudemian *Ergon* Argument', *Ancient Philosophy*, 42 (2022), 471–92 at 490 defends the class of 'intellectualist readings of the *EE*, according to which *eudaimonia* is just theoretical activity according to virtue'.

[59] If they were valuable in themselves, they might conflict with contemplation, which, on this view, is happiness. On a standard eudaemonist picture, there is no reason to have a certain motive or feeling if having it detracts from one's happiness.

the parts of virtue.[60] Theoretical wisdom is only one part of complete virtue (1144ᵃ4–6), but ethical virtue is another. The agent who sacrifices the activity of one part of virtue, ethical virtue, for another part, theoretical wisdom, would not achieve the activity of complete virtue because happiness is a whole that must include both. And even if ethical virtue is a mean that promotes contemplation, its value is not reduced to its instrumental relation to contemplation. Ethically virtuous activity is worthy of pursuit in its own right because it is itself a part of happiness. This supports an indirect promotion account because the account makes happiness unachievable by one who forgoes ethical virtue to promote contemplation.

The indirect promotion account has a further upshot. The function argument makes happiness the activity of complete virtue. One feature of ethical virtue is its aim, promoting contemplation. But ethical virtue has many other features, extensively described earlier in the *EE*. If any of these features resist being reduced to an instrumental relation to contemplation, then acting from virtuous states that most promote contemplation will mean promoting contemplation within or alongside the constraints imposed by these other essential features of virtue. What might these features be?

It might be especially difficult for a direct promotion account to explain the characterization of the virtues as choiceworthy for their own sake and praiseworthy on their own account (1248ᵇ19–24; cf. *EN* 1105ᵃ32). How could justice or moderation be intrinsically choiceworthy and praiseworthy if its value lies only in its ability to promote contemplation? Relatedly, the *EE* describes the connection between virtue and the fine (καλόν) in its characterization of courage: 'For courage is obedient to reason, and reason commands one to choose the fine' (1229ᵃ1–3). Additionally, Aristotle says, 'Virtue causes people to choose everything for the sake of something, and this is that-for-the-sake-of-which, the fine' (1230ᵃ30–1). How exactly Aristotle conceives of the fine is controversial, but in the *Eudemian Ethics*, Aristotle thinks that things other than contemplation can be fine (1249ᵃ5–6). This suggests, then, that Aristotle does not require contemplation to be the virtuous agent's only aim,

---

[60] This is confirmed in *EE* 8. 3 when Aristotle identifies *kalokagathia* with complete virtue (1249ᵃ16–17), having introduced it as arising from (ἐκ) the particular virtues discussed individually earlier in the treatise (1248ᵇ11). For a defence of an inclusive reading of the *EE* 2. 1 function argument, see R. C. Lee, 'The Function Argument in the *Eudemian Ethics*', *Ancient Philosophy*, 42 (2022), 191–214.

or at least that the requirement to promote contemplation is self-effacing—promoting contemplation through not consciously trying to do so. In any case, virtue requires agents to be responsive to features of actions other than the action's relation to contemplation. These aspects of virtue make it hard to see ethical virtue as simply instrumental. On an indirect promotion reading, then, they constrain the agent's promotion of contemplation to only those actions that are fine and intrinsically choiceworthy and praiseworthy.

Besides virtue's restriction to the fine and what is choiceworthy in itself, there are other features of virtue, which, depending on how they fit into Aristotle's considered account, may impose additional constraints on the agent's promotion of contemplation. Prior to *EE* 8. 3, Aristotle had already determined that virtue is the best disposition, brought about by the best things, and productive of the best actions; it is habituated; it is concerned with pleasures and pains; it is concerned with decision; it makes the aim of a decision correct; it is a mean between excess and deficiency; it accords with the correct reason; it is accompanied by practical wisdom (1234^a29–31); it is thought useful for the political craft by preventing citizens from wronging one another (1234^b22–5); and it brings about the harmony of what is good for a particular individual and what is good without qualification, among other things. Perhaps some of these properties may be part of the essence of virtue; others may be necessary properties that follow from its essence. Yet even after describing virtue in these ways, Aristotle regards his account of virtue as true but not clear. What is needed in addition for a true and clear account is the provision that virtue promotes the most contemplation. In case there are multiple states that satisfy all of virtue's previously described necessary properties, *EE* 8. 3 clarifies that the best—that is, the virtuous—state is the one that additionally satisfies the standard of promoting the most contemplation.

On the indirect promotion view, this final criterion in *EE* 8. 3 is not the only essential property of virtue, by reference to which all of virtue's other characteristics are explained. Rather, it is one among virtue's various necessary properties. Its addition does not undo the other characterizations of virtue. Being a good, virtuous person requires choosing courses of action that seek out and promote contemplative activity. However, ethical virtue also imposes motivational requirements on the agent's actions, requires that the agent choose the fine, plays a role carefully designed by the lawmaker to help citizens get along, and so on. A virtuous state could not bid an agent to pursue contemplation in a way that violates virtue's other necessary characteristics without losing its status as a virtue, and happiness requires the activity of complete virtue. These necessary features of virtue provide further constraints on the agent's pursuit of contemplation beyond those imposed by moving from direct to indirect promotion. The shape and boundaries of some of these other characteristics of virtue remain contested, and how these other characteristics turn out will affect how demanding or constrained the requirement to promote contemplation is. Still, *EE* 8. 3 moves towards a clearer picture of how ethical virtue and contemplative activity are related in the *EE*. Contemplation is virtue's defining aim, to be sought alongside virtue's other requirements.

9. Conclusion

The final chapter of the *Eudemian Ethics* contains what seem to be disparate argumentative aims, but I have argued that they are unified by an overarching concern to clarify what virtue is for the good person. Understood dialectically, the chapter is not making a point about natural goods; rather, its aim is to clarify what virtue is and the happy life it enables one to lead. Throughout the chapter's discussion of the standard, mention of natural goods serves to frame Aristotle's own account of virtue as a corrective for Spartan virtue. Though sometimes admired, the Spartans fall short of the ethical ideal of *kalokagathia* because the kind of disposition they have fails to bring together the good, the fine, and the pleasant, as happiness requires. The good person, though—that is, one who exhibits the virtues of the *Eudemian Ethics*—does have the kind of virtue that brings these categories together, genuine virtue. What is distinctive about this kind of virtue is that it orients one's life towards the aim of contemplation.

The lesson to draw, then, from *EE* 8. 3 is that Aristotle's account of virtue's mean requires the addition of a standard in order to be fully true and clear. A consequence of this interpretation is that Aristotle, at least in the *Eudemian Ethics*, regards an account of virtue given only in terms of the mean and the correct reason as falling short of being fully true and clear. Virtue needs additionally a standard—not just the judgement of the wise person—that is explicit in quantitative terms: promote the most contemplation. Indeed, the contrastive framing of *EE* 8. 3 gives reason to think that one's account of virtue should be explicit enough to explain why another group of people often thought to have virtue and who sometimes perform actions that are at least coincidentally fine are not, in fact, virtuous and fall short of the ethical ideal. Even without a standard, Aristotle might say of the Spartans that they fail to choose fine actions for their own sake, but that is only a symptom of their defective virtue; its ultimate explanation is the standard. What the standard allows Aristotle to do is to diagnose the error in the Spartan disposition and prescribe a correction in such terms that even those who do not have complete virtue or agree what it is can see what should be done instead and why.

Creighton University

BIBLIOGRAPHY

Ackrill, J. L., 'Aristotle on *Eudaimonia*', in A. O. Rorty (ed.), *Essays on Aristotle's Ethics* (Berkeley, 1980), 15–33.

Barney, R., 'Comments on Sarah Broadie "Virtue and Beyond in Plato and Aristotle"', *Southern Journal of Philosophy*, 43 suppl. 1 (2005), 115–25.

Bobonich, C., 'The Good or the Wild at Aristotle *Eudemian Ethics* 8. 3?', *Classical Philology*, 118 (2023), 172–93.

Bonasio, G., 'Natural Goods in the *Eudemian Ethics*' ['Natural Goods'], *Ancient Philosophy*, 41 (2021), 123–42.

Bonasio, G., 'The Pleasure Thesis in the *Eudemian Ethics*', *Journal of the History of Philosophy*, 60 (2022), 521–36.

Bourriot, F., *Kalos Kagathos—Kalokagathia: D'un terme de propagande de sophistes à une notion sociale et philosophique: Étude d'histoire athénienne*, 2 vols. (Hildesheim, 1995).

Broadie, S., *Ethics with Aristotle* (Oxford, 1991).

Broadie, S., 'The Good, the Noble, and the Theoretical in *Eudemian Ethics* VIII. 3' ['The Good'], in J. Cottingham and P. M. S. Hacker (eds.), *Mind, Method, and Morality: Essays in Honour of Anthony Kenny* (Oxford, 2010), 3–25.

Buddensiek, F., 'Contemplation and Service of the God: The Standard for External Goods in *Eudemian Ethics* VIII 3' ['Contemplation'], *Bochumer Philosophisches Jahrbuch für Antike und Mittelalter*, 14 (2011), 103–24.

Buddensiek, F., *Die Theorie des Glücks in Aristoteles'* Eudemischer Ethik [*Theorie*] (Göttingen, 1999).
Bywater, I., ed., *Aristotelis Ethica Nicomachea* (Oxford, 1894).
Cagnoli Fiecconi, E., 'Aristotle on Attention', *Archiv für Geschichte der Philosophie*, 103 (2021), 602–33.
Cooper, J. M., *Reason and Human Good in Aristotle* [*Reason*] (Indianapolis, 1986).
Cooper, J. M., and Hutchinson, D. S. (eds.), *Plato: Complete Works* (Indianapolis, 1997).
Davies, P., '"Kalos Kagathos" and Scholarly Perceptions of Spartan Society', *Historia: Zeitschrift für alte Geschichte*, 62 (2013), 259–79.
Devereux, D., '*Theoria* and *Praxis* in Aristotle's Ethics' [*'Theoria'*], in P. Destrée and M. A. Zingano (eds.), *Theoria: Studies on the Status and Meaning of Contemplation in Aristotle's Ethics* (Louvain-la-Neuve, 2014), 155–205.
Dirlmeier, F., *Aristoteles: Eudemische Ethik* (Berlin, 1962).
Ferguson, D., 'The "Belonging to a Kind" Reading of the Eudemian *Ergon* Argument', *Ancient Philosophy*, 42 (2022), 471–92.
Frede, D., 'On the So-Called Common Books of the *Eudemian* and the *Nicomachean Ethics*', *Phronesis*, 64 (2019), 84–116.
Inwood, B., and Woolf, R. (eds.), *Eudemian Ethics* (Cambridge, 2013).
Irwin, T., 'The Wild and the Good' ['Wild'], in G. Di Basilio (ed.), Investigating the Relationship between Aristotle's Eudemian *and* Nicomachean Ethics (London, 2022), 188–206.
Kenny, A., *Aristotle on the Perfect Life* (Oxford, 1992).
Kenny, A., *The Aristotelian Ethics: A Study of the Relationship between the* Eudemian *and* Nicomachean Ethics *of Aristotle* [*Aristotelian Ethics*], 2nd edn (Oxford, 2016).
Kraut, R., *Aristotle on the Human Good* (Princeton, 1989).
Lear, G. R., *Happy Lives and the Highest Good: An Essay on Aristotle's* Nicomachean Ethics (Princeton, 2004).
Lee, R. C., 'The Function Argument in the *Eudemian Ethics*', *Ancient Philosophy*, 42 (2022), 191–214.
Lorenz, H., 'Virtue of Character in Aristotle's *Nicomachean Ethics*', *Oxford Studies in Ancient Philosophy*, 37 (2009), 177–212
Monan, J. D., *Moral Knowledge and Its Methodology in Aristotle* (Oxford, 1968).
Nightingale, A. W., *Spectacles of Truth in Classical Greek Philosophy: Theoria in Its Cultural Context* (Cambridge, 2004).
Pearson, G., '*Phronēsis* as a Mean in the *Eudemian Ethics*', *Oxford Studies in Ancient Philosophy*, 32 (2007), 273–95.
Peterson, S., '*Horos* (Limit) in Aristotle's Nicomachean Ethics' [*'Horos'*], *Phronesis*, 33 (1988), 233–50.

Reeve, C. D. C., *Action, Contemplation, and Happiness: An Essay on Aristotle* [*Essay*] (Cambridge, 2012).
Rowe, C., *Aristotelica: Studies on the Text of Aristotle's Eudemian Ethics* [*Aristotelica*] (Oxford, 2023).
Rowe, C., *Aristotelis Ethica Eudemia* (Oxford, 2023).
Rowe, C., *The Eudemian and Nicomachean Ethics: A Study in the Development of Aristotle's Thought* [*Study*] (Cambridge, 1971).
Rowe, C., '*Sophia* in the *Eudemian Ethics*' ['*Sophia*'], in G. Di Basilio (ed.), *Investigating the Relationship between Aristotle's Eudemian and Nicomachean Ethics* (London, 2022), 122–36.
Simpson, P. (trans. and comm.), *The Eudemian Ethics of Aristotle* [*Eudemian Ethics*] (New York, 2013).
Susemihl, F. (ed.), *Aristotelis Ethica Eudemia* (Leipzig, 1884).
Tuozzo, T. M., 'Contemplation, the Noble, and the Mean: The Standard of Moral Virtue in Aristotle's Ethics' ['Standard'], *Apeiron*, 28 (1995), 129–54.
Verdenius, W. J., 'Human Reason and God in the *Eudemian Ethics*' ['Human Reason'], in P. Moraux and D. Harlfinger (eds.), *Untersuchungen zur Eudemischen Ethik* (Berlin, 1971), 285–97.
Walker, M. D., *Aristotle on the Uses of Contemplation* [*Uses*] (Cambridge, 2018).
Walzer, R. R., and Mingay, J. M. (eds.), *Aristotelis Ethica Eudemia* (Oxford, 1991).
Whiting, J., 'Self-Love and Authoritative Virtue: Prolegomenon to a Kantian Reading of *Eudemian Ethics* VIII 3' ['Self-Love'], in S. Engstrom and J. Whiting (eds.), *Aristotle, Kant, and the Stoics: Rethinking Happiness and Duty* (Cambridge, 1996), 162–99.
Wolt, D., '*Phronêsis* and *Kalokagathia* in *Eudemian Ethics* VIII. 3' ['*Phronêsis*'], *Journal of the History of Philosophy*, 60 (2022), 1–23.
Woods, M., *Aristotle: Eudemian Ethics, Books I, II, and VIII* [*Eudemian Ethics*], 2nd edn (Oxford, 1992).

HOW VIRTUOUS ACTIONS ARE A MEANS TO CONTEMPLATION

SUKAINA HIRJI

1. Introduction

In a number of passages in the *Nicomachean Ethics* [*NE*], Aristotle seems to suggest that ethically virtuous actions are an instrumental means to contemplation. But as many scholars have worried, this view appears to be both implausible on the face of it and in tension with other commitments Aristotle has. The difficulty in understanding the relationship between virtuous actions and contemplation is part of a larger puzzle about the structure of value in Aristotle's ethical theory. Does Aristotle countenance a plurality of independently valuable ends for human beings? Or is the value of all other ends for human beings ultimately reducible to the value of the highest human good? In this paper, I explore what it would mean to accept the face value reading: virtuous actions really are 'for the sake of' contemplation because they instrumentally promote contemplation. Specifically, I argue, virtuous actions are for the sake of the noble insofar as they promote conditions of peace, security, and freedom from necessity, and these are precisely the conditions under which contemplation is possible. On the interpretation I defend, we find in Aristotle a sophisticated theory of value that demonstrates the possibility of being a pluralist while still maintaining that every good is hierarchically organized around some one highest good.

This paper proceeds in three parts. In Section 2, I set up the problem, and consider existing solutions. I divide attempts to construe the relationship between virtuous actions and contemplation into two camps on the basis of the axiology they attribute to

---

I am grateful to audiences at the University of Pennsylvania, NYU, Columbia, Indiana University, the University of Toronto, Washington University in St. Louis, and Princeton. Special thanks to feedback from Eric Brown, Patricia Marechal, Katy Meadows, Susan Sauvé Meyer, Benjamin Morison, Jessica Moss, and Claudia Yau. I am also grateful to Rachana Kamtekar and the referees for *Oxford Studies in Ancient Philosophy* for their helpful comments.

Aristotle. Pluralist views identify a range of distinct and incommensurably valuable goods, including both virtuous actions and contemplation. Monist views claim the goodness of all human goods for Aristotle is reducible in some way to the goodness of contemplation. I argue that at the heart of the debate is a dilemma. Pluralist views can capture common-sense views about virtuous actions, but they struggle to explain how human goods are all for the sake of contemplation. Monist views can capture how all goods are hierarchically ordered under contemplation, but they face the challenge of explaining how the value of paradigmatically virtuous actions is explained by reference to contemplation.

In Section 3, I diagnose the source of the difficulty in making sense of the relationship between virtuous actions and contemplation. I argue that, to make progress, we need to understand how virtuous actions are always instrumental to other, more valuable ends without it being the case that the goodness of acting virtuously is reducible to the goodness of contemplation. I'll argue that the goodness of acting virtuously depends on the goodness of virtuous *actions*, and the goodness of virtuous *actions* depends on the goodness of the external ends at which they aim, and ultimately, on the goodness of contemplation.[1] However, the goodness of acting virtuously is not reducible to the goodness of virtuous *actions*, and so is also not reducible to the goodness of contemplation.

In Section 4, I propose a principled way in which virtuous actions are instrumentally for the sake of contemplation that does not result in either textual inconsistency or implausible consequences. I do this by appeal to a distinction between virtuous actions and acting virtuously. I will argue that virtuous actions, insofar as they are for the sake of the noble, are instrumentally for the sake of bringing about conditions of peace and leisure, and these are precisely the conditions under which contemplation is possible.[2] I clarify that Aristotle is offering us a standard for virtuous actions without offering a decision procedure or a principle of action. Virtuous actions are for the sake of contemplation because they promote the sorts of goods that are *such as to provide* the

---

[1] In Section 3.1, I introduce 'acting virtuously' as a technical term that refers to performing a virtuous action from a virtuous character.
[2] This is, I will argue, a somewhat broader notion of instrumentality than the one that has often been assumed. Roughly, something is instrumental to an end when it produces or otherwise promotes the existence of some end.

conditions necessary for contemplation, even if they do not, *in fact*, always bring about more contemplation. Acting virtuously, by contrast, is its own end, insofar as it is the excellent accomplishment of the human function. I conclude with some reflections on what we can learn from Aristotle about the relationship between an ethical life and a life devoted to philosophy.

2. The puzzle

2.1. *The 'for the sake of' relation*

What is the evidence for thinking that, for Aristotle, virtuous activity is an instrumental means to contemplation (θεωρία)? Perhaps the clearest evidence comes from two commitments Aristotle seems to endorse explicitly: first, everything that is not the highest human good is choiceworthy for the sake of the highest human good, and second, the highest human good is contemplative activity. If everything that is not the highest human good is choiceworthy for the sake of the highest human good, and the highest human good is contemplation, then ethically virtuous actions, along with everything else other than contemplative activity, must be choiceworthy for the sake of contemplation.[3]

We see evidence of the first commitment from the beginning of the *Nicomachean Ethics*. In the opening lines of the text, Aristotle notices that every craft, inquiry, action, and decision seems to aim at some good (*NE* 1094^{a}1–2). Moreover, he observes, there is a hierarchy amongst the ends we pursue: some ends are pursued for the sake of higher-level ends, and these higher-level ends are more choiceworthy than the lower-level ends (1094^{a}2–18). Aristotle continues in *NE* 1. 2 to suppose that if there is some one end that is choiceworthy for its own sake and for the sake of which all other ends are ultimately chosen, this end will be the best good or εὐδαιμονία (hereafter, translated as happiness) (1094^{a}18–23).

---

[3] I will not defend any particular view about what contemplation consists in, although Aristotle seems to conceive of it as a remarkably narrow activity involving the active understanding of eternal objects in the realm of the divine and unchanging. See M. D. Walker, *Aristotle on the Uses of Contemplation* [*Uses*] (Cambridge, 2018), 24–42 for a good discussion of the proper objects of wisdom (σοφία) and contemplation.

Aristotle resumes the discussion in *NE* i. 7, arguing that whatever happiness turns out to be, it must be the most end-like (τέλειον) end: an end that we always choose because of itself and never because of anything else (1097ᵃ25–ᵇ6). Every good that is not happiness, Aristotle insists, is chosen at least in part for the sake of happiness.

A brief note on language. There are two different prepositions typically translated as 'for the sake of', and they are generally taken to be functionally equivalent for Aristotle: χάριν + genitive (as at *NE* 1094ᵃ15, 1097ᵃ15, 1097ᵃ18, 1097ᵇ4–6) and ἕνεκα + genitive (as at 1097ᵃ21); another preposition, διά + accusative (as at *NE* 1094ᵃ19), picks out the end for the sake of which an agent acts.[4] Aristotle does not offer an explanation of this relation other than through examples: medicine is for the sake of health, generalship is for the sake of victory, and building is for the sake of a house, and so on (*NE* 1097ᵃ19–21). A very natural reading of this relation, given the examples, is as instrumental or productive. For example, in arguing that happiness is the most end-like end, Aristotle claims that we choose other ends including pleasure, honour, and other virtues in part 'for the sake of happiness, because we judge that, through them, we will be happy' (αἱρούμεθα δὲ καὶ τῆς εὐδαιμονίας χάριν διὰ τούτων ὑπολαμβάνοντες εὐδαιμονήσειν, *NE* 1097ᵇ4–6). Here, the thought seems to be that happiness is commonly considered to be a result of, or instrumentally promoted by, these other goods.[5] I will note that, by the end of this paper, the instrumentality relation I think we find in Aristotle is broader than a straightforwardly means-ends relationship. I will argue that, when x is 'for the sake of' y in this sense, it is because x is the sort of thing that promotes y.[6]

I turn now to the second commitment, that the highest human good is contemplative activity. In *NE* i. 7, shortly after the passage above where Aristotle identifies happiness as the most end-like end, Aristotle argues that we locate human happiness in the

---

[4] For discussion, see S. S. Meyer, *Ancient Ethics*. (Abingdon, 2007), 89 n. 8, as well as R. Kraut, *Aristotle on the Human Good* [*Human Good*] (Princeton, 1991), 200–3.

[5] I understand the instrumentality relation here as existing when one good produces or promotes the existence of some end. And, Aristotle thinks, when this relation holds, the value of the means depends on the value of the end.

[6] Although this is broader than a pure means-ends relationship, it is much closer to a face value reading of instrumentality than the alternatives I will discuss.

characteristic work or function of human beings. He argues that this characteristic work or function is the activity of the rational part of the soul and concludes that happiness is the activity of the rational part of the soul in accordance with virtue (1097^b24–1098^a18). In *NE* 10. 7, he appears to resume the discussion, arguing that if happiness is activity in accordance with virtue, it is reasonable that it should be in accordance with what is most excellent, this being the virtue of the best element, namely understanding. He concludes that complete happiness consists in contemplative activity (1177^a12–19).[7]

To sum up: Aristotle seems to be committed to two claims: (i) every good that is not itself the highest human good is choiceworthy, at least in part, for the sake of the highest human good, and (ii) contemplation is the highest human good. These two commitments,

---

[7] In this paper, I take as the face value reading of the text that Aristotle uses the language of the highest good and happiness (εὐδαιμονία) interchangeably, and that contemplation is the highest good. For commentators who have maintained that Aristotle's discussion in *NE* 10. 7–8 is in tension with the rest of the *NE*, see e.g. J. Ackrill, 'Aristotle on Eudaimonia' ['Eudaimonia'], in A. O. Rorty (ed.), *Essays on Aristotle's Ethics* (Berkeley, 1980), 15–33; A. W. Adkins, 'Theoria versus Praxis in the Nicomachean Ethics and the Republic', *Classical Philology*, 73 (1978), 297–313; J. M. Cooper, *Reason and the Human Good in Aristotle* [*Reason*] (Cambridge, Mass., 1975), 156–64; W. F. R. Hardie, 'The Final Good in Aristotle's Ethics' ['Final'], in J. M. E. Moravcsik (ed.), *Aristotle: A Collection of Critical Essays* (London, 1967), 297–322; W. Jaeger, *Aristotle*, trans. by R. Robinson (Chicago, 1948), 439–40; W. D. Ross (trans.), *Aristotle Ethica Nicomachea* (Oxford, 1915), 233–4; N. P. White, 'Goodness and Human Aims in Aristotle's Ethics' ['Goodness'], in D. J. O'Meara (ed.), *Studies in Aristotle* (Washington DC, 1981), 242–3; and K. Wilkes, 'The Good Man and the Good for Man in Aristotle's Ethics', in A. O. Rorty (ed.), *Essays on Aristotle's Ethics* (Berkeley, 1980), 341–58 at 341 and 351–2. For attempts to render *NE* 10.7–8 consistent with the rest of the *NE*, see e.g. J. M. Cooper, 'Contemplation and Happiness: A Reconsideration', *Synthese*, 72 (1987), 187–216; D. T. Devereux, 'Aristotle on the Essence of Happiness' ['Essence'], in D. J. O'Meara (ed.), *Studies in Aristotle* (Washington DC, 1981), 247–60; D. Keyt, 'Intellectualism in Aristotle' ['Intellectualism (1983)'], in J. P. Anton and A. Preus (eds.), *Essays in Ancient Greek Philosophy*, 2nd edn (Albany, 1983), 364–87; and J. Whiting, 'Human Nature and Intellectualism in Aristotle', *Archiv für Geschichte der Philosophie*, 68 (1986), 70–95. Commentators who have embraced an 'intellectualist' reading of Aristotle according to which, strictly speaking, *eudaimonia* consists in contemplation alone include Devereux, 'Essence', 260; R. Heinaman, 'Eudaimonia and Self-Sufficiency in the Nicomachean Ethics', *Phronesis*, 33 (1988), 31–53 at 45; A. Kenny, *The Aristotelian Ethics: A Study of the Relationship between the Eudemian and Nicomachean Ethics of Aristotle* (Oxford, 1978), 209; G. R. Lear, 'Happiness and the Structure of Ends' ['Structure'], in G. Anagnostopoulos (ed.), *A Companion to Aristotle* (Malden, 2009), 385–403; and White, 'Goodness', 225–45.

taken together, imply that ethically virtuous actions are a means to contemplation.

Further evidence for thinking that virtuous activity is an instrumental means to contemplation comes from an analogy Aristotle draws between practical wisdom and the medical art in *NE* 6. As a prelude to his discussion of the virtues of the rational part of the soul, Aristotle acknowledges that to say that one ought to choose what is intermediate and what is in accordance with right reason is true, but uninformative. To advise someone to choose what is intermediate or what right reason dictates would be like simply telling a patient to do what the medical art prescribes or what someone who possessed the medical art would do, without filling in the content of what the medical art prescribes. In order for this advice to be informative or action-guiding, one needs to fill in the content of what the intermediate consists in or what right reason is: 'it should be determined what right reason is and what is the standard that fixes it' (ἀλλὰ καὶ διωρισμένον τίς ἐστιν ὁ ὀρθὸς λόγος καὶ τούτου τίς ὅρος, *NE* 6. 1, 1138ᵇ34–5).

In the analogy that Aristotle is drawing here, practical wisdom is likened to the medical art. Although Aristotle does not say so explicitly in this passage, it is clear that the standard (ὅρος) of the medical art is health; health is what the medical art is for and the standard that determines what sorts of treatments are appropriate and in what amounts. Aristotle returns to this analogy in *NE* 6. 13 in considering the question of how practical wisdom (φρόνησις) and contemplation (θεωρία) are related. He insists that practical wisdom is 'not authoritative over wisdom, i.e. over the best part of us, just as the art of medicine is not over health; for it does not use it but provides for its coming into being; it issues orders, then, for its sake, but not to it' (ἀλλὰ μὴν οὐδὲ κυρία γ' ἐστὶ τῆς σοφίας οὐδὲ τοῦ βελτίονος μορίου, ὥσπερ οὐδὲ τῆς ὑγιείας ἡ ἰατρική· οὐ γὰρ χρῆται αὐτῇ, ἀλλ' ὁρᾷ ὅπως γένηται· ἐκείνης οὖν ἕνεκα ἐπιτάττει, ἀλλ' οὐκ ἐκείνῃ, *NE* 6. 13, 1145ᵃ6–9).[8] In the case of medicine, medicine is not superior to health; instead, the medical art is for the sake of health because it provides for its coming into being. Likewise, on the most straightforward way of reading the analogy, practical wisdom is not

---

[8] Translations are my own unless otherwise noted. Greek text from I. Bywater, *Aristotelis Ethica Nicomachea* (Oxford, 1894).

superior to theoretical wisdom; instead, practical wisdom is for the sake of wisdom because it provides for its coming into being.

Aristotle appears to make this point even more explicitly in *Eudemian Ethics* 8. 3. I do not want to lean too heavily on this passage here, given the much-discussed textual difficulties in it, as well as the broader question of the relevance of the *EE* for understanding Aristotle's views in the *NE*.[9] However, it is worth noting that the passage bears a strong resemblance to Aristotle's discussion in *NE* 6. 1. Aristotle again draws an analogy between practical wisdom and health, noting:

ἐπεὶ δ' ἐστί τις ὅρος καὶ τῷ ἰατρῷ, πρὸς ὃν ἀναφέρων κρίνει τὸ ὑγιεινὸν σώματι καὶ μή, καὶ πρὸς ὃν μέχρι ποσοῦ ποιητέον ἕκαστον καὶ εὖ ὑγιαῖνον, εἰ δὲ ἔλαττον ἢ πλέον, οὐκέτι· οὕτω καὶ τῷ σπουδαίῳ περὶ τὰς πράξεις καὶ αἱρέσεις τῶν φύσει μὲν ἀγαθῶν οὐκ ἐπαινετῶν δὲ δεῖ τινα εἶναι ὅρον καὶ τῆς ἕξεως καὶ τῆς αἱρέσεως καὶ [περὶ] φυγῆς <καὶ περὶ> χρημάτων πλήθους καὶ ὀλιγότητος καὶ τῶν εὐτυχημάτων.ἐν μὲν οὖν τοῖς πρότερον ἐλέχθη τὸ ὡς ὁ λόγος· τοῦτο δ' ἐστὶν ὥσπερ ἂν εἴ τις ἐν τοῖς περὶ τὴν τροφὴν εἴπειεν ὡς ἡ ἰατρικὴ καὶ ὁ λόγος ταύτης.

(*EE* 8. 3, 1249ᵃ21–ᵇ5)

Since even the doctor has a principle of determination, by referring to which he decides what is healthy for a body and what is not, and how far each thing ought to be done and is good for health, while, if done less or more, it is no longer so; so also the morally good person must in doing and choosing things that are naturally good but not praiseworthy have a principle for determining his possession and choice and avoidance both in quantity, great and small, of money and in things distributed by fortune. In the preceding discussion we said [this principle of determination] is 'as reason directs'. But this is just as if someone with regard to food should say 'as medicine and its principles direct'.[10]

Aristotle goes on to argue that a human being should live by reference to its governing principle, insisting that just as medicine is for the sake of health, so also:

οὕτω δ' ἔχει κατὰ τὸ θεωρητικόν. οὐ γὰρ ἐπιτακτικῶς ἄρχων ὁ θεός, ἀλλ' οὗ ἕνεκα ἡ φρόνησις ἐπιτάττει (διττὸν δὲ τὸ οὗ ἕνεκα· διώρισται δ' ἐν ἄλλοις), ἐπεὶ κεῖνός γε οὐθενὸς δεῖται. ἥτις οὖν αἵρεσις καὶ κτῆσις τῶν φύσει ἀγαθῶν ποιήσει μάλιστα

---

[9] See C. J. Rowe, *The Eudemian and Nicomachean Ethics: A Study in the Development of Aristotle's Thought*, Proceedings of the Cambridge Philological Society, Suppl. 3 (Cambridge, 1971) for a sustained, albeit controversial, discussion of the relation between these texts.

[10] Translation from Cooper, *Reason*, 135–6 with minor changes. Greek text from R. R. Walzer and J. M. Mingay (eds.), *Aristotelis Ethica Eudemia* (Oxford, 1991).

τὴν τοῦ θεοῦ θεωρίαν, ἢ σώματος ἢ χρημάτων ἢ φίλων ἢ τῶν ἄλλων ἀγαθῶν, αὕτη ἀρίστη, καὶ οὗτος ὁ ὅρος κάλλιστος· ἥτις δ' ἢ δι' ἔνδειαν ἢ δι' ὑπερβολὴν κωλύει τὸν θεὸν θεραπεύειν καὶ θεωρεῖν, αὕτη δὲ φαύλη.

(*EE* 8. 3, 1249^{a}21–^{b}23)

[T]his holds for the contemplative faculty. For god[11] is not a ruler in the sense of issuing commands (and 'that for the sake of which' has two meanings: these have been distinguished elsewhere), since god is in need of nothing, but he is that for the sake of which[12] practical wisdom issues commands so that whatever choice and possession of things good by nature will most produce the contemplation of god—whether goods of the body or money or friends or the other goods—this is best, and this is the finest principle of determination; but whatever hinders the service of god by contemplation, whether by being deficient or by being excessive, this is bad.

Just as health is the standard for medicine, so also, Aristotle seems to claim here, the standard for practical wisdom is contemplation; just as the doctor should guide her actions with a view to what best promotes the patient's health, so also the person with practical wisdom should direct her actions to what best promotes contemplation.[13]

---

[11] Commentators disagree over what 'the god' refers to here. See M. Woods (ed.), *Aristotle: Eudemian Ethics: Books I, II, and VIII*, 2nd edn (Oxford, 1992), 180 and Cooper, *Reason*, 142 n. 56 for discussion. Settling this question is not important for our purposes: on either interpretation, the sense of the passage is that the activity of contemplation provides the standard for the choice and possession of natural goods.

[12] Here, as elsewhere, Aristotle distinguishes between two senses of 'that for which'. The distinction is typically understood as between 'the purpose for which' and the 'beneficiary for whom'. On this way of interpreting the distinction, it is clear that Aristotle has the latter in mind. For a recent challenge to this standard interpretation of the distinction, see J. Gelber, 'Two Ways of Being for an End', *Phronesis*, 63 (2018), 64–86. Gelber proposes that the distinction picks out, on the one hand, the relation between 'something and the aim or objective it is in the business of producing' and, on the other hand, the relation between an instrument and the user of that instrument. On this version of the distinction, 'Aristotle is denying that the orders *phronēsis* makes are for the sake of god as tools for any use god could put them to' (p. 74). The general sense of the passage is clear enough, and the details are not important to settle for my purposes here. For other passages that appear to draw the same distinction, see *Phys.* 2. 2, 194^{a}35, *DA* 2. 4, 415^{b}2, *Metaph.* Λ. 7, 1072^{b}2.

[13] See e.g. M. Scharle, 'Elemental Teleology in Aristotle's *Physics* 2. 8', *Oxford Studies in Ancient Philosophy*, 34 (2008), 147–83 at 158, for whom practical wisdom is for the sake of the god insofar as the god is identical with theoretical contemplation that is promoted by the commands of practical wisdom. Lear, instead, takes practical wisdom to be for the sake of 'god' insofar as god is the object of approximation of practical wisdom (G. R. Lear, *Happy Lives and the Highest Good: An Essay on Aristotle's Nicomachean Ethics* [*Happy*] (Princeton, 2004), 79).

To be sure, many commentators have hoped to resist reading the *NE* 6. 1 passage in light of what Aristotle says in *EE* 8. 3; instead, commentators argue that the *EE* 8. 3 passage either provides us with a rather different ethical view from what we find in the *NE* or simply addresses a different question from what is at issue in *NE* 6. 1. So, for example, Jaeger interprets the *EE* passage as claiming that 'our most pressing duty is to choose all the occupations and activities and goods that further the knowledge of God'; on this reading, Aristotle defends a version of the 'theonomic ethics' found in late Plato,[14] one that is not found in the *NE*. Cooper and Ackrill, instead, argue that the *EE* 8. 3 does not bear on the question raised in *NE* 6. 1. Ackrill argues that Aristotle is not, in the *EE*, addressing the question of what makes actions good or virtuous; his answer to this question is that these actions are done for their own sake by good men. Instead, Ackrill argues, the *EE* passage addresses the distinct question of how and to what extent we should pursue natural goods.[15] As I'll argue in Section 3, I do not think these are distinct questions: what makes actions virtuous is, in part, the sorts of ends at which they aim, and choosing a virtuous action for its own sake is not inconsistent with choosing it for the sake of the good result or consequence at which it aims. It will be an upshot of the view I defend that the *EE* 8. 3 passage can be read as reflecting the very same ethical view we find in the *NE*.

2.2. *The stakes*

Given the evidence above for thinking that Aristotle conceives of virtuous activity as an instrumental means to contemplation, why have commentators resisted this conclusion? There are two serious problems that seem arise for Aristotle if this is his view.

The first problem is that the view that virtuous actions are instrumentally valuable for the sake of contemplation seems to be at odds with Aristotle's insistence in a number of passages that virtuous actions are ends choiceworthy for their own sakes (see *NE* 10. 6, 1176^{b}6–9; 6. 4, 1140^{a}26). As Gauthier and Jolif wonder, 'on ne voit pas... comment les actions morales, dont c'est la nature d'être à elle-mêmes leur propre fin, pourront ultérieurement être

---

[14] Jaeger, *Aristotle*, 242–3.
[15] Ackrill, 'Eudaimonia', 30–1. See Cooper, *Reason*, 140–2 for a similar line.

ordonnées à autre chose pour former une série hiérarchisée' ('we do not see how virtuous actions whose nature is to be their own end will subsequently be ordered to something else to form a hierarchal ordering'); they call this one of Aristotle's 'incohérences foncières' ('fundamental incoherences'), wondering how 'au lieu d'être sa fin à elle-même, l'action morale devient un moyen de *faire* autre chose qu'elle-même, le bonheur' ('instead of being its own end, virtuous action becomes a means of achieving something other than itself, happiness').[16] The apparent textual inconsistency reflects the deeper philosophical question of what the source of value of virtuous actions is. Are virtuous actions ends choiceworthy for their own sake, or are they choiceworthy because of the more valuable ends—like contemplation—that they instrumentally promote? Otherwise put, is the value of virtuous actions explained by the value of contemplation, or are virtuous actions valuable independently of the way they might promote contemplation?[17] Part of the worry here is that, if virtuous actions are instrumental to something further, this appears to trivialize or undermine the way in which virtuous actions are supposed to be ends in themselves.

We might think that it is easy to dismiss the problem by noticing that goods can be valuable in more than one way. It is, after all, easy enough to imagine cases where a just or generous action might be choiceworthy for its own sake and instrumentally promote contemplation. The challenge, however, is to give a principled explanation for how it is true of the *nature* of virtuous actions that they are valuable in these two different ways. How is it true in some

---

[16] R. A. Gauthier and J. Y. Jolif, *L'Éthique à Nicomaque* (Louvain, 1958), 6–7. Translations are my own.

[17] For some important discussion of the relationship between virtuous actions and their ends, see J. Ackrill, 'Aristotle on Action' ['Action'], *Mind*, 87 (1978), 595–601; D. Charles, *Aristotle's Philosophy of Action* [*Action*] (Cornell, 1986), especially 65–6; R. Heinaman, 'Activity and Praxis in Aristotle' ['Activity'], *Proceedings of the Boston Area Colloquium of Ancient Philosophy*, 12 (1996), 71–111; Keyt, 'Intellectualism (1983)', Lear, *Happy*; id., 'Structure'; and J. Whiting, 'Eudaimonia, External Results, and Choosing Virtuous Actions for Themselves' ['External'], *Philosophy and Phenomenological Research*, 65 (2002), 270–90. A great deal has been written about whether Aristotle's claims in *NE* 10.7–8 are consistent with what has come before. I am not here directly concerned with this controversy, though I think it is a desideratum of a successful account of the relationship between virtuous actions and their ends that it render Aristotle's discussions in *NE* 10.7–8 consistent with the rest of the *NE*. See also n. 10 above.

non-accidental way that just, generous, or courageous actions both are ends in themselves and instrumentally promote contemplation?

The second main challenge for the view that virtuous activity is an instrumental means to contemplation is understanding how such a view captures anything like the common-sense conception of virtue. Aristotle does not appear to be offering a revisionary account of what sorts of actions count as virtuous: the sorts of actions he describes as virtuous—paying one's debts, giving money to worthwhile projects, fighting just wars—line up with ordinary Greek conceptions of morality from the period. But if virtuous actions are the sorts of actions that promote contemplative activity, it is not obvious how actions like paying one's debts or fighting just wars turn out to be virtuous. Some commentators have worried that if contemplation really is the ultimate end of human life, Aristotle's view might license us to perform heinous or intuitively immoral actions for the sake of contemplation; indeed, Aristotle's view might generate the result that these actions are actually virtuous.[18]

It might seem like a possible solution is to appeal to an inclusivist conception of happiness. On this sort of view, famously defended by John Ackrill, various ends are 'for the sake of' happiness not because they instrumentally promote happiness, but because they are constituent parts of happiness. So, for Ackrill, both contemplation and ethically virtuous activity turn out to be 'for the sake of' happiness by being constituents of happiness. In fact, although an inclusivist conception of happiness helps with some of the worries for understanding how virtuous actions can be both ends and for the sake of ends beyond themselves, the view does not help with the deeper question of how to understand the proper relationship between virtuous activity and contemplation. Even if both are constituents of *eudaimonia*, contemplation is supremely more valuable. If virtuous activity is not simply an instrumental means to contemplation, to what extent should we pursue it if we are also able to pursue contemplative activity? Indeed, Ackrill acknowledges this worry in his paper, suggesting that Aristotle simply gives us no satisfying story for how to combine

---

[18] For discussions of this worry, see for example Ackrill, 'Eudaimonia'; Hardie, 'Final'; Cooper, *Reason*, 149–50; Keyt, 'Intellectualism (1983)', 368; G. Lawrence, 'Aristotle and the Ideal Life' ['Ideal'], *Philosophical Review* 102 (1993), 1–34.

virtuous activity and contemplation in a happy life. If Aristotle thinks that we should give absolute priority to contemplation such that we engage in or promote other goods only when contemplation is unavailable to be engaged in or promoted, Aristotle can avoid any potential conflicts between virtuous activity and contemplation. However, he would do so at the expense of a deeply revisionary and implausible ethical theory. If, on the other hand, contemplation is not given absolute priority over ethical virtue—if instead Aristotle intends there to be some compromise between the two in a happy life—it is difficult to see what principled, coherent story is possible for Aristotle about when and how to engage in virtuous activity over contemplation, given the supreme value of contemplation. Ackrill himself is pessimistic, concluding that Aristotle is 'in the company of all philosophers who hold that one element in man is supremely valuable, but are unwilling to embrace the paradoxical and extremist conclusions about life that that view implies'.[19]

Another initially plausible solution is to try to explain how virtuous actions can be 'for the sake of' contemplation at the level of an agent's psychology, in terms of what it means to pursue something as an ultimate end. Meyer, for example, defends a view according to which virtuous actions are 'for the sake of' contemplation insofar as they take place in the 'space of permissions' left open by our ultimate commitment to contemplation.[20] On this view, a life devoted to the pursuit of contemplation may still leave open the pursuit of a wide variety of other goals that are valued and pursued for their own sakes, so long as their pursuit is limited or regulated by the agent's commitment to contemplation. A view like this is useful for understanding how an agent coherently conceives of her ends, but I do not think it fully addresses the prior question of what the objective structure of value is. As I understand Aristotle, the agent with practical wisdom appropriately responds to mind-independent facts about value. To have a fully satisfying account of how virtuous actions are 'for the sake of' contemplation we need not only a description of the agent's psychology, but an explanation for why she is getting things right about the world when she conceives of the role of contemplation as she

---

[19] Ackrill, 'Eudaimonia', 33.

[20] S. S. Meyer, 'Living for the Sake of an Ultimate End', in J. Miller (ed.), *Aristotle's Nicomachean Ethics: A Critical Guide* (Cambridge, 2011), 47–65.

does. It is this question about the objective structure of value that I am interested in here.

2.3. *Two strategies*

There are a lot of moving parts in the debate over the relationship between virtuous actions and contemplation, and I cannot do justice to the diversity and sophistication of views that scholars have proposed. In this section, I want to outline broadly two kinds of strategies that scholars have adopted and identify in general terms the challenges faced by each approach.

I suggested in Section 2.2 that an inclusivist conception of happiness does not immediately resolve the question of how virtuous actions and contemplation are properly related. However many goods are components of happiness, we need to make sense of how to select from these goods, given the superior value of contemplation. Rather than carving the debate along inclusivist versus intellectualist lines, I want to suggest that a more helpful division is between those views that are pluralist about value and those that are monist about value. Pluralist views assert that, for Aristotle, there is a range of human goods, including virtuous actions, that are valuable independently of any relation they bear to contemplation. Monist views, by contrast, assert that the value of all other human goods, including virtuous actions, is ultimately explained by some relation those goods bear to contemplation.

Consider, first, pluralist approaches. As we saw in Section 2.2 in the discussion of Ackrill's view, Aristotle's picture looks either unsatisfying or implausible if his view is that virtuous actions and contemplation are valuable in distinct ways, contemplation is immeasurably more valuable than virtuous actions, and there is nothing further to be said about when or whether to choose virtuous actions if they conflict with the pursuit of contemplation. Defenders of a pluralist approach have hoped to find ways to explain how our pursuit of contemplation should be regulated or constrained to avoid implausible scenarios in which we are permitted to act in unethical ways in order to maximize our own contemplation.

Keyt, following Cooper, defends what he calls a 'superstructure' view.[21] The superstructure view says that theoretical activity is the

---

[21] D. Keyt, 'Intellectualism in Aristotle', *Society for Ancient Greek Philosophy Newsletter*, 87 (1978), 1–20.

primary component of the best life, and that moral activity is a secondary component. Keyt's idea is that the moral life sets certain minimal requirements that must be satisfied before one is free to engage in theoretical activity. It may be sometimes permissible to shirk a trivial duty in order to contemplate, but it is not permissible to do any action, however base, to maximize contemplation. Keyt suggests it is up to the man of practical wisdom to determine what to prioritize in cases where there is a potential conflict between virtue and contemplation.

I'm sympathetic to Keyt's picture, and indeed the view I will propose bears some resemblance to his. As it stands, however, Keyt's picture does not help explain the passages from *NE* 6. 1 and *EE* 8. 3 where Aristotle suggests that virtuous actions are in some sense for the sake of contemplation. On Keyt's picture, there is simply no relationship between what makes virtuous actions good and what makes contemplation good.

Kraut defends a somewhat different pluralist view on which contemplation sets a limit on our pursuit of other goods, including virtue. Kraut supports an intellectualist reading of *eudaimonia* according to which the ultimate aim of human life for Aristotle is to use reason well, and this goal can be accomplished in two ways: ideally, by living a contemplative life and, if that option is unavailable, then by developing and exercising the practical virtues in the political arena.[22] For Kraut, contemplation serves as the ultimate aim of human life by being a way of organizing these subordinate ends into a coherent system: contemplation sets the limit for our pursuit of these other lower goods. So, although, like Keyt, Kraut understands Aristotle as recognizing a variety of goods that are valuable independently of their contribution to contemplation, Kraut is able to capture the idea that all goods other than contemplation are choiceworthy, at least in part, for the sake of contemplation, by instrumentally promoting contemplation.

On the face of it, Kraut's view seems poised to respond to both of the challenges we saw in Section 2. On Kraut's view, virtuous actions are ends, but they are also for the sake of contemplation both by instrumentally promoting contemplation and because contemplation regulates or guides our pursuit of these actions. Kraut's view seems to capture both the pluralism of Aristotle's theory and

[22] Kraut, *Human Good*, 7.

the role contemplation plays in structuring and guiding our ends. On his view, although the best life for an individual is one with the most contemplation possible, we are not, on Kraut's interpretation, licensed to perform heinous actions for the sake of maximizing our own happiness; Kraut rejects an egoistic form of eudaemonism.

I think there is much to like about Kraut's view, but it is ultimately unsatisfying. A central worry for his view is how to make sense of the way contemplation is supposed to regulate our pursuit of other intrinsically valuable goods. Again, on Kraut's view, goods like virtuous actions are choiceworthy both in themselves— independently of the way they promote contemplation—and as instrumentally valuable for contemplation. Kraut is not an egoistic eudaemonist—he does not think that we are rationally justified in performing actions only to the extent that they promote our own contemplation. But, once we reject an egoistic form of eudaemonism, it is unclear why we should accept that the virtuous agent should in general pursue virtuous actions only to the extent they instrumentally promote contemplation.[23] Kraut argues that the person whose life is devoted to contemplation will still have prudential reasons to perform virtuous actions insofar as being virtuous is generally conducive to contemplation. And, indeed, the fact that virtuous actions can promote our contemplation explains why we have *some* reason to perform virtuous actions if we want to be happy. But it seems plausible that many—indeed the best—virtuous actions take away from our ability to engage in contemplation. Moreover, as Kraut himself acknowledges, it might be that sometimes the action that would best promote contemplation is a vicious one.[24] Kraut suggests that such cases of conflict between what would promote one's own happiness and what virtue demands will be rare. This seems to me overoptimistic. It is a contingent matter, on Kraut's picture, whether virtuous actions will, in fact, promote contemplation, and it is easy enough to imagine cases where they will not. Kraut's view

---

[23] T. H. Irwin, 'The Structure of Aristotelian Happiness' ['Structure'], *Ethics*, 101 (1991), 382–91.

[24] As Kraut argues, 'I do take him to be assuming that *for the most part* unjust actions become known to others, and that when this is taken into account it will be more in a philosopher's interest to have the virtue of justice rather than the vice of injustice' (Kraut, *Human Good*, 181). This strikes me as a highly defeasible reason for the philosopher to be just.

is, as such, ultimately unable to respond to the second challenge we saw in Section 2; it leaves open the possibility that the life devoted to contemplation will turn out to be a deeply unethical one.[25]

The problem that Kraut's view faces for capturing the commonly held views about virtuous actions arises from the way he responds to the first challenge, how to make sense of how virtuous actions are both ends and for the sake of ends beyond themselves. Kraut's strategy is to identify two apparently unrelated sources of value for virtuous actions: virtuous actions have what we might now think of as a kind of intrinsic moral value, and they have instrumental or prudential value for the agent insofar as having the virtues of character helps an agent contemplate. The deeper problem for Kraut's view is just the familiar problem of reconciling prudential and moral reasons, a problem that arises because of his rejection of eudaemonism; on his view, there is no one ultimate rational aim that is meant to accommodate all our ethical concerns.

Consider now monist strategies. Gabriel Richardson Lear defends a picture on which the value of all other goods in the ethical domain is ultimately explained by the value of contemplation. Her view is meant to explain how we get the sort of structure of value described in *NE* 1. 2 and 1. 7, where there is a hierarchy of ends, with one good, happiness, at the top. Lear argues that the way in which other goods are 'for the sake of' the highest good is not instrumental, but rather a relation of teleological approximation. Roughly, her idea is that when a virtuous agent performs a virtuous action, she aims at grasping practical truth and so in a way aims at contemplation insofar as theoretical truthfulness sets the standard of success for practical truthfulness.[26] Specifically, Lear thinks that virtuous actions express an agent's understanding of her own highest good as lying in contemplation. But by choosing virtuous actions for the sake of contemplation, the virtuous agent is also in a way choosing virtuous actions for their own sake because of the way that they approximate and therefore inherit the intrinsic value from contemplation. So, to take an example, when a virtuous agent

---

[25] The conclusion that the philosophical life is a deeply unethical one has struck most commentators as an untenable position for Aristotle to have held, though it is conceptually possible and not, as far as I can tell, strictly ruled out by anything in the text. However, I assume here that it is philosophically and interpretively unattractive to attribute this view to Aristotle if there is a viable alternative.

[26] See Lear, *Happy*, 4–5.

performs a courageous action, she expresses her concern for the excellent use of reason in leisure, and this orientation towards the excellent and leisurely use of reason is what makes her virtuous actions fine. And because the most excellent and leisurely use of reason is contemplation, the virtuous person's sense of the fine is implicitly guided by the value of contemplation.

Despite its virtues, I worry that Lear's account offers an implausible explanation of the source of value of virtuous actions. As Lear says:

courageous actions are fine because, in being ordered, proportioned, and bounded just as they are, they make clear the agent's commitment to the human good, which he conceives as the excellent, rational use of a peaceful, political life. The appropriateness of his actions to a person committed to the excellent rational use of a leisurely citizen's life is what makes them fine.[27]

Here, Lear relies on the way in which virtuous actions aim at the noble, and the *kalon* seems to track what is noble where this is understood as being opposed to what is necessary.

Even if Lear's story works for courage, it seems less plausible in the case of other virtues. Take generosity. Lear's view suggests that generous actions are fine because they express the virtuous agent's commitment to the excellent and leisurely use of reason. But how does giving wealth away express this commitment? After all, wealth is valuable for an agent precisely because it provides for leisure. Lear's view would make sense if she had a non-egoistic picture like Kraut's, where virtuous actions are valuable in part because they promote the happiness of others. But given her embrace of eudaemonism, it is difficult to see how an agent's giving wealth away could express her appreciation of her *own* leisurely use of reason.[28]

---

[27] Lear, *Happy*, 149.

[28] For a view that shares some similarities with Lear's, see D. Charles, 'Aristotle on Well-Being and Intellectual Contemplation', *Aristotelian Society*, Suppl. 73 (1999), 205–23; and id., 'Eudaimonia, Theoria, and the Choiceworthiness of Practical Wisdom', in P. Destrée and M. Zingano (eds.), *Theoria: Studies on the Status and Meaning of Contemplation in Aristotle's Ethics* (Leuven, 2014), 89–109. Charles, however, argues that these other goods are ends because of the way they resemble the 'focal' good of contemplation. In explaining the value of these goods by the resemblance they bear to contemplation, Charles' view is similar to Lear's and, I think, inherits some of the same problems.

Tuozzo defends a somewhat different monist picture.[29] Tuozzo argues that virtuous actions have a nature and worth that is, in part, dependent on their relation to contemplation. On his picture, choosing a virtuous action for its own sake involves choosing it because of its relation to contemplation. So far, this is much like Lear's view. However, for Tuozzo, virtuous actions are related to contemplation not by a relation of teleological approximation, but instead by a kind of instrumental relation. For Tuozzo, virtuous actions are those actions that best promote the internal psychic conditions necessary for contemplation. In this way, contemplation serves as an indirect standard for virtuous actions. So, for example, self-indulgence is the state in which a person values bodily pleasures more than they are worth, and the self-indulgent person is driven to endlessly pursue these bodily pleasures. The virtue of temperance allows an agent to be freed from the pain of unsatisfied desire and so to direct her attention to loftier pursuits, and to contemplation in particular.

I find unpersuasive the suggestion that the *way* virtuous actions instrumentally promote contemplation is by furnishing us with certain psychic states. It is difficult to evaluate Tuozzo's proposal fully in the absence of more discussion of the particular virtues. Certainly, many vices will involve psychic states that detract from an agent's ability to contemplate. And certainly, particular virtues, like temperance, are likely to create psychic conditions conducive to contemplation. But it is less obvious how the worth of other paradigmatic virtues is explained in this way. Virtues like courage, justice, and generosity do not seem to have as their principal function creating psychic leisure. Indeed, they are virtues that, insofar as they aim to achieve external ends, seem involve a lack of leisure. In many cases, the exercise of these virtues appears to be in tension with our ability to contemplate.

To be clear, I do not take myself to have offered decisive reasons for rejecting any of the above interpretations. Instead, what I have hoped to do is show how the question of the relationship between virtuous actions and contemplation illuminates a broader philosophical question for Aristotle: how to understand the structure of value in his ethical theory. The challenge for understanding his axiology can be thought of as a kind of dilemma. On one horn,

---

[29] T. Tuozzo (1995), 'Contemplation, the Noble, and the Mean: The Standard of Moral Virtue in Aristotle's *Ethics*', *Apeiron*, 28 (1995), 129–54.

Aristotle is a pluralist about value: there is a range of goods—including virtuous actions—that are choiceworthy for their own sakes, independently of the way they are related to contemplation. The worry for this cluster of views is how to explain how there exists a hierarchy of ends with contemplation at the top: how is it that the goods that are choiceworthy independently of the way they are related to contemplation are also reliably choiceworthy for the sake of contemplation? On the other horn, Aristotle is a monist about value: the value of all goods, including virtuous actions, is reducible to or explained by the value of contemplation. On this horn, what *makes* an action good or virtuous is, at least in part, the way it is appropriately related to contemplation. The worry for this cluster of views is how to capture the reputable opinions about virtue: paradigmatically courageous, just, and generous actions are not obviously good or choiceworthy because of the way they are related to contemplative activity.

3. A diagnosis

3.1. *Virtuous actions and their ends*

In Section 2, I identified two apparent challenges for the view that virtuous actions are an instrumental means to contemplation. The first challenge is to make sense of how virtuous actions can be instrumental to contemplation if they are also supposed to be ends and chosen for their own sakes. The second challenge is to square this account of virtuous actions with common-sense opinions about virtue: it isn't obvious how just, generous, or courageous actions are ultimately a means for us to promote our own contemplative activity. In this section, I want to focus on the first challenge. Once we avail ourselves of some of the available resources for addressing this challenge, we will be in a position to address the second challenge.

The question of how to square a virtuous action's being instrumental to contemplation with its being an end and chosen for its own sake is of a piece with a broader question that has itself received much attention from scholars.[30] In some passages, Aristotle

[30] For some important discussion of the relationship between virtuous actions and their ends, see Ackrill, 'Action'; Charles, *Action*, esp. 65–6; Heinaman, 'Activity'; Lear, *Happy*; id., 'Structure'; and Whiting, 'External'.

appears to characterize virtuous actions as ends (see *NE* 10. 6, 1176^{b}6–9; 6. 4, 1140^{a}26–^{b}7). In other passages, he characterizes them as being for the sake of ends beyond themselves (see *NE* 10. 7, 1177^{b}1–4, 16–20). This apparent tension in the way Aristotle describes virtuous actions reflects what appears to be a deeper tension in his ethical theory. On the one hand, Aristotle wants to maintain, for much of the *NE*, that ethically virtuous activity is one of the components of happiness. For this to be true, ethically virtuous activity must be an end or choiceworthy for itself. On the other hand, Aristotle seems to characterize virtuous actions in part in terms of the good external results at which they aim; what makes virtuous actions worth performing seems to be in part that they make some positive difference to the world. If Aristotle wants to maintain that virtuous actions are both ends and for the sake of ends beyond themselves, we need a principled explanation for how this can be the case. More strongly, we need an explanation that holds in virtue of the nature of virtuous actions.

In the face of these worries, a number of scholars have proposed solutions that rely on a distinction between what we might think of as the internal end and the external end of an agent's performing a virtuous action.[31] So the strategy goes, virtuous actions are worthwhile in part for their own sake and in part because they bring about, or aim to bring about, good results or consequences in the world. On this type of view, in passages where Aristotle talks about virtuous actions as having ends outside themselves, he is referring to the external end of the action. In passages where he describes performing a virtuous action as an end, he is referring to the internal end. This sort of strategy is not only helpful for resolving the apparent textual inconsistencies in how Aristotle describes virtuous actions; it is also helpful for seeing how Aristotle's ethical theory is not

---

[31] See S. Hirji, 'Acting Virtuously as an End in Aristotle's *Nicomachean Ethics*', *British Journal of the History of Philosophy*, 26 (2018), 1006–26 for the distinction between virtuous actions and acting virtuously. See Keyt, 'Intellectualism (1978)', 14–15 for the distinction between the internal and external end of an action. Whiting offers an extended discussion of how virtuous actions can be ends and also aim at an external result ('External'). For a distinction between virtuous actions and acting virtuously similar to the one I prefer, see M. Jimenez, 'Aristotle on Becoming Virtuous by Doing Virtuous Actions', *Phronesis*, 61 (2016), 3–32 at 4, 15–18, 21–2. See also S. S. Meyer, 'Aristotle on Moral Motivation', in I. Vasiliou (ed.), *Moral Motivation: A History* (Oxford, 2016), 44–64 for a similar distinction between virtuous actions and virtuous agency, or acting virtuously.

objectionably egoistic. Even though virtuous actions are ends and promote an agent's own happiness, their worth is not reducible to the way they promote an agent's own happiness. Instead, they also often promote external results that benefit the political community more generally, such as security or an even distribution of wealth.

On the interpretation I prefer, Aristotle distinguishes between what we might think of as 'virtuous actions' and 'acting virtuously'. In passages like *NE* 10.7, when Aristotle seems to claim that virtuous actions are not ends but rather are for the sake of actions beyond themselves, Aristotle is referring to the particular political or military actions analogous to the just or temperate actions in *NE* 2. 4 and 6. 12 that can be performed even by a non-virtuous agent and that count as virtuous because of certain features of the actions themselves. As scholars such as Whiting have also argued,[32] these actions count as virtuous because of the good ends they aim to realize: this the sense in which they are choiceworthy for the sake of ends beyond themselves. In these passages, Aristotle is expressing the intuitive idea that what makes an action appropriate or called for in a given circumstance is something about the goodness of the end it aims to achieve.[33] That is, in these passages, he is referring to the *virtuous actions* themselves, which have an external end. Notice that, on this sort of picture, the way that an action is 'for the sake of' an end is not explained by the fact that it is the agent's goal or intention in the action. It is in this way that an action can be virtuous—because of the kind of end it aims at—even if it is not performed from virtuous motives.[34]

---

[32] Whiting, 'External'.

[33] For discussion of the doctrine of the mean, see L. Brown, 'What Is "the Mean Relative to Us" in Aristotle's Ethics?', *Phronesis*, 42 (1997), 77–93, and ead., 'Why Is Aristotle's Virtue of Character a Mean? Taking Aristotle at His Word', in R. Polansky (ed.), *The Cambridge Companion to Aristotle's Nicomachean Ethics* (Cambridge, 2014), 64–80; H. J. Curzer, 'A Defense of Aristotle's Doctrine that Virtue Is a Mean', *Ancient Philosophy*, 16 (1996), 129–38; W. F. R. Hardie, 'Aristotle's Doctrine That Virtue Is a Mean', *Proceedings of the Aristotelian Society*, 65 (1964), 183–204; and S. Leighton, 'The Mean Relative to Us', *Apeiron*, 28 (1995), 67–78. For discussion of the way that virtuous actions are for the sake of the noble, see T. H. Irwin, 'Aristotle's Conception of Morality ['Conception']', *Proceedings of the Boston Area Colloquium in Ancient Philosophy*, 1 (1985), 115–43; Lear, *Happy*; and K. Rogers, 'Aristotle's Conception of Τὸ Καλόν' ['Τὸ Καλόν'], *Ancient Philosophy*, 13 (1993), 355–71.

[34] That being said, when a virtuous agent performs a virtuous action, they should aim at the features that make the action good. This means that their goal or intention should line up with the end of the action, at least at some level of description

Compare this with the *NE* 10. 6 (1176ᵇ6–9) passage where Aristotle seems to claim that virtuous actions are ends. Here, Aristotle argues that 'the actions on the basis of virtue' (αἱ κατ' ἀρετὴν πράξεις) appear to be the sorts of things from which nothing beyond the activity is sought, explaining that 'doing fine and good actions' (τὰ καλὰ καὶ σπουδαῖα πράττειν) is choiceworthy for its own sake. Both of these formulations—the κατά followed by accusative and the infinitive phrase—are plausibly picking out the *acting* rather than the action, which is to say, the activity that is the exercise of virtue, rather than the particular fine or good action that is successfully realized.[35] Likewise, in the *NE* 6. 5 (1140ᵇ4–7) passage where Aristotle contrasts a πρᾶξις ('action') with a ποίησις ('production'), his explanation for why a πρᾶξις has no further end beyond itself is that εὐπραξία ('acting well') is an end. Here again, plausibly, Aristotle has in mind by εὐπραξία the acting rather than the action; we can read εὐπραξία as equivalent to the other adverbial phrases that pick out *acting virtuously*, rather than a virtuous action: this acting well or 'acting virtuously' has an internal end.

On this view, there is a qualified way in which virtuous actions are both ends and for the sake of ends beyond themselves. Specifically, virtuous actions are for the sake of ends beyond themselves because what makes them good or choiceworthy, what makes them the kinds of actions they are, is the external ends they aim to realize. 'Acting virtuously' is an end because it is an excellent accomplishment of the human function: it is the full expression of practical wisdom and character virtue working in harmony. In some passages, Aristotle is focusing on the value of the particular actions themselves, and in other passages he is focusing on the value of the *acting*.

(the agent need not, I think, have a fully articulable appreciation of exactly why the action type in question is good or virtuous; it is enough, I imagine, that they have some sense of what the end is and why it is worthwhile).

[35] My suggestion here is that the phrase αἱ κατ' ἀρετὴν πράξεις picks out not just actions that conform to what virtue demands, but actions that are the exercise of one's virtuous character; if this is right, then these actions are instances of 'acting virtuously'. See Irwin, 'Structure', 390–1 for a discussion of different readings of the *kata* + accusative phrase in Aristotle. See Kraut, *Human Good* and Lawrence, 'Ideal' for defences of the view that an activity can be κατά some virtue only if it is the exercise of that virtue. I do not mean to endorse this stronger claim here; it is enough for my purposes that we can read the κατά locution this way and that the context of the passage invites us to do so here.

Again, the exact details are not important for the purposes of this paper. Here is what matters. First, there is a sense in which, when a virtuous agent performs a virtuous action, she does something that is both an end and for the sake of some end beyond the action itself. Second, the value of her acting depends on the value of her action, which in turn depends on the value of the external end at which the action aims. But again, this is not to say that the value of her acting is in any way *reducible* to the value of her action. Third, the explanation for what makes a virtuous action good is not an egoistic one; although in performing a just action the virtuous agent promotes her own happiness, the just action itself is good because it benefits the political community more generally.

3.2. *Contemplation and the* kalon

On the view I have defended so far, virtuous actions are good because they promote good external ends, and when a virtuous agent performs a virtuous action, she engages in the excellent practically rational activity partly constitutive of her own happiness. Notice that on this picture, insofar as virtuous actions aim at ends beyond themselves, virtuous actions are *always* a means to other, more valuable goods: a just action is good because of the good external results it aims to realize. Contemplation is one of the goods achievable in action; indeed, it is the very best good achievable in action. There is, then, a straightforward way in which virtuous actions might be a means to contemplation.

This, however, is not strong enough to capture what we are after. Again, Aristotle conceives of the structure of value as a hierarchical ordering with contemplation at the top of a chain of ends; all goods other than contemplation are choiceworthy at least in part for the sake of contemplation. What we need to explain is not simply how virtue is *sometimes* an instrumental means to contemplation, but how it is *always* instrumentally for the sake of contemplation. I've argued that virtuous actions aim to bring about a variety of goods or states of affairs: health, security, a just distribution of wealth, and so on. The question, then, is how, in bringing about these ends, virtuous actions also instrumentally promote contemplation.

Here is what I want to suggest. Virtuous actions are instrumentally for the sake of contemplation because, by bringing about other valuable goods in the ethical domain, they bring about the conditions under which contemplation is possible. Specifically, virtuous actions aim ultimately to bring about conditions of peace, leisure, and freedom from necessity, and these are precisely the conditions under which we are free to engage in contemplation, an activity that has no practical benefit beyond itself.

Why think virtuous actions necessarily aim to bring about the conditions under which contemplation is possible? Some evidence comes from Aristotle's discussion of the noble. Aristotle makes clear throughout his ethical works that when the virtuous agent performs a virtuous action, she acts 'for the sake of' the καλόν or noble (see *NE* 1115^{b}11–13, 23–4, 1120^{a}23–4, 1122^{b}6–7, 1116^{b}30–1, 1168^{a}33, *EE* 1216^{a}25–6, 1229^{a}4). There is no consensus amongst scholars about how exactly to understand the concept of the noble in Aristotle's works.[36] It is clearly related to the way in which virtuous actions are chosen for their own sake and the way in which they are good. Moreover, the noble seems to be related to notions of proper arrangement and fittingness (*Top.* 5. 6, 135^{a}13–14, *NE* 2. 9, 1109^{a}26–9).

The noble also seems to be strongly associated with freedom from necessity, and this is the aspect of the noble relevant for our purposes. In the *Rhetoric*, Aristotle explains that 'the noble is whatever is praiseworthy, being choiceworthy for its own sake, or whatever, being good, is pleasant because it is good' (καλὸν μὲν οὖν ἐστιν ὃ ἂν δι' αὑτὸ αἱρετὸν ὂν ἐπαινετὸν ᾖ, ἢ ὃ ἂν ἀγαθὸν ὂν ἡδὺ ᾖ, ὅτι ἀγαθόν, *Rhet.* 1. 9, 1366^{a}33–4).[37] He goes on to describe various virtues of character, claiming that actions are more noble where the reward is honour rather than money, or where the action is chosen for someone else's sake and not to further an individual's own interests (1366^{b}34–1367^{a}17). Victory and honour, Aristotle explains, are noble because they are desirable despite not yielding anything beyond themselves. Similarly, in the *Rhetoric*, Aristotle contrasts the useful with the noble, arguing that the 'useful is what is good for oneself, and the noble is what is good absolutely' (τὸ μὲν γὰρ συμφέρον αὐτῷ ἀγαθόν ἐστι, τὸ δὲ καλὸν ἁπλῶς, *Rhet.* 2. 13, 1389^{b}37–1390^{a}1).

---

[36] See e.g. Irwin, 'Conception'; Lear, *Happy*; Rogers, 'Τὸ Καλόν'.

[37] Here I translate both αἱρετὸν and ἐπαινετὸν normatively rather than indicatively: the idea, I take it, is that whatever is noble wouldn't be noble simply if it was praised or chosen for its own sake when it was not *in fact* praiseworthy or choiceworthy for its own sake.

In all these cases, the noble is contrasted with what is necessary or useful; what is noble need not have some immediate practical benefit to the agent herself.

Aristotle associates the noble with freedom from necessity again in *NE* 10. 6, 1176^{b}2–7, where he draws a contrast between actions that are chosen for the sake of other things and 'necessary' and activities that are chosen for their own sake, explaining that doing noble and excellent actions is one of the things choiceworthy for its own sake. Moreover, he connects a good's being noble and desirable for its own sake to the idea of self-sufficiency, one of the features of happiness.

More evidence of the association of the noble with freedom from necessity comes from *Pol.* 7. 13, 1332^{a}7–28. Here, Aristotle distinguishes between what he calls the 'conditional' and the 'unqualified' exercise of virtue. He illustrates the distinction with two kinds of actions that are both 'from virtue': on the one hand, there are actions that are necessary, while, on the other hand, there are actions that aim at honours and advantage. The former actions are noble merely 'in a necessary way', since it would be more choiceworthy if these actions weren't needed, whereas the latter actions are unqualifiedly noble. Aristotle goes on to explain that the former actions destroy bad things, while the latter supply and are productive of good things. If one puts this all together, the distinction between the complete and conditional exercise of virtue is as follows: the former involves actions that are most noble and unqualifiedly so, and supply and produce good things, whereas the latter involves actions that are necessary, and the nobility they have is 'of necessity'; they are actions that destroy bad things. The best virtuous actions are preparatory and productive of good things, and in *Pol.* 7. 14, 1333^{a}30–7, Aristotle suggests these good things are ultimately peace and leisure.

So far, I have been suggesting that one important aspect of the noble is its association with freedom from necessity, and in particular conditions of peace and leisure. To the extent that virtuous actions aim at the noble, they aim at such conditions where possible. This picture is, I think, borne out by Aristotle's discussion of particular virtues. Consider courage, one of the virtues most clearly associated with the noble. Aristotle tells us that courage is displayed in determining which dangers are most fine to withstand, and that the courageous person acts for the sake of the fine (*NE*

1115ᵇ12, 20–4, 1116ᵃ11, 15, 1116ᵇ3, 31). Aristotle insists that many of the situations that inspire fear do not involve exercises of courage, because the actions in these situations are not chosen for the sake of the fine (see *NE* 1116ᵇ2–3, 22, 1117ᵃ7–8, 15–17). So, for example, actions that we choose under compulsion or to avoid something shameful are not courageous. Likewise, exhibiting the appropriate response to disease or the threat of death at sea falls short of being courageous, because death in these circumstances is not fine (see *NE* 1115ᵃ17–19, 1115ᵇ4–6). Instead, courage is best expressed in situations like war, where an individual faces the greatest and noblest dangers. What makes war different from these other circumstances appears to be the sort of end available to a virtuous agent: in war, a courageous agent is able to act for the sake of victory and the security of her political community.[38] As Aristotle repeatedly tells us, the proper end of war and courageous action is peace (*Pol.* 7. 14, 1333ᵃ30–ᵇ3, 1334ᵃ14–16; *NE* 10. 7, 1177ᵇ4–12).

Return now to the question of how virtuous actions are instrumentally for the sake of contemplation. Here is what I propose: insofar as virtuous actions aim at peace and leisure, they aim at the conditions under which contemplation is possible. Aristotle makes clear that peace is valuable for the sake of leisure (*Pol.* 7. 14, 1334ᵃ14–16; *NE* 10. 7, 1177ᵇ4–6) and that the political community makes possible the pursuit of leisure activities (*Pol.* 7. 14, 1333ᵃ35–6, 1334ᵃ4–5; 7.15 1334ᵃ14–16).[39] However, Aristotle insists, leisure is valuable only if it can be used well (*Pol.* 7. 15, 1334ᵃ36–40).[40] So, for example, in *NE* 10. 6, Aristotle argues that pleasant amusements and relaxation are for the sake of activity, and in particular the activities in accordance with virtue that constitute happiness. Of these activities, Aristotle goes on to say, the best is contemplation. In *Metaph.* A, Aristotle makes clear that philosophy is made possible only because of the conditions of leisure afforded by a well-functioning political community, insisting that 'philosophy only began to be sought when almost all the necessities of life and the things that make for comfort and recreation were present', since 'we do not seek it for the sake of any advantage', but rather

---

[38] See Lear, *Happy*, 153.
[39] See Lear, *Happy*, 159.
[40] Here I follow Lear's discussion closely, esp. at *Happy*, 159–61.

'we pursue this as the only free science, for it alone exists for itself', (*Metaph.* A. 2, 982^{b}22–8).

It should be no surprise that leisure is required for contemplation. After all, contemplation aims at nothing beyond itself; it has no practical benefit beyond the activity itself.[41] That is, when we are living under conditions of serious physical insecurity or material scarcity, we do not have the freedom to engage in an activity that cannot improve these conditions.[42] This is another way to put the point that Aristotle makes in *NE* 10. 8, 1178^{b}8–18, that it would be absurd to think that the gods engage in virtuous actions, since they do not have a material existence and so have no need of virtuous actions.

4. How virtuous actions are for the sake of contemplation

4.1. *Monism and pluralism*

I suggested in Section 2 that there were two worries for interpreting Aristotle as saying that virtuous actions are instrumentally a means to contemplation. The first challenge was to explain how this does not undermine the way in which acting virtuously is also an end and something chosen for its own sake. We wanted some principled explanation of how it can be true of the nature of virtuous actions both that they are valuable in themselves and that they instrumentally promote contemplative activity. The second challenge was how to capture common-sense views about which sorts of actions are ethically virtuous. The actions that Aristotle treats as paradigmatically virtuous—just, generous, courageous actions—do

---

[41] Though see Walker, *Uses* for a defence of the view that, despite Aristotle's apparent insistence to the contrary, contemplation does, in fact, have practical benefits for humans.

[42] Aristotle's position becomes even more attractive and plausible if we are expansive about what counts as contemplative activity. We might think that virtuous actions promote conditions under which some kind of contemplative activity is possible, even if it is not contemplation in the strict sense of being an exercise of wisdom. So for example, we might include as activities that have a contemplative dimension things like going to the theatre, enjoying literature and music, or appreciating art. I have hoped to show the plausibility of Aristotle's view even on a strict interpretation of contemplation, but I am sympathetic to the idea that other intellectual activities we do in leisure might share some of the value of contemplation. I am grateful to an anonymous referee for making this suggestion.

not obviously seem to be the actions best suited to promoting contemplative activity.

To address the first worry, I pointed to a qualified way in which a virtuous action can be both an end and for the sake of an end beyond itself. Virtuous actions are good because of the good ends they aim to achieve, but when a virtuous agent performs a virtuous action, she also fully expresses her practically rational nature, and this activity is itself an end. The value of her acting depends on, but is not reducible to, the value of the end of her action. To address the second worry, I argued that the good ends at which virtuous actions aim—ends like security, health, equal distributions of goods—are ends that make possible the conditions under which we are free from necessity, and these are precisely the conditions under which contemplative activity is possible. So, insofar as virtuous actions aim at the conditions under which contemplation is possible, virtuous actions are instrumentally for the sake of contemplation.[43]

The view I have defended shares important elements with both the pluralist and monist approaches. Ultimately, it is a pluralist view: the value of all goods in the ethical domain is not reducible to the value of contemplative activity. Again, I distinguished between 'virtuous actions' and 'acting virtuously' and argued that what makes 'acting virtuously' an end and choiceworthy for its own sake is not that it promotes contemplative activity, but that it is the full expression of our practically rational nature. Its value depends on, but is not reducible to, the value of virtuous actions, and the value of virtuous actions is in turn explained in terms of what promotes contemplation. What this means is that although the exercise of virtue is valuable independently of the way it promotes

---

[43] What about actions that fall between bringing about the conditions necessary for contemplation (peace, leisure, and so on) and contemplation itself? For example, what about teaching in conditions of peace and leisure in a way that equips students to contemplate? Would this count as a virtuous action, even though it does not bring about conditions of peace and leisure? I think it is plausible that there are actions that don't bring about the conditions of peace and leisure, but still promote contemplation in some more general sense, and as such are 'for the sake of' contemplation. However, there will also be actions that are instrumental to contemplation that do not count as virtuous actions (teaching might be an example of such). Not every action that is 'for the sake of' contemplation will be virtuous, even if every virtuous action will, in some way, be 'for the sake of' contemplation. I am grateful to Rachana Kamtekar for encouraging me to clarify this.

contemplation, there is also a non-contingent way in which it *does* instrumentally promote contemplation, because virtuous actions are the sorts of actions that instrumentally promote contemplation. In this way the view shares important similarities with a monist picture: the exercise of virtue and the ends that virtuous actions aim to achieve—health, peace, leisure, and so on—all help to bring about the conditions under which contemplation is possible. If something like this account is right, Aristotle has a remarkably sophisticated axiology, one that shows the possibility of having a plurality of independently valuable goods that are still hierarchically ordered under some one most valuable good.

It will be helpful with a view to clarifying the details of my account to contrast it with some of the accounts I considered in Section 2.3. Consider first how it compares with the sort of pluralist view defended by Kraut. Again, on Kraut's picture there are a variety of intrinsically valuable goods in the ethical domain, but contemplation sets a limit on our pursuit of other goods, including virtue. So, on Kraut's view, virtue is choiceworthy for the sake of contemplation because it instrumentally promotes contemplation, and our pursuit of it is regulated by contemplation. That being said, Kraut thinks there are clearly instances where we ought to sacrifice some measure of our happiness in the form of contemplation for the sake of virtue. I suggested that Kraut's view doesn't give us a principled story for why virtuous actions aimed at the good of the *polis* also reliably promote our own contemplation. The possibility of conflict between the actions that benefit the *polis* and the actions that best promote an agent's own contemplation seems to be much more expansive than Kraut acknowledges.

Like Kraut, I think there is a non-egoistic explanation for the goodness of virtuous actions. On my view, we should understand virtuous actions in terms of the good ends they aim to bring about in a political community. However, unlike Kraut, on my view, the way that virtuous actions benefit a political community is also the way in which virtuous actions are instrumentally for the sake of contemplation; by bringing about conditions of peace and leisure, virtuous actions allow for the conditions under which contemplative activity is possible. What this means is that it is not merely a contingent matter, as on Kraut's view, that just, generous, or courageous actions instrumentally promote contemplation. The mistake that scholars like Kraut have made is to assume that the way virtuous actions are other-directed or benefit the political community cannot be the same as the way in which they instrumentally promote contemplation.

Now compare my account with the monist views we saw in Section 2.3. On Lear's view, goods other than contemplation are 'for the sake of' contemplation by being teleological approximations of contemplation. On Tuozzo's view, virtuous actions are 'for the sake of' contemplation because they instrumentally promote contemplation by providing the kinds of psychic states necessary for contemplation. The worry I raised for both views is that they are ill-positioned to explain how many paradigmatic instances of virtuous action are for the sake of contemplation in the ways they describe. Like Lear and Tuozzo, I locate the way that virtuous actions are for the sake of contemplation in the way they are for the sake of the noble, and I understand the noble as being closely related to conditions of peace and leisure. However, unlike both, I offer what I take to be a more straightforward explanation of how virtuous actions, by being for the sake of the noble, are for the sake of contemplation: they bring about the conditions necessary for contemplative activity. This more straightforward reading is unavailable to both Lear and Tuozzo because they assume the way that the exercise of virtue benefits the agent herself is by promoting her own contemplation. On my view, because of the distinction between virtuous actions and acting virtuously, we need not assume this. Instead, the external ends of virtuous actions are the conditions under which contemplation is possible more generally in a political community. And in performing the actions that bring about these conditions, the virtuous agent fully expresses her practical rationality and so accomplishes an aspect of the human function.

4.2. *Objections*

The view I have defended here is, by necessity, exploratory: I have hoped to offer the strongest possible case for something like a face value reading of the way that virtuous activity is for the sake of contemplation. I want to close by considering three possible worries for my account. First, we might question whether the relation I have identified between virtuous actions and contemplation is, in fact, an instrumental one. Second, we might wonder whether my account actually resolves the apparent conflicts between virtue and contemplation that it purports to solve. Third, we might be concerned that the account does no better than competing accounts at accommodating the common or reputable opinions; we might worry that any moral theory that uses contemplation as the standard for moral action is *prima facie* implausible.

Take the first worry first. As I explained in setting up the paper, passages like *NE* 6.1 and *EE* 8.3 strongly suggest that virtuous actions are for the sake of contemplation by being instrumentally a means to contemplation. One of the virtues of my account is supposed to be that it does justice to this face value reading. However, we might wonder whether the account I've given strains the instrumental relation we hoped to capture. Again, on my view, it is not the case that virtuous actions directly aim at maximizing or producing contemplative activity. Instead, they are for the sake of contemplation insofar as they aim at freedom from necessity, and this freedom from necessity is what is required for contemplative activity to be possible. Virtuous actions do not always directly promote contemplation. They do not even always directly promote the conditions *necessary* for contemplation. We might worry that the relationship between virtuous actions and contemplation is too indirect to be thought of as an instrumental one.

I think this worry is misplaced. It assumes too narrow a conception of instrumentality to capture what Aristotle himself seems to have in mind. Consider again the analogy with medicine and health. Aristotle clearly thinks that medicine is instrumentally for the sake of health. However, it is not the case that everything a doctor does as an exercise of the medical art is aimed at maximizing health in any particular patient. After all, a doctor might have to consider how to distribute scarce resources amongst a number of patients; it might be better, all things considered, to stabilize the conditions of a number of patients rather than to bring any one patient into full health.[44] Moreover, sometimes a doctor might try her best to make a patient healthier and fail through no fault of her own. At other times, it might not even be appropriate for a doctor to aim to make a patient healthy; an illness might have progressed so far that all a doctor can do is minimize the patient's pain or

---

[44] It is tempting to assume that if we ascribe to Aristotle a consequentialist picture, it must be a maximizing one. But I take Aristotle to have a broadly consequentialist picture that is neither impartialist nor maximizing. In this way, his ethical theory represents an important alternative to the way that contemporary consequentialist theories have developed.

prevent the illness from spreading. Still, it is appropriate to describe the goal of medicine as health and to say that medicine is instrumentally for the sake of health. One way to think about this is that any condition the doctor aims to bring about is a step in the direction of health. A doctor might prescribe a diet to lower blood pressure, or amputate an infected limb, or run a range of tests to identify the cause of a set of symptoms. These are all actions that are *such as* to promote health, even if in some particular case they do not, in fact, bring about health in the patient. Health is the ultimate goal of the art in general, even if it is not realizable in particular cases. So also, I want to suggest, the freedom from necessity required for contemplation is the ultimate goal of ethical virtue even if it is not always realizable. A generous action might involve giving money to someone in need so that they do not have to do a humiliating or exploitative job. A just action might take the form of creating laws that guarantee workers are fairly compensated for their labour. These actions are, I want to suggest, such as to promote conditions of peace and leisure in a political community; these actions all serve to ameliorate conditions of compulsion or material necessity. As such, these actions are all, in the sense relevant here, also 'for the sake of' contemplation.[45]

I suspect one source of confusion in thinking about how virtuous actions are instrumental to other ends is in identifying the level at which the instrumental relation is supposed to apply. When Aristotle makes claims about medicine being for the sake of health or virtuous actions being for the sake of contemplation, I take him to be making claims about the natures of things or about the objective structure of value. Claims made at this level of abstraction are consistent with medicine not always producing health and virtue not always producing contemplation. One way to think about this is in terms of the distinction often made in contemporary ethical theory between a decision procedure and a standard of rightness.[46]

---

[45] To be sure, there are limits to the analogy with medicine. Medicine is for the sake of health in the sense that it aims to produce health. Virtue is for the sake of contemplation in the sense that it aims to produce the conditions necessary for contemplation, rather than contemplation itself. In a way it is not surprising that the analogy runs out here. Contemplation is not the end of a process or a craft, but instead is the kind of activity that is itself an end.

[46] For this distinction, see e.g. C. A. Stark, 'Decision Procedures, Standards of Rightness and Impartiality', *Noûs*, 31 (2002), 478–95. As she describes it, a decision procedure is a method for deliberation, whereas a standard of rightness is an answer

Virtuous Actions 171

Aristotle famously does not give us a clear decision procedure or principle of action. Instead, he exhorts us to act as the virtuous agent does. Some have understood this to be a deficiency or oversight of his view, but I think more charitably that Aristotle was just not principally interested in the question of how we ought to act in some particular instance. He was interested in the prior question of what *makes* certain kinds of actions ethically virtuous, which is to say, what the goods are in the ethical domain that virtuous actions aim to bring about. That is, Aristotle was interested in offering us a kind of standard of rightness.

Turn now to the second worry, about potential conflicts between the pursuit of virtue and the pursuit of contemplation. There are actually a few different concerns here to untangle. One sort of worry we might have is that even if virtuous actions promote the conditions under which contemplation is possible, they are not the sorts of actions *best* suited to bringing about those conditions. After all, there are, in many cases, actions that would more directly bring about contemplation than actions aimed at fighting just wars or equitably distributing material resources. Here, there are two things useful to point out about my account. First, it is a mistake to assume that just because contemplation is the standard for virtuous actions, all virtuous actions must be aimed at *maximizing* contemplative activity. I've argued that Aristotle is giving us a standard of rightness, not a principle of action. What this means is that although just, generous, or courageous actions are the sorts of actions that aim to free us from material necessity and promote peace and leisure, they may not always be the best actions in a particular context to bring about these conditions; the claims Aristotle is making are at the level of the natures of these actions and the kinds of ends that characterize them.[47]

---

to the question 'What kinds of actions are morally right?' Offering a decision procedure makes sense when there is an answer to the prior question of what the standard of rightness is.

[47] One might have a related worry here that the account I am proposing does not adequately explain the non-instrumental value of ethical activity. On the view I am defending, acting virtuously is an end because it is an excellent exercise of our intellectual capacities, and virtuous actions are for the sake of ends beyond themselves. But, so the worry goes, we might think that when we perform a just action, the fact that it is just is enough of a reason to do so; we ought to do the just action simply because it is what justice requires, not because it benefits us by being an excellent accomplishment of the human function, or simply because of its consequences. In fact,

Second, I've argued that Aristotle is a pluralist about value. Even though the ends of virtuous actions instrumentally promote contemplation, this need not exhaust their value. Indeed, it seems to me plausible that the goods virtuous actions aim to achieve—peace, leisure, health, and so on—are worthwhile in important ways independently of how they allow for contemplation. What this means is that there is no simple story for what goods we ought to prioritize in particular cases. This question of how to navigate conflicts between values in particular instances is a question that finds itself at the centre of contemporary moral theories, but I believe it was simply not the sort of question that Aristotle meant to answer. Instead, I have hoped to show that there is no conflict or incoherence at the level of the objective structure of value that Aristotle describes.

A different sort of worry we might have is how to adjudicate conflicts between the actions that best promote my own contemplative activity and the actions that best promote the conditions for contemplation in the wider political community. What does my account say in a case where an agent is choosing between prioritizing her own leisure time to contemplate and fighting for a just political cause? In fact, these sorts of conflicts are inevitable on my account. I do not take Aristotle to have the form of eudaemonism on which an agent ought only do whatever best promotes her own happiness. It is true that when an agent performs a virtuous action, she benefits herself by engaging in an instance of acting virtuously. But it is not the case that doing so *best* promotes her own happiness in cases where she could instead engage in contemplation. Many of the paradigmatic virtuous actions are other-directed, aimed at promoting happiness in the political community more generally. Not only are these conflicts inevitable, but I do not think Aristotle has a general rule for determining when we ought to prioritize our own happiness and when we ought to prioritize the good of the political

---

my hope is that, by seeing the instrumental nature of virtuous actions at the level of a standard of rightness, not a principle of action, my account does not make the value of virtuous actions purely instrumental. The thought here is that a just action is good even if in some particular instance it does not have the desired result. It is good because it is the sort of action that is such as to promote conditions that are valuable for human beings. What this means is that the fact that the action is just is a good enough reason to perform it. However, if we want to spell out *what justice is*, we will need to make reference to the ends that just actions are such as to promote. I am grateful to an anonymous referee for pressing this objection.

community. This might seem unsatisfying, but again I think this is more a reflection of the narrow focus of contemporary ethical theories than a deficiency in Aristotle's own view. Moreover, it seems to reflect the complexity of these decisions in our own lives.

Consider a final worry. Suppose you are convinced by the interpretation I have defended. You still might wonder to what extent I have been successful in vindicating Aristotle's ethical theory. After all, it might seem hopelessly elitist and deeply self-serving for Aristotle to insist that our ultimate ethical aim should be the promotion of philosophy, an activity enjoyed by so few. In closing, I want to emphasize what the view gets right and what Aristotle himself, to some degree, failed to see about his own commitments. To notice that virtuous actions, by promoting conditions of peace and leisure, promote the conditions under which contemplation is possible is to notice the enormous degree of privilege required to be able to engage in philosophy. This is hardly an elitist position. Instead, it is a recognition that people are not free to engage in an activity like philosophy, an activity that rarely yields any practical benefit, until their basic needs are met. Aristotle's ethical theory enjoins us to bring about the conditions of peace, security, and freedom from necessity that make philosophy accessible to those who would otherwise not be able to participate.

University of Pennsylvania

BIBLIOGRAPHY

Ackrill, J., 'Aristotle on Action' ['Action'], *Mind*, 87 (1978), 595–601.

Ackrill, J., 'Aristotle on Eudaimonia' ['Eudaimonia'], in A. O. Rorty (ed.), *Essays on Aristotle's Ethics* (Berkeley, 1980), 15–33.

Adkins, A. W., 'Theoria versus Praxis in the Nicomachean Ethics and the Republic', *Classical Philology*, 73 (1978), 297–313.

Brown, L., 'What Is "the Mean Relative to Us" in Aristotle's Ethics?', *Phronesis*, 42 (1997), 77–93.

Brown, L., 'Why Is Aristotle's Virtue of Character a Mean? Taking Aristotle at his Word', in R. Polansky (ed.), *The Cambridge Companion to Aristotle's Nicomachean Ethics* (Cambridge, 2014), 64–80.

Bywater, I., *Aristotelis Ethica Nicomachea* (Oxford, 1894).

Charles, D., 'Aristotle on Well-Being and Intellectual Contemplation', *Aristotelian Society*, Suppl. 73 (1999), 205–23.

Charles, D., *Aristotle's Philosophy of Action* [*Action*] (Cornell, 1986).
Charles, D., 'Eudaimonia, Theoria, and the Choiceworthiness of Practical Wisdom', in P. Destrée and M. Zingano (eds.), *Theoria: Studies on the Status and Meaning of Contemplation in Aristotle's Ethics* (Leuven, 2014), 89–109.
Cooper, J. M., 'Contemplation and Happiness: A Reconsideration', *Synthese*, 72 (1987), 187–216.
Cooper, J. M., *Reason and the Human Good in Aristotle* [*Reason*] (Cambridge, Mass., 1975).
Curzer, H. J. 'A Defense of Aristotle's Doctrine That Virtue Is a Mean', *Ancient Philosophy*, 16 (1996), 129–38.
Devereux, D. T., 'Aristotle on the Essence of Happiness', in D. J. O'Meara (ed.), *Studies in Aristotle* (Washington DC, 1981), 247–60.
Gauthier, R. A., and J. Y. Jolif, *L'Éthique à Nicomaque* (Louvain, 1958).
Gelber, J., 'Two Ways of Being for an End', *Phronesis*, 63 (2018), 64–86.
Hardie, W. F. R., 'Aristotle's Doctrine That Virtue Is a Mean', *Proceedings of the Aristotelian Society*, 65 (1964), 183–204.
Hardie, W. F. R., 'The Final Good in Aristotle's Ethics' ['Final'], in J. M. E. Moravcsik (ed.) *Aristotle: A Collection of Critical Essays* (London, 1967), 297–322.
Heinaman, R., 'Activity and Praxis in Aristotle ['Activity']', *Proceedings of the Boston Area Colloquium of Ancient Philosophy*, 12 (1996), 71–111.
Heinaman, R., 'Eudaimonia and Self-Sufficiency in the Nicomachean Ethics', *Phronesis*, 33 (1988), 31–53.
Hirji, S., 'Acting Virtuously as an End in Aristotle's *Nicomachean Ethics*', *British Journal of the History of Philosophy*, 26 (2018), 1006–26.
Irwin, T. H., 'Aristotle's Conception of Morality' ['Conception'], *Proceedings of the Boston Area Colloquium in Ancient Philosophy*, 1 (1985), 115–43.
Irwin, T. H., 'The Structure of Aristotelian Happiness' ['Structure'], *Ethics*, 101 (1991), 382–91.
Jaeger, W., *Aristotle*, trans. by R. Robinson (Chicago, 1948).
Jimenez, M., 'Aristotle on Becoming Virtuous by Doing Virtuous Actions', *Phronesis*, 61 (2016), 3–32.
Kenny, A., *The Aristotelian Ethics: A Study of the Relationship between the Eudemian and Nicomachean Ethics of Aristotle* (Oxford, 1978).
Keyt, D., 'Intellectualism in Aristotle' ['Intellectualism (1978)'], *Society for Ancient Greek Philosophy Newsletter*, 87 (1978), 1–20.
Keyt, D., 'Intellectualism in Aristotle' ['Intellectualism (1983)'], in J. P. Anton and A. Preus (eds.), *Essays in Ancient Greek Philosophy*, 2nd edn (Albany, 1983), 364–87.
Kraut, R., *Aristotle on the Human Good* [*Human Good*] (Princeton, 1991).
Lawrence, G., 'Aristotle and the Ideal Life' ['Ideal'], *Philosophical Review*, 102 (1993), 1–34.

Lear, G. R., 'Happiness and the Structure of Ends', in G. Anagnostopoulos (ed.), *A Companion to Aristotle* (Malden, 2009), 385–403.
Lear, G. R., *Happy Lives and the Highest Good: An Essay on Aristotle's Nicomachean Ethics* [*Happy*] (Princeton, 2004).
Leighton, S., 'The Mean Relative to Us', *Apeiron*, 28 (1995), 67–78.
Meyer, S. S., *Ancient Ethics* (Abingdon, 2007).
Meyer, S. S., 'Aristotle on Moral Motivation', in I. Vasiliou (ed.), *Moral Motivation: A History* (Oxford, 2016), 44–64.
Meyer, S. S., 'Living for the Sake of an Ultimate End', in J. Miller (ed.), *Aristotle's Nicomachean Ethics: A Critical Guide* (Cambridge, 2011), 47–65.
Rogers, K., 'Aristotle's Conception of Τὸ Καλόν' ['*Τὸ Καλόν*'], *Ancient Philosophy*, 13 (1993), 355–71.
Ross, W. D. (trans.), *Aristotle* Ethica Nicomachea (Oxford, 1915).
Rowe, C. J., *The Eudemian and Nicomachean Ethics: A Study in the Development of Aristotle's Thought*, Proceedings of the Cambridge Philological Society, Suppl. 3 (Cambridge, 1971).
Scharle, M., 'Elemental Teleology in Aristotle's *Physics* 2. 8', *Oxford Studies in Ancient Philosophy*, 34 (2008), 147–83.
Stark, C. A., 'Decision Procedures, Standards of Rightness and Impartiality, *Noûs*, 31 (2002), 478–95.
Tuozzo, T., 'Contemplation, the Noble, and the Mean: The Standard of Moral Virtue in Aristotle's Ethics', *Apeiron*, 28 (1995), 129–54.
Walker, M. D., *Aristotle on the Uses of Contemplation* [*Uses*] (Cambridge, 2018).
Walzer, R. R., and Mingay, J. M. (eds.), *Aristotelis Ethica Eudemia* (Oxford, 1991).
White, N. P., 'Goodness and Human Aims in Aristotle's Ethics', in D. J. O'Meara (ed.), *Studies in Aristotle* (Washington DC, 1981), 225–46.
Whiting, J., 'Eudaimonia, External Results, and Choosing Virtuous Actions for Themselves' ['External'], *Philosophy and Phenomenological Research*, 65 (2002), 270–90.
Whiting, J., 'Human Nature and Intellectualism in Aristotle', *Archiv für Geschichte der Philosophie*, 68 (1986), 70–95.
Wilkes, K., 'The Good Man and the Good for Man in Aristotle's Ethics', in A. O. Rorty (ed.), *Essays on Aristotle's Ethics* (Berkeley, 1980), 341–58.
Woods, M. (ed.), *Aristotle:* Eudemian Ethics*: Books I, II, and VIII*, 2nd edn (Oxford, 1992).

THOUGHT 'FROM WITHOUT'

The Role of the Agent Intellect in Alexander's *De intellectu*

ROBERT ROREITNER

De anima 3. 4–5 contains a well-known conundrum. Aristotle begins analysing thought in *DA* 3. 4 by analogy with perception, as a kind of 'being affected' (πάσχειν) by the object of thought.[1] But he ends up invoking the so-called 'agent' or 'productive' (ποιητικόν), eternally active intellect (νοῦς) in *DA* 3. 5 as what 'produces everything' (ποιεῖν πάντα), while the 'potential' (δυνάμει) intellect 'becomes everything' (πάντα γίνεσθαι). What is it, then, that 'acts' on my 'potential' intellect when I think, say, the essence of horse: is it the essence (i.e. the object of thought), the agent intellect, or somehow both? Traditionally, most interpretations of Aristotle have been *compatibilist* in one of the following two senses. On the one hand, some interpretations ascribe *complementary* efficient roles to the agent

---

Different versions of this paper were presented at Charles University in Prague, Stanford University, and Central European University in Vienna. I would like to thank the audiences for stimulating discussions, especially István Bodnár, Pantelis Golitsis, Emily Perry, Howard Robinson, Thomas Slabon, Štěpán Špinka, Karel Thein, and Glen Zhou. I am especially grateful to Peter Adamson, Gweltaz Guyomarc'h, and Stephen Menn, who read the paper at an early stage and provided very helpful feedback, as well as to Nicolas Aubin for a consultation of the Arabic material. My thanks also go to the two anonymous referees of *OSAP* for useful comments, the current editor Rachana Kamtekar for her unfailing helpfulness, and Cole Mitchell for his excellent copy-editing. Most of all, though, I would like to thank the former editor Victor Caston, who led the review process in 2020–3 and provided me with two sets of most thorough, deeply probing, and yet encouraging feedback. I am grateful to Alexander von Humboldt-Stiftung for enabling me to work on the paper during my research stay at LMU Munich. The research was supported by the Czech Science Foundation (Grant No. 25–16298S).

[1] The analogy is introduced right away at *DA* 3. 4, 429^{a}13–18; the notion of 'being affected' here is clearly to be understood in its 'preservative' meaning (σωτηρία), distinguished at *DA* 2. 5, 417^{b}2–16 from the ordinary sense of 'being affected' as involving a 'destruction' (φθορά) of some feature by its opposite. For the Greek text of *De anima*, I use A. Förster, *Aristotelis De anima libri tres* (Budapest, 1912). For other texts of Aristotle and Plato I use the Oxford Classical Texts.

intellect and the object of thought, as in most variants of the *abstractionist* account, on which the agent intellect (usually conceived as a constituent part of the human soul) produces, by abstraction, an actual object of thought that then acts on the potential intellect.[2] On the other hand, some interpretations *collapse* the agent intellect with the object of thought, as in the *emanationist* account (influenced by Neoplatonism), on which the essence of horse that we think emanates directly from the transcendent agent intellect eternally thinking everything there is to be thought;[3] since all essences are constituent parts of the agent intellect's thought, being affected by one of them just *is* being affected by (an aspect of) the agent intellect.[4]

These compatibilist approaches have recently been challenged en bloc by interpreters calling into question the very idea of the agent intellect being a genuine *efficient* cause of all of our thinking acts. Some scholars have argued that this intellect is, by Aristotle's lights, an 'efficient' cause only insofar as it is the *final* cause of our

---

[2] See e.g. Aquinas, *In DA* 3. 10, §§728–39; *Summa theol.* 1a qu. 79, art. 3; *Summa contra gentiles* 2. 60, 73–4, 76–8. Cf. e.g. F. Brentano, *Die Psychologie des Aristoteles: Insbesondere seine Lehre vom ΝΟΥΣ ΠΟΙΗΤΙΚΟΣ* (Mainz, 1867), 163–233. For a more recent abstractionist approach, see e.g. M. V. Wedin, *Mind and Imagination in Aristotle* (New Haven, 1988), 160–208.

[3] This emanationist account is traditionally traced back to Avicenna (see e.g. Aquinas, *Summa contra gentiles* 2. 74), although there is a strong empiricist tendency in Avicenna's thought which makes it difficult to class him under the heading of emanationism, as recently stressed by D. Gutas, 'The Empiricism of Avicenna', *Oriens*, 40 (2012), 391–436; D. N. Hasse, 'Avicenna's Epistemological Optimism', in P. Adamson (ed.), *Interpreting Avicenna: Critical Essays* (Cambridge, 2013), 109–19; T. Alpina, 'Intellectual Knowledge, Active Intellect and Intellectual Memory in Avicenna's Kitab al-Nafs and Its Aristotelian Background', *Documenti e Studi sulla Tradizione Filosofica Medievale*, 25 (2014), 131–83; and R. C. Taylor, 'Avicenna and the Issue of the Intellectual Abstraction of Intelligibles', in M. Cameron (ed.), *Philosophy of Mind in the Early and High Middle Ages* (London, 2019), 56–82.

[4] There has been *a tendency to* emanationism among those modern scholars who, like Avicenna, conceive of the agent intellect as eternally thinking everything there is to be thought properly speaking; see e.g. J. Lear, *Aristotle: The Desire to Understand* (Cambridge and New York, 1988), 135–41, 293–306; M. Frede, 'La théorie aristotélicienne de l'intellect agent' ['L'intellect agent'], in G. R. Dherbey (ed.), *Corps et âme: Études sur le de Anima d'Aristote* (Paris, 1996), 377–90; D. Charles, *Aristotle on Meaning and Essence* (Oxford, 2000), 130–43 (cf. D. Charles, *The Undivided Self: Aristotle and the 'Mind-Body' Problem* (New York, 2021), 222 n. 41); or M. F. Burnyeat, *Aristotle's Divine Intellect* [*Divine Intellect*] (Milwaukee, 2008), 37–43. Sometimes the account of the agent intellect as a thinking system of all eternal truths or intelligible essences is combined with a *teleological* conception of its role as the final, rather than a genuinely efficient, cause of our thought (see esp. Frede, 'L'intellect agent', 387, 390, and Burnyeat, *Divine Intellect*, 42–3).

thought, just as the prime mover 'moves' heaven by being an object of its desire.[5] Others have maintained that the agent intellect is indeed introduced as a genuine efficient cause of our thinking—but only our thinking of this intellect itself, not of the essences of material things.[6] And there have been still other readings that are not easily squared with compatibilism.[7]

Both proponents and critics of compatibilism have often called one witness, namely Alexander of Aphrodisias (second/third century CE), the most ancient interpreter of Aristotle's *De anima* whose views are fairly well known to us and the greatest Peripatetic authority of late antiquity. Unfortunately, our only access to Alexander's commentary on Aristotle's *De anima* comes via scanty indirect references and occasional quotations.[8] But we are lucky enough to have Alexander's own treatise *De anima* and a series of short treatises, transmitted as the second book of his *De anima*,[9] where we find an essay entitled *De intellectu* that provides a detailed

---

[5] *Metaph.* Λ. 7, 1072ᵃ23–ᵇ4. See especially V. Caston, 'Aristotle's Two Intellects: A Modest Proposal' ['Two Intellects'], *Phronesis*, 44 (1999), 199–227 at 219–23; cf. e.g. T. K. Johansen, *The Powers of Aristotle's Soul* (Oxford, 2012), 241–2.

[6] See esp. S. Menn, 'From *De Anima* III 4 to *De Anima* III 5' ['From III 4 to III 5'], in G. Guyomarc'h, C. Louguet, and C. Murgier (eds.), *Aristote et l'âme humaine: Lectures de 'De Anima' III offertes à Michel Crubellier* (Leuven, 2020), 95–155.

[7] For one such approach, conceiving of the agent intellect as a *knowledge* (acquired or perhaps inborn), see J. Barnes, 'Aristotle's Concept of Mind', *Proceedings of the Aristotelian Society*, 72 (1971), 101–14; R. M. Polansky, *Aristotle's De anima* (New York, 2007), 458–72; F. A. J. de Haas, 'Aristotle and Alexander of Aphrodisias on Active Intellectual Cognition' ['Active Intellectual Cognition'], in V. Decaix and A. M. Mora-Márquez (eds.), *Studies in the History of Philosophy of Mind; Active Cognition: Challenges to an Aristotelian Tradition* (New York, 2020), 13–36 at 19–23; or E. Berti, 'Aristotle's *Nous Poiêtikos*: Another Modest Proposal', in G. Sillitti, F. Stella, and F. Fronterotta (eds.), *Il NOUS di Aristotele* (Sankt Augustin, 2016), 137–53. A similar approach seems to have already been adopted by Plutarch of Athens (see Philop. *De intellectu* 43. 18–45. 59 Verbeke with *In DA* 535. 5–536. 5 Hayduck), and it may be even more ancient (as suggested by Themistius, *In DA* 102. 33–6 Heinze).

[8] See I. Kupreeva, 'Alexander of Aphrodisias and Aristotle's "De Anima": What's in a Commentary?', *Bulletin of the Institute of Classical Studies*, 55 (2012), 109–29.

[9] Dubbed *Mantissa*, i.e. 'makeweight', by its first editor Ivo Bruns. See R. W. Sharples, 'Alexander of Aphrodisias: What Is a *Mantissa*?', *Bulletin of the Institute of Classical Studies*, Suppl. 83 (2004), 51–69; and R. W. Sharples, *Alexander Aphrodisiensis: 'De Anima Libri Mantissa': A New Edition of the Greek Text with Introduction and Commentary* [*Mantissa*] (Berlin, 2008). We also find arguments drawing on *DA* 3. 4–5 elsewhere in the works ascribed to Alexander; see e.g. the opening of *Quaest.* 1. 25 Bruns.

and broadly Aristotelian account of human thought.[10] Some aspects of Alexander's interpretation are plain enough: he takes the agent intellect of *De anima* 3. 5 to be not a constituent of the human soul but a transcendent divine entity (apparently the prime mover of *Metaphysics* Λ. 6–10), whereas the human soul, including its intellective part, is through and through perishable.[11] But it is less clear what *role* Alexander ascribes to the transcendent intellect with respect to human thought.

Interpreters once understood Alexander's account along traditional compatibilist (abstractionist) lines.[12] But since the pioneering doctoral dissertation of Paul Moraux on Alexander's noetic,[13] the attention of scholars has been drawn to Alexander's circumspection in describing the role of the agent intellect in his *De anima*. Here he analyses the development of the 'potential' or 'material' intellect from the state of a pure potentiality to the acquisition of universal concepts, and apparently also of scientific definitions, without any reference to the agent intellect whatsoever (80. 16–86. 6).

---

[10] It was historically more influential than Alexander's *De anima*. For its Arabic reception, see M. Geoffroy, 'La tradition arabe du Περὶ νοῦ d'Alexandre d'Aphrodise et les origines de la théorie farabienne des quatre degrés de l'intellect' ['La tradition arabe'], in C. D'Ancona and G. Serra (eds.), *Aristotele e Alessandro di Afrodisia nella tradizione araba* (Padua, 2002), 191–231. For its Latin reception, see G. Théry, *Autour du décret de 1210: II. Alexandre d'Aphrodise: Aperçu sur l'influence de sa noétique* (Le Saulchoir, 1926). See also H. J. Blumenthal, 'Alexander of Aphrodisias in the Later Greek Commentaries on Aristotle's De Anima', in J. Wiesner (ed.), *Aristoteles: Werk und Wirkung: Band II Kommentierung, Überlieferung, Nachleben* (Berlin, 1987), 90–106; and E. Kessler, 'Alexander of Aphrodisias and His Doctrine of the Soul: 1400 Years of Lasting Significance', *Early Science and Medicine*, 16 (2011), 1–93.

[11] Cf. e.g. A. C. Lloyd, 'Alexander of Aphrodisias' ['Alexander'], in P. Edwards (ed.), *The Encyclopedia of Philosophy* (New York, 1967), i–ii. 73; or D. Frede, 'Alexander of Aphrodisias', in E. N. Zalta (ed.), *The Stanford Encyclopedia of Philosophy* (Winter 2017 edn), https://plato.stanford.edu/archives/win2017/entries/alexander-aphrodisias/, accessed 20 August 2024.

[12] See e.g. E. Zeller, *Die Philosophie der Griechen in ihrer geschichtlichen Entwicklung III.1* [*Die Philosophie der Griechen*], 5th edn (Leipzig, 1922), 826; or W. D. Ross, *Aristotle*, 6th edn (London, 1995), 158; and more recently R. Sorabji, *The Philosophy of the Commentators, 200–600 AD: Psychology (with Ethics and Religion)* [*Commentators*] (Ithaca, NY, 2005), 104; or H. Busche, 'Alexander von Aphrodisias, Über die Seele', in H. Busche and M. Perkams (eds.), *Antike Interpretationen zur aristotelischen Lehre vom Geist* (Hamburg, 2018), 116–87 at 135–9. For more references, see G. Movia, *Alessandro di Afrodisia: Tra naturalismo e misticismo* [*Tra naturalismo e misticismo*] (Padua, 1970), 36 n. 1.

[13] P. Moraux, *Alexandre d'Aphrodise: Exégète de la noétique d'Aristote* [*Exégète*] (Liège, 1942).

No such reference is made until much later, at 88. 24–89. 11, where Alexander, in contrast to compatibilist interpreters, seems to ascribe only an *indirect* role to the agent intellect.

Meanwhile the details are still in dispute. Moraux argued that the agent intellect comes to be a cause of human thinking mainly as an Avicennean *dator formarum* ('provider of forms') that as such guarantees the existence of potentially intelligible objects in nature (89. 9–11).[14] Other scholars emphasized its role as the supremely intelligible object (88. 24–89. 9), suggesting that the idea is 'as close to what is causality in Neoplatonism as possible'.[15] But the concept of causality here has been shown to have a solid foundation in Aristotle's work.[16] And it has been emphasized how sharply Alexander's account differs from Neoplatonist accounts in making the human material intellect relatively autonomous, that is, in allowing it to develop purely on the basis of experience with natural objects, whose forms it comes to think by exercising its own power to separate them from matter.[17] The role of the agent

[14] Moraux, *Exégète*, 87–93; cf. id., 'Le *De Anima* dans la tradition grecque: Quelques aspects de l'interprétation du traité, de Théophraste à Thémistius' ['De Anima'], in G. E. R. Lloyd and G. E. L. Owen (eds.), *Aristotle on Mind and the Senses: Proceedings of the Seventh Symposium Aristotelicum* (Cambridge, 1978), 281–324 at 300; id., *Der Aristotelismus bei den Griechen: Von Andronikos bis Alexander von Aphrodisias*, iii: *Alexander von Aphrodisias [Aristotelismus bei den Griechen* iii] (Berlin, 2001), 370; or Movia, *Tra naturalismo e misticismo*, 40–2.

[15] P. Merlan, *Monopsychism: Mysticism: Metaconsciousness: Problems of the Soul in the Neoaristotelian and Neoplatonic Tradition* [*Monopsychism*] (The Hague, 1963), 39; cf. Lloyd, 'Alexander'; P. L. Donini, *Tre studi sull'aristotelismo nel II secolo d. C* [*Tre studi*] (Turin, 1974), 41–6.

[16] A. C. Lloyd, 'The Principle that the Cause Is Greater than Its Effect', *Phronesis*, 21 (1976), 146–56 (arguing also against Moraux, *Exégète*, 89–92, who charges a part of the key passage with Platonism that 'has nothing Aristotelian to it'); cf. P. Accattino and P. L. Donini, *Alessandro di Afrodisia: L'anima* [*L'anima*] (Rome, 1996), 288–92.

[17] For the autonomy of the material intellect, see F. M. Schroeder, 'The Analogy of the Active Intellect to Light in the "De Anima" of Alexander of Aphrodisias' ['Analogy'], *Hermes*, 109 (1981), 215–25; and esp. M. Tuominen, 'Aristotle and Alexander of Aphrodisias on the Active Intellect' ['Active Intellect'], in V. Hirvonen, T. J. Holopainen, and M. Tuominen (eds.), *Mind and Modality* (Leiden, 2006), 55–70 at 63–6; and M. Tuominen, 'Receptive Reason: Alexander of Aphrodisias on Material Intellect' ['Receptive Reason'], *Phronesis*, 55 (2010), 170–90; cf. e.g. F. A. J. de Haas, 'Intellect in Alexander of Aphrodisias and John Philoponus: Divine, Human or Both?', in J. Sisko (ed.), *Philosophy of Mind in Antiquity* (Abingdon, 2018), 299–316 at 300–6. Contrast B. C. Bazán, 'L'authenticité du "De Intellectu" attribué à Alexandre d'Aphrodise' ['L'authenticité'], *Revue philosophique de Louvain*, 71 (1973), 468–87, who interprets the account of Alexander's *De anima* as an 'implicit' and 'imperfect' articulation of

intellect can thus be only indirect.[18] It has recently been proposed that the whole passage (88. 24–89. 11) should be interpreted entirely in terms of *final* causality (the agent intellect being the final cause of both natural compounds and human thought).[19]

Now if the emphasis scholars have laid on the relative autonomy of the human material intellect and on the indirectness or finality of the agent intellect's role in Alexander's *De anima* points in the right direction, this raises a new set of questions concerning the relation between this treatise and *De intellectu*. As already noted by Moraux, there appears to be a wide gulf between the two accounts:[20] in sharp contrast to Alexander's *De anima*—which seems not to ascribe any direct role to the agent intellect—*De intellectu* emphatically invokes such a role when insisting that the material intellect is enabled to think objects like the essence of horse *only by thinking the transcendent agent intellect*. There has been a long-standing dispute as to how exactly this contrast should be understood and what consequences should be drawn from it for questions concerning the dating and authorship of *De intellectu*. Some scholars have maintained that *De intellectu* must come from a later author misinterpreting the account of Alexander's *De anima*,[21] and maybe even

---

the same doctrine that we find in *De intellectu* (see especially p. 484), where, according to Bazán, the illumination coming from the agent intellect must *precede* abstraction and separation of forms from matter. For a similar approach, see also A. P. Fotinis, *The De Anima of Alexander of Aphrodisias: A Translation and Commentary* (Washington DC, 1979), 322.

[18] Cf. e.g. M. Gabbe, 'Themistius on Concept Acquisition and Knowledge of Essences', *Archiv für Geschichte der Philosophie*, 92 (2010), 215–35 at 229. For an overview of different interpretations combined with a sceptical perspective on how much we can actually learn from Alexander's elliptical remarks about the causal role of the agent intellect in *De anima*, see R. W. Sharples, 'Alexander of Aphrodisias: Scholasticism and Innovation' ['Scholasticism and Innovation'], in W. Haase (ed.), *Aufstieg und Niedergang der Römischen Welt*, ii. xxxvi: *Philosophie, Wissenschaften, Technik* (Berlin, 1987), 1176–1243 at 1206–8; and M. Bergeron and R. Dufour, *Alexandre d'Aphrodise: De l'âme [De l'âme]* (Paris, 2008), 50–5.

[19] See G. Guyomarc'h, 'Alexander of Aphrodisias and the Active Intellect as Final Cause' ['Active Intellect'], *Elenchos*, 44 (2023), 93–117. Cf. id., *L'unité de la métaphysique selon Alexandre d'Aphrodise [L'unité de la métaphysique]* (Paris, 2016), 270–9.

[20] See Moraux, *Exégète*, 132–42; cf. e.g. Sorabji, *Commentators*, 104. Averroes, in his *Long Commentary* 3. 36. 81–127, 482–4 Crawford, also notices a contrast between the two accounts of the relation between the material and the agent intellect, but it is a different contrast from (although not unrelated to) the one on which modern scholarship has focused. For more on Averroes' understanding, see n. 154 below.

[21] This is the original position of Moraux, *Exégète*, 132–42.

from a considerably later author systematically misreading Alexander through the lens of Plotinus.[22] At least one interpreter has argued that *De intellectu* is more likely to express Alexander's mature views.[23] And still other scholars have come to the conclusion that *De intellectu* must contain Alexander's early ideas, whereas *De anima* represents his mature position.[24]

Each of these judgements has been premised on a certain understanding of the doctrine of *De intellectu* itself. But none of these interpretations has been very charitable, to say the least. Most scholars have found in *De intellectu* a 'bizarre' (Sharples)[25] and 'paradoxical' (Accattino)[26] account according to which the material intellect *first* thinks the agent intellect—i.e. effectively, the prime mover of *Metaphysics* Λ. 6–10—and *then* tries to *imitate* it by abstracting and thinking enmattered forms.[27] Even if one can devise considerations that might have led an interpreter of Aristotle to such a curious idea, it hardly seems to provide a philosophically interesting, let alone respectable view.[28]

---

[22] See F. M. Schroeder and R. B. Todd, *Two Greek Aristotelian Commentators on the Intellect: The* De Intellectu *Attributed to Alexander of Aphrodisias and Themistius' Paraphrase of Aristotle* De Anima, *3. 4–8* [*Two Commentators*] (Toronto, 1990); F. M. Schroeder, 'The Provenance of the "De Intellectu" Attributed to Alexander of Aphrodisias' ['Provenance'], *Documenti e Studi sulla Tradizione Filosofica Medievale*, 8 (1997), 105–20; F. M. Schroeder and R. B. Todd, 'The *De Intellectu* Revisited', *Laval théologique et philosophique*, 64 (2008), 663–80.

[23] Bazán, 'L'authenticité'.

[24] This was originally suggested by Donini, *Tre studi*, 60–1, and afterwards accepted also by Moraux, 'De Anima', 305 (cf. Moraux, *Aristotelismus bei den Griechen* iii, 392–3); Accattino and Donini, *L'anima* (cf. P. Accattino, *Alessandro di Afrodisia: De intellectu* [*De Intellectu*] (Turin, 2001), 14–15; id., 'Alessandro di Afrodisia interprete del De Anima di Aristotele' ['Alessandro interprete'], *Studia Graeco-Arabica*, 4 (2014), 275–88); M. Rashed, 'A "New" Text of Alexander on the Soul's Motion' ['A "New" Text'], *Bulletin of the Institute of Classical Studies*, Suppl. 68 (1997), 181–95 at 192–5; R. W. Sharples, *Alexander of Aphrodisias: Supplement to On the Soul* [*Alexander: Supplement*] (London, 2004); cf. id., 'Peripatetics on Soul and Intellect' ['Peripatetics on Soul'], *Bulletin of the Institute of Classical Studies*, Suppl. 94 (2007), 607–20 at 616.

[25] See Sharples, *Alexander: Supplement*, 29 n. 65; cf. id., 'Scholasticism and Innovation', 1213, where the same idea is characterized more cautiously as 'problematic'.

[26] See Accattino, *De Intellectu*, 46; id., 'Alessandro interprete', 283.

[27] See also Bazán, 'L'authenticité', 482; Moraux, 'De Anima', 302–3; id., *Aristotelismus bei den Griechen* iii, 389; Movia, *Tra naturalismo e misticismo*, 42–4; Sharples, 'Scholasticism and Innovation', 1213; Accattino and Donini, *L'anima*, xxviii.

[28] The situation is not improved by D. Papadis, *Die Seelenlehre bei Alexander von Aphrodisias* [*Seelenlehre bei Alexander*] (Bern, 1991), 334–82, who, idiosyncratically,

The only fully fledged alternative in the literature has been the interpretation developed by Frederic Schroeder in a series of articles and a book. A key insight on Schroeder's part has been that the author of *De intellectu* conceives the involvement of the agent intellect as *simultaneous* with our separating and thinking enmattered forms rather than, as standardly assumed, temporally prior to it. This observation is worthy of more attention than has been paid to it, even though much more discussion is needed of how such a simultaneity is possible and what evidence for it can be found in *De intellectu*. But Schroeder connects this insight with several assumptions that make the resulting account, if anything, even less philosophically appealing than the more typical accounts and historically quite irrelevant. According to Schroeder, the author—writing considerably later than Alexander—is fatally misled by Plotinus into conceiving the role of the agent intellect along strict emanationist lines.[29]

This paper argues that the account of human thought developed in *De intellectu* and the role of the agent intellect therein need to be reconsidered. The author of this treatise would not have been at all happy with the 'paradoxical' and 'bizarre' account, which can at most provide a very clumsy 'solution' to a single isolated difficulty in Aristotle's account. Nor is the issue a peripheral deadlock pertaining to the late ancient dialogue between Platonism and Aristotelianism. The account of *De intellectu* is far more sophisticated and philosophically interesting than that, and it has considerable historical

conceives the agent intellect in Alexander's view as a 'part of the human soul' (cf. id., '"L'intellect agent" selon Alexandre d'Aphrodise', *Revue de Philosophie Ancienne*, 9 (1991), 133–51). This leaves it, if anything, even more unclear how this agent intellect should become 'the first moving cause' for the potential intellect (cf. id., *Seelenlehre bei Alexander*, 366–80).

[29] Unlike in Alexander's *De anima*, where, as Schroeder puts it, illumination is conceived as a 'joint effect of the *illuminans* and the *illuminatum*', the author of *De intellectu* allegedly conceives illumination as the effect of the *illuminans* alone. For the account of illumination in Alexander's *De anima*, see Schroeder, 'Analogy', together with F. M. Schroeder, 'The Potential or Material Intellect and the Authorship of the De Intellectu: A Reply to B.C. Bazán' ['Potential Intellect'], *Symbolae Osloenses*, 57 (1982), 115–25. For the relation between the account of illumination in Alexander's *De anima* and in Plotinus, see id., 'Light and the Active Intellect in Alexander and Plotinus' ['Light and the Active Intellect'], *Hermes*, 112 (1984), 239–48. For the account of illumination in *De intellectu* contrasted with that of *De anima* as allegedly influenced by Plotinus' account, see Schroeder and Todd, *Two Commentators*; Schroeder, 'Provenance'; Schroeder and Todd, 'The *De Intellectu* Revisited'.

importance. The idea of the agent intellect being *the final cause* of human thinking plays a key role in the treatise, and although the author undeniably believes that Aristotle is committed to conceiving the agent intellect as also *directly involved* in our thinking of enmattered forms (so that it is itself thought by us), this can be properly understood only within a teleological framework.[30]

The author of *De intellectu* wants us to conceive of the agent intellect not as a *thinking subject foreign* to us, an inscrutable god, but as the perfect *act of thought* that is *our proper* ultimate goal— notwithstanding that it has always existed independently from us as a self-standing substance. This act of thought *becomes ours* insofar as we manage to *genuinely think* something, e.g. the essence of horse, but as long as our thought is concerned with an *enmattered* form, the agent intellect is never *fully* ours. Our thought falls short of it to the extent that it fails to be perfectly the same as its object, and so *qua* our ultimate goal the agent intellect remains transcendent and out of our reach.

In contrast to the widespread 'bizarre' and 'paradoxical' interpretation, this paper argues that our thinking of the agent intellect does not temporally precede our thinking of enmattered forms, but is simultaneous with it and, so to speak, built into it; the agent intellect is not thought as something foreign to us (e.g. as a god to be worshipped or imitated), but as our proper—more or less perfectly attained—fulfilment, for this is how it comes to be present in us, even if we fail to be aware of its external origin. This, to be sure, is not to be understood in emanationist terms (there is no trace of any Neoplatonist influence to be found in *De intellectu*): there is literally nothing in the agent intellect that could emanate from it, for it is a perfect act of self-thinking, void of any other content. When we come to think the essence of horse, bronze, or fire, the specific content of our thought is determined by our previous perceptual experience and our processing of it, which is in no way supernatural; it is only the fact that this content ultimately comes to *be thought* that presupposes an involvement of the agent intellect, because neither the object nor our thinking capacity can, according to the author, produce a genuine thought. Thought can come to us only from without—but it is

---

[30] The importance of final causality in at least one section of *De intellectu* has been emphasized by de Haas, 'Active Intellectual Cognition', 29–31.

our thought (and is thought by us as such); indeed, it is we and our experience that determine both *when* the thought comes and *what* it is a thought *of*.

One of my contentions will be that we can better understand and appreciate the account of the agent intellect developed in *De intellectu* within the context of the Peripatetic school debate. Very far from being a mere—more or less confused—misinterpretation of Alexander's *De anima*, the account provides a crisp and sophisticated way of dealing with a set of traditional Peripatetic difficulties propounded by Theophrastus. The solutions offered here are recognizably novel with respect to both Theophrastus himself and what we know about the author's immediate predecessor. The author's emphasis on human autonomy (that is, on our thought being *up to us*) brings his solutions into close proximity with those we find articulated in Alexander's *De anima*, rather than the one account contradicting the other on this point (as has been widely believed). This shows, incidentally, that the traditional attribution of *De intellectu* to Alexander remains by far the best available hypothesis. What is perhaps most valuable about *De intellectu* is that it gives us a glimpse of what was at stake in the Peripatetic debates about intellect before and during Alexander's time.

After outlining the structure of *De intellectu*, I begin by reconstructing the reasons that the author finds in Aristotle for believing *that* a transcendent intellect needs to be involved in order for us to think anything (Section 2). I then turn to his view of *how* the agent intellect is involved, beginning with the first key passage (108. 19–24) that has been taken as the chief justification for both the 'bizarre and paradoxical' and the Neoplatonizing reading (Section 2). I argue that, in fact, the passage primarily treats the agent intellect as the *final* cause of our thinking. The main question, then, is how this teleological framework is compatible with the idea (fully articulated later in the treatise) that we already need to *think* the agent intellect in order to think anything whatsoever. I start by explaining why it is more promising to understand our thinking of the agent intellect as *simultaneous* with our thinking of each enmattered form rather than temporally prior to it (Section 3). To provide background for the author's account, I then briefly analyse a set of difficulties about human thought raised by Theophrastus, who unmistakably understood the agent intellect as a genuine efficient cause of our thinking (Section 4). I show how these difficulties can shed light on what the author of *De intellectu* is trying to achieve, with special emphasis on the notion of *autonomy*: against (apparently) all of his predecessors, the author is willing to defend the claim that our thinking is *up to us*. This context will help us understand and appreciate the key idea that, in each genuine act of thinking, we think the agent intellect as our proper—more or less perfectly attained—fulfilment, that is, as our own thought. This idea is brought out by a close analysis of the author's fullest account of the agent intellect's involvement (110. 25–112. 5), which shows how the key idea of the agent intellect being thought as one's proper fulfilment is here developed step by step as the author's response to a set of inherited difficulties (Section 5). The proposed interpretation is then corroborated by a detailed analysis of another, undeservedly understudied part of *De intellectu* (109. 4–110. 3), containing the author's account of our and the agent intellect's own self-thinking (Section 6). I argue that already at this point the author is responding to Theophrastus' *aporiai* and anticipating the idea that the agent intellect is, in each genuine act of thinking, thought by us as our own thought.

1. Need for an intellect 'from without'

De intellectu divides naturally into three parts: (A) a summary of Aristotle's noetic (106. 19–110. 3); (B) a discussion of Aristotle's motivation for introducing the so-called 'intellect from without' (110. 4–112. 5); and (C) a discussion of difficulties raised against the notion of the intellect from without (112. 5–113. 24).[31] The question of whether these are parts of a single treatise or instead

---

[31] C is concerned with 'difficulties *they raise* against the intellect from without that [according to them] must necessarily change place, but since it is non-bodily, it can neither be in a place nor move and come from one position to another' (ἀπορίας ἃς ἐπιφέρουσιν τῷ θύραθεν νῷ ἀνάγκην ἔχοντι τόπον ἀλλάττειν, οὐ δυναμένῳ δέ, εἴ γέ ἐστιν ἀσώματος, οὔτε ἐν τόπῳ εἶναι οὔτε μεταβαίνειν καὶ ἄλλοτε ἐν ἄλλῳ γίνεσθαι, 112. 6–8). These difficulties have been traced by scholars to Atticus, as reported by Stob., *PE* 15. 9. 13. For the larger context of the debate, see Rashed, 'A "New" Text'; id., *Alexandre d'Aphrodise: Commentaire perdu à la 'Physique' d'Aristote (Livres IV–VIII): Les scholies byzantines* (Berlin, 2014), 369–74; and S. Menn, 'Atticus, Alexander, Porphyry: Εἴσκρισις and the Neo-Platonic Interpretation of the Third Hypothesis of the *Parmenides*: With Some Implications for Instantaneous Creation' (forthcoming).

three (fragmentary) treatises put together by a later editor[32] can be left aside for the purposes of this paper. We will see that while there surely are differences of emphasis, there is a solid doctrinal unity underlying all the three parts.

Already in the manuscripts, A is divided into (A1) an account of the material intellect (106. 19–107. 20); (A2) an account of the dispositional intellect (107. 21–8); and (A3) an account of the agent intellect (107. 29–110. 3). This traditional division of the text (followed by modern translators and interpreters)[33] is potentially misleading because the final segment of A (109. 4–110. 3, which I call A4) is no longer really a discussion of the agent intellect, but rather a discussion of self-thinking both at the level of the dispositional intellect (109. 4–23, A4a) and at the level of the agent intellect (109. 23–110. 3, A4b). The traditional treatment of A4 as a mere part of the author's discussion of the agent intellect, which suggests that A4a serves as only a background for A4b, may be partly responsible for the fact that the distinctive account of human self-thinking in A4a has not been appreciated (more on that in Section 6).

Accattino has convincingly and helpfully divided Part B into a brief passage summing up a predecessor's account of Aristotle's motivation for introducing the intellect from without (B1 = 110. 4–25)[34] and a longer section in which the author seems to be adding

---

[32] See Schroeder's 'analytical' approach as defended in Schroeder and Todd, *Two Commentators*; Schroeder, 'Provenance'; Schroeder and Todd, 'The *De Intellectu* Revisited'.

[33] Inspired by the first sentence 'Intellect, according to Aristotle, is of three types' (Νοῦς ἐστι κατὰ Ἀριστοτέλη τριττός, 106.19). For the Greek text of *De intellectu* and the rest of *Mantissa*, I use Sharples, *Mantissa*. For other ancient commentators on Aristotle, I use the Commentaria in Aristotelem Graeca series. All translations are mine.

[34] The origin of this interpretation has been a notorious question of scholarship. Three main kinds of approach to the key opening lines of B1 (110. 4–6) have been proposed: (1) Zeller suggested an emendation identifying the reported teacher with Aristocles of Messene (Zeller, *Die Philosophie der Griechen*, 814 n. 1, 815 n. 3; cf. e.g. Burnyeat, *Divine Intellect*, 36), but the support is tenuous, and what we know of Aristocles does not really suggest any kinship with B1 or C1 (cf. M. L. Chiesara (ed.), *Aristocles of Messene: Testimonia and Fragments* (Oxford, 2001), xvi). (2) P. Moraux, 'Aristoteles, der Lehrer Alexanders von Aphrodisias', *Archiv für Geschichte der Philosophie*, 49 (1967), 169–82 (cf. id., *Der Aristotelismus bei den Griechen: Von Andronikos bis Alexander von Aphrodisias*, ii: *Der Aristotelismus im 1. und 2. Jh. n. Chr* [*Aristotelismus bei den Griechen* ii], vi: *Peripatoi* (Berlin, 1984), 399–425; id., 'Ein neues Zeugnis über Aristoteles, den Lehrer Alexanders von Aphrodisias', *Archiv für Geschichte der Philosophie*, 67 (1985), 266–9; P. Accattino,

some reflections of his own on the topic (B2 = 110. 25–112. 5).³⁵ If this division is sound, then B has a similar internal structure to C's, where the author's report of a solution to the difficulty (C1 = 112. 5–113. 12) is very clearly followed by his objections and a brief proposal of an alternative solution (C2 = 113. 12–24). For ease of reference, I will speak of the originator of the reported account in both B1 and C1 as 'the teacher'. For a basic orientation to the structure and contents of *De intellectu*, the reader is invited to consult the Appendix as needed.

We will be primarily concerned with the author's descriptions of how the agent intellect is involved in human thought, as offered in A3 (Section 2) and B2 (Sections 3–4), and with his account of

'Alessandro di Afrodisia e Aristotele di Mitilene', *Elenchos*, 6 (1985), 67–74; id., *De Intellectu*; Sharples, 'Scholasticism and Innovation', 1211) argued that the reference to 'Aristotle' in the text of 110. 4 should be understood as being not to the Stagirite, but to the Peripatetic of the same name from Mytilene whom we know about through Galen and who also seems to be mentioned by Alexander at *In Metaph.* 166. 19–20 Hayduck (cf. I. Kupreeva, 'Aristotelianism in the Second Century AD: Before Alexander of Aphrodisias' ['Aristotelianism before Alexander'], in A. Falcon (ed.), *Brill's Companion to the Reception of Aristotle in Antiquity* (Leiden, 2016), 138–59 at 142–3). (3) Improving on Moraux's original position in id., *Exégète*, 143–9 (cf. P. Thillet, *Alexandre d'Aphrodise: Traité du destin* (Paris, 1984), xviii), Schroeder and Todd, on the one hand (see Schroeder and Todd, *Two Commentators*, 22–31; cf. Schroeder and Todd, 'The *De Intellectu* Revisited'), and Opsomer and Sharples, on the other (see J. Opsomer and R. W. Sharples, 'Alexander of Aphrodisias, *De Intellectu* 110. 4: "I Heard This from Aristotle": A Modest Proposal', *Classical Quarterly*, 50 (2000), 252–6; cf. Sharples, *Alexander: Supplement* or R. Dufour, *Alexandre d'Aphrodise: De l'âme II (Mantissa)* [*Mantissa*] (Quebec, 2013), 23), proposed two ways of construing the text (with a slight emendation in the former case and without any emendation in the latter) in such a way that the account reported in B1 turns out not to be ascribed to any person in particular (the author merely reports an anonymous interpretation of Aristotle).

³⁵ For this division of B into B1 and B2, see Accattino, *De Intellectu*, 10–11, 50, who is followed on this point by Sharples, *Alexander: Supplement* (cf. id. *Mantissa*, 2); cf. also J. Söder, 'Alexander von Aphrodisias, Über den Geist' ['Über den Geist'], in H. Busche and M. Perkams (eds.), *Antike Interpretationen zur aristotelischen Lehre vom Geist* (Hamburg, 2018), 193–4; and de Haas, 'Active Intellectual Cognition', 28. Moraux (see e.g. id., *Aristotelismus bei den Griechen* iii, 393; id., *Aristotelismus bei den Griechen* ii, 412; id., 'De Anima', 294–5), in contrast, took for granted that B as a whole is a report of what the author heard from someone else (cf. Sharples, 'Scholasticism and Innovation', 1211–13; id., 'Peripatetics on Soul', 616–17; or Kupreeva, 'Aristotelianism before Alexander', 151–2), that is—in Moraux's view—from Aristoteles of Mytilene; moreover, following Trabucco (F. Trabucco, 'Il problema del "de philosophia" di Aristocle di Messene e la sua dottrina', *Acme*, 11 (1958), 97–150 at 120–4), Moraux thinks that in B as a whole the author reports Aristoteles' account of a *communis opinio*. The argument of the present paper can also be understood as providing additional support for Accattino's division.

human self-thinking in A4 insofar as this account arguably presupposes the involvement of the agent intellect as well (Section 6). Section 4 will provide a broader perspective on how the author's account of the agent intellect's involvement fits within the Peripatetic tradition, including the teacher's account reported in B1 and C1 (and the criticism of it in C2). But before plunging into the intricacies of *how* exactly the agent intellect is involved in human thinking, it will be worth tracing, in the remainder of the present section, the author's reasons for believing *that* the agent intellect needs to be involved in the first place.

The first thing to be cleared up is a peculiarity common to all three parts of *De intellectu*, namely the idea that the agent intellect comes to be involved in our thought as 'intellect from without'. Not only are Parts B and C introduced as two discussions of the 'intellect from without', but already A3's account of the agent intellect culminates in an identification of it with the 'intellect from without' (see 108. 19–109. 4).

This notion is not found in Aristotle's *De anima* but instead derives from *Generation of Animals* 2. 3,[36] where Aristotle deals with a set of questions about whether soul belongs to the embryo, how it does so, where it comes from, and when.[37] More specifically, he is interested in whether some part of the soul pre-exists its coming to be in the embryo (*GA* 2. 3, 736^{b}15–17) and whether, if coming from the male parent, it came to be in that parent 'from without' or not (*GA* 2. 3, 736^{b}19–20). Famously, Aristotle answers:

λείπεται δὴ τὸν νοῦν μόνον θύραθεν ἐπεισιέναι καὶ θεῖον εἶναι μόνον· οὐθὲν γὰρ αὐτοῦ τῇ ἐνεργείᾳ κοινωνεῖ <ἡ> σωματικὴ ἐνέργεια.

(*GA* 2. 3, 736^{b}27–9 Drossaart Lulofs)

It remains that intellect alone comes from without and is alone divine; for in its activity the bodily activity has no share.

---

[36] There are two further occurrences of 'intellect from without' in the corpus which may have inspired the author's reading: namely *De iuv.* 8, 472^{a}22–4 and *GA* 2. 6, 744^{b}21–6. The latter is suspected to be a corruption by P. Moraux, 'À propos du nous thurathen chez Aristote' ['Nous thurathen'], in A. Mansion (ed.), *Autour d'Aristote* (Louvain, 1955), 255–95 at 288–95. That may not be so, but Moraux seems right in his judgement that the passage can only be misleading when it comes to interpreting the key occurrence of the notion in *GA* 2. 3.

[37] For the place of these questions within the larger context of *GA* 2. 1–3, see S. Connell, 'How Does a Living Animal Come to Be from Semen? The Puzzles of Aristotle's *Generation of Animals* II 1–3', in D. Lefebvre (ed.), *The Science of Life in Aristotle and the Early Peripatos* (Leiden, forthcoming).

The precise meaning of this claim (including the key notion of 'from without', θύραθεν), its implications, and its role in Aristotle's overall discussion all remain controversial.[38] However, at least this much is clear: in *De intellectu* we find an ingenious interpretation of Aristotle's notion, which is at least *prima facie* more compelling as a way of articulating and highlighting a key move made by Aristotle in *DA* 3. 4–5 than as an exegesis of *GA* 2. 3 (indeed, the author shows no interest whatsoever in that chapter's questions).[39] Here is how the author explains the notion of 'intellect from without' at the end of A3:

νοῦς μὲν γὰρ καὶ τῶν ἄλλων ἕκαστον τῶν νοουμένων εἰδῶν ὅταν νοῆται, ἀλλ' οὐ θύραθεν οὐδ' ἔξωθεν νοῦς ὤν, ἀλλ' ὅτε νοεῖται γινόμενος. οὗτος δέ, νοῦς ὢν καὶ πρὸ τοῦ νοεῖσθαι, εἰκότως ὅταν νοηθῇ, θύραθέν τέ ἐστι καὶ λέγεται.

(109. 1–4)

For also each of the other objects of thought is intellect when it is being thought, but it is not intellect from without or from outside; rather it becomes intellect when it is being thought. This [i.e. the agent intellect], in contrast, which is intellect already before being thought [by us], is—and is rightly called—from without when it is thought [by us].

---

[38] The passage was at the heart of a longstanding controversy between Eduard Zeller (intellect *pre-exists*, as something non-individual, its coming to be a part of an individual human soul) and Franz Brentano (each human intellect is *created de novo* at some point of embryogenesis). The most representative pieces are E. Zeller, 'Über die Lehre des Aristoteles von der Ewigkeit des Geistes', *Sitzungsberichte der Königlich Preussischen Akademie der Wissenschaften*, 49 (1882), 1033–55; and F. Brentano, *Aristoteles Lehre vom Ursprung des menschlichen Geistes* (Leipzig, 1911). Interest in this passage was renewed by its close analysis in Moraux, 'Nous thurathen', which argued that 'intellect from without' constitutes merely one horn of an *aporia* that Aristotle seeks to eliminate. A similar reservation concerning Aristotle's commitment to 'intellect from without' was expressed e.g. by W. Charlton, 'Aristotle on the Place of Mind in Nature', in A. Gotthelf and J. G. Lennox (eds.), *Philosophical Issues in Aristotle's Biology* (Cambridge, 1987), 408–23 at 413–16. Caston, 'Two Intellects', 215–16 provides, in sharp contrast to *both* Zeller and Brentano, a 'fully traducian' reading of the claim. The passage and its reception are helpfully discussed by S. Connell, '"*Nous* Alone Enters from Outside": Aristotelian Embryology and Early Christian Philosophy', *Journal of Ancient Philosophy*, 2 (2021), 109–38, who expresses a sympathy with Alexander's understanding. For an earlier alternative approach developed already by Theophrastus, see R. Roreitner, 'Human Ontogeny in Aristotle and Theophrastus', *Apeiron*, 57 (2024), 427–77.

[39] For the historical background, motivation, and influence of this notion of intellect from without (also found in Alex. Aphr., *DA* 90. 19–91. 4), see R. Roreitner, '*Nous thurathen*: Between Theophrastus and Alexander of Aphrodisias', *British Journal for the History of Philosophy*, 33 (2025).

The agent intellect is thought by us as intellect 'from without' because it pre-exists—*qua* intellect—our act of thinking it, unlike other objects of our thought. Clearly, this has nothing to do with Aristotle's embryology. The idea derives instead from the contrast Aristotle draws at the end of *DA* 3. 4 in response to the question of whether intellect is itself intelligible (raised at *DA* 3. 4, 429^{b}26–9):

καὶ αὐτὸς δὲ νοητός ἐστιν ὥσπερ τὰ νοητά. (i) ἐπὶ μὲν γὰρ τῶν ἄνευ ὕλης τὸ αὐτό ἐστι τὸ νοοῦν καὶ τὸ νοούμενον· ἡ γὰρ ἐπιστήμη ἡ θεωρητικὴ καὶ τὸ οὕτως ἐπιστητὸν τὸ αὐτό ἐστιν. τοῦ δὲ μὴ ἀεὶ νοεῖν τὸ αἴτιον ἐπισκεπτέον. (ii) ἐν δὲ τοῖς ἔχουσιν ὕλην δυνάμει ἕκαστόν ἐστι τῶν νοητῶν. ὥστ' ἐκείνοις μὲν οὐχ ὑπάρξει νοῦς (ἄνευ γὰρ ὕλης δύναμις ὁ νοῦς τῶν τοιούτων), ἐκείνῳ δὲ τὸ νοητὸν ὑπάρξει.

(*DA* 3. 4, 430^{a}2–9 Ross)

And it [i.e. intellect] is intelligible just as the objects of thought are. (i) In the case of [objects] without matter, that which thinks is the same as that which is thought, for the theoretical knowledge and that which is known in this way are the same thing. The reason of not always thinking is yet to be explored. (ii) In [objects] having matter, each of the objects of thought is in potentiality.[40] And so intellect will not belong to them—for the intellect of such objects is a potentiality [for them] without matter—while being intelligible will belong to it [i.e. the intellect].

This important passage cannot be discussed here in its own right.[41] For our purposes it suffices to note that, by the author's lights, the agent intellect has in effect already been introduced in (i). As he puts it near the beginning of A3, this intellect is nothing other than 'the object intelligible by its own nature' (τὸ τῇ αὑτοῦ φύσει νοητόν, 107. 34), and that description is applicable only to 'the immaterial form' (τὸ ἄϋλον εἶδος, 108. 2), which is what the author takes to be the referent of 'the [objects] without matter' (τὰ ἄνευ ὕλης) at *DA* 3. 4, 430^{a}3.[42]

---

[40] Or, on an alternative construal (for which, see Menn, 'From III 4 to III 5', 119–23; cf. S. Menn, 'Aristotle's Theology', in C. Shields (ed.), *The Oxford Handbook of Aristotle* (New York, 2012), 422–64 at 443–4; C. Shields, *Aristotle: De Anima* (Oxford, 2016); F. D. Miller, *Aristotle: On the Soul* (Oxford, 2018)): 'In the case of [objects] which have matter, [the intellect] is each of the objects of thought in potentiality.'

[41] There is a close parallel to it at *Metaph.* Λ. 9, 1074^{b}38–1075^{a}5. For an insightful analysis, and an overview of existing interpretations, see Menn, 'From III 4 to III 5', 111–24. A very different approach (less congruent to *De intellectu*) is offered by S. Kelsey, *Mind and World in Aristotle's* De Anima [*Mind and World*] (Cambridge, 2022), 122–44.

[42] What he means is a form that on its own exists without any matter. In this respect, the author's understanding is to be contrasted with the influential idea that

Thought 'From Without' 193

Now why should such a form be itself an intellect? The answer is provided by the general account of thought that the author extracts from *DA* 3. 4. A form is being thought for exactly as long as it is separated from matter, and as such it is one and the same as the intellect thinking it.[43] In the case of objects having matter, the form must first be separated and become one and the same as a human intellect; indeed, upon separation, the form itself 'becomes intellect' (νοῦς γίνεται, 108. 6).[44] But an immaterial form clearly

---

'the [objects] without matter' include enmattered forms *qua* separated from matter by thought (for which, see e.g. L. Judson, *Aristotle, Metaphysics Lambda* (New York, 2019), 293–4, 318–23; or Kelsey, *Mind and World*, 122–4). His understanding is, however, problematic in that immaterial substances are never described by Aristotle as *forms*. Rather, Aristotle seems to reserve this notion for the formal causes of hylomorphic compounds. For a criticism of this influential move on Alexander's part (also prominent in Alexander's *De anima*), see E. E. Ryan, 'Pure Form in Aristotle', *Phronesis*, 18 (1973), 209–24; or, more recently, Judson, *Aristotle, Metaphysics Lambda*, 281–2. The author's understanding of (i), moreover, leads to a puzzle, for Aristotle speaks of a *plurality* of objects without matter (and this is echoed in *De intellectu* on at least two occasions), whereas there seems to be a *single* agent intellect. For more on this issue, see Section 5.

[43] This account is ultimately derived from the analogy with perception from which *DA* 3. 4 begins (429ᵃ13–18; cf. *De intellectu* 108. 10–13): the senses already are 'receptive of the form' (δεκτικὸν τοῦ εἴδους, 429ᵃ15–16), namely a form 'without the matter' (ἄνευ τῆς ὕλης, 424ᵃ18–19), as explained at *DA* 2. 12, 424ᵃ17–28. The exact meaning of this notion is notoriously controversial. For a critical discussion of two extreme approaches (no material change is involved, or no material particles are received) and an alternative approach (form is received in a different pair of contraries), see V. Caston, 'The Spirit and the Letter: Aristotle on Perception', in R. Salles (ed.), *Metaphysics, Soul, and Ethics: Themes from the Work of Richard Sorabji* (Oxford, 2005), 245–320 at 300–7, and V. Caston, 'Aristotle on the Transmission of Information: Receiving Form without the Matter', in D. Bennett and J. Toivanen (eds.), *Philosophical Problems in Sense Perception: Testing the Limits of Aristotelianism*, Studies in the History of Philosophy of Mind (Cham, 2020), 15–55. For another recent account, see K. Corcilius, 'The Gate to Reality: Aristotle's Basic Account of Perception', in C. Cohoe (ed.), *Aristotle's On the Soul: A Critical Guide* (Cambridge, 2022), 122–54. In Alexander's *De anima*, he distinguishes between the meanings of 'without the matter' applicable in the two cases: intellect not only does not receive the form as if it were itself a kind of matter (which is true of perception as well); it also does not receive the form 'as [the latter] being in matter and with matter' (ὡς ἐν ὕλῃ ὄντα καὶ μεθ' ὕλης, *DA* 83. 22–3 Bruns), which is exactly what perception does (see *DA* 83. 13–84. 14; cf. 86. 28–87. 24). No such contrast is to be found in A; something along these lines is introduced only in B1 (on which, more below).

[44] 'For intellect in actuality is nothing other than the form which is being thought, so that even each of those beings which are not intelligible simply [on their own] becomes intellect, when it is being thought' (ὁ γὰρ κατ' ἐνέργειαν νοῦς οὐδὲν ἄλλο ἢ τὸ νοούμενον εἶδός ἐστιν, ὥστε καὶ τούτων ἕκαστον τῶν οὐκ ὄντων ἁπλῶς νοητῶν νοῦς, ὅταν νοῆται, γίνεται, 108. 7–9). Cf. 109. 1–3, 7–8.

needs no such assistance, for it is already on its own perfectly separate from any matter. So, if being separate from matter coincides with being thought and being intellect, then an immaterial form is constantly being thought without this thinking depending on anything beyond this form itself, and it is itself an intellect or thought thinking itself.[45]

I say 'intellect *or thought*', for although I keep to the traditional translation of *nous* as 'intellect' throughout this paper, it is important to bear in mind that the term need not refer to a *subject* of thought; it can also refer to the *grasp* of some object, which can be either fully actual, as in an active thought of that object, or merely dispositional with respect to such a thought.[46] When an immaterial form is identified as itself being *nous*, the meaning of active thought comes to the foreground. The point is that when we come to think this form, it does not *become* a thought in us; instead, it comes to us as already being a thought, i.e. as a thought 'from without'.[47] The 'intellect from without', with which the author identifies the 'agent intellect', is an active thought that exists independently from human thinkers, but that can, under certain circumstances, come to be present in them as their own thought.

By our author's lights, then, Aristotle in effect first introduces the 'intellect from without' in *DA* 3. 4, and only in *DA* 3. 5 identifies it *as* the 'agent intellect', in connection with our thinking of enmattered forms. As for the rationale behind this identification, the closing passage of *DA* 3. 4 (quoted above) is again crucial. Like many after him, the author believes that Aristotle's account of '[objects] having matter' in (ii) provides the ultimate reason *why* something like the agent intellect needs to be involved in our thinking of enmattered forms:

---

[45] See 108. 16–19. In modern discussion, this line of thought has been emphasized as the key to Aristotle's argument in *Metaph*. Λ. 7, e.g. by J. G. DeFilippo, 'Aristotle's Identification of the Prime Mover as God', *Classical Quarterly*, 44 (1994), 393–409; and Menn, 'Aristotle's Theology', 443–4.

[46] The importance of this fact for Plato's and Aristotle's theology has been emphasized by S. Menn, 'Aristotle and Plato on God as *Nous* and as the Good', *Review of Metaphysics*, 45 (1992), 543–73; and id., *Plato on God as* Nous (Carbondale, 1995). In this paper, we will see how important it is for *De intellectu*'s account of human thought.

[47] In what follows, I continue using 'intellect' as the traditional placeholder for *nous*; it should, however, not be taken as anything more than that.

ἔστι δὲ οὗτος τὸ τῇ αὑτοῦ φύσει νοητὸν καὶ ἐνεργείᾳ τοιοῦτον· τοῦτο γὰρ ποιητικόν τε τοῦ νοεῖν καὶ εἰς ἐνέργειαν ἄγον τὸν ὑλικὸν νοῦν. . . . τὰ μὲν γὰρ ἔνυλα εἴδη ὑπὸ τοῦ νοῦ νοητὰ γίνεται ὄντα δυνάμει νοητά. χωρίζων γὰρ αὐτὰ τῆς ὕλης ὁ νοῦς, μεθ' ἧς ἐστιν αὐτοῖς τὸ εἶναι, ἐνεργείᾳ νοητὰ αὐτὸς αὐτὰ ποιεῖ.

(107. 34–108. 5; cf. 108. 14–15)

This [sc. the agent intellect] is the object intelligible by its own nature and in actuality. For this is what produces thinking and what leads the material intellect into actuality. . . . For the enmattered forms become intelligible by the agency of intellect, while being [on their own] intelligible [only] in potentiality: it is by separating these [forms] from the matter with which they have their being that intellect itself makes them intelligible in actuality.

It is far from clear in this passage *how* exactly the agent intellect is supposed to 'lead the material intellect into actuality'.[48] But Aristotle's account of '[objects] having matter' in (ii) is obviously taken to provide the ultimate reason *why* some such leading will be needed: it is because the enmattered forms are on their own intelligible only in potentiality, and thus need to be made intelligible in actuality by intellect, which must separate them from matter in order to think them.[49]

So much is clear from the quoted passage, which thus anticipates a rich tradition of compatibilist approaches to *DA* 3. 4–5.[50] But it is worth noting that the passage not only fails to spell out *how* the agent intellect is supposed to be involved, but in fact falls short of really *explaining* why such an intellect is needed. It turns out that this shortcoming marks A3 as a whole and is closely connected to

[48] When the author says that 'the enmattered forms become intelligible objects by the agency of *intellect*' (108. 3), it is not clear *which* intellect he means. Some interpreters have thought he speaks of the agent intellect (see e.g. Geoffroy, 'La tradition arabe', 206); others have thought he must have in mind the material intellect (see e.g. Accattino, *De Intellectu*, 11, 43, Sharples, *Alexander: Supplement*, 28). In Section 5, we will see that a part of the author's strategy in B2 is to ascribe certain characteristics to intellect precisely *without* specifying the kind of intellect in question. This may be his intention already here. What is clear is only that the agent intellect must somehow be involved in order for the separation, and so the thinking, to take place.

[49] That is why, among other things, the intelligibility of intellect does not imply that whatever has an intelligible essence has an intellect, as Aristotle worried at *DA* 3. 4, 429^{b}27–8 (echoing Plato, *Parm.* 132 C 9–11). The reason is just that the essence present in, say, Bucephalus is only *potentially* intelligible, and so only potentially an intellect.

[50] The reading is premised on one possible construal of (ii) (cf. n. 40 above). Menn, 'From III 4 to III 5', 119–23 offers an alternative to this traditional reading on which (ii) can be in no way used to motivate the notion of the agent intellect.

the fact that A3, rather surprisingly, stops short of spelling out any contrast between thought and perception.[51] This lapse may leave the reader puzzled: if even in the case of perception, as the author insists, the perceptual object in actuality (τὸ κατ' ἐνέργειαν αἰσθητόν) is one and the same as perception in actuality (τῇ κατ' ἐνέργειαν αἰσθήσει, 108. 11–12), then before the object is actually perceived, it is a perceptual object only in potentiality, and yet this clearly does not imply in the author's mind anything like an 'agent sense'.[52] The author would perhaps reply that something actual is needed, at least in the case of sight: colours can become actually perceived only *in light*. But this analogy, highlighted at the very outset of A3, cannot take us very far on its own: whatever light is on the author's account, it is certainly not an active perception or an 'agent sense'. So then why should the agency of *an intellect* be needed for potential objects of thought to become actual?

We should keep these shortcomings of A3 in mind when in Section 2 we come to its only description of *the way* in which the agent intellect is supposed to be involved. But first let us see how the gaps in answering the why-question are filled in by B1, which is introduced as tackling exactly this question.[53] It does so under the *prima facie* somewhat confusing heading of Aristotle's motivation for introducing the 'intellect from without'. But that heading should no longer surprise us once the author's understanding of 'intellect from without' has been taken on board.

The answer reported in B1 goes beyond the account of A3 in at least two respects.[54] First, it explicitly states the key *contrast* between perceptual and intelligible objects: perceptual objects are already 'in actuality' before being perceived, which allows them to

---

[51] There are only *analogies*: an analogy with light at 107. 29–34, echoing *DA* 3. 5, 430ᵃ15–17 (on which, more below), and a general analogy with perception at 108. 10–13, drawing on *DA* 3. 4, 429ᵃ13–18.

[52] For an overview of the medieval tradition of postulating an 'agent sense' in parallel to the agent intellect and its sources in Aristotle, I refer the reader to R. Roreitner, *Aristotle on the Nature and Causes of Perception* [*Nature and Causes*] (Cambridge, 2025), §5.5.

[53] Given the shortcomings of the overview given in A3, B turns out to be a natural continuation (or deepening) of A.

[54] For a detailed analysis of the argument of B1, I refer the reader to R. Roreitner, 'What Is New in Alexander's Noetic? Early Peripatetic Disagreements about the Material and the Agent *Nous*', in C. Bobonich et al. (eds.), *Human and Divine* Nous *from Ancient to Byzantine and Renaissance Philosophy and Religion: Key Themes, Intersections, and Developments* (Leiden, forthcoming).

Thought 'From Without' 197

act on the senses and make them actual as well (110. 13–14), whereas 'none of the objects thought by us is intelligible in actuality' (ἐνεργείᾳ δὲ νοητὸν τούτων τῶν νοουμένων ὑφ' ἡμῶν οὐδέν ἐστιν, 110. 16–17), which means that none can produce thinking. It cannot do so because:

[**Actuality Principle**] οὐ γὰρ οἷόν τε ποιητικόν τι εἶναί τινος μὴ ὂν αὐτὸ ἐνεργείᾳ.

(110. 15–16)

it is impossible for something to be the producer of something else if it is not itself in actuality [in the relevant respect].[55]

While Bucephalus' colour is capable of producing an act of seeing (by assimilating the sense of sight to itself), his equinity is not as such capable of producing an act of thought. So, since equinity is on its own unable to assimilate intellect to itself, it is apparently necessary for intellect to make equinity more intellect-like first (by separating it from matter). Otherwise, the sameness between equinity and intellect required for the one to be thought by the other can never be secured.

The second respect in which B1 goes beyond A3 concerns the reason why *another* intellect, in addition to the material one, is needed for this to happen. B1 offers a somewhat richer description of what the actualization of potentially intelligible objects consists in, namely 'separating and abstracting things that are in actuality perceptible from that with which they are perceptible and capturing them on their own' (χωρίσαι καὶ ἀφελεῖν [τὰ ἐνεργείᾳ αἰσθητὰ] τούτων, σὺν οἷς ὄντα ἐστὶν αἰσθητά, καὶ ὁρίσασθαι καθ' αὐτά, 110. 19–20). But more importantly, B1 provides an explanation of why this act of separation presupposes *another* intellect:

εἰ δὴ αὕτη ἐστὶν ἡ τοῦ νοῦ τοῦ δυνάμει πρότερον ὄντος ἐνέργεια, δεῖ δὲ τὸ γινόμενον καὶ ἀγόμενον ἐκ τοῦ δυνάμει εἰς ἐνέργειαν ὑπό τινος γίνεσθαι ἐνεργείᾳ ὄντος, δεῖ τινα εἶναι καὶ νοῦν ποιητικὸν ἐνεργείᾳ ὄντα.

(110. 20–3)

---

[55] The principle (restated more fully at 110. 21–2, quoted below) is, as it stands, somewhat ambiguous, for it does not spell out the relevant kind of actuality. The potentially intelligible enmattered form (say, Bucephalus' horse form) is surely something actual. And having an actual colour does not guarantee that the thing can actually be seen by a perceiver in its proximity (who can see the former only in light).

If, then, this [act of separation] is an activity of the intellect *which was previously in potentiality*, and what comes to be and is being brought from potentiality to actuality must come to be by the agency of something which is in actuality, then there also has to be an agent intellect which is in actuality.

Here, unlike in A3, we have a clear statement of the need for *another* intellect as an efficient cause acting on the material intellect and thereby enabling it to make the enmattered forms intelligible in actuality. The rationale can be spelled out thus:

Problem of Two Potentialities: the account of *De anima* 3. 4 leaves us with a picture in which one potentiality (the potential 'material' intellect) is faced with another potentiality (the potentially intelligible form) such that each side lacks the actuality required by *Actuality Principle* to actualize the other side; hence, their encounter cannot as such produce actual thought.[56]

B1 is the earliest extant articulation of this line of reasoning, which underlies most compatibilist approaches to *DA* 3. 4–5.[57] But it allows for a wide range of understandings of *the way* in which the agent intellect is supposed to be involved. Indeed, we will see that two very different ways of fleshing out this overall framework are contained in B (and, again, in C).[58] The 'bizarre' and 'paradoxical' account represents in turn just one, rather uncharitable way of interpreting the alternative to the teacher's account contained in B2.

In what follows, I will call into question two key assumptions behind this standard interpretation. First, the author's account is made unnecessarily paradoxical by assuming that we think the agent intellect *before* thinking any enmattered form. And second,

---

[56] This problem has been discussed more often with respect to Alexander's *De anima*. Moraux, *Exégète*, 73–7 argued that the relative autonomy ascribed to material intellect in *De anima* founders on this problem. The same point was repeated by Bazán, 'L'authenticité', and used to argue that *De anima* represents an earlier stage of Alexander's thought that the account of *De intellectu* seeks to overcome. Moraux's statement of the problem has been called into question first by Schroeder, 'Potential Intellect', and more recently by Tuominen, 'Active Intellect', 63–9, and especially by Tuominen, 'Receptive Reason', which argue that in *De anima* Alexander develops a robust account of 'receptive reason' that allows him at least to mitigate the alleged problem without invoking any direct involvement of the agent intellect. Cf. Guyomarc'h, 'Active Intellect'.

[57] In Section 4 we will see that Theophrastus already understood the agent intellect as an efficient cause of human thinking, but that he arrived at the need of such a cause by a very different route.

[58] More on that in Sections 4–5.

Thought 'From Without'   199

most of the bizarreness comes from the incorrect tacit assumption that in thinking the agent intellect we are grasping the immaterial form, i.e. the loftiest object of thought, as it is in itself. I will argue that, according to the account of B2, the material intellect thinks the agent intellect *simultaneously* with thinking each enmattered form and that it thinks it *as its own*—imperfectly attained—*fulfilment*, i.e. as its own thought. It turns out that the treatment of the *Problem of Two Potentialities* in B1 was based on an incorrect and unquestioned assumption, namely that the potentiality on the side of the material intellect is a passive one in the sense that it can only be actualized by way of being affected.

Before inquiring into the details of B2's account, however, we need to have a look at how the author describes the involvement of the agent intellect in A3. We will see that this section not only falls short of properly motivating any direct involvement of the agent intellect (as suggested above), but also stops short of actually claiming any such involvement and focuses instead on a *teleological* relation between the material and the agent intellect.

2. Teleological framework

Everything the author says in A about *how* the agent intellect is involved is contained in the following densely packed sentence:

τοῦτο δὴ τὸ νοητόν τε τῇ αὑτοῦ φύσει καὶ κατ' ἐνέργειαν νοῦς, αἴτιον γινόμενον τῷ ὑλικῷ νῷ τοῦ κατὰ τὴν πρὸς τὸ τοιοῦτο εἶδος ἀναφορὰν χωρίζειν τε καὶ μιμεῖσθαι καὶ νοεῖν καὶ τῶν ἐνύλων εἰδῶν ἕκαστον καὶ ποιεῖν νοητὸν αὐτό, θύραθέν ἐστι λεγόμενος νοῦς ὁ ποιητικός, οὐκ ὢν μόριον καὶ δύναμίς τις τῆς ἡμετέρας ψυχῆς, ἀλλ' ἔξωθεν γινόμενος ἐν ἡμῖν, ὅταν αὐτὸν νοῶμεν.

(108. 19–24)

This thing which is both the object intelligible by its own nature and intellect in actuality comes to be the cause for the material intellect of the fact that, by reference to this kind of form, it separates and imitates and thinks each of the enmattered forms too and makes it intelligible; this is the agent intellect which is said [to come] 'from without' because it is not a part or a capacity of our soul, but comes from outside whenever we think it.

The participial clause here (αἴτιον γινόμενον... αὐτό)—together with two passages from B2 (on which, more in Section 5)—has become the key support for the 'bizarre' and 'paradoxical' interpretation.

This is because it has been widely understood as saying that the material intellect first thinks 'the object intelligible by its own nature' (i.e. the agent intellect) and then in an act of imitation (μιμεῖσθαι) establishes a connection between this object and the forms separated from matter which thus come to be thought too (καὶ τῶν ἐνύλων εἰδῶν ἕκαστον).[59] At the same time, the alleged assertion here that the material intellect 'imitates' the agent intellect has been used by Schroeder as a key piece of support for his alternative claim that there is a discernible Neoplatonist influence behind *De intellectu*.[60]

The received text, however, is more difficult than is usually recognized. First, it does not really say what interpreters often read in it, namely that the material intellect somehow imitates the agent intellect. If μιμεῖσθαι has a grammatical object, as one would expect, it must be the same as the object of χωρίζειν[61] ('separating') and νοεῖν ('thinking'), and this is clearly 'each of the enmattered forms'. But what would it mean for the material intellect to 'imitate' enmattered forms? Sometimes interpreters refer to the passage as if it were *in fact* the agent intellect which is imitated by the material intellect.[62] Schroeder and Todd even *translate* the passage in such a way that it appears as if enmattered forms were *not* the natural candidate for the grammatical object of μιμεῖσθαι and paraphrase it as saying that the human intellect imitates the agent intellect. But their translation is strained, to say the least.[63]

---

[59] One may, then, think of the passage as echoing Aristotle's account of how perishable sublunar beings 'imitate' the eternal and divine ones at *GC* 2. 10, 336ᵇ27–337ᵃ7, *Metaph*. Θ. 8, 1050ᵇ24–30, or *DA* 2. 4, 415ᵃ23–ᵇ7.

[60] See Schroeder and Todd, *Two Commentators*, 64–5; Schroeder, 'Provenance', 112.

[61] In other occurrences in *De intellectu*, the object of χωρίζειν is duly expressed, see 108. 4, 108. 14, 108. 17, 110. 19 (111. 18—the only apparent exception—is a substantivized infinitive).

[62] See e.g. Bazán, 'L'authenticité', 482: 'Pour les rendre intelligibles, l'homme doit établir entre les formes immergées dans la matière et cet "intellect par nature" une relation d'imitation (μιμεῖσθαι) qui s'accomplit précisément par la séparation (χωρίζειν)' ('To make them intelligible, humans must establish between the forms immersed in matter and this "intellect by nature" a relation of imitation (μιμεῖσθαι) which is accomplished precisely by means of separation (χωρίζειν).'). To retrieve this from the text, one would need to assume that the object of μιμεῖσθαι is not expressed, which seems to presuppose that the object of χωρίζειν is also not expressed (but see n. 61 above). Still, the sentence would be strange because even if τῶν ἐνύλων εἰδῶν ἕκαστον ('each of the enmattered forms') is not *grammatically* the object of χωρίζειν, it is clearly the actual object of the separation, so that the position of μιμεῖσθαι between χωρίζειν and νοεῖν as having an entirely different object remains disturbing.

[63] See Schroeder and Todd, *Two Commentators*, 64. Here is the crucial part of the sentence in their translation that makes it seem as if there were no difficulty with

Paolo Accattino, in contrast, notices the problem[64] and provides a subtle interpretation of what the author might mean by an 'imitation' of enmattered forms, preserving the key idea that the agent intellect serves as the model of the process and must be thought by the material intellect before the latter begins to separate and think enmattered forms.[65] The suggestion is that the material intellect is *reproducing* (μιμεῖσθαι) the enmattered form in such a way as to *become* as *similar* as possible to the object intelligible by its own nature, i.e. the pure form. So the *reproduction* of the enmattered form is, in fact, an *imitation* of the object intelligible by its own nature.[66] This interpretation allows Accattino to ascribe to the author of *De intellectu*—on the basis of this very passage—the 'ingenious but paradoxical' idea that 'the first thought of man has to be concerned with nothing other than the god of [*Metaphysics*] *Lambda*'.[67] This idea is also identified in the same passage, and

μιμεῖσθαι and no implication of temporal priority: 'it becomes the cause of the material intellect's separating, imitating and thinking with reference to such a form *and* of its also making each of the enmattered forms itself an object of thought' (emphasis added). The idea, it seems, is to take the καί after νοεῖν, not as an adverb going with τῶν ἐνύλων εἰδῶν ἕκαστον (the agent intellect 'becomes the cause...of separating, imitating and thinking *also* each of the enmattered forms'), but as a conjunction that coordinates ποιεῖν with the three preceding verbs (χωρίζειν—μιμεῖσθαι—νοεῖν). Yet the way Schroeder and Todd then need to construe καὶ τῶν ἐνύλων εἰδῶν ἕκαστον καὶ ποιεῖν νοητὸν αὐτό is highly questionable. First, there is one καί too many (they translate the first καί conjunctively and the second καί adverbially, but one cannot have a double καί in Greek meaning 'and...also'). Second, the last word αὐτό seems superfluous as well: the interpretation of it as 'itself' seems strained and it remains obscure what it is supposed to add. The same objections can be raised against Dufour, *Mantissa*, 20, in whose translation the second καί and αὐτό are simply omitted ('devenant cause...du fait que ce dernier, en référant chacune des formes dans la matière à une telle forme, les sépare, les imite, les pense et les rend intelligibles'). Thanks to Victor Caston for a discussion of these grammatical issues.

[64] As Moraux, *Exégète*, 128, did before (for more on his understanding, see n. 81 below).
[65] Accattino, *De Intellectu*, 44–5.
[66] Cf. P. Accattino and P. C. Ghiggia, *Alessandro di Afrodisia: De anima II (Mantissa)* [*Mantissa*] (Alessandria, 2005), 190 n. 30, where *this* is claimed to be the idea behind μιμεῖσθαι: the material intellect acquires a capacity to think that 'consists essentially in *reproducing* (this seems to me the meaning of *mimeisthai* at 108.21) from perceptible entities the forms intelligible in act, separating them from the matter with which they exist' ('consiste essenzialmente nel *riprodurre* (questo mi pare il significato di *mimeisthai* in 108, 21) a partire dagli enti sensibili delle forme intelligibili in atto, separandole dalla materia con la quale esse esistono').
[67] Accattino, *De Intellectu*, 46; cf. Accattino and Ghiggia, *Mantissa*, 190 n. 30.

characterized as 'bizarre', by Robert Sharples[68] (who follows Accattino's interpretation of μιμεῖσθαι),[69] and indeed by most readers of *De intellectu* regardless of how they construe the difficult sentence.[70]

I would offer the following points. First, there is some evidence in the Arabic translation indicating that the sentence may be at one or two points corrupt. Second, even if we keep to the received text, there is nothing in the sentence that strongly suggests the 'bizarre' and 'paradoxical' account. For all we know, the author may have in mind here a purely *teleological* relation to the agent intellect; and even if he is assuming that one must already think the agent intellect in order to think enmattered forms (as is unmistakably affirmed in B2), there is nothing to suggest (here or elsewhere) that the former *temporally precedes* the latter.[71]

To cut a long story short, we have a very respectable Arabic translation (which comes from approximately the same time as the most ancient Greek manuscript[72] and which usually seems to follow the original meticulously),[73] and this translation suggests, at least *prima facie*, that the translator's text (i) had δέχεσθαι in place

---

[68] Sharples, *Alexander: Supplement*, 29 n. 65.
[69] Sharples, *Alexander: Supplement*, 30 n. 66.
[70] The most significant exception is Schroeder and Todd, *Two Commentators*, but their reading of the present passage seems hardly defensible: see n. 63 above. According to Papadis, *Seelenlehre bei Alexander*, 368–9, the sentence describes the agent intellect as *a part of the human soul*; but this reading can appear plausible only so long as one omits 108. 22–4 (as Papadis does), where the author clearly precludes this interpretative option.
[71] At the end of the quoted passage, the author does, to be sure, speak of our thinking of the agent intellect, but it is not obvious whether he takes this to be a precondition of our thinking of enmattered forms or instead the climax of our intellectual development. Even if he did have in mind here a precondition of our thinking of enmattered forms, that would in no way suggest that it is temporally prior to this thinking.
[72] Codex Venetus bibliothecae S. Marci 258 (V): see I. Bruns, *Alexandri Aphrodisiensis De anima liber cum Mantissa* [*De anima cum Mantissa*] (Berlin, 1887), v–x; and Sharples, *Mantissa*, 9–11. M. Rashed, 'Nicolas d'Otrante, Guillaume de Moerbeke et la "Collection Philosophique"', *Studi Medievali*, 43 (2002), 693–717 at 715–16, dates it to 850/860.
[73] The Arabic translation is by Isḥāq ibn Ḥunayn (d. 910/911). The text was edited by Finnegan (J. Finnegan, *Texte arabe du PERI NOY d'Alexandre d'Aphrodise* (Beirut, 1956)) and Badawī ('Abd al-Raḥmān Badawī, *Commentaires sur Aristote perdus en grec et autres épîtres* (Beirut, 1972). Since then, new manuscripts have been discovered, and we will have to wait for a new edition currently being prepared by Michael Chase. On the Arabic version and its reception, see Geoffroy, 'La tradition arabe'.

Thought 'From Without' 203

of μιμεῖσθαι, and (ii) lacked the καί before τῶν ἐνύλων εἰδῶν.[74] If this should prove to be the right reading, it would be much easier to interpret the text. (i) Instead of the surprising and isolated μιμεῖσθαι (which gave rise to much ungrounded speculation about the involvement of the agent intellect), there would be a perfectly intelligible sequence χωρίζειν (separating)—δέχεσθαι (receiving)—νοεῖν (thinking), each term having 'each of the enmattered forms' for its grammatical object. (ii) The text would not be saying that each of these forms is thought *too*, and so it would not imply that the immaterial form is thought by the material intellect, let alone that it is thought temporally prior to the enmattered forms.

The first and more radical emendation does not, however, have a sufficiently strong textual basis to be confidently embraced: the evidence of the Arabic translation on this point is inconclusive, and it seems much easier to explain a change from μιμεῖσθαι into δέχεσθαι, as the *lectio facilior*, than the other way round.[75] And

---

[74] The translation of 108. 19–22 reads as follows (I quote from Badawī's edition): *fa-hāḏā l-maʿqūlu bi-ṭabīʿati-hi, llaḏī huwa ʿaqlun bi-l-fiʿl, iḏā ṣāra ʿillatan li-l-ʿaqli l-hayūlānī li-l-intizāʿi wa-t-taqabbuli wa-t-taṣawwuri li-kulli wāḥidin mina ṣ-ṣuwari l-hayūlāniyyāti wa-kulli maʿqūlin bi-taraqqī-hi naḥwa tilka ṣ-ṣūrati, qīla fī-hi inna-hu l-ʿaqlu l-mustafād al-fāʿil*. The verbal noun *taqabbul* corresponds here to the Greek μιμεῖσθαι (Finnegan's edition reports an alternative reading in the Istanbul manuscript Jarullah 1279 which has *tanaqqul* ('to be transferred', 'to shift') instead of *taqabbul*; that, however, makes no good sense and is best interpreted as a corruption from *taqabbul*, which seems to be why Badawī does not even bother describing this variant). *Taqabbul* would be a quite natural translation of Greek δέχεσθαι ('to receive'). Indeed, the root *qbl* seems to be reserved by the translator for δέχεσθαι and its derivatives. At 107. 17–19, for instance, δύναμις δεκτική ('receptive capacity') is translated as *qūwa qābila*; λαμβάνειν ('to receive', 'to grasp') and its derivatives, in contrast, are usually rendered as *'aḫaḏa* and its derivatives: see 108. 15; cf. e.g. 107. 21 and 111. 8, 12, 13. The discrepancy between the received Greek text and the Arabic translation has been noticed by F. W. Zimmermann and H. V. B. Brown, 'Neue arabische Übersetzungstexte aus dem Bereich der spätantiken griechischen Philosophie', *Der Islam*, 50 (1973), 313–30 at 317 n. 25; and by Geoffroy, 'La tradition arabe', 212 n. 42. Both articles suggested emendations of the Arabic text, reading either *tamaṯṯul* ('assimilating oneself to something else') or *taqlīd* ('following authority') instead of *taqabbul*. But these emendations are purely conjectural (moreover, *taqlīd* is not a natural translation for μιμεῖσθαι at all). Cf. H. A. Davidson, *Alfarabi, Avicenna, and Averroes, on Intellect: Their Cosmologies, Theories of the Active Intellect, and Theories of Human Intellect* (Oxford, 1992), 21–2, who translates the verb in question as 'abstracting', but without quoting the Arabic. Thanks to Peter Adamson for a discussion of this issue. For a possible explanation of the received Arabic text, see n. 75 below.

[75] Thanks to Victor Caston for insisting on the second point. As for the first: the occurrence of *taqabbul* in place of μιμεῖσθαι at 108. 21, as surprising as it has seemed to interpreters, is, in fact, not unique. In the Arabic translation of Themistius'

there is no real need for this radical measure, for the author's use of μιμεῖσθαι can be satisfyingly explained and interpreted as saying nothing essentially different from what the more natural δέχεσθαι would say (more on that below).

But the second possible emendation appears attractive: the possibility of the penultimate καί in a sequence of τε καί...καί...καί... καί having been added erroneously certainly appears more plausible.[76] And it appears attractive because the καί in question causes difficulties that are much harder to handle than μιμεῖσθαι. It would need to be interpreted adverbially (as most scholars have done),[77] but this introduces an unexpected slip on the author's side. The text says, in effect, that not only the enmattered forms, but also the object intelligible by its own nature is *separated*, imitated, and thought by the material intellect; and it says this immediately after the author went out of his way to emphasize that this object does *not* derive its property of being intelligible 'from an intellect that would *separate* it from matter' (παρὰ τοῦ χωρίζοντος αὐτὸ τῆς ὕλης νοῦ, 108. 17–18). Deleting the third καί, as the Arabic translation suggests, saves the author from this slip. However, if we accept this emendation, the text can hardly support the 'bizarre' and 'paradoxical' account, for it will not even touch upon the idea that separating and thinking enmattered forms presupposes thinking the agent intellect.

But even if we retain the received Greek text, there is still no real support to be found for the 'bizarre' and 'paradoxical' account. This account is certainly not supported by the author's use of

In DA and of Aristotle's *Physics*—which are likely also to come from Isḥāq ibn Ḥunayn—we encounter something similar. Where the Greek text of Themist. *In DA* (drawing on *DA* 2. 4, 415ª26–ᵇ3) says that the reproductive power desires the divine and *imitates* it (ὀρέγεται τοῦ θείου καὶ μιμεῖται ἐκεῖνο, 53. 12–13 Heinze), the translator uses *tataqabbalu* for μιμεῖται. And likewise in the Arabic translation of *Phys.* 2. 2, 194ª22 and 2. 8, 199ª16, where Aristotle speaks of art imitating nature (and where the corruption into δέχεσθαι would make no sense at all). It is, therefore, quite possible that *taqabbul* at 108. 21—which scholars thought to be in need of emendation if it is to translate the Greek μιμεῖσθαι (cf. n. 74 above)—in fact represents an unusual but acceptable way of rendering the Greek verb. Thanks to Nicholas Aubin for a discussion of these passages.

[76] Especially if the scribe understood the 'reference' to the immaterial form in terms of it being thought—perhaps because he was looking over his shoulder to B2, where the idea that the material intellect needs to think the agent intellect in order to think an enmattered form is unambiguously expressed.

[77] For two exceptions, see n. 63 above. Söder, 'Über den Geist', 215 does not translate the καί at all (although he prints it in Greek).

μιμεῖσθαι. If it occurred in the original text, it was, I submit, most probably intended to emphasize the fact that enmattered forms are received by the intellect quite differently from how they are present in the material objects. The author explained at the very outset of A1 that the first intellect is not 'material' in the sense of being able literally to receive forms in the way in which matter receives them and then as a result literally become what it thinks.[78] The material intellect is, instead, similar to the receptacle in Plato's *Timaeus* in that it never really becomes what it receives.[79] Now Plato says that the 'figures that enter and depart' the receptacle are only 'imitations of those that always exist' (τὰ δὲ εἰσιόντα καὶ ἐξιόντα τῶν ὄντων ἀεὶ μιμήματα, 50 C 4–5), and that the respective part of the receptacle 'appears to be...earth and air insofar as it receives imitations of these' (φαίνεσθαι...γῆν τε καὶ ἀέρα καθ᾽ ὅσον ἂν μιμήματα τούτων δέχηται, 51 B 4–6). Similarly, one may insist, the intellect does not receive the form that it thinks in the way matter would receive it, but rather 'portrays' or 'imitates' it while remaining something different from it (it only 'portrays', for example, the form of horse without really becoming horse).[80] That seems to be a perfectly sound point, which can indeed be helpfully articulated in terms of 'imitation' without carrying any implication whatsoever for how the agent intellect may or may not be involved.[81] The

---

[78] See 106. 20–3; cf. 107. 17. Cf. *DA* 3. 4, 429ᵃ15–16, where Aristotle (drawing on *DA* 2. 12, 424ᵃ21–4) describes intellect as 'being in potentiality like [its object] but not it' (δυνάμει τοιοῦτον ἀλλὰ μὴ τοῦτο).

[79] See *Tim.* 50 B 5–51 A 4, which is clearly in the background of Aristotle's description of the potential intellect at *DA* 3. 4, 429ᵃ20–2 (cf. V. Caston, 'Aristotle's Argument for Why the Understanding Is Not Compounded with the Body', *Proceedings of the Boston Area Colloquium in Ancient Philosophy*, 16 (2000), 135–75 at 156–8; or Menn, 'From III 4 to III 5', 104–7).

[80] As, for instance, one can imitate people speaking from a distance by remaining close but speaking quietly (see *Mant.* 15, 147. 4–5), or as birds can imitate the voices of other animals and perhaps even the sounds of non-living things (*In Metaph.* 3. 20–2). The classic Peripatetic example of art imitating nature (most clearly articulated in *Phys.* 2. 2) may fall under the same rubric, insofar as it is important to emphasize the extent to which art production can never really become natural; cf. *In Metaph.* 103. 37–104. 3: art can at most imitate nature because the former is rational (λογική) whereas the latter non-rational (ἄλογος). Thanks to Stephen Menn for a discussion of what μιμεῖσθαι can mean in *De intellectu*.

[81] Moraux, *Exégète*, 128–32 already sought a more innocent interpretation of μιμεῖσθαι. But in sharp contrast to the reading proposed above, he understood μιμεῖσθαι in terms of 'identifying itself with' or 'completely assimilating oneself to'. It is, however, doubtful whether μιμεῖσθαι is an apt verb for emphasizing identity and complete assimilation (cf. Donini, *Tre studi*, 61). In any case, Moraux's

idea of 'portraying' or 'imitating', rather than literally receiving, may be an anticipation of the most distinctive move of B2, which sees the author insisting emphatically that the human intellect is *not passive* but productive in its grasping (λαμβάνειν) of enmattered forms. But in any case, this idea has no obvious implications for the involvement of the agent intellect.

The only unquestionable and explicit description of the agent intellect's involvement in our passage, then, comes under the notion of 'reference' (ἀναφορά). The material intellect is said to do everything it does 'by reference to this kind of form' (κατὰ τὴν πρὸς τὸ τοιοῦτο εἶδος ἀναφοράν, 108. 20–1), that is, to the immaterial form which turned out to be the agent intellect. Does this description support the 'bizarre' and 'paradoxical' account? Evidently not, for having reference to something else does not imply having an articulate thought of it. This is demonstrated by the two other uses of the term in *De intellectu*: in C2 (113. 15–16), the author improves on the idea from C1 (113. 6–8) and speaks of providence as realized by 'things here' (τὰ ἐνταῦθα) having reference (ἀναφορά) to the divine things (ἐπὶ τὰ θεῖα). Neither in C1 nor in C2 does this idea of 'reference' imply, absurdly, that everything in the sublunar world has some grasp of the divine things.

It seems more likely that the author's talk of 'reference' here is an expression of a principle identified by Gweltaz Guyomarc'h:

Principle of Maximal Causality: 'Among a set of things instantiating a property ϕ, what is supremely ϕ is necessarily cause of being-ϕ in the rest of the set.'[82]

Guyomarc'h has convincingly argued that this principle governs Alexander's *teleological* account of the role of the agent intellect in

---

circumspection concerning the meaning of μιμεῖσθαι did not prevent him from insisting that, according to this passage, each of us thinks the agent intellect before even acquiring the capacity to abstract enmattered forms (see Moraux, *Exégète*, 129).

[82] See Guyomarc'h, *L'unité de la métaphysique*, esp. 104–11, 279–96 ('le principe de causalité du maximum'; the English label and formulation is given in Guyomarc'h, 'Active Intellect', 103); cf. P. Golitsis, *Alexander of Aphrodisias: Commentary on Aristotle, Metaphysics (Books I–III): Critical edition with Introduction and Notes* (Berlin, 2022), xxxi–xxxiv. The principle draws on Aristotle, *Metaph.* α. 1, 993^{b}23–31, where Aristotle claims that 'most true is that which is the cause of truth for what comes after it' (ἀληθέστατον τὸ τοῖς ὑστέροις αἴτιον τοῦ ἀληθέσιν εἶναι, 993^{b}26–7 Ross; cf. *Post. An.* 1. 2, 72^{a}25–32), and is most fully expounded in Alexander's commentary on this passage (*In Metaph.* 147. 3–149. 13).

his *De anima*.⁸³ And the two uses of 'reference' in *De intellectu* seem to correspond neatly to the two key senses of finality which appear to be in play in *De anima*: the agent intellect is (a) the final cause of actualization for all enmattered forms (and so of their potential intelligibility for us), and (b) the ultimate final cause of all thinking acts. Neither of these roles presupposes that the agent intellect has been thought by something beyond itself (or that it is *directly* involved in any other way).⁸⁴

All that our passage in A3 says unambiguously is that if there existed no immaterial form (identical to the eternal thought of itself), then no enmattered form could ever be thought.⁸⁵ What the author may mean is that the grasp of an enmattered form is, at the end of the day, nothing other than an imperfect realization of the separateness and identity characteristic of the object intelligible by its own nature: this is what we ultimately aim at *qua* thinkers and what we only approximate in separating and thinking an enmattered form. But in any case, when, towards the end of our sentence, the author describes the agent intellect as coming 'from outside *whenever we think it*', he may very well be referring to the—rarely achieved—climax of human intellectual development rather than

---

⁸³ See Guyomarc'h, *L'unité de la métaphysique*, 270–9, and, in more detail (and with an explicit emphasis on finality), id., 'Active Intellect'. The principle is explicitly formulated at *DA* 88. 26–89. 1 Bruns: 'For in all things that which is something in the highest degree and primarily is also the cause of being such for other things' (ἐν πᾶσιν γὰρ τὸ μάλιστα καὶ κυρίως τι ὂν καὶ τοῖς ἄλλοις αἴτιον τοῦ εἶναι τοιούτοις). And it is applied to the agent intellect as 'that which is intelligible in the highest degree and by its own nature' (τὸ μάλιστα δὴ καὶ τῇ αὑτοῦ φύσει νοητόν, 89. 4–5).

⁸⁴ A teleological relation is, indeed, what the notion of ἀναφορά often expresses in Alexander (see e.g. the four occurrences in his *DA*: 28. 8–10; 39. 9–10; 73. 23–4; 76. 12–14; cf. *Mant.* 17, 151. 4–7; 19, 157. 11–13; 20, 164. 3–5, 165. 29–32; 168. 14–15; 23, 174. 13–14), although it is more general and can also articulate a different kind of asymmetric dependence (see e.g. *In Metaph.* 67. 28–30, where all assertions that something is or isn't white are said to have ἀναφορά to a single concept of white). There is a nice illustration of this more general meaning in Alexander's tripartite distinction at *In Metaph.* 2. 3–11 between (a) actions having their goal beyond themselves (and so having an essential ἀναφορά to this goal), (b) virtuous actions that are desirable through themselves but only for living beings that, unlike the gods, are endowed with passions (and thus have an essential ἀναφορά to passions), and (c) theoretical activity that has no ἀναφορά to anything beyond itself. In fact, Alexander's *De anima* and *De intellectu* both suggest that the description of (c) here is somewhat simplified, for theoretical thought directed towards enmattered forms does have an essential ἀναφορά to something else, namely the object intelligible by its own nature that exists eternally as the agent intellect. Thanks to Pantelis Golitsis for a discussion of ἀναφορά in Alexander.

⁸⁵ Cf. Alex. Aphr., *DA* 89. 6–7.

to something that must precede its first and imperfect steps. The contemplation of the immaterial form, in which the object is perfectly identical to the thinking act, is something that all our cognitive activities are ultimately directed at, though without any guarantee that we will ever reach that goal.[86]

Now it can hardly be denied that in B2 the author goes significantly further than this: he asserts that no one can think an enmattered form without somehow already thinking the agent intellect.[87] This distinctive claim seems to be motivated by the *Problem of Two Potentialities*, first formulated, as we have seen, in B1. The fact that this problem is not fully articulated in A3 may explain why the author is satisfied here with what looks like a purely teleological account of the involvement of the agent intellect. But I do not want to insist on this purity too much. If the adverbial καί before τῶν ἐνύλων εἰδῶν is retained (despite the embarrassment it causes), A3 seems already to take an additional step, for the key sentence will then imply that not only enmattered form, but also the agent intellect is somehow thought. The key question—which in any case awaits us in B2—is whether and how that step can be combined with an understanding of the agent intellect as the ultimate goal of our thought. This seems impossible on the 'bizarre' and 'paradoxical' interpretation, for then this goal will be unqualifiedly reached before our intellectual development even starts. What I wish to argue is that the account of B2 seeks a solution to the *Problem of Two Potentialities* within *an overall teleological framework* (as laid down in A3): the agent intellect comes to be thought by the material intellect simultaneously with each enmattered form, but it is thought as the material intellect's own imperfectly attained fulfilment. What is new in B2 is the idea that the ultimate goal is *already attained*—albeit imperfectly—in each genuine act of thinking an enmattered form. This surprising twist, I will argue, is exactly what provides the author with his distinctive solution to the *Problem*.

---

[86] Cf. de Haas, 'Active Intellectual Cognition', 28. This paper constitutes a rare exception to the 'bizarre' and 'paradoxical' approach. From de Haas's brief remarks on our passage (at p. 27), it is not quite clear how he reads it (evidently it is the agent intellect that he takes to be 'imitated'), but he tends to an overall teleological understanding.

[87] See 110. 31–111. 2, 111. 24–36, discussed in Section 5.

In Sections 4–5, we will see how the idea of the agent intellect being thought as the material intellect's *own*—more or less perfectly attained—*fulfilment* is articulated in B2 and how it responds to difficulties deriving from Theophrastus. But first, in Section 3, we will explore how this thinking can be *simultaneous* with the thinking of enmattered forms rather than preceding it in time and give reasons for attributing such an account to the author of *De intellectu*.

3. The first moment of thought

In B2 as in A3, the author will invoke the agent intellect as the cause of our separating the enmattered forms, making them intelligible in actuality and so thinking them. But since it is supposed to play this causal role *qua* object of our thinking, the *prima facie* impression is that we must think the agent intellect *before* we think any enmattered form. The only assumption needed here is that separating such a form and making it intelligible in actuality temporally precedes the act of thinking this form. Since separation already presupposes thinking the agent intellect, it would follow that we must think it *before* we think any enmattered form.

But whether this conclusion is really warranted depends on what exactly separating and making intelligible in actuality amounts to. The picture drawn in B1 may suggest that there are four temporally distinct events: (1) the agent intellect acts on the material intellect (whatever this acting consists in);[88] (2) the activated material intellect acts on the potential objects of thought ('abstracting' and 'separating' them); (3) the activated objects of thought act on the material intellect; (4) the material intellect thinks these objects. But there are reasons to doubt this analysis into four temporally distinct events. Aristotle's claim behind (3) is that to think *is* to be affected by the object in question, which suggests that (3) and (4) may, in fact, coincide as just two descriptions of one and the same event. Moreover, the account discussed in C1 clearly understands (1) and (2)/(4) as also being just two descriptions of one and the

---

[88] See 110. 20–4. Significantly, the agent intellect is conceived here as acting on the material intellect rather than on the potential objects of thought (as in most abstractionist accounts).

same event: roughly, (1) spells out the true nature of what we experience as (2) and/or (4).[89] Meanwhile, however, the relation between (2) and (3)/(4) remains unclear in B1 and C1. Since (3) and (4) are likely to coincide in a single event, and the author of *De intellectu* removes (3) from the picture anyway (insisting that there is nothing passive about thought), we can limit ourselves to the relation between (2) and (4).

The *prima facie* impression that (2) and (4) are two temporally distinct events—i.e. that there is first a process of separating and abstracting the potential objects of thought, and only when this process has been completed do the activated objects begin to be thought by the material intellect—is never explicitly confirmed, but also not precluded, by B1 or C1. There are, however, implicit problems raised by the analogy of light (in B1, as already in A3): in Aristotle's and Alexander's view, light becomes present in the entire illuminated medium at once and instantly, and similarly, the mediation of colours from the coloured objects via the illuminated medium to the organ of sight takes no time at all.[90] So although there is nothing unusual about a colour being 'activated' by illumination at moment T_1 and seen only at a later moment T_2, (a) these moments can never be two *immediately successive* events, for some interval of time must separate them, and (b) they *need not* be two temporally distinct events at all, for colours can be (and often are in the Aristotelian picture) seen immediately upon their activation by light, in which case both instantaneous events take place in the same moment T. We may still want to speak of them as two events insofar as one conditions the other (and not the other way round); but we may perhaps also speak of a single instantaneous event with two causally distinct aspects.

Now, there is at least one point directly relevant to this issue on which the author of *De intellectu* is (in both A3 and B2) clearer than the teacher reported in B1 and C1: there can be no interval of time between any two events of separating and thinking an enmattered form, i.e. between (2) and (4). Such an interval is impossible

---

[89] See 112. 16–18: when the agent intellect 'takes hold of' (λάβηται) the material intellect, 'then it is active as through an instrument...and then we are said to think' (τότε καὶ ὡς δι' ὀργάνου... ἐνήργησεν, καὶ τότε λεγόμεθα νοεῖν ἡμεῖς). More on this in Section 4.

[90] See Aristotle, *De sensu* 6, 446^{b}27–447^{a}11, and Alex. Aphr., *In De sensu* 131. 13–135. 22; cf. Alex. Aphr., *DA* 43. 8–11; *Mant.* 15, 143. 23–35; *In Meteor.* 129. 3–9.

for the simple reason that there is no way for an enmattered form to exist separately from matter and on its own other than in being thought by a material intellect. This observation is explicitly stated in Alexander's *De anima*,[91] and although there is no equally explicit passage in *De intellectu*, the author makes it clear enough that he takes the point for granted. This is the case already in his very first description of separation. Having said that enmattered forms are made intelligible in actuality by intellect that separates them from matter,[92] the author continues:

καὶ τότε ἕκαστον αὐτῶν, ὅταν νοῆται, ἐνεργείᾳ τε νοητὸν καὶ νοῦς γίνεται οὐ πρότερον οὐδὲ τῇ αὐτῶν φύσει ὄντα τοιαῦτα.

(108. 5–7)

and each of them at the very moment when it comes to be thought becomes an intelligible object in actuality and intellect, being such neither prior to this nor by its nature.

An enmattered form is separated from matter and becomes intelligible in actuality at the very same moment in which it comes to be thought. The fact that no interval of time can separate (2) from (4) is also reflected in other passages, such as the following:

ὁ γὰρ νοῦς τὸ εἶδος τοῦ νοουμένου λαμβάνων καὶ χωρίζων αὐτὸ τῆς ὕλης κατ' ἐνέργειαν ἐκεῖνό τε νοητὸν ποιεῖ καὶ νοῦς αὐτὸς κατ' ἐνέργειαν γίνεται.

(108. 14–15)

For as the intellect grasps and separates the form of the object that it thinks from the matter, it both makes it intelligible in actuality and becomes itself intellect in actuality.

What is not entirely clear from these (and other) descriptions of separation in A3 and B2 is whether it, i.e. (2), should be understood as a temporally extended process or as an instantaneous event. The present tense of most descriptions may *prima facie* suggest the former, but that is far from conclusive. The whole analysis of the agent intellect and its role in human thought is governed by Aristotle's analogy with light (this is what A3 starts from and what both B1 and B2 strongly emphasize), and the present tense is regularly used in speaking of the illumination and transmission of colours to express what are, in fact, instantaneous events. Given this

---

[91] Most clearly and famously at *DA* 90. 6–11; cf. already 88. 14–16.
[92] See 107. 34–108. 5, quoted and discussed in Section 1.

analogy and the reasons for thinking that activated objects of thought cannot exist without already being thought, it becomes very natural to expect separation, as the event of activating an object of thought, to be *an instantaneous event coinciding with the first moment of thinking* the object in question.[93]

There is only a single passage in B2 that explicitly addresses the temporal relation between separation (abstraction) and thinking (grasping). Unfortunately, the author articulates his thought with a not entirely transparent set of particles:

πρότερον γὰρ ποιεῖ τῇ ἀφαιρέσει νοητόν, εἶθ' οὕτως λαμβάνει τούτων τι ὃ νοεῖ τε καὶ ὁρίζεται, ὅτι τόδε τί ἐστι. καὶ γὰρ εἰ ἅμα χωρίζεται καὶ λαμβάνει, ἀλλὰ τὸ χωρίζειν προεπινοεῖται· τοῦτο γάρ ἐστιν αὐτῷ τὸ ληπτικῷ εἶναι τοῦ εἴδους.

(111. 15–19)

For [the intellect] first produces an object of thought [in actuality] by abstraction and then in this way grasps some such object which it thinks and captures as a this. For although it separates and grasps simultaneously, separating is, nevertheless, prior in account; that is because this [i.e. separating] is what being capable of grasping the form consists in.

The grammar here has posed difficulties to translators and interpreters. The passage has most often been read in line with the schoolbook precept that while εἰ καί means 'although' and introduces something the author recognizes as true or at least possible, καί εἰ means 'even if' and introduces an unreal scenario which should as such confirm the case under consideration.[94] Yet the universality of this precept has long been called into question.[95] And the truth is that the quoted passage presents a more complex set of particles, and this combination turns out to have a specific,

---

[93] The present tense can also be explained in different, less deflationary ways. (a) In most cases the author speaks of *a plurality* of forms being separated—each of them presumably in a different moment of time. From this perspective, one may speak of a temporally extended period of separation in the sense of the period within which all members of a certain class of forms have been separated; this is perfectly compatible with each such separation being an instantaneous event. (b) A still different explanation of the present tense would be as follows: separation occurs instantaneously and so coincides with the first moment of thinking the form in question; but one can also insist that separation *continues to occur* throughout the entire time of thinking that form insofar as it is *retained in its separated state*.

[94] Thus, even Schroeder and Todd, *Two Commentators*, 54 have 'For even if it separates', seemingly contrary to the best interests of their interpretation.

[95] See e.g. J. D. Denniston, *Greek Particles*, ed. by K. J. Dover, 2nd edn (London, 1996), 301–2; cf. H. W. Smyth, *A Greek Grammar for Colleges* [*Greek Grammar*] (New York, 1920), 538 (§2374).

well-established role in writings ascribed to Alexander, and indeed already in Aristotle. Roughly, the writer uses καὶ γὰρ εἰ... [+ indicative] ἀλλά... [+ indicative] in order to justify a claim by addressing what appears to be an objection to it. Importantly for the meaning of our passage, the apparent objection, introduced by καὶ γὰρ εἰ (and formulated in the indicative mood), is in *all* cases that I have found (there are dozens of them in Alexander) something the writer *accepts*; in the clause introduced by ἀλλά, he then explains why the mentioned fact does *not* constitute any real objection to or problem for the main claim.[96]

This, I submit, is also how we should read the quoted passage. The author is here providing a support for his key claim (to be discussed in Section 5) that thinking is not passive but productive, and he does so by insisting on the priority (πρότερον) of the abstraction by which intellect produces an object intelligible in actuality and the posteriority (εἶθ') of the grasping, thinking, and capturing of this object. Against this justification one could object (καὶ γὰρ εἰ...) that separation and grasping *are, in fact, simultaneous*. This our author seems to accept as true, but he explains why it does not cause any problem for his claim (ἀλλ'...), namely because although separation and grasping are simultaneous, the notion of separation is, nevertheless, *conceptually* prior to that of grasping. And the author goes on to spell out this notion of conceptual priority. The

---

[96] Take, for example, Alex. Aphr., *De mixt.* 13, 228. 17–21 Bruns: Alexander is explaining why Anaxagoras' claim that everything is mixed with everything must be wrong by saying that neither affections nor the forms of substances are separable. He formulates what could be seen as an objection to the latter claim: for even though (καὶ γὰρ εἰ) these [i.e. the forms of substances] are themselves substances, too.... And he explains why in fact this is no real objection:...yet (ἀλλ') they do not exist on their own. There are two further occurrences in *Mantissa* (8, 127. 11–12; 25, 182. 1–2; cf. 23, 175. 12–13 with optative), and two occurrences in his *De anima* (6. 8–11, 84. 4–6). There are also numerous examples elsewhere: see e.g. the following passages from *In Metaph.*: 64. 3–10; 77. 30–4; 148. 6–10; 212. 13–15; 234. 28–35; 263. 5–7; 276. 11–13; 309. 8–10; 316. 7–9; 323. 20–1; 359. 10–11; 368. 29–33; 434. 1–4. This combination of particles with the same function is, as mentioned above, already to be found in Aristotle, although there are only three occurrences. The clearest one is probably *GA* 1. 18, 732[b]19–22, where Aristotle makes an observation about insects as a key piece of support for his main claim that male sperm does not come from all bodily parts: insects provide the weightiest evidence, he says, for even though (καὶ γὰρ εἰ) it is not the case with all insects, it is true that (ἀλλ') in most cases during copulation 'the female extends a part of itself into the male' (τὸ θῆλυ εἰς τὸ ἄρρεν μέρος τι αὑτοῦ ἀποτείνει, 732[b]21–2 Drossaart Lulofs). See also *Post. An.* 1. 32, 88[a]18–22 and *Metaph.* B. 6, 1002[b]25–9.

point is that separation is included in the notion of what it is to be capable of grasping the form of something, and not the other way round. Presumably, it is insofar as the object in question is a hylomorphic compound, so that its form can only be grasped *when separated* from matter, that this inclusion obtains.

There is, as mentioned above, powerful evidence suggesting that if the author uses καὶ γὰρ εἰ... ἀλλά... with indicatives, he is dealing with a claim that he accepts as true. When he wishes to address a claim that is merely possible or admissible only for the sake of argument (which is far less frequent), he uses the optative.[97] But even if this were not so, i.e. even if the author were treating simultaneity as merely possible in the quoted passage, we would still have strong reasons to conclude that this is something he actually accepts as true. One such reason comes from his extensive use of the light analogy. For Aristotle, as noted above, illumination need not temporally precede the act of seeing, and when understood as including the illumination of the organ of sight, it is standardly simultaneous with the first moment of seeing. Indeed, the author of B2 claims that colours are seen 'along with' light (σὺν αὐτῷ) and similarly that enmattered forms are thought 'along with' the agent intellect.[98] In addition to these hints suggesting that the author actually took separation, thinking of enmattered forms, and thinking of the agent intellect to be simultaneous, there is one more consideration in favour of simultaneity: it allows us, as we will see in Section 5, to arrive at a more charitable reconstruction of how the author conceives the involvement of the agent intellect.

Before continuing, however, I should like to pre-empt one potential misunderstanding. Isn't it just obvious that the separation of an enmattered form (which activates it as an object of thought) must be a temporal process preceding the temporally extended activity of thinking? Such a separation surely presupposes a lengthy period of accumulating and processing experience (standardly

---

[97] See e.g. *In Metaph.* 300. 28–301. 1 where Alexander is allowing for the sake of argument against the relativists that the number two is both even and odd (cf. 400. 34–401. 1). However, not all occurrences with the optative (which are significantly less numerous) imply that the claim under consideration is deemed false by the author: it is also used to express something that is genuinely possible (thus, apparently, at *Mant.* 23, 175. 12–13) or to express more cautiously something the author in fact accepts (thus, e.g. at *In Metaph.* 206. 22–8).

[98] See 111. 32–4. More on this in Section 5.

with the assistance of a teacher): it is only through this time-consuming process that we finally become capable of grasping an enmattered form separately from its matter.[99] This much should be uncontroversial. The question is what exactly 'separation' (χωρίζειν), as used in *De intellectu*, refers to within this framework. One could understand it as somehow covering the whole process, perhaps beginning with the reception of perceptual forms 'without matter' in perception (*De anima* 2. 12), passing through the retention of *phantasmata* which 'are like percepts except without matter' (ὥσπερ αἰσθήματά ἐστι, πλὴν ἄνευ ὕλης, 3. 8, 432^{a}9–10),[100] and through 'inductive' processes that gradually purify the universal in question from all accidental features (as described most famously in Arist. *Metaph.* A. 1 and *Post. An.* 2. 19). But one can also see all of these as mere *preconditions* of the separation proper, which can only be an instantaneous event: this event occurs when a form, present to us in its enmattered state via *phantasmata*, memories, and experience, comes to be thought apart from matter and so becomes one and the same as the thinker's intellect, and indeed itself 'becomes intellect'.[101] A form cannot be thought *more or less* apart from matter and cannot be *more or less* intellect; either it is thought apart from matter and is intellect, or it isn't: there is nothing in between and so no room for this separation being, *stricto sensu*, a change (κίνησις) that takes place in time. Thus, we can speak of separation in a looser and in a stricter sense—one involving time, the other not—and we need to ask which of these is intended in the key passages of *De intellectu*.

To be more precise, the loose/strict distinction is not that important as long as we are concerned with a *teleological* account of the material intellect's dependence on the agent intellect (as is, I argued, primarily the case in A3). It is perfectly plausible to maintain that *both* the separation in a stricter sense and the separation in a looser sense are performed 'by reference to' the immaterial form.

---

[99] For an account of this process that draws on *Post. An.* 2. 19 and *Metaph.* A. 1, see Alex. Aphr., *DA* 82. 19–84. 14.

[100] What does Aristotle mean? I take him to mean that whereas percepts exist only as far as the respective matter is physically present to the perceiver (i.e. the object is acting on her), *phantasmata* are retained (and can be activated) even without this presence.

[101] See *De intellectu* 108. 6–9, 109. 1–3, and 109. 7–8. Cf. Alex. Aphr., *DA* 88. 10–16, 90. 4–11.

It is a perfectly Aristotelian thought to claim that already the specifically human way of perceiving and retaining *phantasmata* is thoroughly determined by the goal of arriving at thinking, and, ideally, thinking in the sense most properly pertaining to the immaterial form itself.[102] Here, however, we are not concerned with something intellect *performs* properly speaking, but rather with activities of the perceptive part of the human soul and the way it is determined (or co-opted) by human rationality. When it comes to 'separation' as an act of the intellect itself, and indeed as the most distinctive of its acts whereby it is to be contrasted with the perceptive part (as in B2), and when the author claims that this act presupposes an act of thinking the agent intellect, it becomes at the very least more charitable, I submit, to understand him as referring to separation strictly conceived, i.e. the instantaneous event of a form coming to be grasped separately from matter and so becoming the same as one's intellect. The agent intellect is not thought *before* the form; rather—as the author maintains, using Aristotle's light analogy (111. 32–4)—the latter is thought 'along with' the former. The moment of separation of an enmattered form whereby our thinking of that form begins must also be the first moment of our thinking of the agent intellect—whatever that amounts to. That the author has separation strictly speaking in mind is also suggested by the fact that, unlike Alexander's *De anima*, *De intellectu* is entirely silent about the processes that fall under separation in a looser sense. That difference is perfectly understandable, given that *De intellectu* is not about the soul as a whole, but only intellect and its proper activities.

Once we take seriously the possibility that in B2 the author has separation strictly speaking in mind, we will see that not even here, when tackling the *Problem of Two Potentialities*, does he necessarily embrace the paradoxical idea that we must *first* engage in thinking the most sublime object of thought *before* we can even begin to

[102] For how rationality determines the functioning of the human perceptive capacity, and indeed the structure of the human body, see e.g. P. J. van der Eijk, 'The Matter of Mind: Aristotle on the Biology of "Psychic" Processes and the Bodily Aspects of Thinking', *Medicine and Philosophy in Classical Antiquity: Doctors and Philosophers on Nature, Soul, Health and Disease* (Cambridge, 2005), 206–37; J. G. Lennox, 'The Place of Mankind in Aristotle's Zoology', *Philosophical Topics*, 27 (1999), 1–16; and S. Connell, 'Thinking Bodies: Aristotle on the Biological Basis of Human Cognition', in P. Gregoric and J. L. Fink (eds.), *Encounters with Aristotelian Philosophy of Mind* (New York, 2021), 223–48.

think enmattered forms.[103] It remains to be seen whether this insight will also allow us to spell out his account in a less bizarre and more compelling way. That will largely depend on what exactly the act of thinking the agent intellect (construed as simultaneous with the act of thinking each enmattered form) amounts to.

4. Theophrastean *aporiai*

Before discussing B2's account in its own right, it will be worth familiarizing ourselves with a more ancient set of difficulties concerning human intellect deriving from reflections on Aristotle's *De anima* recorded by his pupil and successor in the Lyceum Theophrastus, in what was known in late antiquity both as his *De anima* 2 and as his *Physics* 5, a work preserved only in quotations and reports by Themistius and Priscianus.[104] One thing that becomes clear from examining these fragments is that Theophrastus already went beyond a purely teleological understanding of the agent intellect and understood it as a genuine *efficient* cause of human thinking, although the considerations which led him to this view are recognizably different from those recorded in B1. It is not the *Problem of Two Potentialities* (of which there is no trace in our testimonies), but an apparent tension between passivity and autonomy of human thinking, that brings Theophrastus to embrace a

[103] Contrast de Haas, 'Active Intellectual Cognition', 29–31, which explicitly ascribes a looser understanding of separation to the author of B2. This leaves de Haas with only one potential alternative to the 'bizarre' and 'paradoxical' understanding, namely that the agent intellect assists the material intellect in separating enmattered forms *in some other unspecified way*, whereas it comes to *be thought* by us only later. This, however, appears unlikely, because, as is noted by most interpreters of *De intellectu*, the author of B2 is very explicit about the fact that some kind of thinking of the agent intellect is presupposed by our thinking of enmattered forms (more on that front in Section 5). Moreover, the point of C2 is precisely that the entire involvement of the agent intellect in our thought is to be understood in terms of it being thought by us.

[104] See Barbotin's attempt at reconstructing the train of thought in the part of this book that is concerned with intellect: E. Barbotin, *La théorie aristotélicienne de l'intellect d'après Théophraste* (Louvain, 1954). The fragments are also assembled and analysed in P. Huby, *Theophrastus of Eresus: Sources for His Life, Writings, Thought and Influence: Commentary: Psychology* (Leiden, 1999). For an insightful discussion of what we can learn about the part of Theophrastus' treatise that is concerned with perception, see V. Caston, 'Theophrastus on Perceiving', *Rhizomata*, 7 (2019), 188–225.

robustly efficient understanding of the causal role of the agent intellect. We will see that this Theophrastean passivity/autonomy dilemma sheds light on what is going on in B and C. The author's account of the involvement of the agent intellect in B2 and C2 can be understood as a sophisticated and novel way of resolving this dilemma—differing both from how Theophrastus himself tends to resolve it and from the solution articulated in B1 and C1. It will turn out that—contrary to the standard view of *De intellectu* as denying (in sharp contrast to Alexander's *De anima*) autonomy to human intellect—autonomy, i.e. the idea that thinking is *up to us*, is its very central concern (which directly connects it to Alexander's *De anima*), and the author's novelty consists precisely in emphasizing this aspect of the human intellect much more than either Theophrastus or the teacher reported in B1 and C1 did before him.

As a supplement to the key dilemma about passivity and autonomy, Theophrastus also formulated a set of difficulties concerning the identity of the 'material' intellect through its development and as it passes from one object to another. With these difficulties (and Theophrastus' tentative answer to them) as background, we can better appreciate the most distinctive idea of B2, that the material intellect thinks the agent intellect as its own fulfilment, albeit more or less perfectly attained (Section 5), as well as the author's account of self-thinking in A4 (Section 6).

Both of our late ancient sources record the following *aporia*, which clearly governed a significant part of Theophrastus' discussion of intellect in *Physics* 5. Theophrastus describes here an apparent conflict between, on the one hand, the claim that thinking is a kind of being affected and, on the other hand, the claim that thinking is up to intellect:

[**Passivity/Autonomy Aporia**] πῶς δέ ποτε γίνεται τὰ νοητὰ καὶ τί τὸ πάσχειν αὐτόν; δεῖ γάρ, εἴπερ εἰς ἐνέργειαν ἥξει καθάπερ ἡ αἴσθησις. ἀσωμάτῳ δὲ ὑπὸ σώματος τί τὸ πάθος ἢ ποία μεταβολή; καὶ πότερον ἀπ' ἐκείνου ἡ ἀρχὴ ἢ ἀπ' αὐτοῦ; τῷ μὲν γὰρ πάσχειν ἀπ' ἐκείνου δόξειεν ἄν (οὐδὲν γὰρ ἀφ' ἑαυτοῦ τῶν ἐν πάθει)· τῷ δὲ ἀρχὴν πάντων εἶναι καὶ ἐπ' αὐτῷ τὸ νοεῖν, καὶ μή ὥσπερ ταῖς αἰσθήσεσιν, ἀπ' αὐτοῦ. (Themist., *In DA* 108. 1–6 Heinze; cf. Priscianus, *Metaphr.* 27. 8–14 Bywater).[105]

---

[105] At 108. 1 I read αὐτόν, which is Wimmer's emendation of αὐτό in Priscianus instead of αὐτῶν found in Themistius. Instead of ὑπὸ σώματος, at 108. 2–3 Priscianus (27. 10) has ὑπ' ἀσωμάτου. The way in which Theophrastus proposes to resolve the

Thought 'From Without' 219

And how can it be that it [i.e. intellect] becomes the objects of thought? And what is it for it to be affected?[106] For it has to [be affected], if it is going to come into actuality, just like the perceptive capacity. But what affection could there be for something incorporeal from a body or what kind of change [could it undergo]? And is the principle [of coming into actuality] from that [which acts on intellect], or from it [i.e. intellect itself]? On the one hand, the fact that it is affected would suggest that it is from that [which acts on intellect] (for none of the things undergoing affection does so from itself). On the other hand, the fact that intellect is the principle of everything and thinking is up to it (and not as in the case of the senses) would suggest that it is from it.

At the heart of this *aporia* is an apparent conflict identified by Theophrastus between Aristotle's recurrent claim that thinking is a kind of being affected,[107] which implies that what acts on the intellect is in this sense prior to it, and the idea that thinking is 'up to intellect' (combined with the Anaxagorean claim that intellect is 'the principle of everything'), which seems to imply, on the contrary, that no object can be prior to intellect.[108] If thinking consists for us in being affected by what we think, then apparently thinking

---

dilemma (as we will see below) seems to support Themistius' version. But this issue is not crucial for our present purposes.

[106] It is only the second part of the question (concerning 'being affected') that is developed in this fragment and addressed in another one quoted below. The first part (concerning 'becoming objects of thought') seems to have been addressed later in *Physics* 5 in the fragments discussed already above (dispersed through Priscianus, *Metaphr.* 29. 18–31. 13).

[107] See Arist., *DA* 3. 4, 429^{a}13–15, 429^{b}24–5, 29–31; cf. 3. 5, 430^{a}24.

[108] The second horn apparently draws on Aristotle's claim (at *DA* 2. 5, 417^{b}24–6 and 3. 4, 429^{b}7–8) that thinking (unlike perception) is *up to the knower*. It is far from obvious, however, why this claim should contradict the idea that thinking is a kind of being affected: the knower's autonomy may well consist in something like the power of letting the object act on her intellect whenever the knower wishes. A genuine conflict arises only when we interpret Aristotle's claim as being not (only) about the knower, but (also) about intellect itself. That is apparently what Theophrastus did (one can compare the notion of noetic self-motion developed by M. V. Wedin, 'Aristotle on the Mind's Self-Motion', in M. L. Gill and J. G. Lennox (eds.), *Self-Motion: from Aristotle to Newton* (Princeton, 1994), 80–116). He may have found support at *DA* 3. 4, 429^{b}6–8: the phrase 'this occurs when he/it can be active through himself/itself' (τοῦτο δὲ συμβαίνει ὅταν δύνηται ἐνεργεῖν δι' αὑτοῦ) at 429^{b}7 can *prima facie* be read as ascribing autonomy either to the knower or to the intellect itself. Theophrastus seems to have taken it the latter way (although *DA* 2. 5, 417^{b}24–6 supports the former reading). He apparently believed that this understanding is supported by the Anaxagorean idea that intellect is the principle of everything (echoed at *DA* 3. 4, 429^{a}18–20), for which, see also Priscianus, *Metaphr.* 29. 12–15 quoted and discussed below.

is not up to the intellect in us, but rather, in an important sense, up to the object we think.[109] But if what we think is natural compounds, like horse or flesh (or their essences), this would imply that intellect is affected by and dependent on something other than intellect—an implication that Theophrastus finds at odds with the idea that thinking is up to intellect.

How can this apparent tension be resolved? The first thing to notice from the perspective of *De intellectu* is that Theophrastus is not willing to solve the *Passivity/Autonomy Aporia* by denying the claim corresponding to the first horn, i.e. that thinking is for us a kind of being affected. It is surely not any ordinary kind of being affected, but to claim that our intellect is entirely impassive appears to be a non-starter, because this would seem to make it impossible to explain how thinking comes about (as Aristotle objects to Anaxagoras):[110]

πῶς οὖν παθητικός; εἰ γὰρ ὅλως ἀπαθής, φησίν, οὐδὲν νοήσει.
(Priscianus, *Metaphr.* 28. 16–17 Bywater)

In what sense then is it capable of being affected? [It has to be in some sense,] for if it were entirely impassive, he [i.e. Theophrastus] says, it would think nothing.

The impassivity of intellect, introduced by Aristotle at *DA* 3. 4, 429ª15 and emphasized at 429ª29–ᵇ5, is compatible, Theophrastus insists, with the classification of thinking as a kind of being affected. We only need to take seriously Aristotle's distinction between different kinds of passivity drawn at 2. 5, 417ᵇ2–16:

ἀπαθὴς γὰρ ὁ νοῦς, φησὶν ὁ Θεόφραστος, εἰ μὴ ἄρα ἄλλως παθητικός, καὶ ὅτι τὸ παθητικὸν ἐπ' αὐτοῦ οὐχ ὡς τὸ κινητόν, ἀτελὴς γὰρ ἡ κίνησις, ἀλλ' ὡς ἐνέργειαν. ταῦτα δὲ διαφέρει, χρῆσθαι δὲ ἀναγκαῖον ἐνίοτε τοῖς αὐτοῖς ὀνόμασιν.
(Priscianus, *Metaphr.* 28. 20–3 Bywater;
cf. Themist., *In DA* 108. 15–17 Heinze)[111]

---

[109] Compare the case of perception: what I hear, for instance, is entirely determined by which objects in my environment are making sounds right now and what kind of sounds they are making.

[110] See Arist., *DA* 1. 2, 405ᵇ19–23 and 3. 4, 429ᵇ22–5.

[111] At 28. 20, I read ἀπαθής with Themistius instead of ἀπαθές in Priscianus; at 28. 21, I read παθητικός, καὶ ὅτι τὸ παθητικὸν ἐπ' αὐτοῦ and κινητόν with Themistius instead of ᾗ τὸ παθητικόν and κινητικόν in Priscianus; at 28.22, I read ἐνέργειαν with Themistius instead of ἐνέργεια in Priscianus.

For intellect is impassive, says Theophrastus, unless 'capable of being affected' is [understood] in some other way, and [he says] that 'being capable of being affected' is not to be understood in the sense of 'being movable', for motion is incomplete, but in the sense of [passive] activity; and these differ, although sometimes it is necessary to use the same words [for what is not exactly the same].

We can, Theophrastus maintains, retain Aristotle's classification of thinking as a kind of being affected if we keep in mind that thinking is not a passive process (motion) but a complete passive activity.[112] We will see that in B2 the author goes far beyond this idea and denies straightaway any applicability of the category of being affected to thinking.[113] This move will lead him to a very different solution to the *Passivity/Autonomy Aporia* from the one hinted at by Theophrastus himself.

Theophrastus makes his key move in the following passage:

ἐπεί φησί τὸ ὑφ' ἑτέρου κινοῦντος τὴν ἐνέργειαν εἶναι τοῦ νοῦ καὶ ἄλλως ἄτοπον, καὶ πρότερόν τι ποιεῖν ἐστιν ἕτερον τοῦ νοῦ, καὶ οὐκ ἐφ' ἑαυτῷ τὸ νοεῖν, εἰ μή τις ἄλλος ὁ κινῶν νοῦς.

(Priscianus, *Metaphr.* 29. 12–15 Bywater)

[To claim] that the activity of intellect is caused by something else moving [it], is absurd for other reasons too, but [above all] it means to make something else to be prior to intellect and thinking not to be up to it, unless it is some other intellect that moves [it].

The first part of this quotation restates the second horn of the original dilemma. We have seen why it is unavoidable to ascribe a certain passivity to our intellect insofar as it is acted upon or moved

---

[112] The idea of thinking as a complete passive activity seems to be drawing on *DA* 2. 5, 417^{b}2–9, where Aristotle introduces the notion of being affected that is not 'a destruction by the contrary' (φθορά τις ὑπὸ τοῦ ἐναντίου) but 'rather a preservation' (σωτηρία μᾶλλον, 417^{b}3). Theophrastus may also have in mind *DA* 3. 7, 431^{a}6–7, where the contrast between motion and complete activity is fully spelled out. The scholarly discussion of these Aristotelian passages is too rich to be even listed here. For two recent contributions (including good overviews of the debates), see, on *DA* 2. 5, A. Anagnostopoulos, 'Aristotle's First Moves Regarding Perception: A Reading of (Most of) *De Anima* 2.5', *Archiv für Geschichte der Philosophie*, 105 (2023), 68–117, and, on *DA* 3. 7, K. Corcilius, '*De Anima* III 7: The Actuality Principle and the Triggering of Mental Episodes', in G. Guyomarc'h, C. Louguet, and C. Murgier (eds.), *Aristote et l'âme humaine: Lectures de 'De Anima' III offertes à Michel Crubellier* (Leuven, 2020), 185–219. For the notion of complete passive activity in *De anima*, see Roreitner, *Nature and Causes*.

[113] This is another point of contact with Alexander's *De anima*. See e.g. 83. 12–84. 14.

by what it thinks. But saying that it is moved by something else conflicts with the assumption that thinking is up to intellect. It is the final clause of the quoted sentence which suggests a way out of the dilemma: it can be solved if we assume that what acts upon our intellect is not something *un*intelligent but *another intellect*.[114]

Unfortunately, it is difficult to learn anything certain from our sources about Theophrastus' further moves.[115] But conveniently enough for our present purposes, what we have seen is just enough to appreciate how different is the resolution to the *Passivity/ Autonomy Aporia* proposed by the author of *De intellectu*. Moreover, this background allows us to understand better the teacher's position reported in B1 and C1, as well as the author's reservations with respect to it, as expressed in B2 and more explicitly in C2. Indeed, the account of B1 and C1 can be understood as providing *the same kind of* solution to the *Passivity/Autonomy Aporia* as Theophrastus himself, and both together can be sharply contrasted with the kind of solution provided in B2 and C2. Let me explain.

First, the teacher's position reported in B1 and C1 resembles Theophrastus' solution in its assumption that the agent intellect *acts on* the material intellect and the latter is affected by the former. In B1's explanation of what prompted Aristotle to introduce the intellect from without, the material intellect is supposed to play the role of that which is affected (τὸ πάσχον), and this assumption is never questioned here—unlike in B2. In C1 we are given a more concrete account of how the agent intellect is supposed to act on the material intellect: it acts on it in the same sense in which an artisan acts on her instrument when she takes hold of it (τούτου τοῦ ὀργάνου λάβηται, 112. 16–17) and by means of it performs her work

---

[114] Cf. S. Magrin, 'Theophrastus, Alexander, and Themistius on Aristotle's *De anima* III. 4–5', in R. Wisnovsky et al. (eds.), *Vehicles of Transmission, Translation, and Transformation in Medieval Textual Culture* (Turnhout, 2011), 49–74 at 58–9.

[115] How, for instance, can we think other objects beyond the 'moving intellect' itself, such as the essence of horse? There are some hints dispersed through Priscianus, *Metaphr.* 32. 25–37. 4 concerning Theophrastus' reflections on the latter part of *DA* 3. 4. But it is particularly difficult to extract reports of Theophrastus from Priscianus' own reflections here, let alone reconstruct Theophrastus' account. What is noteworthy is the complete absence of anything that would resemble the *Problem of Two Potentialities* and Theophrastus' reluctance to call enmattered forms 'objects of thought' (νοητά) at all.

(δί ὀργάνου...ἐνήργησεν, 112. 17–18; διὰ τῆς ἡμετέρας δυνάμεως ἐνεργήσῃ, 112. 23–4).[116] This account of how the agent intellect acts on the material intellect, then, allows the teacher to provide an even more 'revisionist' interpretation of what it means to say that our thinking is 'up to intellect'. Like Theophrastus, the teacher believes that our thinking is not up to *our* intellect, and so not really up to *us*. Indeed, 'our' intellect is just an instrument of the divine intellect, which it uses to perform its own activities of thinking enmattered forms: this is what *we call* our thinking, but what is here referred to as our intellect is, in fact, a compound of the material intellect (which alone is properly ours) and *an activity of the agent intellect*, and what we describe as our thinking is, in reality, the activity of the agent intellect *using our intellect* as its instrument (112. 16–21, 23–30).[117]

So the two key points of Theophrastus' tentative solution (our intellect is affected by the agent intellect, and so our thinking is up to intellect but not really up to us) are taken over and, indeed, radicalized by the teacher, as reported in B1 and C1. And both points are passionately opposed by the author of B2 and C2. This is more plainly detectable in C2, where the author protests that according to the reported account 'thinking will not be up to us and will not be our own work' (τὸ μὴ ἐφ' ἡμῖν εἶναι τὸ νοεῖν μηδ' εἶναι τοῦτο ἡμέτερον ἔργον, 113. 16–17).[118] But both points of disagreement are, as we will see, already central to the argument of B2: the author goes out of his way here to deny that our thinking could be classified as any kind of being affected—even being affected by the agent intellect—and to insist that our thinking (while it depends on a direct involvement of the transcendent agent intellect) remains in a robust sense *our own* work and something that is *up to us*, not just

---

[116] See 112. 16–30 as a whole; cf. 113 1–2.

[117] The idea here of 'our' intellect being a kind of 'compound' (σύνθετος) of the material intellect and an activity of the agent intellect is likely to be drawing on Theophrastus as well, namely on his account of intellect as being 'somehow mixed out of the agent and the potential' (μικτὸν...πως...ἐκ τε τοῦ ποιητικοῦ καὶ τοῦ δυνάμει) recorded by Themist., *In DA* 108. 18–28 (see 108. 24 Heinze). For an overview of existing interpretations of this Theophrastean idea and an insightful discussion of it, see M. Gabbe, 'Theophrastus and the Intellect as Mixture', *Elenchos*, 29 (2008), 61–90.

[118] Cf. Aristotle's definition of a compulsory act in *NE* 3. 1 as 'that whose principle is outside' (οὗ ἡ ἀρχὴ ἔξωθεν, 1110ᵃ1; cf. 1110ᵇ2, 16).

'up to intellect'.[119] We will see that although this is most probably a conscious departure from Theophrastus, Theophrastus' own solution—and the idea of thinking being 'up to intellect' but with two different kinds of intellect involved, in particular—can help us better understand and appreciate the author's chief move: once we allow our thinking to be described as being 'up to intellect' without qualification, we may want to take a further step and ask whether it also makes sense to say that 'intellect' without qualification is what each of us truly is.[120]

But Theophrastus' discussion in *Physics* 5 will not only be helpful in bringing out the *Passivity/Autonomy Aporia* that both the author of *De intellectu* and the teacher were trying to resolve. For our sources also contain a set of difficulties subordinated to this overarching *aporia* which seem to have directly inspired the author's solution. We have seen that Theophrastus started with a pair of closely connected questions: (1) How can intellect become what it thinks? (2) What can 'being affected' mean for it?[121] He first addressed issues pertaining to 'being affected' and the apparent conflict with autonomy and then returned to those concerning 'becoming'. These latter issues were spelled out in a later part of *Physics* 5 whose fragments are dispersed throughout Priscianus' *Metaphrasis* 29. 18–31. 13. Here Theophrastus was raising and partly addressing difficulties concerning the identity of our intellect through the process of its development and as it passes from one object to another. What does it mean to say that the intellect in us *becomes* the objects it thinks? If its actuality *qua* intellect consists in its being one and the same as an object of thought, does this mean that whenever it does not think anything, it fails to be intellect

---

[119] Accattino, who was the first to suggest reading B2 as the author's own addition to the account reported in B1, also notices a connection between the argument of B2 and the emphasis in C2 on the idea that thinking is up to us (see Accattino, *De Intellectu*, 53, 55).

[120] Cf. Arist., *EN* 10. 7, 1178^{a}2–8.

[121] The questions are closely interconnected because Theophrastus seems to be assuming that intellect becomes its object as a result of being affected by it and assimilated to it. In being affected, the perceiver or the thinker is assimilated to what she perceives or thinks: see Arist., *DA* 2. 5 417^{a}17–21, 418^{a}3–6. Cf. again *DA* 3. 4, 429^{a}13–18, where the idea of thinking as a kind of being affected is closely linked to that of the intellect as being 'in potentiality like [its object]' (δυνάμει τοιοῦτον, 429^{a}16). Later at 429^{b}5–9, Aristotle speaks of the intellect 'when it has become each [of its objects]' (ὅταν...ἕκαστα γένηται, 429^{b}5–6).

or even to exist at all?[122] That seems absurd, Theophrastus maintains, and:

[**Stability Problem**] καὶ γὰρ ἄτοπον... εἰ δυνάμει μὲν ὢν μηδέν ἐστιν, ἐνεργείᾳ δὲ ἕτερος ὅταν μὴ ἑαυτὸν νοῇ, τῷ δὲ ἄλλο καὶ ἄλλο νοεῖν οὐδέποτε ὁ αὐτός. ἄκριτος γάρ τις αὕτη γε καὶ ἄτακτος ἡ φύσις

(Priscianus, *Metaphr.* 30. 22–5 Bywater)

it is also absurd... if [intellect], being [everything] potentially, is nothing [in actuality], while in actuality it is some other [intellect] whenever it does not think [just] itself, and as it thinks a different [object] each time, it is never the same [intellect]. [This is absurd, indeed,] for it [i.e. such an intellect] would be an indistinguishable and disordered nature.

The difficulty seems to be as follows. If the intellect in us becomes the object it thinks on each occasion of thinking, then it becomes *something else*—or at least a different intellect—each time; but this means that there is no stability in it and it resembles matter (something 'indistinguishable and disordered')[123] rather than intellect. This threat would be precluded only in the case of the intellect's pure self-thinking. But apparently, pure self-thought is not something our intellect is capable of: it would mean effectively collapsing our intellect with the divine intellect.

We will see (in Section 6) that a very similar dilemma can be identified as background for the author's distinctive account of self-thinking in A4. Either our intellect is entirely absorbed in the object it thinks on each occasion, so that there remains no room for its self-thinking (because there remains no 'self' to be thought), or it thinks purely itself, which seems beyond human capacity (and

---

[122] 'For if it [i.e. intellect], he says, becomes the things when it is active, and then it is both [i.e. intellect and things] in the highest degree, it would seem that intellect is the things.... Does it mean that whenever it [i.e. intellect] does not think, then, since it is not the things, it is also not intellect?... And does it mean that it is nothing before thinking?' (εἰ γὰρ ἐνεργῶν, φησί, γίνεται τὰ πράγματα, τότε δὲ μάλιστα ἑκάτερόν ἐστι, τὰ πράγματα ἂν εἴη ὁ νοῦς... ἆρα οὖν, ὅταν μὴ νοῇ, μὴ ὢν τὰ πράγματα οὐδὲ νοῦς ἐστιν;...ἆρα οὖν οὐδέν ἐστι πρὶν νοεῖν; Priscianus, *Metaphr.* 29. 18–20, 22–3, 26–7 Bywater).

[123] In his *Metaphysics*, Theophrastus characterizes the θεωρία ('study') of nature as 'more disordered' (ἀτακτοτέρα) than the θεωρία of the principles (1, 4^{a}3–5 Gutas; cf. Arist., *Meteor.* 1. 1, 338^{b}19–21), and he associates 'the disordered' (τὸ ἄτακτον) with the Platonic dyad (24. 1, 11^{b}2–5 Gutas). Cf. 17, 8^{a}11–12 Gutas, where Theophrastus describes matter as something ἀόριστον ('indeterminate'; cf. Aristotle's *Metaph.* Z. 10, 1036^{a}8–9 where matter is described as ἄγνωστος ('unknowable')).

which would *a priori* exclude the possibility of thinking an enmattered form).

Moreover, we find in Theophrastus at least a hint at how this *Stability Problem* (or at least one aspect of it) can perhaps be resolved; and this hint points us directly to the account of self-thinking and the agent intellect's involvement developed in A4 and B2, respectively. In a passage which seems to have been located shortly after the formulation of the *Stability Problem* quoted above, Theophrastus is reported (by Priscianus, *Metaphr.* 31. 11–13) to have focused on the character of the 'coming to be' involved in the development of the intellect in us and to have asked whether it is to be understood as a coming to be of a disposition (ἕξις) or of a substance (οὐσία). He rejected the second option, apparently because it would imply that each time we come to think something or acquire the power to think something, the intellect in us becomes something different, in the manner of an indistinguishable and disordered nature like matter. Theophrastus' tentative conclusion was that:

ἔοικε δὲ μᾶλλον ἕξεως, αὕτη δὲ οἷον τελεοῦν τὴν φύσιν.
(Priscianus, *Metaphr.* 31. 13 Bywater)

it rather seems to be [a coming to be of] a disposition, but [of] such a disposition that it, so to speak, perfects the nature.[124]

In other words, the intellect in us comes to be the object it thinks in such a way that it is not changed into something substantially different (into something else or another intellect). Rather, it acquires, while remaining the same intellect, a disposition, albeit not just any old disposition: it must acquire a disposition that 'perfects its nature'.[125] The object thought by the intellect comes to be present in it as its own fulfilment.

I want to argue that this kind of response to the *Stability Problem* is taken over and further developed by the author of *De intellectu*. He believes that, in each act of our thinking, the agent intellect comes to be present in the material intellect and thought by it as its own—more or less perfectly attained—fulfilment. The idea is not, as we will see, that the content of our thought (say, the essence of

---

[124] The text is difficult, and the proposed translation provides just one possible understanding of it.
[125] Theophrastus is here clearly drawing on Arist., *DA* 2. 5, 417^{b}5–7 and 12–16.

horse) comes 'from above'. The form comes from the natural world and from it alone, after a sufficient amount of experience has been assembled and processed. The point is not merely that the form and the material intellect are not enough to produce a genuine thought, as implied by the *Problem of Two Potentialities*; but moreover, if our intellect were to think the form alone, it would in fact end up being an indistinguishable and disordered nature that becomes a different thing each time it thinks something new. Fortunately, in each act of thinking an enmattered form we also of necessity think the agent intellect as our own thought, even as it comes from without, and this not only allows our thinking to come about, but also guarantees to our intellect a stability of self-thinking as it passes from one enmattered form to another. In this way A4 and B2 work jointly towards a solution to the *Stability Problem*. And this solution, as we will see, dovetails with the author's novel way of resolving the *Passivity/Autonomy Aporia*.

5. Autonomy of thought

Let us now finally turn to the intricate argument of B2. It begins by emphatically affirming what is already familiar to us from A3, but what was conspicuously absent in B1, namely that there is something intelligible by its own nature, and that this object is itself an intellect (110. 25–30). But the author quickly goes beyond A3 by unambiguously stating that such an object needs to be thought by us if we are ever to think an enmattered form, and that in this way the agent intellect is directly involved in the development of the material intellect:

ἔστιν τι καὶ καθ' αὑτὸ νοητὸν τῇ αὑτοῦ φύσει τοιοῦτον ὄν. τοῦτο δὴ καὶ αὐτὸ ὁ δυνάμει νοῦς τελειούμενος καὶ αὐξόμενος νοεῖ.

(110. 30–1)

there is also something intelligible by itself, being such by its own nature. This is what the potential intellect thinks too as it is being perfected and is developing.

The author believes that we think the agent intellect not only at the climax of our intellectual development, but very early on and indeed somehow throughout that development. Standardly, interpreters read this passage as recalling the 'bizarre' and 'paradoxical' doctrine from 108. 19–24.[126] But in fact, it goes beyond A3, and it does so without providing any support whatsoever for the 'bizarre and paradoxical' account. What the passage suggests is not that we first think the agent intellect and then start to think enmattered forms, but rather that we think the agent intellect somehow throughout the time in which various enmattered forms are, one after another, separated and thought by us. And as we saw in Section 3, this does not necessarily mean that we start thinking the agent intellect *before* we start thinking the first enmattered form. It is at least equally possible that the process of development referred to in the quoted passage begins with the first moment of grasping an enmattered form and that the act of thinking the agent intellect is always *simultaneous* with the act of thinking some such form.[127]

Good Peripatetic that he is, the author then compares (at 110. 31–111. 2) intellect with the capacity to walk (ἡ περιπατητικὴ δύναμις), although the comparison is rather confusing.[128] Just as the capacity

[126] See Accattino, *De Intellectu*, 50; Sharples, *Alexander: Supplement*, 34; or id., *Mantissa*, 153. Sharples introduces an unnecessary complication here by asking how the aorist participle αὐξόμενος is to be explained (he responds, in both works, that it is used proleptically). This complication is reflected in Accattino and Ghiggia, *Mantissa*, 33, who also translate αὐξόμενος as if it were an aorist participle (in contrast to Accattino, *De Intellectu*, 50, translating it, duly, as a present participle; cf. e.g. Schroeder and Todd, *Two Commentators*, 53, 69; or Dufour, *Mantissa*, 24). This complication becomes important for de Haas, 'Active Intellectual Cognition', 29, who rejects Sharples' proleptic reading and infers from the quoted sentence that 'the potential intellect has to be advanced to a certain level before it will think the productive intellect'. This leads de Haas to distinguish (at pp. 29–31), in contrast to other interpreters, two stages in B2: (1) the material intellect is advanced by the agent intellect; (2) the material intellect thinks the agent intellect (cf. n. 146 below). Yet the textual basis for this speculation is poor. The idea seems to be that αὐξόμενος is a participle from second aorist ηὖξον; but I don't think the second aorist ever occurs: ηὖξον is used as an alternative form of the imperfect together with ηὔξανον, and αὐξάνω has a regular sigmatic aorist ηὔξησα (cf. the entry αὐξάνω in LSJ, or Smyth, *Greek Grammar*, 689). What has confused interpreters here is apparently the fact that the author forms the participle, not from the more usual ν-form αὐξάνω, but from the less usual shortened form αὔξω. This, however, is not that uncommon; in fact, αὔξω and its derivations are regularly used in *Mantissa* and other writings ascribed to Alexander. See e.g. *Mant.* 1, 105. 10–12, 26–7; 3, 126. 7–9; or *DA* 36. 21–37. 3; *De mixt.* 233–8 is an excellent sample of Alexander's free variation between the two forms of the verb (the participles αὐξόμενον and αὐξανόμενον are used interchangeably throughout the passage).

[127] The statement that the potential intellect thinks the agent intellect 'as it is being perfected and is developing' (110. 31) would thus mean that the former thinks the latter each time that it comes to separate and think some enmattered form.

[128] It may be inspired by Arist., *GA* 2. 3, 736ᵇ24, although here walking is contrasted *with* thought. That is also the case at Alex. Aphr., *DA* 82. 5–11, where

Thought 'From Without' 229

to walk in a human being is brought to actuality and perfected without her being affected (οὐ κατὰ πάθος τι), so:

καὶ ὁ νοῦς τελειωθεὶς τά τε φύσει νοητὰ νοεῖ καὶ τὰ αἰσθητὰ δὲ νοητὰ αὐτῷ ποιεῖ, ἅτε ὢν ποιητικός.

(111. 1–2)

the intellect too, when it has been perfected, both thinks the objects intelligible by nature and makes the perceptible objects intelligible to itself, due to its productivity.

Even if we leave aside for now the sudden occurrence of the objects intelligible by nature *in the plural* here,[129] it is far from obvious how the comparison is supposed to work. But the author is at least clear as to what the comparison should bring out about the material intellect: like the human being learning to walk, the material intellect is *not affected* when developing and thinking, but is instead *productive*.[130] This is a very surprising claim, given Aristotle's classification of thinking, like perceiving, as a kind of being affected by the object of thought,[131] and also his characterization of the potential intellect, in contrast to the agent intellect, as passive.[132] But the author means what he says, and he goes out of his way to emphasize the non-passivity of human intellect in what

---

Alexander contrasts the acquisition of expert knowledge with the capacity to walk. But since his point is to contrast the acquisition of expert knowledge with what he calls the 'natural' intellect, there is an implicit analogy between intellect and walking present here as well.

[129] The status of these objects (they appear once more in *De intellectu*, at 112. 3) and their relation to the agent intellect is notoriously unclear. The author's oscillation between singular and plural has a much discussed parallel in Alexander's *DA* 87–90 (cf. Philop., *De intellectu* 82. 15–24 Verbeke), interpreted by Merlan, *Monopsychism*, 41, and Donini, *Tre studi*, 28–35, as anticipating Plotinus' account of divine intellect embracing a plurality of contents; for a more cautious explanation, see e.g. Sharples, 'Scholasticism and Innovation', 1210–11. I return to this notorious issue at the end of the present section.

[130] The comparison here is often related to the contrast Alexander draws at *DA* 82. 5–10 between the natural development of the capacity for walking and the development of intellect: see Accattino and Donini, *L'anima*, 273; Accattino, *De Intellectu*, 50–2; Sharples, *Alexander: Supplement*, 34–5 n. 77. But while it is clear that the comparison is used in a very different way in the present passage, there is not necessarily any contradiction between the two passages. The point of the present passage is not (*pace* Accattino, *De Intellectu*, 51) that the intellect is developed 'naturally', which would indeed contradict the point made in Alexander's *De anima*, but that it is not affected while being developed, which in contrast seems perfectly in line with what Alexander maintains throughout the noetic section of *De anima*.

[131] Arist., *DA* 3. 4, 429^{a}13–18, 429^{b}24–5, 29–31.

[132] Arist., *DA* 3. 5, 430^{a}11–13, 24–5.

follows (111. 2–22). We will see that his move can be much better understood and appreciated against the background of Theophrastus' *Passivity/Autonomy Aporia*.

The claim is somewhat easier to understand with respect to enmattered forms. The author draws a contrast with perception that goes far beyond the contrast drawn in B1 (where it underlay the *Problem of Two Potentialities*). Unlike perception, which consists in (or at least presupposes) *being affected* by something else (*viz.* the perceptible object), the material intellect instead *produces* its object by abstracting an enmattered form from matter.[133] One can, to be sure, say that the material intellect, like perception, 'receives' or 'grasps' (λαμβάνειν) its object, but this 'receptivity' does not imply any genuine passivity because, unlike the object of perception, the object grasped in thought is produced by the intellect rather than acting on it.

It is worth noting just how far, even at this stage, the author goes beyond both Theophrastus and the teacher. Theophrastus duly contrasted (in line with Arist., *DA* 2. 5, 417ᵇ2–16) the relevant kind of being affected from the kinetic and destructive kind; but that contrast is common to perception and thought, and neither Theophrastus nor the teacher seems to have ever entertained the idea of classifying human thought as productive *rather than* passive. The author of B2 underscores this feature by another surprising comparison, which in effect makes human thought resemble nutrition more than perception: the activity of the intellect is compared to that of fire, which turns other things into fire and thus nourishes itself by them in assimilating them to itself rather than being assimilated to them, as in the case of perception (111. 19–22).[134]

So much is relatively clear, and although the move seems novel, it is not unconnected with what we know from Theophrastus. As we have seen, Aristotle's associate and successor had already rejected the idea of intellect being affected *by something other* than

---

[133] The author's denial of passivity here (i.e. intellect cannot be passive 'in the sense of coming to be by the agency of something else and being affected by it like perception', ὡς ὑπὸ ἄλλου γίνεσθαι καὶ πάσχειν, καθάπερ ἡ αἴσθησις, 111.3) closely echoes the first horn of the *Passivity/Autonomy Aporia*.

[134] Cf. Arist., *DA* 2. 4, 416ᵃ9–12, 21–9, and contrast 2. 5, 417ᵃ7–9. See also *Metaph.* a. 1, 993ᵇ24–31, where fire is the primary example of the *Principle of Maximal Causality* then applied to truth (cf. Alex. Aphr., *In Metaph.* 147. 16–148. 2).

intellect (cf. ὑπὸ ἄλλου at 111.3). What is significantly more difficult to understand is how the author can move from here to his much stronger claim about the activity of the material intellect being *toto caelo* productive, with no room at all for passivity.[135] According to Theophrastus, our intellect is affected by another 'moving' intellect, and so our thinking is still essentially a kind of being affected. Now the author of B2 goes out of his way to emphasize that if we are to think anything at all, we need to think the object intelligible by its own nature; and with respect to it, our intellect is clearly not productive (see 110. 25–7). Does there remain then any alternative to saying—much like Theophrastus—that with respect to this object our intellect *is* passive, so that the contrast with perception cannot be as sharp as the author claimed, and so that his comparisons with walking and fire are at the very least misleading because they belie this essential passivity of our intellect?

The remainder of B2 (111. 22–112. 5) seems intended to address exactly this kind of concern. And the final sentence reveals the author's confidence that it can be disarmed:

ἴδιον γὰρ τοῦ νοῦ τὸ ποιητικόν, καὶ τὸ νοεῖν αὐτῷ ἐνεργεῖν ἐστιν οὐ πάσχειν.

(112. 4–5)

It is being productive that is proper to intellect, and thinking is not being affected for it but being active.[136]

The challenge confronting the reader of the difficult passage that precedes this concluding claim[137] is to work out how the author thinks it can be justified. We are, I submit, in a much better position to appreciate what is going on here if we approach the passage

---

[135] This difficulty seems to lie behind Sharples' judgement (Sharples, 'Scholasticism and Innovation', 1212 n. 135) that there is a *confusion* in B2 between, on the one hand, the agent intellect and, on the other hand, the material intellect itself described as agent (ποιητικός). The difficulty is entirely ignored by Moraux, who states that the receptivity of the potential intellect with respect to the agent intellect is just like the receptivity of perception with respect to perceptible objects (Moraux, *Aristotelismus bei den Griechen* ii, 414–15).

[136] This goes far beyond Arist., *DA* 2. 5, 417^{b}2–16 (cf. 3.7, 431^{a}4–7) and its reflection in Theophrastus. First, Aristotle and Theophrastus contrast complete activity with motion, not with being affected, and their point is exactly the opposite, namely that the contrast with motion is precisely why we can understand perception and thought as a kind of being affected. Second, in Aristotle and Theophrastus, being a non-kinetic activity has nothing to do with being a case of producing (ποιεῖν).

[137] A text which certainly 'doesn't sparkle with clarity', as Accattino, *De Intellectu*, 54, puts it.

as the author's attempt at providing a novel resolution to the *Passivity/Autonomy Aporia*. To put it schematically, instead of reaffirming (with Theophrastus and the teacher) the passivity of human thought at the cost of its autonomy (i.e. by acknowledging that our thinking is *governed by another intellect*), the author seeks to preserve a more robust autonomy for our thinking (it is *up to us*) by rejecting the idea of its being passive.

He starts at 111. 22–9 by arguing for a claim which at least *prima facie* conflicts with Aristotle's insistence on the priority of what is knowable over knowledge in *Cat.* 7 (7^{b}22–35), namely that 'if intellect did not exist, nothing would be intelligible' (ὥστε μὴ ὄντος νοῦ, οὐδὲν ἂν εἴη νοητόν, 111.25).[138] This would follow:

οὔτε γὰρ ὁ φύσει (αὐτὸς γὰρ ἦν μόνος τοιοῦτος), οὔτε τὸ ὑπὸ τούτου γινόμενον. οὐκ ὢν γὰρ οὐδ' ἂν ποιοῖ.

(111. 25–7)

because neither what is [intelligible] by its nature[139] [would exist]—for only it [i.e. intellect] was [agreed to be] such—nor what becomes [intelligible] by its agency; for if it did not exist, it would not produce anything.

One could take the referent of 'its' and 'it' in the last line to be the human intellect.[140] But the context, in fact, suggests that Aristotle has in mind the 'intellect' previously identified as 'what is intelligible by its nature'.[141] Now, this intellect could be straightforwardly identified as the agent intellect.[142] Alternatively, the author may be intentionally referring to 'intellect' without qualification (we will see another instance of this strategy below): if there were no intellect whatsoever, there would be neither any object intelligible by nature, because only (a certain kind of) intellect is such,

---

[138] Accattino, *De Intellectu*, 54, makes this claim less striking by adding qualifications to it: if the *human* intellect did not exist, nothing would be intelligible for *humans*. But this is close to a tautology, and one may wonder why the author did not make these qualifications himself.

[139] This is how ὁ φύσει is understood by Sharples, *Alexander: Supplement*, in contrast to Schroeder and Todd, *Two Commentators*, and Accattino, *De Intellectu*, who understand it as 'intellect by nature'.

[140] So Accattino, *De Intellectu*, 54. Sharples, *Alexander: Supplement*, 36 n. 84, rejects this reading, but it is not clear what alternative he has in mind.

[141] If the meaning of ὁ φύσει is 'what is naturally so [i.e. intelligible]', then the latter clearly cannot as such be Aristotle's referent, given the masculine οὐκ ὢν in the last clause.

[142] Schroeder and Todd, *Two Commentators*, 54, interpret the pronouns as referring to the agent ('natural') intellect.

nor any other intelligible object, for each such object is made intelligible in actuality *by intellect* (that is, it seems, by the human intellect somehow relating to the agent intellect).

In any case, the text that follows sees the author proceed to explain how the production of intelligible objects by intellect takes place, and here he explicitly distinguishes between the complementary roles of the agent and the human intellect, the one becoming an associate (συνεργός) of the other:

συνεργὸς δ' ἂν γίνοιτο τῷ ἐν ἡμῖν ὁ φύσει τε νοῦς καὶ θύραθεν, ὅτι οὐδ' ἂν τὰ ἄλλα νοητὰ ἦν ὄντα δυνάμει μὴ ὄντος τινὸς τῇ ἰδίᾳ φύσει νοητοῦ.

(111. 27–9)

The intellect by nature and from without will become an associate of the intellect in us, for if there were nothing intelligible by its own nature, other things—which are [intelligible] in potentiality—could not be intelligible [in actuality] either.

What is first clear is that the author does not wish to reverse the priority of object over knowledge propounded by Aristotle in *Categories* 7. 'Nothing would be intelligible' if 'intellect did not exist' *because* it would mean that there is nothing intelligible by its own nature and *this* would in turn imply—in line with the *Principle of Maximal Causality*—that nothing else can be intelligible either.[143] The idea seems to be that the object intelligible by its own nature is the only instantiation of intelligibility proper and that the intelligibility of enmattered forms is somehow derivative from it and measured by it: when thinking an enmattered form, we are *eo ipso* falling some way short of thinking what alone is truly intelligible.[144] The only reason why this can be phrased in terms of a priority of intellect over what is intelligible is that what is truly intelligible turns out to be a self-standing intellect.[145]

But the author has good reasons for making the point in these (potentially misleading) terms. (1) He believes that the relation of our acts of thinking enmattered forms to the object intelligible by

---

[143] Cf. Alex. Aphr., *DA* 89. 4–7, where Alexander identifies the agent intellect as that which is intelligible in the highest degree and by its own nature, 'for if there were nothing intelligible by its nature, no other thing would become intelligible, either' (εἰ γὰρ μὴ ἦν τι νοητὸν φύσει, οὐδ' ἂν τῶν ἄλλων τι νοητὸν ἐγίνετο, 89. 6–7 Bruns).

[144] More below on what this can mean concretely.

[145] The author does *not* seem to assume that this object is intellect *prior to* being intelligible.

its own nature is *not purely* conceptual or teleological: we cannot think the former without actually *thinking* the latter. (2) At the same time, he wants to resist the idea that our intellect *is affected* by the object intelligible by its own nature, as the parallel with perception would suggest. (3) He thinks this can be achieved when it is emphasized that the object intelligible by its own nature comes to us *as an associate intellect* which *cooperates* or *is active along with* (συνεργεῖν) our intellect, rather than *acting on* it.

Unlike the perceiver who is affected (πάσχειν) by the perceptible object, the material intellect is *active along with* (συνεργεῖν) the agent intellect, and so 'thinking is not being affected for it but being active (ἐνεργεῖν)' (112.4–5)—*even with respect to the object intelligible by its own nature*. The material intellect encounters the object intelligible by its own nature not as something *other* than itself by which it would be affected—as the perceiver encounters the perceptible object (cf. 111. 3–4)—but as a fellow intellect with which it is *active together*. There seems to be an intentional contrast here between, on the one hand, the notion of the agent intellect as an associate (συνεργός) of our intellect and, on the other hand, Theophrastus' notion of the former as the mover (κινῶν) of the latter (together with C1's notion of the former as using the latter as its instrument). While Theophrastus' (and C1's) notion necessitates a revisionary account of autonomy (thinking is *up to intellect*, but not up to *us*), the author's notion makes it at least conceivable that our thinking is genuinely up to us, even as it presupposes a direct involvement of the transcendent agent intellect.

In order to see just what kind of autonomy can, on this basis, be ascribed to our intellect, we need to understand more about our intellect's relation to the agent intellect and more about the latter's involvement. The fullest description of the agent intellect in *De intellectu* is contained in the immediately subsequent passage:

(i) τοῦτο δὴ τῇ αὐτοῦ φύσει νοητὸν ὂν ἐν τῷ νοοῦντι γενόμενον διὰ τοῦ νοηθῆναι νοῦς τέ ἐστι γεγενημένος ἐν τῷ νοοῦντι καὶ θύραθεν νοεῖται καὶ ἀθάνατος καὶ ἐντίθησιν τὴν ἕξιν τῷ ὑλικῷ ὥστε νοεῖν τὰ δυνάμει νοητά. (ii) ὡς γὰρ τὸ φῶς, ποιητικὸν ὂν τῆς κατ' ἐνέργειαν ὄψεως, καὶ αὐτὸ ὁρᾶται καὶ τὰ σὺν αὐτῷ, καὶ δι' αὑτοῦ τὸ χρῶμα, οὕτως δὲ καὶ ὁ θύραθεν νοῦς αἴτιος γίνεται τοῦ νοεῖν ἡμῖν, νοούμενος καὶ αὐτός, (iii) οὐ ποιῶν αὐτὸν νοῦν, ἀλλὰ τὸν ὄντα νοῦν τῇ αὐτοῦ φύσει τελειῶν καὶ ἄγων ἐπὶ τὰ οἰκεῖα.

(111. 29–36)

(i) When this thing, being intelligible by its own nature, comes to be in that which thinks (in the sense of being thought by it), it is an intellect that has come to be in that which thinks and is thought from without and is immortal and gives the material [intellect] the disposition to think objects intelligible in potentiality. (ii) For as light, which produces vision in actuality, is seen itself, as also are the things [seen] along with it, and the colour is seen through it, so the intellect from without also becomes the cause of thinking for us as itself being thought [along with enmattered forms] too; (iii) it does not make it [i.e. the material intellect] to be intellect, but it perfects it as something which already is intellect by its nature and brings it to the things which are proper to it.

We should first note that this passage confirms that, according to the author, no one can think an enmattered form without somehow already thinking the agent intellect.[146] What is new and potentially enlightening in it is the descriptions in (i) and (iii) of how the agent intellect comes to be present in the material intellect. But before analysing these descriptions, we need to revisit—one last time—the 'bizarre' and 'paradoxical' reading, because (i) has become the third main piece of support for it (after 108. 19–24 and 110. 30–1).

This stems from the fact that (i) on its own can easily be read as distinguishing two temporally distinct events: first, the material intellect thinks the agent intellect, and then—endowed with its newly acquired disposition—it begins to think the enmattered forms. But this reading appears plausible only if (i) is taken out of context. For in (ii) the author hastens to spell out his thought by means of Aristotle's light analogy, which he fleshes out in a way that allows him to bring out the *simultaneity* between one's thinking of the agent intellect and one's thinking of each enmattered form.[147] Thus, when the quoted passage is taken as a whole,

---

[146] De Haas, 'Active Intellectual Cognition', 31, asks whether the characteristic of giving the material intellect the disposition to think objects intelligible in potentiality may not be 'more loosely added' to the preceding characteristics in (i), so that—contrary to how B2 is standardly read—the material intellect would be allowed to think enmattered forms *without thinking* the agent intellect (the same suggestion has already been made at p. 29 with respect to 110.30–1, but that was based on a misparsing of the participle αὐξόμενος; see n. 126 above). The answer is provided by (ii)—omitted by de Haas—and is an emphatic 'no': the agent intellect enables the material intellect to think enmattered forms precisely by being an object thought by it, just as light is said to be seen along with the colours revealed by it.

[147] The *comparatum* part of this passage has become the target witness in Schroeder's case against the authenticity of *De intellectu* and for its alleged Plotinian influence: see Schroeder and Todd, *Two Commentators*, Schroeder, 'Provenance',

I submit, it testifies against rather than in support of the 'bizarre' and 'paradoxical' reading.

But what more can we learn from the passage about the involvement of the agent intellect? In (i) the author speaks of the agent intellect not only as being intelligible by its own nature, but also as being 'intellect that has come to be ($\gamma\epsilon\gamma\epsilon\nu\eta\mu\acute{\epsilon}\nu o\varsigma$) in that which thinks'. In Section 6, we will see that this may be an echo of the author's distinctive account of human self-thinking according to which intellect is being thought along with each object of thought, and there are reasons—partly derived from Theophrastus' *Stability Problem*—to believe that this would be impossible if only the material intellect and an enmattered form (coming to be one and the same) were involved.

In (iii), the author elaborates further on how the intellect in question comes to be present in our intellect, and here his description echoes Theophrastus' tentative solution to the *Stability Problem*, while ultimately leading to a very different resolution of the *Passivity/Autonomy Aporia*. The author rejects the idea that the agent intellect acts on the material intellect in the sense of making ($\pi o\iota\epsilon\hat{\iota}\nu$) it something it was not before. The material intellect already *is* intellect, and the agent intellect—in coming to be intellect in it, and so becoming its associate ($\sigma\upsilon\nu\epsilon\rho\gamma\acute{o}\varsigma$)—merely 'perfects it as something which already is intellect by its nature' (111. 35). Thus, rather than acting on the material intellect as something else or as another intellect (and assimilating it to itself or using it as an instrument), the agent intellect comes to be present in the material

and Schroeder and Todd, 'The *De Intellectu* Revisited'. It is the idea that light is itself seen in an act of vision which Schroeder identifies as decisively influenced by Plotinus' account of illumination from *Enn*. 4. 5. 7, contrasting this account with the one provided by Alex. Aphr., *DA* 42. 19–43. 11 (see Schroeder, 'Light and the Active Intellect'). Schroeder's diagnosis has been called into question by Accattino and Donini, *L'anima*, 181–3 and Accattino, *De Intellectu*, 51–2, cf. V. Caston, *Alexander of Aphrodisias: On the Soul. Part I: Soul as Form of the Body, Parts of the Soul, Nourishment, and Perception* (London, 2012), 156. This is not the place to discuss the issue in detail. Roughly, I agree with Schroeder that there is an interesting difference between the account of illumination in B2 and that in Alexander's *De anima* and that it neatly reflects the contrast between, on the one hand, *De intellectu*'s distinctive claim that the agent intellect is thought in any act of human thinking and, on the other hand, *De anima*'s more cautious and reserved characterization of the agent intellect's causation as the most intelligible object. But like Accattino and Donini, I am not convinced this should be explained by Plotinus' influence. Rather, I believe the distinctive doctrine of *De intellectu* is better understood as a set of responses to the traditional Aristotelian difficulties propounded by Theophrastus.

intellect as the material intellect's *own fulfilment*—while at the same time, it seems, remaining a self-standing transcendent entity.[148]

One way to make sense of these claims is as follows. It would be a mistake to conceive the agent intellect as a *subject* of thought distinct from ours. It is rather an *act* of thought, perfectly identical with its object, this object being nothing other than the act itself. More to the point, as the act of thinking that which is intelligible by its own nature, it is the most perfect act of thinking there is. In this sense, it is the final goal of our intellect—the most perfect fulfilment of it—and this is not contravened by the fact that it already existed before we did or that it is a self-standing substance entirely independent from whether we think it or not. This is a key peculiarity of intellect: while our activities of locomotion or perception *come into being* when we perform them, the activity of thinking is something that has always already existed and *becomes our* activity only when we engage in it—without this in any way affecting its status as a self-standing act. Once we learn to see the agent intellect not as *another* intellect (as Theophrastus and the teacher seem to have it), but as *the very fulfilment* of our intellect (notwithstanding that it has always already existed and will continue existing independently from us), we will find a novel way out of the *Passivity/Autonomy Aporia*: the agent intellect is not an 'agent' acting on our intellect in the way that a perceptible object acts on the perceiver; it is our very fulfilment, and so something that is *up to us*, although ultimately it can come to us only 'from without'. This sounds like sheer paradox until we take seriously the idea that what is coming to us 'from without' is nothing short of our true self.

Against the standard reading, I have argued that, according to the account of *De intellectu*, the agent intellect does not directly intervene in the process of our accumulating and processing experience. That process is fully autonomous, and the agent intellect is merely the final cause of it. The agent intellect comes to be directly involved only in the moment when an enmattered form is separated from matter and becomes an actual object of thought. The claim is that in this climactic moment the form can come to be thought *only along with* the agent intellect, never alone. The rationale seems directly connected to the *Problem of Two Potentialities* as outlined in B1: the

---

[148] For the author's explicit statement to the effect that coming to be present in us as an object of our thought allows the agent intellect to remain transcendent, see the final part of C2 (113. 19–24).

process of accumulating and processing experience can never culminate in an act of thinking, given the involvement of only the material intellect and the potentially intelligible form; this is because neither is endowed with the level of actuality needed for the production of the activity of thinking. But the author of B2 goes significantly beyond the framework of the *Problem* as outlined in B1 by insisting that the material intellect is *not* a passive capacity that would need to be *acted upon* by the agent intellect. Rather, the material intellect is productive inasmuch as it is what separates the form simultaneously with the agent intellect coming to it from without as *its own activity of thinking*—thinking now directed to this very form.

The act of thinking an enmattered form can thus occur only as a result of a cooperation between the material and the agent intellect. Without the agent intellect the material intellect could never come actually to think anything; and without the material intellect, the agent intellect would think itself only as the object intelligible by its own nature, and no enmattered forms would ever be thought. This is also why the agent intellect plays a double role in each act of thinking an enmattered form: it comes to be present in the material intellect as an actual thought, i.e. *its very fulfilment*, which can come to it only from without; but it also *remains transcendent and out of our reach* precisely insofar as the thought in question is concerned with an enmattered form, for the agent intellect on its own will think only itself as the object intelligible by its own nature.

The reason why our thought, when directed at an enmattered form, cannot simply coincide with the agent intellect is, presumably, that insofar as a thought is concerned with an enmattered form, it cannot be perfectly the same as its object and thus can only be an imperfect thought—unlike the agent intellect itself. As for why such a thought cannot be perfectly the same as its object, this is because the enmattered form must be thought as separated from matter and indeed becomes the same as the thought precisely insofar as it has been separated, whereas 'it has its being with a certain kind of matter' (ἐπὶ ὕλῃ τινὶ τὸ εἶναι ἔχει, Alex. Aphr., *DA* 88. 13 Bruns; cf. 90. 4–11), and hence to that extent the enmattered form as such remains beyond the reach of thought.[149] So, while our

---

[149] The same point is also made in Alex. Aphr., *Quaest*. 1. 25, 39. 24–31: only an immaterial form can be simply identical to thought, whereas an enmattered form can only be qualifiedly (πως) the same, precisely because intellect cannot 'grasp the

Thought 'From Without' 239

thought, when we separate and grasp an enmattered form, can come to us only from without, this thought of ours points beyond itself insofar as it is a merely imperfectly attained thought.

If this is true, then whenever the material intellect (i.e. the capacity for thought) thinks an enmattered form, the agent intellect (i.e. the act of thought) comes to be present in it as its very fulfilment—but imperfectly attained, so that the perfect self-thought of the agent intellect itself remains the final goal of the material intellect, a goal which is not as such reached until the material intellect comes to think the object intelligible by its own nature *under that description*, and so comes to be at last engaged in that act of thinking which is perfectly identical to its object.[150] Attaining this goal is not only inessential for thinking enmattered forms; it seems to be a very rare achievement—if it is accessible to human beings at all.[151]

If this is indeed what the author has in mind in the quoted passage from B2, his account raises further questions. I mention three of them.

(1) In what sense exactly do we *think the agent intellect* in episodes of thinking directed at enmattered forms? The first thing to emphasize is that we are not, of course, aware of thinking the agent intellect, i.e. the object intelligible by its own nature, as such: we don't think it under that description.[152] What our thought is

---

form with its matter' (μετὰ τῆς ὕλης τὸ εἶδος λαμβάνειν, 39. 29 Bruns) and so misses something about its being. The point is not made in so many words in *De intellectu*; but the author comes close to it, for example, at 108. 14–18, where τὸ νοούμενον is conceived as including both the form and the matter, from which only the form comes to be one and the same as the intellect and thus comes to be the thought strictly speaking (cf. e.g. 108. 7–9), so that something of what was to be thought must have been left out; for the idea of the forms 'having their being with matter' (μεθ' ἧς [sc. ὕλης] ἐστιν αὐτοῖς τὸ εἶναι) from which they are separated in thought, see also 108. 4–5.

[150] This description fits well the author's dominant talk of a single object intelligible by its own nature, identified with the agent intellect. Below I come to the question of how to understand the two passages in which the author seems to speak of a plurality of such objects.

[151] At *DA* 90. 11–91. 6, Alexander provides an arresting analysis of this event. There is comparatively very little in *De intellectu*, where we find only the two telegraphic remarks (110. 33–111. 2, 112. 3–4) about the perfected material intellect coming to be capable of thinking both enmattered *and immaterial* forms. More on what this can mean below.

[152] Thanks to Victor Caston for observing that he is unaware of ever having thought of the agent intellect prior to encountering interpretations of Aristotle's *De*

directed at as such is an enmattered form, which lies beyond the reach of the agent intellect itself. But each such thought is simultaneously a self-thought: not only the form, but also the thought (or intellect) is thought in it. And that, I submit, is where the agent intellect comes in according to the author of *De intellectu*: it is thought exactly as our thought, notwithstanding that it comes to us from without, directed (due to its presence in us) to the enmattered form in question. We will return to this picture in Section 6, when discussing the author's account of self-thinking in A4.

(2) How can the agent intellect come to be present in us and yet remain transcendent? When we think it as our own thought of an enmattered form, we evidently think it in one of its effects or manifestations, or (as Plotinus would put it) in one of its external, secondary activities.[153] We don't yet think it as what it intrinsically is, independently from its causal role *qua* agent intellect. The per se nature of the agent intellect, i.e. the perfect self-thinking activity which *is* the object intelligible by its own nature, remains transcendent to us.

(3) How can the author maintain both that the material intellect is unaffected by the agent intellect and that the former's encounter with the enmattered form is insufficient for producing the activity of thinking? Although the author does not say it in so many words, he seems committed to the view that the agent intellect is not the efficient cause of our thinking of enmattered forms, but in addition to being the final cause of this activity, the agent intellect is the very core of its *form*.[154] There is substantially more to the form of

---

anima, like Alexander's, although he is pretty sure he had many thoughts beforehand. For present purposes, we can disregard the fact that many instances of what we call 'thoughts' nowadays would probably not count as genuine cases of νοεῖν by the lights of Arist., *DA* 3. 4–5.

[153] For a distinction between primary (internal) and secondary (external) activity of the divine intellect, however, we need not go all the way to Plotinus. We already find it in the account reported in C1. The author's key innovation is to say that the secondary activity of divine intellect *is* our proper activity and that it is in this way that we think it.

[154] This idea, incidentally, comes close to Averroes' account of the agent intellect as 'form for us' (for this notion, see R. C. Taylor, 'The Agent Intellect as "Form for Us" and Averroes's Critique of al-Fârâbî', *Proceedings of the Society for Medieval Logic and Metaphysics*, 5 (2005), 18–32). In fact, it is hardly accidental that, in the *Long Commentary on De Anima*, Averroes refers to *De intellectu* (contrasted with Alexander's *De anima*) as a support for his account: the agent intellect becomes *causa secundum formam intellectus materialis in actione eius propria* ('the formal cause

a thought than the form that is thought in it due to separation from matter, and this 'more' can come only from without. Indeed, no form could even be separated from matter, and so be thought, were it not for the immaterial form identical to eternal pure self-thought and its availability to us as potentially *our own* thought of any enmattered form we manage to direct it to.

With these tentative answers on the table, we can finish our discussion of B2. In the rest of the section, the author drives home what has been the main message throughout, namely that the material intellect is *not passive*—not even with respect to the agent intellect which comes to it as its own, more or less perfectly attained fulfilment:

ἔστιν οὖν φύσει μὲν νοητὸν ὁ νοῦς, τὰ δὲ ἄλλα τὰ νοητὰ τέχνῃ τούτου καὶ τούτου ποιήματα, ἃ ποιεῖ οὐ παθὼν καὶ γενόμενος ὑπό τινος ὁ δυνάμει (ἦν γὰρ νοῦς καὶ πρὸ τοῦ ἐνεργεῖν), ἀλλὰ αὐξηθεὶς καὶ τελειούμενος. τελειωθεὶς δὲ τά τε φύσει νοητὰ νοεῖ καὶ τὰ κατὰ τὴν οἰκείαν ἐνέργειαν καὶ τέχνην. ἴδιον γὰρ τοῦ νοῦ τὸ ποιητικόν, καὶ τὸ νοεῖν αὐτῷ ἐνεργεῖν ἐστιν οὐ πάσχειν.

(111. 36–112. 5)

So intellect is something intelligible by nature, while the other intelligible objects are [intelligible] by its craft and are produced by it, and the potential [intellect] produces them not as [itself] being affected and brought about by something (for it was intellect already before being active), but as developing and being perfected. Once it has been perfected, it thinks both the objects intelligible by their nature and those [that are intelligible] on the basis of its activity and craft. For it is being productive that is proper to intellect, and thinking is not being affected for it but being active.

The first sentence contains the same kind of ambiguity we have already encountered at 111. 25–7. *Which* intellect does the author have in mind when characterizing it as something intelligible by its own nature?

Some interpreters assume that he is talking about the agent intellect.[155] Others argue that the author must be talking about the material intellect for what follows to make any sense.[156] As natural as the dilemma may seem, it is probably ill-posed, and realizing this turns out to be important for our understanding of the argument

of the material intellect in its proper activity', 3. 36, 152–4, 484 Crawford; Averroes has just quoted the crucial sentence from A3 108. 19–22, significantly, without any trace of μιμεῖσθαι or of the καί after νοεῖν).

[155] This is how I read Schroeder and Todd, *Two Commentators*, 71–7.

[156] See Accattino, *De Intellectu*, 54–5, followed by Sharples, *Alexander: Supplement*, 37–8 n. 91.

of B2 as a whole. The indeterminacy of 'intellect' (ὁ νοῦς) at the beginning of the quoted passage (111. 36) seems intentional, as is strongly suggested by the specification 'the potential [intellect]' (ὁ δυνάμει) in its second part (112. 1–2). It is intellect *without qualification* that is claimed to be intelligible by nature (cf. 111. 25–7) and this, I submit, points to a key idea behind the argument of B2. When the material intellect thinks—in each of its acts—the object intelligible by its own nature, i.e. the agent intellect, it thinks nothing other than *its own*—more or less perfected—*nature as intellect*. And thinking its own nature or itself cannot be a case of being affected.

If this is indeed what the author has in mind, then his idea resembles, at least to a certain extent, Theophrastus' solution of the *Passivity/Autonomy Aporia*. Theophrastus' key move was to say that human thought can be seen as both passive and autonomous, provided that we understand autonomy as being 'up to intellect' *broadly conceived*, that is, not primarily our own 'material' intellect. The author of B2 similarly speaks of intellect *broadly conceived* as being intelligible by its own nature: this applies to the agent intellect independently of the material intellect, but it also applies, secondarily, to the material intellect insofar as each of its thoughts involves an act of thinking the agent intellect as its own fulfilment, i.e. as its own thought coming from without. The author thus goes beyond Theophrastus' solution by exploiting the idea that the agent intellect is not just *another* intellect, let alone a *moving* intellect, but is the very fulfilment of the material intellect, notwithstanding that it exists as a self-standing entity. Once this idea is taken seriously, one can insist that what is brought to the material intellect by the agent intellect's involvement is, in fact, its own fulfilment or self, which means this cannot be a case of being affected. Indeed, it becomes possible to maintain that thinking is genuinely *up to us* (as is done emphatically in C2).

In the closing passage of B2, the author seems once more to echo *and reject* the first horn of the *Passivity/Autonomy Aporia*: it is *not* the case that the material intellect comes to think when 'being affected and brought about by something' (παθὼν καὶ γενόμενος ὑπό τινος, 112. 1). This rejection allows him to draw the momentous conclusion that intellect is essentially productive, and its thinking does not consist in being affected but in being active. The material intellect is not affected by the agent intellect but rather cooperates with it when the latter comes to be present in the former as the former's own thought—thought concerned with an enmattered form. That object lies beyond the reach of the agent intellect as such, and thought can come to be concerned with it in us only at the cost of thought's perfection.

With this in mind, we can close the present section by returning to the notorious exegetical question that first arose at 110. 33–111. 2 and that recurred in the last-quoted passage (112. 3–4).[157] These two places in *De intellectu* are where the author speaks of objects intelligible by their nature in the plural, which contrasts with his standard invocation of the object intelligible by its own nature in the singular, identified as the agent intellect. The issue cannot be fully discussed here, but we are in a position to evaluate at least a few tentative suggestions as to how it could be resolved.

The first thing to notice is that both passages are unique in a further respect: they are the only two passages in *De intellectu* that speak of the material intellect when it has been perfected, where 'perfection' seems to be conceived in the maximally demanding way, as implying the power to think at will *anything there is to be thought*. This perspective then suggests an easy way of resolving the apparent tension between the singular and the plural. When speaking of 'objects intelligible by their nature' (plural), in conjunction with objects which are only potentially intelligible (plural), the author is clearly echoing the contrast with Arist., *DA* 3. 4, 430^{a}3–9 between '[objects] without matter' and '[objects] having matter' (quoted in Section 1). The plural is thus used, as in Aristotle, to mark a general *category* of objects. The question of *how many* objects without matter there are evidently belongs to a different inquiry, namely that of first philosophy. It may be, then, that in these two remarks the author of *De intellectu* merely wishes to distinguish two general categories of objects of thought, without committing himself to any definite view about their respective number: the point would just be that when our intellect is brought to perfection, it can think the object(s) without matter in isolation, as object(s) distinct from enmattered forms, rather than thinking the object(s) without matter *along with an enmattered form* as its own thought of this form. This point would be perfectly compatible with the idea that there really is only one such object—or at

---

[157] Cf. n. 129 above.

any rate, that only one such object can be proved to exist in the present inquiry.[158]

All the same, one may wish to press the question further and ask what it would mean for the author's account were he to admit a plurality of objects intelligible by their nature. He could, of course, adopt the straightforward approach of taking the agent intellect to be one of these objects.[159] But that appears rather unsatisfactory, especially once the author has emphasized the role of the agent intellect *qua* the object intelligible by its own nature. If there are more such objects, why does only one of them play the role of the agent intellect? Alternatively, it could be that the entire plurality of objects intelligible by their nature play the role of the agent intellect, somehow jointly enabling us to think enmattered forms, so that as long as the material intellect thinks its own thought of an enmattered form coming from without, there is simply no way of determining which of the objects intelligible by their nature this thought comes from. Only when the material intellect has been perfected and has become capable of thinking the objects intelligible by nature on their own does it become capable of distinguishing between them and thinking one of them to the exclusion of others.

This solution is, to say the least, speculative. Fortunately, however, we don't need to rely on it. First, as noted above, it may be that the author opts to remain agnostic about the number of immaterial forms in the present context because he is aware of its limitations. More importantly, it is possible that the author's actual position was that there is strictly speaking only one object intelligible by its own nature,[160] so that the plurality scenario would remain a pure conceptual possibility. This is a highly controversial matter, and so once again it cannot be decided here. It is worth noting, though, that the unicity of immaterial form, as the single object of desire common to all heavenly spheres, has been identified

---

[158] If there were no such object, human thinking would not be possible; but it is possible; therefore, there is at least one such object. When asking whether more such objects exist, we will have to start from a different set of phenomena, namely the motion in the universe, and the motion of heavenly spheres in particular.

[159] As in the account shared by several Arabic thinkers which identifies the agent intellect with the lowest heavenly intelligence. If the author identifies the agent intellect with the mover of the first sphere, he could still admit that there are many other such intellects moving the lower spheres.

[160] Cf. Donini, *Tre studi*, 60.

by scholars in the treatise *On Principles*, preserved in an Arabic translation as Alexander's work.[161]

Either of the suggested answers will work for our purposes, and so there is no need to dwell on this issue any longer. Instead, we may proceed to discuss what is perhaps the most understudied part of *De intellectu*, namely the author's account of self-thinking in A4. We will see that it corroborates the picture which has emerged so far.

6. Self-directedness of thought

We have seen (in Section 2) that in A3 the author primarily focuses on a teleological description of the agent intellect's involvement. The text may or may not have also hinted at the need for the material intellect *to think* the agent intellect in order to think any enmattered form (depending on whether there was an adverbial καί after νοεῖν at 108. 21 or not); but even if it did, this was still at best a promissory note to be cashed out later in B2. This makes perfect sense, because only in B1 is the *Problem of Two Potentialities* posed (as shown in Section 1) and with it the need for a direct involvement of the agent intellect. I want to suggest now that in what comes after A3's discussion of the agent intellect—namely in A4, which has not been properly marked out as its own section—the author develops a distinctive account of human self-thinking that *anticipates* the account of B2. It does so by, in effect, identifying a need for the direct involvement of the agent intellect as described in B2 that is independent of the *Problem of Two Potentialities*. If this is true, then A4 will corroborate the interpretation of B2 proposed in Section 5, and the case for the unity of A and B will be further strengthened.[162] Moreover, A4 will again highlight the importance of Theophrastus' *aporiai* (introduced in Section 4)

---

[161] See I. M. Bodnár, 'Alexander's Unmoved Mover', in C. Cerami (ed.), *Nature et sagesse: Les rapports entre physique et métaphysique dans la tradition aristotélicienne* (Louvain-la-Neuve, 2018), 387–416. The same idea may also be expressed in Alex. Aphr., *Quaest.* 1. 25, 40. 3–10. Cf. also I. M. Bodnár, 'Alexander of Aphrodisias on Celestial Motions', *Phronesis*, 42 (1997), 190–205.

[162] As against the 'analytical' approach, for which, see Schroeder and Todd, *Two Commentators*; Schroeder, 'Provenance'; Schroeder and Todd, 'The *De Intellectu* Revisited'.

insofar as the *Stability Problem* helps us appreciate what the author may be up to here.

The account of self-thinking at the level of the dispositional intellect in A4a (= 109. 4–23) is, in fact, an interpretation of Aristotle's claim at *DA* 3. 4, 429^{b}6–10 that the intellect capable of thinking through itself can also think itself (αὐτὸν νοεῖν, 429^{b}9),[163] as well as of his answer to the question raised at 429^{b}26 as to whether intellect is itself intelligible (i.e. 3. 4, 430^{a}2–9, quoted in Section 1). Accordingly, the account of A4a falls naturally into two parts.

In the first part (109. 4–14), the author argues that human intellect does not think itself insofar as it is intellect, but 'insofar as intellect in actuality is the same as the objects thought in actuality' (ᾗ ὁ κατ' ἐνέργειαν νοῦς ὁ αὐτός ἐστι τοῖς κατ' ἐνέργειαν νοουμένοις, 109. 6–7).[164] Since human intellect comes to be the same as the objects it thinks—and, indeed, 'the objects that it thinks become, in being thought, intellect' (ταῦτα ἃ νοεῖ ἐν τῷ νοεῖσθαι νοῦς γίνεται, 109. 8)— in thinking them it somehow thinks itself. What is somewhat surprising is the author's assertion (109. 11–14) that the reason in this case is the same as in the case of perception, which also perceives itself insofar as it becomes in actuality the same as the perceptual objects in actuality.[165] This parallelism underlines the fact that the author's account here must be compatible with the caveat (introduced in Section 5) that, in the case of enmattered forms, intellect is not *perfectly* the same as the object it thinks. It becomes the same as each form *only insofar as* the latter is separated from matter, but

---

[163] A4, together with Alex. Aphr., *DA* 86. 14–28 (see esp. 17–18), provides strong evidence against Bywater's emendation at 429^{b}9 (αὐτὸς δι' αὐτοῦ instead of αὐτὸς δὲ αὐτόν; followed e.g. by W. D. Ross (ed.), *Aristotelis De anima* [*De anima*] (Oxford, 1961); D. W. Hamlyn, *Aristotle, De Anima: Books II and III*, 2nd edn (Oxford, 1993); and Shields, *Aristotle: De Anima*; cf. Accattino, *De Intellectu*, 47.

[164] More below on the excluded option.

[165] It is surprising, at least from the perspective of Alexander's *De anima*, in which the author insists that the kind of sameness between perception and the object perceived is quite different from the kind of sameness between thought and the object of thought, so that perception is of itself in a very different sense from that in which thought is of itself (87. 1–11). In its reluctance to draw any explicit contrast between perception and thought A4 is in line with A3. V. Caston, 'Higher-Order Awareness in Alexander of Aphrodisias' ['Higher-Order Awareness'], *Bulletin of the Institute of Classical Studies*, 55 (2012), 31–49 at 48–9, finds a similar kind of contrast between Alexander's *De anima* and his analysis of higher-order awareness in *Quaest.* 3. 7. We will see, however, that the second part of A4a already points *beyond* the analogy with perception.

the form 'has its being with matter' (cf. 108. 4–5). What matters for the account of A4a is that the form is thought precisely *insofar as* it becomes one and the same as intellect, so that, in thinking it, intellect somehow thinks itself. It should be noted that the author never qualifies the *kind of sameness* between intellect and the separated form. He does not say, for instance, that intellect becomes this form *only extrinsically*.[166] What makes the sameness imperfect is that the form has its being with matter, but insofar as it is separated from matter, it seems to be simply identical to the intellect thinking it: it 'becomes intellect', as the author puts it (109. 8; cf. 108. 6–9 and 109. 1–3). This, as we will see, is where Theophrastus' *Stability Problem* becomes pressing.

What follows at 109. 14–23 is usually treated by interpreters as merely repeating, in different words, the point of 109. 4–14.[167] But this approach is doubtful for at least two reasons. First, it fails to respect the grammatical structure of 109. 4–23. The first part is introduced by a μέν ('on the one hand') clause:

οὐ καθὸ νοῦς ἐστιν... ἀλλὰ καὶ ταύτῃ μέν, ᾗ...

(109. 5–6)

[the intellect can think itself] not insofar as it is intellect..., but, on the one hand, insofar as...

And although this is rarely respected by translations and commentaries,[168] there is little doubt that this μέν is complemented by the δέ introducing the second part:

---

[166] As in the account of Alexander's *De anima* according to Caston, 'Higher-Order Awareness', 46–8.

[167] Schroeder and Todd, *Two Commentators*, 68, find the whole passage worthy of no more than a single laconic sentence. Sharples, *Alexander: Supplement*, 31, translates it with no comment at all (the same goes for Dufour, *Mantissa*; and Söder, 'Über den Geist'). Accattino, *De Intellectu*, 47–8 sees in this section only an additional indirect support for the claim of 109. 4–14 that the intellect does not think itself insofar as it is intellect, but insofar as it comes to be one and the same as an object of thought. In Accattino's view, at 109. 14–23 the author returns to the idea that the intellect could think itself insofar as it is intellect, and explains at 109. 19–22 why this cannot be so. But Accattino's assumption that at 109. 14–18 the author is simply returning to the idea that the intellect could think itself insofar as it is intellect seems, as we will see, unlikely.

[168] One exception is Sharples, whose translation (unlike that of Todd and Schroeder, Accattino (and Ghiggia), Dufour, and Söder) faithfully reflects this structure. Unfortunately, Sharples makes no comment about the content of the second part.

ἔτι δὲ λέγοιτ' ἂν αὐτὸν νοεῖν ὁ νοῦς οὐχ ᾗ νοῦς ἐστιν, ἀλλ' ᾗ...

(109. 14–15)

Further, on the other hand, one could say that the intellect thinks itself not insofar as it is intellect, but insofar as...

This suggests that what is said in the second part is not just paraphrasing what has already been said, but is intended to make a new and complementary point.

109. 14–23 is also unlikely to be a mere repetition, because what it says does sound novel indeed. Intellect does not think itself 'insofar as it is intellect but insofar as it too is intelligible' (οὐχ ᾗ νοῦς ἐστιν, ἀλλ' ᾗ καὶ αὐτὸς νοητός, 109. 15). The καί here has mostly been understood by scholars as simply introducing a second aspect of the intellect: it is not only intellect, but *also* intelligible.[169] And so the passage has been usually taken as merely repeating the point made before, i.e. that intellect thinks itself insofar as it comes to be one and the same as the object of thought. But what follows suggests that the author has something different and more interesting in mind. He explains:

ὡς γὰρ νοητοῦ ἀντιλήψεται, ὥσπερ καὶ τῶν ἄλλων ἑκάστου τῶν νοητῶν, οὐχ ὡς νοῦ.

(109. 15–17)[170]

... for [the intellect] grasps [itself] as an object of thought, just as it also grasps each of the other objects of thought, and not as intellect.

The idea seems to be that, besides the enmattered form that becomes one and the same as the intellect, the intellect also thinks itself as *yet another* object of thought.[171] This suggests that already in the preceding sentence the καί had a different function from that which has usually been assumed. Rather than merely repeating the point that intellect thinks itself insofar as it comes to be one and the same as the object thought by it, it seems to have introduced a

---

[169] Thus, Todd and Schroeder have 'in so far as it is itself *also* an object of thought' (cf. Söder, 'Über den Geist', 219), while Accattino, *De Intellectu*, Sharples, *Alexander: Supplement*, and Accattino and Ghiggia, *Mantissa* do not translate the καί at all. The only exception is Dufour, *Mantissa*, 22, who duly translates 'en tant qu'il est *lui aussi* intelligible' (my emphasis), but without explaining what this means and implies.

[170] Cf. Arist., *DA* 3. 4, 429^{b}28–9: ἢ μεμιγμένον τι ἕξει, ὃ ποιεῖ νοητὸν αὐτὸν ὥσπερ τἆλλα.

[171] That the author has in mind primarily enmattered forms in the first part of A4a is clear from 109. 8: εἴ γε ταῦτα ἃ νοεῖ ἐν τῷ νοεῖσθαι νοῦς γίνεται—a condition that is not met in the case of an object intelligible by its nature. Cf. 109. 13–14.

Thought 'From Without' 249

new complementary point (as the μέν—δέ structure indicates): intellect thinks itself only insofar as not just the enmattered form separated from matter but also *it itself* is intelligible. It is, to be sure, far from clear what this new point amounts to. But it is important to recognize it as such, especially since the author repeats it twice more in what follows.

He first provides a justification of the assumption that there are two different aspects of intellect involved, i.e. its 'being intellect' and its 'being intelligible':[172]

συμβέβηκε γὰρ τῷ νῷ εἶναι καὶ νοητῷ· ἐπεὶ γάρ ἐστι τῶν ὄντων τι καὶ αὐτός, καὶ οὐκ ἔστιν αἰσθητός, λείπεται νοητὸν αὐτὸν εἶναι.

(109. 17–18)

for being intelligible also belongs to the intellect; for since it [i.e. the intellect] too is one of the beings, and it is not perceptible, it remains that it is intelligible.[173]

The intelligibility of intellect is here clearly *not* derived from it becoming the same as the forms it thinks. Instead, the author focuses on the intellect's being something over and above these forms, and he argues that this specific 'being' must be intelligible. It is not obvious how exactly the argument here should be combined with the author's characterization of the material intellect in A1, drawing on Arist., *DA* 3. 4, 429ᵃ18–27, as 'none of the beings in actuality'.[174] If the very being of the material intellect consists

---

[172] Unfortunately, neither Accattino, *De Intellectu*, nor any other interpreter makes any comment about this passage.

[173] The explanation offered here of why being intelligible belongs (συμβέβηκε) to intellect is surprising. Given that it comes from Alexander's *De anima*, one would expect that intellect 'happens' (συμβαίνει) to be thought insofar as it comes to be one and the same as an intelligible object. Instead, however, the author says that intelligibility belongs to intellect insofar as it is itself a being *other than* enmattered forms (which come to be the same as intellect when being thought by it). This consideration must also be behind the (falsely familiar) claim closing A4a that 'intellect comes to be thinking itself incidentally as it progresses from the material intellect' (γίνεται οὖν κατὰ συμβεβηκὸς αὐτὸν νοῶν ὁ νοῦς οὗτος ἀπὸ τοῦ ὑλικοῦ νοῦ προϊών, 109. 22–3). Again, the thought seems not to be that intellect happens to think itself insofar as it comes to be one and the same as what it thinks; rather, intellect happens to think itself *as it progresses*. For more on what the author may have in mind, see n. 182 below.

[174] See 106. 27–107. 11, especially the conclusion: οὐδὲν ἄρα τῶν ὄντων ἐστὶν ἐνεργείᾳ, δυνάμει δὲ πάντα. τοῦτο γάρ ἐστιν αὐτῷ τὸ εἶναι νῷ ('hence it [i.e. the material intellect] is none of the beings in actuality, but it is in potentiality all of them, for this is what it is for it to be an intellect', 107. 9–11).

in being everything in potentiality, and if it thinks itself only insofar as it comes to be one and the same as an enmattered form, that is, insofar as its potential being is actualized in one way or another, then it is not clear how exactly this intellect should be understood as one among the beings that it can think and how exactly it should 'think itself as one of the objects of thought' (αὐτὸν... νοεῖν ὡς ἕν τι τῶν νοητῶν), as the author puts it a few lines below (119. 21–2). We find at least some hints in the rest of A4a.

The author goes on to explain why the intellect in question cannot think itself 'insofar as it is intellect' (ᾗ νοῦς ἐστιν, 109. 15). It cannot do so because this would imply that it cannot think *anything beyond* what is intellect,[175] so that it would *exclusively* think itself (109. 19–20).[176] The author seems to have in mind Aristotle's distinction from *Metaphysics* Λ. 9, 1074^{b}35–1075^{a}5 between, on the one hand, cognitive acts we humans are familiar with, which are primarily directed at their objects but at themselves only 'on the side' (ἐν παρέργῳ), and, on the other hand, the divine activity of thinking, which is primarily directed at itself.[177] Indeed, this is what the author seems to have already had in mind at 109. 5–6 when claiming that if intellect were to think itself insofar as it is intellect, 'thinking and being thought would belong to it together and in the same respect' (ἅμα γὰρ καὶ κατὰ ταὐτὸν αὐτῷ τὸ νοεῖν ἔσται

---

[175] The author must mean anything beyond what is *by its nature* intellect, as becomes clear in what follows at 109. 20–2.

[176] 'For if it were thought by itself as intellect and insofar as it is intellect, it could not think anything other, which is not intellect, so that it would think exclusively itself' (εἰ γὰρ ὡς νοῦς καὶ καθὸ νοῦς ἐστιν ἐνοεῖτο ὑφ' αὑτοῦ, οὐδὲν ἂν ἄλλο, ὃ μὴ νοῦς ἦν, ἐνόει, ὥστε αὐτὸν ἂν ἐνόει μόνον). The claim can perhaps be better appreciated against the background of Aristotle's argument for the intellect having no nature of its own except for being potential at *DA* 3. 4, 429^{a}18–27 (thanks to Peter Adamson for this suggestion). The idea would be that if intellect were able to think itself independently from becoming one and the same as some form, it would have a kind of gigantic blind spot which would make it unable to think anything beyond itself, just as the tongue full of a bitter moisture cannot properly taste anything other than bitterness, as happens when we are sick (cf. Arist., *DA* 2. 10, 422^{b}5–10).

[177] There has been much discussion as to whether it is directed at itself *to the exclusion of* anything else, or whether this thinking includes a plurality of essences. For an overview of this discussion, and a defence of an inclusivist reading, see Judson, *Aristotle, Metaphysics Lambda*, 311–34; for a recent defence of an exclusivist reading, see e.g. F. Baghdassarian, 'L'intellection divine en *Métaphysique* Λ 7 et 9: Les indices d'un approfondissement d'Aristote par lui-même', in G. Guyomarc'h and F. Baghdassarian (eds.), *Réceptions de la théologie aristotélicienne: D'Aristote à Michel d'Éphèse* (Louvain-la-Neuve, 2017), 33–58. The author of *De intellectu* seems to have a decidedly exclusivist understanding.

καὶ νοεῖσθαι).[178] The point, then, seems to be that if intellect were to think itself insofar as it is intellect, this could not be a human intellect capable of thinking enmattered forms, but must instead be a divine intellect limited to itself as the exclusive object of its thinking—this would be the divine kind of self-thinking to which the author turns in A4b (= 109. 23–110. 3).[179] But:

νοῶν δὲ τὰ νοητά, ἃ μή ἐστιν νοῦς πρὸ τοῦ νοεῖσθαι, καὶ αὐτὸν ὡς τοιοῦτον νοεῖ ὡς ἕν τι τῶν νοητῶν.

(109. 20–2)

while it thinks objects of thought which are not intellect before being thought, it thinks itself too as being such, that is, as one of the objects of thought.

If taken in isolation, this sentence could perhaps be understood as merely repeating the point of 109. 4–14 that the intellect thinks itself only insofar as it becomes one and the same as an enmattered form thought by it. But the larger context as reviewed above suggests that this is not what the author means. What he means to say is that the intellect under consideration thinks itself as being itself an object of thought too, in addition to the form thought by it. In other words, the passage as a whole suggests that, according to the author, the structure of human self-thinking is more complex than one would guess after reading 109. 4–14 alone. It is not only (a) the thinking intellect and (b) an enmattered form as the object of its thought that play a role here (becoming one and the same). There is a third item involved, namely (c) the intellect as itself also being an object of thought.

The text also contains, at least implicitly, a justification of this tripartite structure that is interesting and that can help us better understand the author's larger motivation. Roughly, the idea seems

---

[178] This seems to be a reference to *Metaph. Λ.* 9, 1075^{a}3–5 Ross: 'since then in the case of objects having no matter that which is thought is not distinct from intellect, these will be the same, and thinking will be one and the same as that which is thought' (οὐχ ἑτέρου οὖν ὄντος τοῦ νοουμένου καὶ τοῦ νοῦ, ὅσα μὴ ὕλην ἔχει, τὸ αὐτὸ ἔσται, καὶ ἡ νόησις τῷ νοουμένῳ μία).

[179] '[The first intellect] has something more than this [i.e. our intellect], for it thinks nothing other than itself' (πλέον τι παρὰ τοῦτον ἔχει. οὐδὲν γὰρ ἄλλο ἢ αὐτὸν νοεῖ, 109. 24–5). The claim is explained at 109. 25–31, and the first sentence of the conclusion picks up on 109. 19–20: 'It will, thus, be *insofar as it is intellect* that it thinks itself as intelligible' (καθὸ μὲν ἄρα νοῦς ἐστιν, αὐτὸν ὡς νοητὸν νοήσει, 109. 31). Cf. Alex. Aphr., *Quaest.* 1. 25, 39. 31–40. 3.

to be that if (i) the intellect *qua* being thought were indistinguishable from the intellect *qua* thinking, this would be a case of pure self-thinking with no room left for any object different from the intellect to be thought by it.[180] But if (ii) the intellect *qua* being thought were indistinguishable from the object of thought (i.e. an enmattered form) that becomes one and the same as the intellect thinking it, there would remain no room for self-thinking: the thought would be fully absorbed in the object and there would remain no 'self' whatsoever to be thought.[181] Our self-thinking can be a concomitant of thinking enmattered forms and our thinking of enmattered forms can be a case of self-thinking, *only if*, besides the thinking intellect and the enmattered form thought by it, there is also—as a third item—intellect as an object of thought. Indeed, the grammatical structure of A4 underlined above suggests that the author wants to make just these two complementary claims: (i) our intellect can think itself only while thinking an enmattered form (109. 4–14), but (ii) besides this form and the intellect thinking it, there must also be intellect as an object of thought (109. 14–23).

We can better understand the motivation behind this complication, I submit, by attending to Theophrastus' *Stability Problem*. If our intellect were entirely absorbed in the object it thinks on each occasion, it would be something 'indistinguishable', becoming a different thing each time, and there would remain no room for any *self*-thinking, because intellect would have no stability whatsoever. This is a picture that one might fear to have emerged from the μέν-segment of A4a (drawing on Arist., *DA* 3. 4, 430ᵃ6–9). And that, I submit, is why the author adds a δέ-segment. He makes clear here that a pure self-thinking (as implied at *DA* 3. 4, 430ᵃ3–6) is beyond human reach: it is a privilege of what is intelligible by its own nature to think itself and purely itself. What he proposes

---

[180] This seems to be the case with 'the [objects] without matter' (τὰ ἄνευ ὕλης) at Arist., *DA* 3. 4, 430ᵃ3–6; cf. Theophrastus as quoted by Priscianus, *Metaphr.* 30. 23 (discussed in Section 4).

[181] This worry can be understood as a reaction to Aristotle's solution for 'the [objects] having matter' (τὰ ἔχοντα ὕλην) at *DA* 3. 4, 430ᵃ6–9. Let it be taken for granted that these objects do not have intellect because they contain objects of thought *only in potentiality*; but how can the intellect which becomes some of these objects of thought in actuality *also* think *itself*, and how can it continue thinking itself when it passes from one object to another? Cf. Theophrastus' queries quoted by Priscianus, *Metaphr.* 29. 18–20, 22–3, 26–7 (discussed in Section 4).

seems to be a middle path between the full absorption that makes self-thinking impossible and the pure self-thinking that is incompatible with thinking enmattered forms and that is inaccessible to us *qua* human beings. The idea seems to be that, in each act of thinking an enmattered form, our intellect also thinks *intellect as a stable object of thought*.

In any case, A4 leaves unexplained the status of intellect *qua* object of thought. In light of the author's identification of the agent intellect as the object intelligible by its own nature in A3 (and even more emphatically in B2; cf. A4b, 109. 26), it seems plausible to suppose that what he refers to is in effect nothing more than the agent intellect being thought by the material intellect in each act of thinking an enmattered form as the material intellect's own thought, even as it comes 'from without'. Or in other words, it seems plausible to hold that the role of intellect *qua* object of thought presupposed by the account of A4a is intended to be filled in by B2's depiction of the agent intellect as directly involved in each act of our thinking. This seems to be the most distinctive feature of *De intellectu*'s account, and so it is not very surprising also to find a trace of it in the author's account of human self-thinking.[182] Moreover, it is not surprising that the account is not yet fully spelled out in A4: at this point the author has not introduced the main reason *why* the agent intellect needs to be involved in each act of our thinking, let alone explained *how* it can be involved without undermining the aspect of our thought so dear to the author, namely its being *up to us*. Given A4's limited purposes, it seems sufficient to work out the tripartite structure of human self-thinking, which will prove a perfect match with the author's account of the agent intellect that is still to come in B2.

---

[182] We can return now to the closing claim of A4a according to which 'intellect comes to be thinking itself incidentally as it progresses from the material intellect' (γίνεται οὖν κατὰ συμβεβηκὸς αὐτὸν νοῶν ὁ νοῦς οὗτος ἀπὸ τοῦ ὑλικοῦ νοῦ προϊών, 109. 22–3). As already pointed out (in n. 173 above), the idea seems not to be that intellect happens to think itself insofar as it comes to be one and the same as what it thinks, but rather that it happens to think itself *as it progresses*. One potential way of understanding this claim is that in intellect *qua* object of thought, the material intellect happens to think itself because, although the former comes to the latter from without, the former is the *terminus ad quem* of the latter's progress, i.e. its proper fulfilment.

7. Conclusion: Alexander's account(s) of the agent intellect

Let us take stock. If our proposed reconstruction of A4 is on the right track, then the author is in effect offering a way of overcoming Theophrastus' *Stability Problem*. We don't need to worry about the intellect becoming a different intellect, let alone a different kind of thing, every time it comes to think a new object, if we are assured that as it thinks this object, it always thinks intellect as its own fulfilment even as this intellect comes to it from without.[183] This way of resolving the *Stability Problem* prepares the way for the author's resolution of the *Passivity/Autonomy Aporia*, which is worked out in B2: our intellect is not passive—not even with respect to the agent intellect—precisely because the latter comes to be present in our intellect as its own, more or less perfectly attained, fulfilment. The agent intellect thus not only has no direct involvement in the activities of accumulating and processing experience presupposed by our thinking; it comes to us in the culminating moment as *our own* thought—thought concerned with the form in question, and thus imperfect and pointing beyond itself to the agent intellect as a self-standing and perfectly transparent self-thought yet to be reached.

If this is correct, then we can see why the way of contrasting *De intellectu*'s account of the agent intellect with the one developed in Alexander's *De anima* (88. 24–89. 11) that has become standard since Moraux can be very misleading. It has been widely held that while in *De anima* Alexander makes the material intellect *autonomous* by allowing it to separate and think enmattered forms on its own and without any direct involvement of the agent intellect, the author of *De intellectu* presupposes a radical *intervention* of the agent intellect, either as, paradoxically, the very first explicit object of our thought, which we then try to imitate when processing experience and separating enmattered forms, or even as the direct source of the contents of our thought from which 'emanates' whatever we think. The aim of this paper has been to show that, on the

---

[183] Cf. again the final lines of C2 (113. 18–24) for the author's explicit statement to the effect that the agent intellect comes to be present in us insofar as it is thought by us. This certainly does not mean that in each act of thought concerned with an enmattered form we are aware of the agent intellect as such. Instead (as argued in Section 5), we think the agent intellect precisely as our own thought, which is now concerned with the form in question but can be directed at other objects as well.

contrary, the autonomy of human thought is a principal concern of the author of *De intellectu*.

The agent intellect is introduced in A3 primarily as the final cause of our thought. In B, to be sure, the author makes it clear—unlike Alexander in his *De anima*—that this cannot be all there is, because final causality is not enough to resolve the *Problem of Two Potentialities*, necessitating a *direct* involvement of the agent intellect in each act of thought. This problem, which the author inherits, seems ultimately to motivate the idea that in our thinking of each enmattered form, the agent intellect, as the final cause of our intellect, comes to be already *present*—presumably as the core of the thought's form. Yet since the thought still exhibits complexity insofar as it is directed at an enmattered form, which can never be perfectly one and the same as thought, we cannot avoid falling short of fully attaining our ultimate goal *qua* thinkers, namely the perfect self-thought characteristic of the agent intellect itself. The author goes out of his way in B2 to interpret the direct involvement of the agent intellect as not implying any *passivity* whatsoever on the part of the human thought and as compatible with our thought being genuinely *up to us* (a feature emphasized most in C2). From this perspective, *De intellectu*, far from contradicting Alexander's *De anima*, turns out to be its close accomplice in a breakaway from the preceding Peripatetic tradition, insofar as that tradition had conceived our thought as being up to a divine intellect rather than up to us.

This is certainly not to say that there are no differences between the two accounts worth exploring. If, for instance, we interpret the role of the agent intellect in Alexander's *De anima* in purely teleological terms,[184] then the account of *De intellectu* will differ from it precisely insofar as it maintains that when an enmattered form is separated from matter and activated as an object of thought, the agent intellect is already thought as well—as our intellect's own thought. This contrast seems to be ultimately motivated by *De intellectu*'s recognition of the *Problem of Two Potentialities*: a genuine act of thinking cannot (unlike an act of perception) be produced by the object of thought and it cannot be produced by the material intellect as such either; it can come only from without, even as its content is determined by experience, and there needs to

---

[184] See Guyomarc'h, 'Active Intellect'.

be a long process of accumulating and processing experience that culminates in it. This allows the author to offer a novel and thought-provoking answer to the problem that his teacher at least was already wrestling with. It is, in contrast, an at least *prima facie* disquieting feature of Alexander's *De anima* that it fails to offer any such answer.[185]

This does not necessarily mean we should treat *De intellectu* as a more advanced stage of Alexander's thought than his *De anima*.[186] It has been argued that the account of *De anima* is based on a conscious *rejection* of the very terms of the *Problem*.[187] And if that is true, it would allow us to keep to the current majority view on which *De intellectu* represents an earlier stage of Alexander's thought, abandoned at some point—for better or for worse—in favour of the account of *De anima*. If, however, our proposed reconstruction is on the right track, it takes away some of the pressure interpreters have felt to prioritize the account of *De anima* as more advanced; for the account of *De intellectu* turns out to be considerably more sophisticated and philosophically respectable than the 'bizarre' and 'paradoxical' reading would have it. If it does represent an earlier stage, then the advance to the account of *De anima* was not terribly dramatic, for much is already anticipated here. And if *De anima* was written earlier, then *De intellectu* can be seen as an attempt to provide a solution to the *Problem of Two Potentialities* within the framework laid down in the earlier work, rather than an abandonment of it. It becomes, in any case, much easier to see both *De anima* and *De intellectu* as works of the same author, ingenious as Alexander of Aphrodisias was.[188]

I take one point to be, unlike matters of authorship and chronology, established firmly. It seems hopeless to try to explain the specificity of *De intellectu* with a Neoplatonist influence. We have seen that all of the alleged pieces of support for this approach are

---

[185] This point is made by Moraux, *Exégète*, 73–7.

[186] As proposed by Bazán, 'L'authenticité', whose interpretation of *De intellectu* is, however, very different from the one offered in this paper: it is a version of the 'bizarre' and 'paradoxical' account prized for how it resolves the *Problem of Two Potentialities*.

[187] See the references in n. 56 above.

[188] If *De intellectu* is not by Alexander, this would seem to imply that Alexander had a truly ingenious disciple (or predecessor) who remained entirely anonymous. The principle of parsimony puts pressure on the sceptic of Alexandrian authorship, and lays the *onus demonstrandi* on her side.

better explained as attempts to provide a genuinely Peripatetic account that would solve major difficulties handed down by the school. Whatever we think about its relation to Alexander's *De anima*, *De intellectu* is part and parcel of the Peripatetic school's debate over intellect. Indeed, it helps us gain a much richer understanding of that debate than would otherwise be accessible to us. That is not to deny that there are striking parallels between the doctrine of *De intellectu* and some of Plotinus' key ideas. Indeed, I take these parallels worthy of a close examination. The point is that if there was any influence, it must have run in the other direction.

Last but not least, the conflict between Alexander's approach and his Peripatetic predecessors, which *De intellectu* helps us appreciate, is not unrelated to recent discussions of the agent intellect and of the reasons Aristotle may have had for introducing it in *De anima* 3. 5. The account of *De intellectu* may not strike every reader as the best available interpretation of Aristotle, but it has its indisputable merits, not least because it manages to challenge *both* compatibilist and purely teleological interpretations at one blow. It deserves to be taken seriously as probably the earliest extant respectable attempt to solve a conundrum with which readers of Aristotle are still wrestling today.

Charles University, Prague

Appendix

The Contents of *De Intellectu*

(A Schematic Overview)

(A) Summary of Aristotle's Noetic (106. 19–110. 3)
  (A1) *Material Intellect* (106. 19–107. 20)
    - a potentiality different from both the matter and the senses
  (A2) *Dispositional Intellect* (107. 21–8)
    - a readiness to think
  (A3) *Agent Intellect* (107. 29–109. 4)
    - the cause of dispositional intellect (107.29–34)
    - object intelligible by its own nature = immaterial form (107. 34–108. 19)

- all human thought makes 'reference' to it (108. 19–22)
- intellect 'from without', separate, and imperishable (108. 22–109. 4)

  (A4*) *Self-Thinking at the Level of*
- dispositional intellect (109. 4–23)
- agent intellect (109. 23–110. 3)

(B) Discussion of Aristotle's Motivation for Introducing Intellect 'From Without' (110. 4–112. 5)

  (B1) *The Teacher's Account of Aristotle's Motivation* (110. 5–25)
- three factors of coming to be: the subject, the agent, and the result (110. 5–13)
- the *Actuality Principle* and the *Problem of Two Potentialities* (110. 13–25)

  (B2) *The Author's Elaboration and Alternative* (110. 25–112. 5)
- agent intellect is the object intelligible by its own nature (110. 25–30)
- when being developed, human intellect is not affected, but perfected: it is productive (110. 30–111. 2)
- productivity of intellect contrasted with passivity of perception, despite shared receptivity (111. 2–15)
- intellect's productivity is conceptually prior to its receptivity (111. 15–22)
- no intelligibility without intellect (111. 22–9)
- the causality of the agent intellect: as our thought, as object of our thought, and as our fulfilment (111. 29–36)
- conclusion: intellect is productive, not passive (111. 36–112. 5)

(C) Discussion of a Platonist Objection to the Notion of Intellect 'From Without' (112. 5–113. 24)

  (C1) *The Teacher's Solution* (112. 5–113. 12)
- objection: the idea of coming from without implies locomotion, which is incompatible with the intellect's non-bodily nature (112. 5–8)
- agent intellect is present in all matter; material intellect is a potentiality supervening on a mixture of bodies (112. 8–16)

- agent intellect uses material intellect as its instrument—this is what we call our thinking (112. 16–30)
- starting and ceasing to be involved in human thought neither implies locomotion on the agent intellect's part nor compromises its eternity (112. 30–113.6)
- different options for how the agent intellect organizes sublunar world in cooperation with heavenly bodies and nature (113. 6–12)

(C2) *The Author's Objections and Sketch of an Alternative* (113. 12–24)
- objections against immanence, primary providence, and lack of human spontaneity
- alternative: agent intellect as an object of our thought

Greek text: Sharples, *Mantissa*, 42–52; or Bruns, *De Anima cum Mantissa*, 106–14.

English translation: Sharples, *Alexander: Supplement*, 24–44.

BIBLIOGRAPHY

Accattino, P., *Alessandro di Afrodisia: De intellectu [De Intellectu]* (Turin, 2001).

Accattino, P., 'Alessandro di Afrodisia e Aristotele di Mitilene', *Elenchos*, 6 (1985), 67–74.

Accattino, P., 'Alessandro di Afrodisia interprete del De Anima di Aristotele' ['Alessandro interprete'], *Studia Graeco-Arabica*, 4 (2014), 275–88.

Accattino, P., and Donini, P. L., *Alessandro di Afrodisia: L'anima [L'anima]* (Rome, 1996).

Accattino, P., and Ghiggia, P. C., *Alessandro di Afrodisia: De anima II (Mantissa) [Mantissa]* (Alessandria, 2005).

Alpina, T., 'Intellectual Knowledge, Active Intellect and Intellectual Memory in Avicenna's Kitab al-Nafs and Its Aristotelian Background', *Documenti e Studi sulla Tradizione Filosofica Medievale*, 25 (2014), 131–83.

Anagnostopoulos, A., 'Aristotle's First Moves Regarding Perception: A Reading of (Most of) *De Anima* 2.5', *Archiv für Geschichte der Philosophie*, 105 (2023), 68–117.

Badawī, ʿAbd al-Raḥmân, *Commentaires sur Aristote perdus en grec et autres épîtres* (Beirut, 1972).

Baghdassarian, F., 'L'intellection divine en *Métaphysique Λ* 7 et 9: Les indices d'un approfondissement d'Aristote par lui-même', in G. Guyomarc'h and F. Baghdassarian (eds.), *Réceptions de la théologie aristotélicienne: D'Aristote à Michel d'Éphèse* (Louvain-la-Neuve, 2017), 33–58.

Barbotin, E., *La théorie aristotélicienne de l'intellect d'après Théophraste* (Louvain, 1954).

Barnes, J., 'Aristotle's Concept of Mind', *Proceedings of the Aristotelian Society*, 72 (1971), 101–14.

Bazán, B. C., 'L'authenticité du "De Intellectu" attribué à Alexandre d'Aphrodise' ['L'authenticité'], *Revue philosophique de Louvain*, 71 (1973), 468–87.

Bergeron, M., and Dufour, R., *Alexandre d'Aphrodise: De l'âme* [*De l'âme*] (Paris, 2008).

Berti, E., 'Aristotle's *Nous Poiêtikos*: Another Modest Proposal', in G. Sillitti, F. Stella, and F. Fronterotta (eds.), *Il NOUS di Aristotele* (Sankt Augustin, 2016), 137–53.

Blumenthal, H. J., 'Alexander of Aphrodisias in the Later Greek Commentaries on Aristotle's De Anima', in J. Wiesner (ed.), *Aristoteles: Werk und Wirkung: Band II Kommentierung, Überlieferung, Nachleben* (Berlin, 1987), 90–106.

Bodnár, I. M., 'Alexander of Aphrodisias on Celestial Motions', *Phronesis*, 42 (1997), 190–205.

Bodnár, I. M., 'Alexander's Unmoved Mover', in C. Cerami (ed.), *Nature et sagesse: Les rapports entre physique et métaphysique dans la tradition aristotélicienne* (Louvain-la-Neuve, 2018), 387–416.

Brentano, F., *Aristoteles Lehre vom Ursprung des menschlichen Geistes* (Leipzig, 1911).

Brentano, F., *Die Psychologie des Aristoteles: Insbesondere seine Lehre vom ΝΟΥΣ ΠΟΙΗΤΙΚΟΣ* (Mainz, 1867).

Bruns, I., *Alexandri Aphrodisiensis De anima liber cum Mantissa* [*De anima cum Mantissa*] (Berlin, 1887).

Burnyeat, M. F., *Aristotle's Divine Intellect* [*Divine Intellect*] (Milwaukee, 2008).

Busche, H., 'Alexander von Aphrodisias, Über die Seele', in H. Busche and M. Perkams (eds.), *Antike Interpretationen zur aristotelischen Lehre vom Geist* (Hamburg, 2018), 116–87.

Caston, V., *Alexander of Aphrodisias: On the Soul. Part I: Soul as Form of the Body, Parts of the Soul, Nourishment, and Perception* (London, 2012).

Caston, V., 'Aristotle on the Transmission of Information: Receiving Form without the Matter', in D. Bennett and J. Toivanen (eds.),

Philosophical Problems in Sense Perception: Testing the Limits of Aristotelianism, Studies in the History of Philosophy of Mind (Cham, 2020), 15–55.

Caston, V., 'Aristotle's Argument for Why the Understanding Is Not Compounded with the Body', *Proceedings of the Boston Area Colloquium in Ancient Philosophy*, 16 (2000), 135–75.

Caston, V., 'Aristotle's Two Intellects: A Modest Proposal' ['Two Intellects'], *Phronesis*, 44 (1999), 199–227.

Caston, V., 'Higher-Order Awareness in Alexander of Aphrodisias' ['Higher-Order Awareness'], *Bulletin of the Institute of Classical Studies*, 55 (2012), 31–49.

Caston, V., 'The Spirit and the Letter: Aristotle on Perception', in R. Salles (ed.), *Metaphysics, Soul, and Ethics: Themes from the Work of Richard Sorabji* (Oxford, 2005), 245–320.

Caston, V., 'Theophrastus on Perceiving', *Rhizomata*, 7 (2019), 188–225.

Charles, D., *Aristotle on Meaning and Essence* (Oxford, 2000).

Charles, D., *The Undivided Self: Aristotle and the 'Mind-Body' Problem* (New York, 2021).

Charlton, W., 'Aristotle on the Place of Mind in Nature', in A. Gotthelf and J. G. Lennox (eds.), *Philosophical Issues in Aristotle's Biology* (Cambridge, 1987), 408–23.

Chiesara, M. L. (ed.), *Aristocles of Messene: Testimonia and Fragments* (Oxford, 2001).

Connell, S., 'How Does a Living Animal Come to Be from Semen? The Puzzles of Aristotle's *Generation of Animals* II 1–3', in D. Lefebvre (ed.), *The Science of Life in Aristotle and the Early Peripatos* (Leiden, forthcoming).

Connell, S., '"*Nous* Alone Enters From Outside": Aristotelian Embryology and Early Christian Philosophy', *Journal of Ancient Philosophy*, 2 (2021), 109–38.

Connell, S., 'Thinking Bodies: Aristotle on the Biological Basis of Human Cognition', in P. Gregoric and J. L. Fink (eds.), *Encounters with Aristotelian Philosophy of Mind* (New York, 2021), 223–48.

Corcilius, K., '*De Anima* III 7: The Actuality Principle and the Triggering of Mental Episodes', in G. Guyomarc'h, C. Louguet, and C. Murgier (eds.), *Aristote et l'âme humaine: Lectures de 'De Anima' III offertes à Michel Crubellier* (Leuven, 2020), 185–219.

Corcilius, K., 'The Gate to Reality: Aristotle's Basic Account of Perception', in C. Cohoe (ed.), *Aristotle's On the Soul: A Critical Guide* (Cambridge, 2022), 122–54.

Davidson, H. A., *Alfarabi, Avicenna, and Averroes, on Intellect: Their Cosmologies, Theories of the Active Intellect, and Theories of Human Intellect* (Oxford, 1992).

DeFilippo, J. G., 'Aristotle's Identification of the Prime Mover as God', *Classical Quarterly*, 44 (1994), 393–409.
de Haas, F. A. J., 'Aristotle and Alexander of Aphrodisias on Active Intellectual Cognition' ['Active Intellectual Cognition'], in V. Decaix and A. M. Mora-Márquez (eds.), *Studies in the History of Philosophy of Mind; Active Cognition: Challenges to an Aristotelian Tradition* (New York, 2020), 13–36.
de Haas, F. A. J., 'Intellect in Alexander of Aphrodisias and John Philoponus: Divine, Human or Both?', in J. Sisko (ed.), *Philosophy of Mind in Antiquity* (Abingdon, 2018), 299–316.
Denniston, J. D., *Greek Particles*, ed. by K. J. Dover, 2nd edn (London, 1996).
Donini, P. L., *Tre studi sull'aristotelismo nel II secolo d. C* [*Tre studi*] (Turin, 1974).
Dufour, R., *Alexandre d'Aphrodise: De l'âme II (Mantissa)* [*Mantissa*] (Quebec, 2013).
Finnegan, J., *Texte arabe du PERI NOY d'Alexandre d'Aphrodise* (Beirut, 1956).
Förster, A., *Aristotelis De anima libri tres* (Budapest, 1912).
Fotinis, A. P., *The De Anima of Alexander of Aphrodisias: A Translation and Commentary* (Washington DC, 1979).
Frede, D., 'Alexander of Aphrodisias', in E. N. Zalta (ed.), *The Stanford Encyclopedia of Philosophy* (Winter 2017 edn), https://plato.stanford.edu/archives/win2017/entries/alexander-aphrodisias/, accessed 20 August 2024.
Frede, M., 'La théorie aristotélicienne de l'intellect agent' ['L'intellect agent'], in G. R. Dherbey (ed.), *Corps et âme: Études sur le de Anima d'Aristote* (Paris, 1996), 377–90.
Gabbe, M., 'Themistius on Concept Acquisition and Knowledge of Essences', *Archiv für Geschichte der Philosophie*, 92 (2010), 215–35.
Gabbe, M., 'Theophrastus and the Intellect as Mixture', *Elenchos*, 29 (2008), 61–90.
Geoffroy, M., 'La tradition arabe du Περὶ νοῦ d'Alexandre d'Aphrodise et les origines de la théorie farabienne des quatre degrés de l'intellect' ['La tradition arabe'], in C. D'Ancona and G. Serra (eds.), *Aristotele e Alessandro di Afrodisia nella tradizione araba* (Padua, 2002), 191–231.
Golitsis, P., *Alexander of Aphrodisias: Commentary on Aristotle, Metaphysics (Books I–III): Critical edition with Introduction and Notes* (Berlin, 2022).
Gutas, D., 'The Empiricism of Avicenna', *Oriens*, 40 (2012), 391–436.
Guyomarc'h, G., 'Alexander of Aphrodisias and the Active Intellect as Final Cause' ['Active Intellect'], *Elenchos*, 44 (2023), 93–117.
Guyomarc'h, G., *L'unité de la métaphysique selon Alexandre d'Aphrodise* [*L'unité de la métaphysique*] (Paris, 2016).

Hamlyn, D. W., *Aristotle, De Anima: Books II and III*, 2nd edn (Oxford, 1993).
Hasse, D. N., 'Avicenna's Epistemological Optimism', in P. Adamson (ed.), *Interpreting Avicenna: Critical Essays* (Cambridge, 2013), 109–19.
Huby, P., *Theophrastus of Eresus: Sources for His Life, Writings, Thought and Influence: Commentary: Psychology* (Leiden, 1999).
Johansen, T. K., *The Powers of Aristotle's Soul* (Oxford, 2012).
Judson, L., *Aristotle, Metaphysics Lambda* (New York, 2019).
Kelsey, S., *Mind and World in Aristotle's* De Anima [*Mind and World*] (Cambridge, 2022).
Kessler, E., 'Alexander of Aphrodisias and His Doctrine of the Soul: 1400 Years of Lasting Significance', *Early Science and Medicine*, 16 (2011), 1–93.
Kupreeva, I., 'Alexander of Aphrodisias and Aristotle's "De Anima": What's in a Commentary?', *Bulletin of the Institute of Classical Studies*, 55 (2012), 109–29.
Kupreeva, I., 'Aristotelianism in the Second Century AD: Before Alexander of Aphrodisias' ['Aristotelianism before Alexander'], in A. Falcon (ed.), *Brill's Companion to the Reception of Aristotle in Antiquity* (Leiden, 2016), 138–59.
Lear, J., *Aristotle: The Desire to Understand* (Cambridge, 1988).
Lennox, J. G., 'The Place of Mankind in Aristotle's Zoology', *Philosophical Topics*, 27 (1999), 1–16.
Lloyd, A. C., 'Alexander of Aphrodisias' ['Alexander'], in P. Edwards (ed.), *The Encyclopedia of Philosophy* (New York, 1967), i–ii. 73.
Lloyd, A. C., 'The Principle that the Cause Is Greater than Its Effect', *Phronesis*, 21 (1976), 146–56.
Magrin, S., 'Theophrastus, Alexander, and Themistius on Aristotle's *De anima* III. 4–5', in R. Wisnovsky, F. Wallis, J. Fumo, and C. Fraenkel (eds.), *Vehicles of Transmission, Translation, and Transformation in Medieval Textual Culture* (Turnhout, 2011), 49–74.
Menn, S., 'Aristotle and Plato on God as *Nous* and as the Good', *Review of Metaphysics*, 45 (1992), 543–73.
Menn, S., 'Aristotle's Theology', in C. Shields (ed.), *The Oxford Handbook of Aristotle* (New York, 2012), 422–64.
Menn, S., 'Atticus, Alexander, Porphyry: Εἴσκρισις and the Neo-Platonic Interpretation of the Third Hypothesis of the *Parmenides*: With Some Implications for Instantaneous Creation' (forthcoming).
Menn, S., 'From *De Anima* III 4 to *De Anima* III 5' ['From III 4 to III 5'], in G. Guyomarc'h, C. Louguet, and C. Murgier (eds.), *Aristote et l'âme humaine: Lectures de 'De Anima' III offertes à Michel Crubellier* (Leuven, 2020), 95–155.
Menn, S., *Plato on God as* Nous (Carbondale, 1995).

Merlan, P., *Monopsychism: Mysticism: Metaconsciousness: Problems of the Soul in the Neoaristotelian and Neoplatonic Tradition* [*Monopsychism*] (The Hague, 1963).
Miller, F. D., *Aristotle: On the Soul* (Oxford, 2018).
Moraux, P., *Alexandre d'Aphrodise: Exégète de la noétique d'Aristote* [*Exégète*] (Liège, 1942).
Moraux, P., 'À propos du nous thurathen chez Aristote' ['Nous thurathen'], in A. Mansion (ed.), *Autour d'Aristote* (Louvain, 1955), 255–95.
Moraux, P., 'Aristoteles, der Lehrer Alexanders von Aphrodisias', *Archiv für Geschichte der Philosophie*, 49 (1967), 169–82.
Moraux, P., *Der Aristotelismus bei den Griechen: Von Andronikos bis Alexander von Aphrodisias*, ii: *Der Aristotelismus im 1. und 2. Jh. n. Chr* [*Aristotelismus bei den Griechen* ii] (Berlin, 1984).
Moraux, P., *Der Aristotelismus bei den Griechen: Von Andronikos bis Alexander von Aphrodisias*, iii: *Alexander von Aphrodisias* [*Aristotelismus bei den Griechen* iii] (Berlin, 2001).
Moraux, P., 'Le *De anima* dans la tradition grecque: Quelques aspects de l'interprétation du traité, de Théophraste à Thémistius' ['De Anima'], in G. E. R. Lloyd and G. E. L. Owen (eds.), *Aristotle on Mind and the Senses: Proceedings of the Seventh Symposium Aristotelicum* (Cambridge, 1978), 281–324.
Moraux, P., 'Ein neues Zeugnis über Aristoteles, den Lehrer Alexanders von Aphrodisias', *Archiv für Geschichte der Philosophie*, 67 (1985), 266–9.
Movia, G., *Alessandro di Afrodisia: Tra naturalismo e misticismo* [*Tra naturalismo e misticismo*] (Padua, 1970).
Opsomer, J., and Sharples, R. W., 'Alexander of Aphrodisias, *De Intellectu* 110.4: "I Heard This from Aristotle": A Modest Proposal', *Classical Quarterly*, 50 (2000), 252–6.
Papadis, D., '"L'intellect agent" selon Alexandre d'Aphrodise', *Revue de Philosophie Ancienne*, 9 (1991), 133–51.
Papadis, D., *Die Seelenlehre bei Alexander von Aphrodisias* [*Seelenlehre bei Alexander*] (Bern, 1991).
Polansky, R. M., *Aristotle's De anima* (New York, 2007).
Rashed, M., *Alexandre d'Aphrodise: Commentaire perdu à la 'Physique' d'Aristote (Livres IV–VIII): Les scholies byzantines* (Berlin, 2014).
Rashed, M., 'A "New" Text of Alexander on the Soul's Motion' ['A "New" Text'], *Bulletin of the Institute of Classical Studies*, Suppl. 68 (1997), 181–95.
Rashed, M., 'Nicolas d'Otrante, Guillaume de Moerbeke et la "collection philosophique"', *Studi Medievali*, 43 (2002), 693–717.
Roreitner, R., *Aristotle on the Nature and Causes of Perception* [*Nature and Causes*] (Cambridge, 2025).
Roreitner, R., 'Human Ontogeny in Aristotle and Theophrastus', *Apeiron*, 57 (2024), 427–77.

Roreitner, R., 'Nous thurathen: Between Theophrastus and Alexander of Aphrodisias', *British Journal for the History of Philosophy*, 33 (2025).
Roreitner, R., 'What Is New in Alexander's Noetic? Early Peripatetic Disagreements about the Material and the Agent *Nous*', in C. Bobonich et al. (eds.), *Human and Divine Nous from Ancient to Byzantine and Renaissance Philosophy and Religion: Key Themes, Intersections, and Developments* (Leiden, forthcoming).
Ross, W. D. (ed.), *Aristotelis De anima* [*De anima*] (Oxford, 1961).
Ross, W. D., *Aristotle*, 6th edn (London, 1995).
Ryan, E. E., 'Pure Form in Aristotle', *Phronesis*, 18 (1973), 209–24.
Schroeder, F. M., 'The Analogy of the Active Intellect to Light in the "De Anima" of Alexander of Aphrodisias' ['Analogy'], *Hermes*, 109 (1981), 215–25.
Schroeder, F. M., 'Light and the Active Intellect in Alexander and Plotinus' ['Light and the Active Intellect'], *Hermes*, 112 (1984), 239–48.
Schroeder, F. M., 'The Potential or Material Intellect and the Authorship of the De Intellectu: A Reply to B.C. Bazán' ['Potential Intellect'], *Symbolae Osloenses*, 57 (1982), 115–25.
Schroeder, F. M., 'The Provenance of the "De Intellectu" Attributed to Alexander of Aphrodisias' ['Provenance'], *Documenti e Studi sulla Tradizione Filosofica Medievale*, 8 (1997), 105–20.
Schroeder, F. M., and Todd, R. B., 'The *De Intellectu* Revisited', *Laval théologique et philosophique*, 64 (2008), 663–80.
Schroeder, F. M., and Todd, R. B., *Two Greek Aristotelian Commentators on the Intellect: The* De Intellectu *Attributed to Alexander of Aphrodisias and Themistius' Paraphrase of Aristotle* De Anima*, 3. 4–8* [*Two Commentators*] (Toronto, 1990).
Sharples, R. W., *Alexander Aphrodisiensis: 'De Anima Libri Mantissa': A New Edition of the Greek Text with Introduction and Commentary* [*Mantissa*] (Berlin, 2008).
Sharples, R. W., 'Alexander of Aphrodisias: Scholasticism and Innovation' ['Scholasticism and Innovation'], in W. Haase (ed.), *Aufstieg und Niedergang der Römischen Welt*, ii. xxxvi: *Philosophie, Wissenschaften, Technik* (Berlin, 1987), 1176–243.
Sharples, R. W., *Alexander of Aphrodisias: Supplement to On the Soul* [*Alexander: Supplement*] (London, 2004).
Sharples, R. W., 'Alexander of Aphrodisias: What Is a *Mantissa*?', *Bulletin of the Institute of Classical Studies*, Suppl. 83 (2004), 51–69.
Sharples, R. W., 'Peripatetics on Soul and Intellect' ['Peripatetics on Soul'], *Bulletin of the Institute of Classical Studies*, Suppl. 94 (2007), 607–20.
Shields, C., *Aristotle: De Anima* (Oxford, 2016).
Smyth, H. W., *A Greek Grammar for Colleges* [*Greek Grammar*] (New York, 1920).

Söder, J., 'Alexander von Aphrodisias, Über den Geist' ['Über den Geist'], in H. Busche and M. Perkams (eds.), *Antike Interpretationen zur aristotelischen Lehre vom Geist* (Hamburg, 2018), 189–235.

Sorabji, R., *The Philosophy of the Commentators, 200–600 AD: Psychology (with Ethics and Religion)* [*Commentators*] (Ithaca, NY, 2005).

Taylor, R. C., 'The Agent Intellect as "Form for Us" and Averroes's Critique of al-Fârâbî', *Proceedings of the Society for Medieval Logic and Metaphysics*, 5 (2005), 18–32.

Taylor, R. C., 'Avicenna and the Issue of the Intellectual Abstraction of Intelligibles', in M. Cameron (ed.), *Philosophy of Mind in the Early and High Middle Ages* (London, 2019), 56–82.

Théry, G., *Autour du décret de 1210: II. Alexandre d'Aphrodise: Aperçu sur l'influence de sa noétique* (Le Saulchoir, 1926).

Thillet, P., *Alexandre d'Aphrodise: Traité du destin* (Paris, 1984).

Trabucco, F., 'Il problema del "de philosophia" di Aristocle di Messene e la sua dottrina', *Acme*, 11 (1958), 97–150.

Tuominen, M., 'Aristotle and Alexander of Aphrodisias on the Active Intellect' ['Active Intellect'], in V. Hirvonen, T. J. Holopainen, and M. Tuominen (eds.), *Mind and Modality* (Leiden, 2006), 55–70.

Tuominen, M., 'Receptive Reason: Alexander of Aphrodisias on Material Intellect' ['Receptive Reason'], *Phronesis*, 55 (2010), 170–90.

van der Eijk, P. J., 'The Matter of Mind: Aristotle on the Biology of "Psychic" Processes and the Bodily Aspects of Thinking', *Medicine and Philosophy in Classical Antiquity: Doctors and Philosophers on Nature, Soul, Health and Disease* (Cambridge, 2005), 206–37.

Wedin, M. V., 'Aristotle on the Mind's Self-Motion', in M. L. Gill and J. G. Lennox (eds.), *Self-Motion: From Aristotle to Newton* (Princeton, 1994), 80–116.

Wedin, M. V., *Mind and Imagination in Aristotle* (New Haven, 1988).

Zeller, E., *Die Philosophie der Griechen in ihrer geschichtlichen Entwicklung III.1* [*Die Philosophie der Griechen*], 5th edn (Leipzig, 1922).

Zeller, E., 'Über die Lehre des Aristoteles von der Ewigkeit des Geistes', *Sitzungsberichte der Königlich Preussischen Akademie der Wissenschaften*, 49 (1882), 1033–55.

Zimmermann, F. W., and Brown, H. V. B., 'Neue arabische Übersetzungstexte aus dem Bereich der spätantiken griechischen Philosophie', *Der Islam*, 50 (1973), 313–30.

INDEX LOCORUM

Alexander of Aphrodisias

De anima, ed. Bruns
6. 8–11: 213 n. 96
28. 8–10: 207 n. 84
36. 21–37. 3: 228 n. 126
39. 9–10: 207 n. 84
42. 19–43. 11: 235 n. 147
43. 8–11: 210 n. 90
73. 23–4: 207 n. 84
76. 12–14: 207 n. 84
82. 5–10: 229 n. 130
82. 5–11: 228 n. 128
82. 19–84. 14: 215 n. 99
83. 12–84. 14: 221 n. 113
83. 13–84. 14: 193 n. 43
83. 22–3: 193 n. 43
84. 4–6: 213 n. 96
86. 14–28: 246 n. 163
86. 28–87. 24: 193 n. 43
87. 1–11: 246 n. 165
88. 10–16: 215 n. 101
88. 13: 238–9
88. 14–16: 211 n. 91
88. 24–89. 11: 254–5
88. 26–89. 1: 207 n. 83
89. 4–5: 207 n. 83
89. 4–7: 233 n. 143
89. 6–7: 207 n. 85, 233 n. 143
90. 4–11: 215 n. 101, 238–9
90. 6–11: 211 n. 91
90. 11–91. 6: 239 n. 151
90. 19–91. 4: 191 n. 39

De intellectu
80. 16–86. 6: 180–1
87–90: 229 n. 129
88. 24–89. 9: 181–2
88. 24–89. 11: 180–2
89. 9–11: 181–2
106. 19: 188 n. 33
106. 19–107. 20: 188
106. 19–110. 3: 187–8
106. 20–3: 205 n. 78
106. 27–107. 11: 249 n. 174
107. 9–11: 249 n. 174
107. 17 205 n. 78
107. 17–19: 203 n. 74
107. 21: 203 n. 74
107. 21–8: 188
107. 29–34: 196 n. 51
107. 29–110. 3: 188
107. 34: 192
107. 34–108. 5: 195, 211 n. 92
108. 2: 192
108. 3: 195 n. 48
108. 4: 200 n. 61
108. 4–5: 238 n. 149, 246–7
108. 5–7: 211
108. 6: 193–4
108. 6–9: 215 n. 101, 246–7
108. 7–9: 193 n. 44, 238 n. 149
108. 10–13: 193 n. 43, 196 n. 51
108. 11–12: 195–6
108. 14: 200 n. 61
108. 14–15: 195, 211
108. 14–18: 238 n. 149
108. 15: 203 n. 74
108. 16–19: 194 n. 45
108. 17: 200 n. 61
108. 17–18: 204
108. 19–22: 203 n. 74, 240 n. 154
108. 19–24: 199, 227–8, 235
108. 19–109. 4: 190
108. 20–1: 206
108. 21: 203 n. 75, 245–6
108. 22–4: 202 n. 70
109. 1–3: 193 n. 44, 215 n. 101, 246–7
109. 1–4: 191
109. 4–14: 246–7, 251–2
109. 4–23: 188, 246–7
109. 4–110. 3: 186–8
109. 5–6: 247, 250–1
109. 7–8: 193 n. 44, 215 n. 101
109. 8: 246–7, 248 n. 171
109. 11–14: 246–7
109. 13–14: 248 n. 171
109. 14–15: 248
109. 14–18: 247 n. 167
109. 14–23: 247–8, 251–2
109. 15: 248, 250–1
109. 15–17: 248
109. 17–19: 249

109. 19–20: 250–1
109. 19–22: 247 n. 167
109. 20–2: 250 n. 175, 251
109. 22–3: 249 n. 173, 253 n. 182
109. 23–110. 3: 188, 250–1
109. 24–5: 251 n. 179
109. 25–31: 251 n. 179
109. 26: 253
110. 4: 188 n. 34
110. 4–6: 188 n. 34
110. 4–25: 188–9
110. 4–112. 5: 187–8
110. 15–16: 197
110. 16–17: 196–7
110. 19: 200 n. 61
110. 19–20: 197
110. 20–3: 197–8
110. 20–4: 209 n. 88
110. 21–2: 197 n. 55
110. 25–7: 230–1
110. 25–30: 227
110. 25–112. 5: 186–9
110. 30–1: 227, 235
110. 31: 228 n. 127
110. 31–111. 2: 208 n. 87, 228–9
110. 33–111. 2: 239 n. 151, 243
111. 1–2: 229
111. 2–22: 229–30
111. 3: 230 n. 133
111. 3–4: 234
111. 8: 203 n. 74
111. 12: 203 n. 74
111. 13: 203 n. 74
111. 15–19: 212
111. 18: 200 n. 61
111. 19–22: 230
111. 22–9: 232
111. 22–112. 5: 231
111. 24–36: 208 n. 87
111. 25: 232
111. 25–7: 232, 241–2
111. 27–9: 233
111. 29–36: 234–5
111. 32: 214 n. 98
111. 32–4: 215–16
111. 35: 236–7
111. 36: 241–2
111. 36–112. 5: 241
112. 1: 242–3
112. 1–2: 241–2
112. 3: 229 n. 129
112. 3–4: 239 n. 151, 243
112. 4–5: 231, 234
112. 5–113. 12: 188–9

112. 5–113. 24: 187–8
112. 6–8: 187 n. 31
112. 16–17: 222–3
112. 16–18: 210 n. 89
112. 16–21: 222–3
112. 16–30: 223 n. 116
112. 17–18: 222–3
112. 23–4: 222–3
112. 23–30: 222–3
113. 1–2: 223 n. 116
113. 3: 230–1
113. 6–8: 206
113. 12–24: 188–9
113. 15–16: 206
113. 16–17: 223–4
113. 18–24: 254 n. 184
113. 19–24: 237 n. 148
119. 21–2: 249–50

De mixtione, ed. Bruns
228. 17–21: 213 n. 96
233–8: 228 n. 126

In Aristotelis Analyticorum priorum librum unum, ed. Wallies
15. 15–22: 36–7

In Aristotelis Metaphysica commentaria, ed. Hayduck
2. 3–11: 207 n. 84
3. 20–2: 205 n. 80
64. 3–10: 213 n. 96
67. 28–30: 207 n. 84
77. 30–4: 213 n. 96
80. 8–81. 22: 24 n. 47
103. 37–104. 3: 205 n. 80
147. 3–149. 13: 206 n. 82
147. 16–148. 2: 230 n. 134
148. 6–10: 213 n. 96
166. 19–20: 188 n. 34
206. 22–8: 214 n. 97
212. 13–15: 213 n. 96
234. 28–35: 213 n. 96
263. 5–7: 213 n. 96
276. 11–13: 213 n. 96
300. 28–301. 1: 214 n. 97
309. 8–10: 213 n. 96
316. 7–9: 213 n. 96
323. 20–1: 213 n. 96
359. 10–11: 213 n. 96
368. 29–33: 213 n. 96
400. 34–401. 1: 214 n. 97
434. 1–4: 213 n. 96

In Aristotelis meteorologicorum libros commentaria, ed. Hayduck
129. 3–9: 210 n. 90

Index Locorum

In librum de sensu commentarium, ed. Wendland
131. 13–135. 22: 210 n. 90

Mantissa
105. 10–12: 228 n. 126
105. 26–7: 228 n. 126
126. 7–9: 228 n. 126
127. 11–12: 213 n. 96
143. 23–35: 210 n. 90
147. 4–5: 205 n. 80
151. 4–7: 207 n. 84
157. 11–13: 207 n. 84
164. 3–5: 207 n. 84
165. 29–32: 207 n. 84
168. 14–15: 207 n. 84
174. 13–14: 207 n. 84
175. 12–13: 213 n. 96, 214 n. 97
182. 1–2: 213 n. 96

Quaestiones, ed. Bruns
39. 24–31: 238 n. 149
39. 31–40. 3: 251 n. 179

Ammonius
In Aristotelis De interpretatione commentarius, ed. Busse
57. 29–32: 36–7

Aquinas
In libros De anima exposition
3. 10, §§ 728–39: 178 n. 2

Summa contra gentiles
2. 60, 73–4: 178 n. 2
2. 60, 76–8: 178 n. 2
2. 74: 178 n. 3

Summa theologica
1a qu. 79, art. 3: 178 n. 2

Arethas
Scholia in Porphyrii eisagogen, ed. Share
49. 14: 41 n. 82

Aristophanes
Clouds
101: 115 n. 36

Aristotle
Categories
2^b20–1: 42
7^b22–35: 232

De anima
405^b19–23: 220 n. 110
415^a23–$^b7$: 200 n. 59
415^a26–$^b3$: 203 n. 75

415^a26–$^b7$: 125 n. 50
415^b2: 146 n. 12
415^b10–14: 43–4
416^a9–12: 230 n. 134
417^a7–9: 230 n. 134
417^a17–21: 224 n. 121
417^b2–9: 221 n. 112
417^b2–16: 230, 231 n. 136
417^b5–7: 226 n. 125
417^b12–16: 226 n. 125
417^b24–6: 219 n. 108
418^a3–6: 224 n. 121
422^b5–10: 250 n. 176
424^a17–28: 193 n. 43
424^a18–19: 193 n. 43
424^a21–4: 205 n. 78
429^a13–15: 219 n. 107
429^a13–18: 177 n. 1, 193 n. 43, 196 n. 51, 224 n. 121, 229 n. 131
429^a15: 220
429^a15–16: 193 n. 43, 205 n. 78
429^a16: 224 n. 121
429^a18–27: 249–50, 250 n. 176
429^a20–2: 205 n. 79
429^a29–$^b5$: 220
429^b5–6: 224 n. 121
429^b5–9: 224 n. 121
429^b6–8: 219 n. 108
429^b6–10: 246
429^b7–8: 219 n. 108
429^b9: 246
429^b22–5: 220 n. 110
429^b24–5: 219 n. 107, 229 n. 131
429^b26: 246
429^b26–9: 192
429^b27–8: 195 n. 49
429^b28–9: 248 n. 170
429^b29–31: 219 n. 107, 229 n. 131
430^a2–9: 192, 246
430^a3: 192
430^a3–6: 252 n. 180, 252–3
430^a3–9: 243–4
430^a6–9: 252 n. 181, 252–3
430^a11–13: 229 n. 132
430^a15–17: 196 n. 51
430^a24: 219 n. 107
430^a24–5: 229 n. 132
431^a4–7: 231 n. 136
431^a6–7: 221 n. 112
432^a9–10: 214–15

De generatione animalium
732^b19–22: 213 n. 96
732^b21–2: 213 n. 96

736^{b}15–17: 190
736^{b}19–20: 190
736^{b}24: 228 n. 128
736^{b}27–9: 190
744^{b}21–6: 190 n. 36

De generatione et corruptione
323^{b}17: 37 n. 73
336^{b}27–337^{a}7: 200 n. 59

De ideis, ed. Fine
80. 16–81. 8: 54, 57–8

De insomniis
461^{a}1: 126 n. 53

De iuventute et senectute, de vita et morte, de respiratione
472^{a}22–4: 190 n. 36

De sensu
446^{b}27–447^{a}11: 210 n. 90
447^{a}14–16: 126 n. 53

Eudemian Ethics
1214^{a}1–7: 121
1216^{a}15: 101 n. 10
1216^{a}25–6: 162
1219^{a}36: 103
1219^{a}39–40: 120, 131–2
1219^{b}30: 110 n. 28
1219^{b}33: 110 n. 28
1219^{b}38–9: 110 n. 28
1219^{b}40–1220^{a}3: 110 n. 28
1220^{a}5: 103
1220^{a}5–7: 101
1220^{b}21–6: 129
1221^{b}31: 110 n. 28
1222^{a}8–9: 128
1222^{b}5–9: 107
1227^{b}13–17: 127 n. 55
1227^{b}17–19: 127 n. 55
1227^{b}35–1228^{a}1: 127 n. 55
1229^{a}1–3: 132–3
1229^{a}4: 162
1230^{a}30–1: 132–3
1234^{a}28–31: 127–8
1234^{a}29–31: 133
1234^{b}22–5: 133
1235^{b}31–6: 117–18
1235^{b}33: 120–1
1236^{a}1–2: 117 n. 38
1236^{a}28–9: 21
1237^{a}2: 117–18, 120 n. 43
1237^{a}4–5: 117 n. 39
1237^{a}6–7: 120–1
1237^{a}27–8: 121–2

1246^{b}24–7: 127 n. 55
1246^{b}28: 127 n. 55
1248^{b}9–12: 103
1248^{b}9–1249^{a}17: 102–3, 119 n. 42
1248^{b}11: 132 n. 60
1248^{b}11–12: 118 n. 41
1248^{b}17–19: 119
1248^{b}19–21: 118
1248^{b}19–24: 132–3
1248^{b}20–1: 112–13
1248^{b}20–4: 100–1
1248^{b}27–8: 117–18, 120 n. 43
1248^{b}27–31: 95–6, 100–1
1248^{b}32–4: 117–18
1248^{b}37–8: 119
1248^{b}40–1: 113
1249^{a}1–2: 116–17, 119
1249^{a}5–6: 132–3
1249^{a}6–7: 100–1, 102 n. 11, 112–13
1249^{a}7–10: 102 n. 11
1249^{a}8–11: 120
1249^{a}13: 119 n. 42, 120
1249^{a}13–14: 119 n. 42
1249^{a}14: 120
1249^{a}14–16: 112–13, 119
1249^{a}16–17: 102–3, 114–15, 132 n. 60
1249^{a}18–22: 114–15, 120–1
1249^{a}20–1: 121 n. 44
1249^{a}21–^{b}5: 145
1249^{a}21–^{b}23: 145–6
1249^{a}23: 114–15, 122
1249^{a}23–^{b}7: 99, 108, 122–3, 129
1249^{a}23–^{b}25: 102–3
1249^{a}23–^{b}27: 131 n. 58
1249^{b}1: 103–4, 112–13
1249^{b}4: 128
1249^{b}4–7: 110–11
1249^{b}7–25: 122–3, 128
1249^{b}18: 124
1249^{b}18–21: 95, 99, 110–11
1249^{b}18–25: 110, 126
1249^{b}19: 103–4, 129–30
1249^{b}19–21: 126 n. 52
1249^{b}21–5: 110–11
1249^{b}23: 123 n. 46, 126
1249^{b}23–5: 107 n. 19, 126 n. 52
1249^{b}24: 121 n. 44, 123 n. 46
1249^{b}24–5: 104
1249^{b}26: 116–17

Metaphysics
982^{b}22–8: 164–5
987^{b}21–2: 21 n. 42
987^{b}29–33: 21 n. 42

989^{b}24–6: 28 n. 54
990^{b}13–14: 54, 57–8
993^{b}23–31: 206 n. 82
993^{b}24–31: 230 n. 134
993^{b}26–7: 206 n. 82
996^{b}13–14: 43–4
998^{b}9–11: 21 n. 42
998^{b}22–7: 40 n. 80
1001^{a}4–^{b}1: 23 n. 44
1002^{b}25–9: 213 n. 96
1017^{b}14–16: 43–4
1030^{a}21–^{b}3: 21
1036^{a}8–9: 225 n. 123
1050^{b}24–30: 200 n. 59
1072^{a}23–^{b}4: 179 n. 5
1072^{b}2: 146 n. 12
1074^{b}35–1075^{a}5: 250–1
1074^{b}38–1075^{a}5: 192 n. 41
1075^{a}3–5: 251 n. 178
1079^{a}9–10: 54, 57–8

Meteorologica
338^{b}19–21: 225 n. 123

Nicomachean Ethics
1094^{a}1–2: 141–2
1094^{a}2–18: 141–2
1094^{a}15: 142
1094^{a}18–23: 141–2
1094^{a}19: 142
1097^{a}15: 142
1097^{a}18: 142
1097^{a}19–21: 142
1097^{a}21: 142
1097^{a}25–^{b}6: 141–2
1097^{b}4–6: 142
1097^{b}24–1098^{a}18: 142–3
1103^{a}4–10: 101
1105^{a}32: 132–3
1109^{a}26–9: 162
1110^{a}1: 223 n. 118
1110^{b}2: 223 n. 118
1110^{b}16: 223 n. 118
1115^{a}18–19: 163–4
1115^{b}4–6: 163–4
1115^{b}11–13: 162
1115^{b}12: 163–4
1115^{b}20–4: 163–4
1115^{b}23–4: 162
1116^{a}11: 163–4
1116^{a}15: 163–4
1116^{b}2–3: 163–4
1116^{b}3: 163–4
1116^{b}22: 163–4
1116^{b}30–1: 162
1116^{b}31: 163–4
1117^{a}7–8: 163–4
1117^{a}15–17: 163–4
1120^{a}23–4: 162
1122^{b}6–7: 162
1131^{a}24–9: 120
1138^{b}20: 128
1138^{b}21–34: 108
1138^{b}34–5: 144
1139^{a}5–10: 126–7
1139^{a}12: 124
1140^{a}4–7: 160
1140^{a}26: 147–8
1140^{a}26–^{b}27: 157–8
1144^{a}4–6: 131–2
1144^{a}5: 103
1144^{b}23–4: 126–7
1145^{a}6–9: 144–5
1153^{a}14: 121 n. 44
1153^{b}14–15: 121 n. 44
1153^{b}14–26: 106
1168^{a}33: 162
1176^{b}2–7: 163
1176^{b}6–9: 147–8, 157–8, 160
1177^{a}12–19: 142–3
1177^{b}1–4: 157–8
1177^{b}4–6: 164–5
1177^{b}4–12: 163–4
1177^{b}16–20: 157–8
1178^{a}2–8: 224 n. 120
1178^{b}8–18: 165

Physics
194^{a}22: 203 n. 75
194^{a}35: 146 n. 12
199^{a}16: 203 n. 75

Politics
1332^{a}7–28: 163
1333^{a}30–7: 163
1333^{a}30–^{b}3: 163–4
1333^{a}35–6: 164–5
1333^{b}12–18: 113 n. 33
1333^{b}18–21: 116 n. 37
1334^{a}4–5: 164–5
1334^{a}14–16: 163–5
1334^{a}36–40: 164–5

Posterior Analytics
72^{a}25–32: 206 n. 82
88^{a}18–22: 213 n. 96

Rhetoric
1366^{a}33–4: 162–3

1366ᵇ34–1367ᵃ17: 162–3
1389ᵇ37–1390ᵃ1: 162–3

Topics
121ᵃ10–14: 42
121ᵃ14–17: 42 n. 84
135ᵃ13–14: 162

Averroes

Commentarium Magnum in Aristotelis De Anima Libros, ed. Crawford
36. 152–4: 240 n. 154
36. 484: 240 n. 154

Boethius

De Trinitate
2. 83: 44 n. 87

Damascius

De principiis, ed. Westerink
1. 81. 17–19: 2 n. 3
2. 56. 9–16: 2
2. 56. 13–14: 2 n. 3
2. 56–99: 2 n. 3
2. 62. 11: 2 n. 3
2. 62. 12: 27–8
2. 62. 24: 27 n. 52
2. 62. 27–63. 1: 27 n. 52
2. 74. 23–79. 6: 27 n. 52
2. 75. 7: 27 n. 52
2. 174. 3: 2 n. 3
3. 150. 2–3: 27 n. 52
3. 152. 13–15: 27–8

David

In Porphyrii Isagogen commentarium, ed. Busse
158. 2–9: 41 n. 82

Elias

In Porphyrii Isagogen commentarium, ed. Busse
70. 15–17: 41 n. 82

Eusebius

Praeparatio evangelica
14. 8. 1. 1: 11 n. 27

Herodianus

Grammatici Graeci, ed. Lentz
3. 2, 513.6: 37 n. 73

Iamblichus

Protrepticus, ed. Pistelli
53. 1: 118 n. 41
55. 1–3: 109

Isocrates

Antidosis
220: 115 n. 36
261–9: 116–17

Panathenaicus
183: 116

Numenius of Apamea, ed. Des Places
fr. 27: 11 n. 27

Philoponus

Commentaire sur le de Anima d'Aristote, ed. Verbeke
82. 15–24: 229 n. 129

In Aristotelis libros De generatione et corruptione commentaria, ed. Vitelli
44.12–18: 28 n. 53

Plato

Apology
20 A 8–B 2: 115

Cratylus
389 B 8–11: 23 n. 44
401 C 7–8: 5 n. 10

Epinomis
981 D 2–3: 11 n. 27

Euthyphro
11 A 7–8: 1 n. 2

Gorgias
484 C 8–D 2: 116–17

Hippias Major
300 A 9–B 2: 23–4

Laches
186 C 3–4: 115

Laws
823 A 4–5: 11 n. 27

Meno
72 B 1–2: 1 n. 2

Parmenides
132 C 9–11: 195 n. 49
135 A 8: 1 n. 1
135 B 7: 1 n. 1
136 B 6: 3 n. 8
142 B 1: 40 n. 79
142 B 5–7: 77 n. 36
142 B 6: 40 n. 79
142 C 5–6: 40 n. 79
143 D 1–5: 15 n. 35
144 B 4–5: 76–7

Index Locorum

144 B 4–C 1: 77
144 E 4: 76–7

Phaedo
65 D 13: 1 n. 2
68 A 8: 1 n. 2
75 D 1: 23 n. 44
76 A 8–9: 1 n. 2
79 A 6: 28–30
100 B 3–D 7: 23–4
100 D 5–6: 9 n. 22
102 D 6–7: 30 n. 57, 38 n. 74
104 B 6–C 1: 30 n. 57, 38 n. 74

Phaedrus
247 C 2: 24 n. 45
247 E 2: 23 n. 44

Philebus
58 A 2: 1 n. 2

Politicus
261 E 1–7: 9 n. 22
262 C 6–D 6: 76
263 A 2–B 11: 25
263 B 7–10: 77 n. 33
266 A 9–10: 77 n. 33
288 B 3–4: 11 n. 27

Protagoras
328 B 1–3: 115

Republic
405 A 7: 115 n. 36
476 A 1–3: 15 n. 35
476 C 7–D 3: 26
477 A 6: 26
477 A 6–9: 26
478 D 5–7: 26
478 E 1–2: 3–5, 26
478 E 2: 26
478 E 7–479 D 5: 26
486 A 9: 1 n. 2
508 D 4: 1 n. 2
509 B 5–9: 20–1
509 B 7–8: 44 n. 87
509 B 9–10: 45 n. 91
509 D 1–4: 28 n. 54
516 C 2: 44 n. 87
518 C 9: 45 n. 91
521 D 5: 1 n. 2
523 A 3: 1 n. 2
524 B 7–C 1: 15 n. 35
525 B 3: 1 n. 2
525 C 6: 1 n. 2
526 E 3–4: 45 n. 91
526 E 5: 1 n. 2
532 C 6: 45 n. 91

533 B 1–2: 1 n. 2
533 D 6–9: 9 n. 22
534 A 3: 1 n. 2
534 B 3–4: 1 n. 2
585 D 3: 5 n. 10

Sophist
218 B 7–C 1: 10
218 C 5–7: 53–4, 56
225 B 1: 76–7
225 B 9–11: 76–7
226 A 1–4: 77 n. 33
236 E 1–2: 53–4
236 E 2: 55–6
236 E 5: 37–8
237 A 3–4: 56
237 A 4–B 3: 56
237 B 7–8: 37–8
237 D 1–4: 28–30
239 B 4: 37 n. 73
242 C 4: 24
242 C 4–6: 10 n. 23
242 C 6: 11 n. 27
243 C 5: 21 n. 43
243 D 1: 10
243 D 6–244 B 5: 12
243 D 8–244 A 2: 10
243 D 9–E 2: 10 n. 23
243 E 3–4: 24
243 E 4–6: 14 n. 33
243 E 5: 21 n. 43
244 A 5–6: 10 n. 23
244 B 6–245 D 11: 10
245 E 6–249 D 4: 10
246 A 1–2: 10 n. 23
246 B 6–C 4: 26–7
246 B 9–C 2: 10–12
246 E 5–9: 28–30
247 A 5–B 4: 31 n. 58
247 A 9–10: 31 n. 58
247 B 1–4: 31 n. 58
247 D 8–E 4: 32 n. 64
248 A 7–8: 10–12
248 A 7–13: 26–7
249 B 12: 62 n. 13
249 D 3–4: 10–12
249 D 4–E 4: 62 n. 13
249 D 6–8: 12
249 D 9–264 B 8: 63 n. 15
249 E 6–250 A 2: 21 n. 43, 24
250 A 8–9: 12, 14 n. 34
250 A 8–D 3: 9–10, 15–17
250 A 9: 15 n. 37
250 A 11: 15 n. 37, 24–5
250 A 11–12: 12, 14–15

250 A 11–B 7: 16–17
250 A 11–B 11: 9–10, 34
250 B 1: 15 n. 37
250 B 2: 14–15, 15 n. 37
250 B 2–7: 12
250 B 3: 19–20
250 B 5: 15 n. 37
250 B 7: 16, 19–20
250 B 8: 16
250 B 8–C 8: 12–13
250 B 10: 1 n. 1
250 B 10–11: 16
250 B 11: 15 n. 37
250 C 1–2: 14 n. 34
250 C 2: 1 n. 1
250 C 3: 16
250 C 3–4: 13, 14 n. 34, 16
250 C 5: 13 n. 31
250 C 6: 14, 16, 23 n. 44
250 C 6–7: 13, 16, 19 n. 40
250 C 12–D 3: 13, 19 n. 40
250 D 2: 14
250 D 4: 13
250 E 1–2: 19 n. 40
250 E 1–4: 13
251 E 9: 9 n. 22
251 E 10: 1 n. 1
252 A 2: 1 n. 1
252 A 5–10: 31 n. 60
252 B 4: 21 n. 43
252 B 5: 21 n. 43
252 D 2–3: 9 n. 22
252 D 2–10: 30 n. 57
252 D 2–11: 62 n. 13
252 E 2: 9 n. 22
254 B 8–D 2: 59
254 C 3–4: 1 n. 1
254 C 4–6: 34–5, 59
254 C 5–8: 59
254 D 1–2: 59, 84, 86–7
254 D 4: 1 n. 1, 55, 87–8
254 D 4–5: 12 n. 30, 60
254 D 4–255 E 7: 59
254 D 4–257 A 12: 59–68
254 D 7–8: 19 n. 40
254 D 10: 16, 24, 33–6
254 D 14–15: 60
254 E 3: 22–3
254 E 4: 9 n. 22
254 E 17–255 E 7: 60
255 A 7: 62 n. 13
255 A 7–B 1: 16
255 B 3: 9 n. 22

255 B 8–C 4: 16
255 B 8–C 8: 25
255 B 11–15: 62
255 C 8–E 2: 60
255 C 9: 61 n. 12
255 C 12–13: 60
255 C 13–14: 31
255 C 13–D 5: 31
255 D 1: 60, 61 n. 12
255 D 3: 60–1
255 D 4–6: 60
255 D 6–7: 60–1
255 D 9: 23 n. 44, 75 n. 29
255 E 1: 22–3
255 E 4–6: 60–1
255 E 5: 23 n. 44
255 E 8: 34–6
255 E 8–256 D 10: 62, 85–6
255 E 8–256 E 8: 59
255 E 8–257 A 12: 55
255 E 11–12: 67
255 E 11–15: 35
256 A 1: 1 n. 1, 9 n. 22, 16, 24, 34–8
256 A 1–2: 35, 62
256 A 3–6: 35
256 A 3–B 5: 62
256 A 7: 9 n. 22, 35–7
256 A 7–8: 35–6, 42
256 A 10: 36–7, 64
256 A 10–B 4: 63, 66–7
256 A 12: 14 n. 33, 21 n. 43
256 B 1: 9 n. 22, 35–6, 63 nn.15, 16
256 B 1–2: 25, 35–6
256 B 2: 9 n. 22, 63 n. 15
256 B 2–3: 35–6
256 B 3–4: 35–6
256 B 6: 64
256 B 6–7: 62
256 B 6–C 3: 19 n. 40
256 B 10: 9 n. 22
256 C 2–3: 23 n. 44
256 C 4: 36–7
256 C 4–5: 35
256 C 6–10: 62
256 C 7–11: 35
256 C 11–D 9: 62
256 C 11–D 8: 35
256 D 5: 30
256 D 5–6: 36
256 D 5–9: 38 n. 74
256 D 7–257 A 5: 65
256 D 8: 30, 36–7
256 D 8–9: 30, 35–6, 66–7

Index Locorum

256 D 9: 16, 36–7, 39
256 D 11–E 1: 30 n. 56
256 D 11–E 3: 66–7
256 D 11–E 4: 35
256 D 12: 66
256 D 12–E 1: 75 n. 29
256 D 12–E 2: 34
256 D 12–E 3: 28, 40–2
256 D 12–E 4: 38 n. 74
256 E 1: 23 n. 44
256 E 3: 11 n. 27
256 E 3–4: 34, 39
256 E 5: 66–7
256 E 5–6: 36–7, 86–7
256 E 6: 34, 37–8, 42
256 E 6–7: 34–8, 66
256 E 7: 36–8
257 A 1–2: 59
257 A 1–7: 56
257 A 4–5: 64
257 A 4–6: 66
257 A 4–9: 22–3
257 A 6: 64
257 A 9: 23 n. 44
257 A 11–258 E 8: 56
257 B 1: 67
257 B 1–C 4: 55–6, 68–72
257 B 1–258 E 5: 55–6, 59, 68
257 B 3–4: 38 n. 74, 69, 78 n. 39
257 B 3–C 3: 36–7
257 B 4: 78
257 B 6–7: 78 n. 39
257 B 6–8: 69
257 B 6–C 3: 78 n. 39
257 B 9–C 3: 30, 78
257 C 1–2: 64
257 C 5–258 A 10: 55–7, 68, 70 n. 25, 72–80
257 C 7: 23 n. 44, 30 n. 56
257 C 7–8: 75–7
257 C 7–E 5: 30 n. 56
257 D 4: 23 n. 44, 30 n. 56, 75 n. 29
257 D 7: 75, 82
257 D 31: 23 n. 44
257 E 2: 75–6
257 E 2–4: 75–6, 83
257 E 6–7: 75, 82–3
258 A 1: 21 n. 43
258 A 1–2: 78–9
258 A 1–3: 14 n. 33
258 A 4–5: 78–9
258 A 6–259 A 1: 30
258 A 7–9: 78–9
258 A 7–10: 75
258 A 8: 23 n. 44
258 A 8–9: 75 n. 29, 78–9
258 A 11: 23 n. 44, 67, 75 n. 29, 81 n. 46
258 A 11–B 3: 81–3
258 A 11–C 5: 80–1
258 A 11–E 5: 55–7, 68, 72–3, 80–7
258 B 2: 82
258 B 3: 81–3
258 B 5: 82
258 B 6–7: 81–2
258 B 10: 67, 81–2
258 B 10–C 3: 83–4, 86–7
258 B 11–C 3: 19–20
258 C 3: 81–4
258 D 4–E 3: 84
258 D 5: 84
258 D 7: 30 n. 56, 75 n. 29
258 D 7–E 2: 30 n. 56
258 E 2: 85
258 E 2–3: 84
258 E 3: 85
258 E 6: 37–8
258 E 6–7: 85–6
258 E 6–259 A 1: 37–8
258 E 6–259 D 8: 85–6
259 A 1–B 1: 86
259 A 2: 86
259 A 4–5: 22–3
259 A 4–B 7: 42
259 A 5–6: 28, 40–2
259 A 6–7: 39
259 A 6–8: 24
259 A 8–B 1: 86
259 B 1: 87 n. 51
259 B 1–2: 22–3, 85–6
259 B 1–6: 85–6
259 B 2–4: 23–4, 42
259 B 4–6: 86–7
259 C 8: 85–6
260 D 5–261 A 3: 88
260 E 2–3: 88
262 A 1: 89
262 A 3: 90 n. 57
262 C 8–D 6: 57–8
262 E 5–6: 89
262 E 6–7: 28–30
263 A 2–9: 37–8
263 A 2–D 5: 28–30
263 A 5: 28–30, 89
263 A 11: 28–30
263 B 3: 89
263 B 4–5: 28–30

263 B 4–12: 37–8
263 B 4–13: 89
263 B 7: 90
263 B 7–9: 37–8
263 B 7–10: 57–8
263 B 9: 90
263 B 11: 37–8, 90
263 B 11–12: 37–8
263 B 12: 37–8
263 C 1: 28–30
263 C 9–11: 28–30
263 D 1: 28–30
263 D 6–264 B 8: 88
264 A 7–8: 88 n. 54
266 A 1–4: 76–7
266 A 2: 77 n. 33
268 B 4: 37 n. 73

Symposium
210 B 1–211 B 3: 23–4
211 A 7–8: 24 n. 45

Theaetetus
142 B 7: 115 n. 36
184 C 1–3: 9 n. 22
185 B 2: 15 n. 35
185 C 9–10: 3 n. 8
189 A 6–8: 28–30

Timaeus
27 D 5–28 A 4: 28 n. 54
48 E 3–4: 28 n. 54
50 B 5–51 A 4: 205 n. 79
50 C 4–5: 204–6
50 D 7: 45 n. 91
51 A 3: 45 n. 91
51 A 7: 45 n. 91
51 B 4–6: 204–6
52 A 8: 45 n. 91
52 B 3–5: 24 n. 45
52 D 3: 1 n. 2

Plotinus

Enneads
2. 6. 1. 1–5: 2 n. 3
3. 7. 3. 9: 2 n. 3
4. 5. 7: 235 n. 147
6. 2. 1. 6: 2 n. 3
6. 2. 1. 10: 2 n. 3
6. 2. 1. 13: 2 n. 3
6. 2. 1. 18: 2 n. 3
6. 2. 2. 28: 2 n. 3
6. 2. 7. 6: 2 n. 3
6. 2. 7. 17: 2 n. 3
6. 2. 7. 41: 2 n. 3
6. 2. 7. 43: 2 n. 3
8. 25: 2 n. 3

Porphyry

In Aristotelis Categorias commentarium, ed. Busse
86. 7–13: 41 n. 82

In Aristotelis Physica commentaria, ed. Smith
129. 61–72: 41 n. 82

Isagoge, ed. Busse
6. 5. 11: 41 n. 82

Priscianus

Metaphrasis in Theophrastrum, ed. Bywater
27. 8–14: 218 n. 105
28. 16–17: 220
28. 20–3: 220–1
29. 12–15: 219 n. 108, 221
29. 18–20: 225 n. 122, 252 n. 181
29. 18–31. 13: 219 n. 106, 224–5
29. 22–3: 225 n. 122, 252 n. 181
29. 26–7: 225 n. 122, 252 n. 181
30. 22–5: 225
30. 23: 252 n. 180
31. 11–13: 226
31. 13: 226
32. 57–37. 4: 222 n. 115

Proclus

In Platonis Parmenidem commentaries
628. 24–5 Luna-Segonds = 628. 18–19 Steel: 2 n. 3
763. 18 Luna-Segonds = 763. 13 Steel: 2 n. 3
800. 12–13 Luna-Segonds = 800. 10 Steel: 2 n. 3

In Platonis Timaeum commentaria
3. 8. 18–19 Diehl = 4. 10. 17–19 van Riel: 2 n. 3

Seneca

Epistles
58. 8–14: 41 n. 83
58. 9. 13–14: 41 n. 83

Simplicius

In Aristotelis Physica commentaria, ed. Diels

18. 6: 27 n. 52
19. 16: 27 n. 52
94. 5–13: 41 n. 82
136. 10–11: 2
136. 22: 27–8

Stobaeus
15. 9. 13: 187 n. 31

Themistius
In libros Aristotelis De anima paraphrasis, ed. Heinze
53. 12–13: 203 n. 75
108. 1–6: 218–19
108. 15–17: 220
108. 18–28: 223 n. 117

Theophrastus
Metaphysics, ed. Gutas
4^a3–5: 225 n. 123
8^a11–12: 225 n. 123
11^b2–5: 225 n. 123

Thucydides
4. 40: 116

Xenophon
Lacedaemonion Politeia
10. 1–4: 116
Memorabilia
1. 6. 13: 115 n. 36
3. 5. 15: 116

Notes for Contributors to Oxford Studies in Ancient Philosophy

1. Articles should be submitted with double line-spacing throughout. At the stage of initial (but not final) submission footnotes may be given in small type at the foot of the page. Page dimensions should be A4 or standard American quarto (8½″ × 11″), and ample margins (minimum 1¼″ or 32 mm) should be left.

2. Submissions should be made as an **anonymized** PDF file attached to an e-mail sent to the Editor. Authors are asked to supply an accurate word-count (*a*) for the main text, and (*b*) for the notes. The e-mail which serves as a covering letter should come from the address to be used for correspondence on the submission. A postal address should also be provided. If necessary, arrangements for alternative means of submission may be made with the Editor. Authors should note that the version first submitted will be the one adjudicated; unsolicited revised versions cannot be accepted during the adjudication process.

The remaining instructions apply to the final version sent for publication, and need not be rigidly adhered to in a first submission.

3. In the finalized version, the text should be double-spaced and in the same type size throughout, **including displayed quotations and notes**. Notes should be numbered consecutively, and preferably supplied as footnotes rather than endnotes. Any acknowledgements should be placed in a final note attached to the last word of the article. Wherever possible, references to primary sources should be built into the text.

4. **Use of Greek and Latin.** Relatively familiar Greek terms such as *psuchē* and *polis* (but not whole phrases and sentences) may be used in transliteration or likewise a few, isolated terms where translation would be prejudicial. Wherever possible, Greek and Latin should not be used in the main text of an article in ways which would impede comprehension by those without knowledge of the languages; for example, where appropriate, the original texts should be accompanied by a translation. For further details or instructions, please consult the Editor. Greek must be supplied in an accurate form, with all diacritics in place, and should be in a Unicode font.

5. For citations of Greek and Latin authors, house style should be followed. This can be checked in any recent issue of *OSAP* with the help of the Index Locorum. The most exact reference possible should normally be employed, especially if a text is quoted or discussed in detail: for example, line references for Plato (not just Stephanus page and letter) and Aristotle (not just Bekker page and column).

6. In references to books, the first time the book is referred to give the initial(s) and surname of the author (first names are not usually required), and the place and date of publication; where you are abbreviating the title in subsequent citations, give the abbreviation in square brackets, thus:

> T. Brickhouse and N. Smith, *Socrates on Trial* [*Trial*] (Princeton, 1981), 91–4.

Give the volume-number and date of periodicals, and include the full page-extent of articles (including chapters of books):

> D. W. Graham, 'Symmetry in the Empedoclean Cycle' ['Symmetry'], *Classical Quarterly*, NS 38 (1988), 297–312 at 301–4.

> G. Vlastos, 'A Metaphysical Paradox' ['Metaphysical'], in G. Vlastos, *Platonic Studies*, 2nd edn (Princeton, 1981), 43–57 at 52.

Where the same book or article is referred to on subsequent occasions, usually the most convenient style will be an abbreviated reference:

> Brickhouse and Smith, *Trial*, 28–9.

Do *not* use the author-and-date style of reference.

7. Authors are asked to supply *in addition*, at the end of the article, a full list of the bibliographical entries cited, alphabetically ordered by (first) author's surname. Except that the author's surname should come first, these entries should be identical in form to the first occurrence of each in the article, including where appropriate the indication of abbreviated title:

> Graham, D. W., 'Symmetry in the Empedoclean Cycle' ['Symmetry'], *Classical Quarterly*, NS 38 (1988), 297–312.

The names of any additional authors should also be inverted:

> Vogt, K. M., and Vlasits, J. (eds.), *Epistemology after Sextus Empiricus* [*Epistemology*] (Oxford, 2020).

8. If there are any unusual conventions contributors are encouraged to include a covering note for the copy-editor and/or printer. Please say whether you are using single and double quotation marks for different purposes (otherwise the Press will employ its standard single quotation marks throughout, using double only for quotations within quotations).

9. Authors should send a copy of the final version of their paper in electronic form by attachment to an e-mail. The final version should be provided as a Microsoft Word file. This file must be accompanied by a second file, a copy in PDF format of the final version, to which it must correspond **exactly**. If necessary, arrangements for alternative means of submission may be made with the Editor. With final submission authors should also send, in a separate file, a brief abstract and a list of no more than ten keywords.